OUR TIMES
VOLUME III

From a photograph by Harris and Ewing ©

CHARLES EVANS HUGHES

MARK SULLIVAN

OUR TIMES

1900-1925

Introduction by Dewey W. Grantham

III

Pre-War America

New York

CHARLES SCRIBNER'S SONS

INTRODUCTION TO VOLUME III

PRE-WAR AMERICA

Readers of this third volume of Mark Sullivan's *Our Times* will soon discover that its subtitle, *Pre-War America*, is misleading.* Except for the chapter on popular songs, which deals with the years 1900-1914, the chronological focus is the first decade of the century, with emphasis on the second administration of Theodore Roosevelt. Little space is given to the immediate pre-war years, a period that Sullivan later wrote about in his fourth volume. The framework of this book—and much of its substance—is provided by Roosevelt and the politics of his presidency. The volume begins somewhat arbitrarily, it seems, with two chapters on William Howard Taft and his special relationship with Roosevelt. Sullivan's opening sketch of Taft (who is pictured as the proverbial jovial fat man) apparently is intended as a device to give his political chronicle greater symmetry, since he ends his discussion of politics in the book with T.R.'s selection of Taft as his successor in the White House. Several chapters on nonpolitical subjects are included, some of them interspersed in odd places as if the author had deliberately sought to rend the fabric of his political narrative.

Sullivan obviously finds Theodore Roosevelt a congenial, indeed a fascinating, subject, and he dwells upon his political methods, his style, and his uses of power. He devotes a long chapter to one of the twenty-sixth Presi-

---

* A more comprehensive discussion of Mark Sullivan and the writing of *Our Times* is contained in the general introduction to Volume I of this edition.

dent's most important domestic reforms, the enactment
of an effective railroad regulatory law. He recounts several of Roosevelt's more amusing controversies, including
the furors over simplified spelling and nature-fakers, and
suggests why T.R.'s contemporaries found him so much
fun. Sullivan saw nothing inconsistent in his attempt to
write history from the point of view of the average man
and in the emphasis that he gave to the activities of such
a conspicuous figure as Theodore Roosevelt. Ordinary
people needed leaders to inspire them, in the writer's
opinion, and Roosevelt not only reflected many of their
own ideas and ideals in his own thinking but also trans-
lated popular impulses into political action.

Despite the attention Sullivan gives to the politics of
the Roosevelt administration, there are some surprising
gaps in his coverage. Roosevelt's much-publicized diplomacy is virtually passed over, and his conservation program, one of his most constructive achievements, is
scarcely mentioned. Although Roosevelt's reforms are described, the broad reform impulse of this period is not
analyzed. These were the years when the progressive
movement was having a strong effect upon municipal and
state politics, when new intellectual currents were gathering force, and when settlement houses, the social gospel,
and other vehicles of reform were making themselves felt.
Sullivan neglected all of this. It should be noted, however, that he was not endeavoring to write a comprehensive political history. He wanted to portray politicians
and the political process as the average American saw
them, and especially as he followed them in the newspapers. The result was almost certain to be a fragmented
and sensational treatment. Sullivan gives some attention
to the reform journalists whom T.R. labeled "muckrakers,"
but his appraisal of these writers is not well-balanced. He
is too insistent in distinguishing between the early "litera-

ture of exposure," with which he himself was identified, and later muckraking, which he regards as sensational and commercial. He is critical of Upton Sinclair, for instance, on the ground that he had not, in the manner of the reform journalist, reported facts, but instead had used fiction as a medium of exposure.

Sullivan writes of the Roosevelt era with great élan. His volume is crowded with interesting sketches, shrewd insights, and entertaining anecdotes. But he is not always fair in his evaluation of Roosevelt's opponents. Thus he is very critical of Robert M. La Follette, the Wisconsin progressive who sometimes disagreed with what he regarded as Roosevelt's vacillating reformism. The historian Harold Underwood Faulkner, in commenting on this volume in 1931, expressed resentment at "a certain smugness" in Sullivan's attitude "toward some of the great men of his day, particularly those of liberal or progressive tendencies." Yet Faulkner conceded that Sullivan had "resurrected some interesting stories" and that he got "very close to important social history, which in the past, unfortunately, has been ignored by many reputable historians."

Got "very close to important social history"! That—and not the discussion of politics—would prove to be Mark Sullivan's most enduring contribution as the author of *Our Times*. The third volume of the series is less distinctive in this respect than some of the other volumes, but, even so, almost half of its pages are concerned with social and cultural matters.

The most notable of the book's efforts to deal with the culture of the period is the encyclopedic chapter on popular songs. The editors at Scribner's were appalled when Sullivan produced a chapter that ran almost a hundred pages in print; they warned him that it would disrupt his narrative, destroy its proportion, and amount to "a work in itself." But Sullivan would not yield, and the comprehensive assortment of sentimental ballads, ethnic songs, and ragtime tunes found its way into Volume III. The result is one of the most revealing segments of popular culture in all of *Our Times*. "To the historian," observes Sullivan, "some songs constitute an index to manners, vogues, even morals, the events and subjects that engaged national interest, the times of economic, philologic, and other changes." Sullivan's determination to get at the sources of popular culture in the early twentieth century is revealed in his work on "Casey Jones," a song he barely mentions in the third volume of *Our Times*. Of his long search for the identity of the composer and ultimately of Casey Jones himself, Sullivan wrote: "During eighteen months I chased this will-o'-the-wisp of melody from the Pacific Coast to the honkytonks of the Middle South." Sullivan is not always perceptive in his commentary on the songs dealt with in this chapter, underestimating, for example, the contribution of black Americans to authentic American music. But he understood the importance of popular songs as an expression of and a guide to mass culture, and he sought to relate them to the social milieu of the period.

Characteristically, Sullivan includes in this volume isolated chapters on several newsworthy developments of the time. One of these—"An Emancipation"—is a well-written account of Dr. Charles W. Stiles and the successful campaign to eradicate hookworm in the South. Another is the story of James Hazen Hyde, the Equitable Life Assurance Society, and the famous New York investigation of insurance scandals. When Sullivan wrote to the hero of that investigation, Charles Evans Hughes, to ask for his recollections of the probe, he described the treatment he hoped to give the episode in *Our Times*. "I want to write a compact statement," he said, "which shall include every material consequence of that investigation, as well as every amusing or entertaining detail of it." That was an apt description of Sullivan's handling of many other episodes in his history.

The final three chapters of this volume relate, in chronological order, some of the sensational happenings of the years 1906, 1907, and 1908. These chronological chapters are somewhat fuller than similar ones in the first two volumes. They enable the author to present a parade of foibles that range from the notorious American visit of Maxim Gorky to Fred Merkle's ill-fated failure to touch second base during a crucial National League baseball game on September 23, 1908. And on that note of serendipity, the reader may wish to savor *Our Times* for himself.

Dewey W. Grantham
Vanderbilt University

CONTENTS

CONTENTS

ILLUSTRATIONS

Pre-War America

TWO FRIENDS

Who Later Became Foes, Their Friendship Determining the Presidency of the United States for One Term, and Their Estrangement Determining It for Two, and the Whole of Their Relationship Changing the Direction of History to a Degree of Which the Consequences Would Be Difficult to Estimate. Roosevelt, Finding Taft Radiating Usefulness in the Philippines, Tries to Bring Him Back to Washington.

THEODORE ROOSEVELT and William Howard Taft began their friendship when both occupied subordinate government posts in Washington, from 1890 to 1892, sharing a zeal for public service which Roosevelt expressed as Civil Service Commissioner, Taft as Solicitor-General. They lived near each other, met frequently at the homes of each other and of mutual friends, walked to their offices together occasionally — passing the White House, then occupied by Benjamin Harrison, and turning unconsciously to glimpse its unfailing glamour (though it was Roosevelt alone of the two whose thrill was associated with a personal dream). After advancement in their careers separated them from Washington and from each other, they kept their friendship alive through letters and occasional meetings. As crises arose in Roosevelt's turbulent upward climb, he would, said Taft later, "frequently write me to secure my judgment."[1]

Roosevelt went on to become Police Commissioner of New York City, Assistant Secretary of the Navy,

[1] Both had a trait more common then than later, a continuous concern about the country, as if the nation's affairs were a personal responsibility of the individual. Even when Roosevelt was in private life, a head-line in the daily papers about national affairs, especially in the field of foreign relations, would cause him to write to his friends, giving his own views and asking theirs.

Rough Rider Colonel in the Spanish-American War, Governor of New York, and Vice-President. Taft, going forward more ponderously through paths more

Roosevelt and Taft on the south portico of the White House just before leaving for the Capitol, where Roosevelt gave up, and Taft took over, the Presidency.

serene, passed from the post of Solicitor-General to become a Federal judge and Dean of the Law School of the University of Cincinnati. In 1900, he went to Manila as president of the second Philippine Commission. When Roosevelt succeeded to the Presidency, through the death of McKinley in 1901, among the subordinates he inherited was Taft, usefully radiating good-will in the task of governing our Far Eastern possession.

II

Until Dewey's victory at Manila Bay, hardly one American in a hundred had known what or where the Philippines were; probably a smaller proportion had ever dreamed that we should one day govern a Malaysian people seven thousand miles away. Like a youth to whom some dramatic event has brought sudden consciousness of manhood, we had mingled emotions, a rather chanticleer pride in our newly realized strength, subdued somewhat by a sober disquiet over our unanticipated responsibilities.

The Filipinos, thinking of us merely as successors to the Spaniards who had oppressed them for three hundred years, undertook to drive our troops from the Archipelago. On both sides the fighting had been cruel. The Filipinos' treatment of prisoners, frequently indescribably dreadful, led to reprisals by the Americans. Open warfare had ceased with the capture of the Filipino leader, Aguinaldo, by General Funston in 1901, but the situation had remained unstable and there was never-ending apprehension of a new insurrection.

The conditions constituted a summons to the very highest talent America could provide, for a function in which we were wholly without experience. Our youthful nation had to improvise the equivalent of a Roman legate or a British viceroy, and had to adapt the institution to our national spirit, which would not countenance exploitation of our ward. In our solemn exaltation we felt that "the first governor of the Philippines ought to combine the qualities which would make a first-class

President of the United States with the qualities which would make a first-class Chief-Justice of the United States."[2]

To meet this demand on the resources of American public life, President McKinley had picked Taft,[3] had instructed him to prepare as speedily as possible a sound foundation for Filipino self-government, and had secured from him a promise to remain with the task until the Filipinos should be safely on their way to their new destiny.

Taft, on arriving at Manila, was interviewed by a group of American newspaper correspondents who had been long enough in the Islands to be slightly disillusioned, and to feel homesick. One of them wrote:

We ought to ship this splendid fellow back. It's a shame to spoil his illusion that folks the world over are just like the folks he knows out in Ohio. He makes me think of pies, hominy, fried chicken, big red apples, "Mr. Dooley," frosty mornings, oysters on the half-shell, the oaks and the pines, New England town meetings, the little red schoolhouse, cyclopedias on the instalment plan, the square deal, and a home run with the bases full — out here where man wears his shirt outside his breeches to keep cool in midwinter, picks his dinner off a banana tree out of the window, conceals his bolo and his Mauser and his thoughts behind a smile of friendship varnished with Spanish manners, and is in the Four Hundred if he can sign his name with a scrawl. . . . Oh, but wasn't the Judge and his laugh good — and won't he be easy for them !

From the beginning, a relation of affection and confidence existed between this jovial fat man from Cin-

---

[2] The words were quoted, and indorsed, in an article by Theodore Roosevelt in *The Outlook,* 1901. The passage was prophetic; nine years later, Taft was President; twenty years after, he was Chief Justice.

[3] Then a judge on the Federal Circuit Bench. Taft went to the Philippines in the summer of 1900 as head of the newly formed Philippine Commission. When President McKinley decided, a year later, to place a civil governor over those sections which had been pacified by the military, he gave the post to Taft.

cinnati, U. S. A., and the heterogeneous tribes of little
brown men of the Archipelago; between this blue-eyed,
kindly, humor-loving giant, son of uncounted generations of Northwestern European civilization — and the

Taft at Manila watching an American innovation, a baseball game.

dark-skinned, black-eyed, in some cases primitive children of the tropical East, long suspicious of the white
men from Spain who had ruled them for centuries, and
hardly less suspicious of the white soldiers from America who had just put down their insurrection. Toward
them Taft practised a frankness, informality, and un-
pretentiousness they had never known in either their

white rulers or their own chieftains. He encouraged them to call on him and Mrs. Taft, he disarmed them by the openness and freedom of his talk, charmed them by his simplicity, endeared himself to them by the heartiness of his manner, the joviality of his infectious laugh. He devoted himself with genuine pleasure to a social accomplishment at which he had an adeptness remarkable for one of his dimensions, translating his skill with the American waltz and two-step into the steps of the Filipino *rigodon*, and appearing regularly, dressed in a starched white linen suit, at the soirées of Manila society. When he travelled about the Islands, as he did frequently, *fiestas* were given by the towns he visited, at which he always led out for the first dance the *señora* of the local *presidente*.

In his formal rôle of Governor-General, Taft was honest, humane, sympathetic — a new experience for the Filipinos who had learned to hate foreign rulers. Taft believed in the Filipinos, spoke of them as "little brown brothers," had a generous enthusiasm for them, felt that with wise guidance they could within a reasonable time follow in the footsteps of their cousins the Japanese.

The sympathetic heart of the new Governor, and the honesty of his mind, were quickly sensed by the racial intuitiveness of the Filipinos, who would have expressed their notion of Taft with a single American word. Not having the word, an elderly Filipino, driven to symbolize his opinions about various men whose names were mentioned to him, used the device of a stick with which he drew scratches in the sand. In each case the scratch was crooked or wavering, until Taft was mentioned, when the Filipino's face lighted up and he vigorously drew a sharply defined line, absolutely straight.[4]

4 This anecdote is told by Oscar King Davis in "Released for Publication."

III

With disturbing unexpectedness there came to Taft in the Philippines late in 1902, from Roosevelt in the White House, a cable saying: "On January first there will be a vacancy on the Supreme Court to which I earnestly desire to appoint you. . . ."

To Taft the offer brought turmoil of spirit. "All his life his first ambition had been to attain the Supreme Bench; to him it meant the crown of the highest career that a man can seek, and he wanted it as strongly as a man can ever want anything."[5]

Mrs. Taft, however, "had always been opposed to a judicial career for him," regarding it as "settlement in a 'fixed groove' I had talked against so long."[6] Several of Taft's friends and relatives, including an elder brother, Charles P. Taft, to whom he was devoted, had come to feel that Taft's talents, and the tide of public service upon which he was embarked, were capable of carrying him on to the Presidency. Immurement on the Supreme Court would take him out of the current that might lead to the more exalted office.

This ambition Taft himself did not share. For him the Presidency had little allure; the politics incident to the office repelled him. A year before Roosevelt's offer of a Supreme Court berth, Taft had written his brother:[7] "The horrors of a modern Presidential campaign and the political troubles of the successful candidate, rob the office of the slightest attraction for me."

[5] The quotation is from Mrs. Taft — "Recollections."

[6] "Recollections," Mrs. William Howard Taft. Taft's mother (Mrs. Alphonso Taft), unlike his wife, always wanted him to go on the Supreme Bench, and never wished him to run for the Presidency. At one of the several times when Taft was making a choice between the two careers, his mother said: "I do not want my son to be President. A place on the Supreme Bench, where my boy would administer justice, is my ambition for him. His is a judicial mind and he loves the law."

[7] August 27, 1901.

Taft had, however, one reason of his own for fore-going, at this time, the opportunity to go on the Supreme Court. His reason was his feeling of obligation to the Filipinos, the sense of duty which told him he should

From a photograph © by Harris and Ewing.
The Taft figure at a later date — the first of our golf-playing Presidents.

remain with them until they should be securely on their way to stability. This conviction coincided with Mrs. Taft's preference. Although she "remembered the year of illness and anxiety we had just been through," although she "yearned to be safe in Washington" and "weakened just a little" in her determination that her husband should avoid the "fixed groove" of the Court, nevertheless her conclusive judgment was that "acceptance was not to be thought of."[8]

Taft cabled his decision to Roosevelt, as well as to his immediate superior, Secretary of War Elihu Root: "Great honor deeply appreciated but must decline.[9] . . . Conditions here would make my withdrawal violation of duty.[10] All [conditions] render most unwise change of Governor.[9] Nothing would satisfy individual taste more than acceptance.[9] I long for a judicial career but if it must turn on my present decision I am willing to lose it."[10]

With his decision made and his renunciation on its way to Washington, Taft turned from the vista Roosevelt's offer had opened to him of a career as a justice of the hallowed Supreme Court, and busied himself with the pressing problems of his viceroyalty.

At his desk a month later he put aside matters of state in Zamboango and Bayombong to read and re-read a letter that had just completed its long journey from Washington. It was from his chief, President Roosevelt, and ran:

Dear Will, I am awfully sorry, old man, but[11] . . . I shall have to put you on the Supreme Court. I am very sorry. But after all, old fellow, if you will permit me to say so, I am

8 "Recollections," Mrs. William H. Taft.
9 From Taft's cable to Roosevelt.
10 From Taft's cable to Root.
11 Throughout this volume, for the purpose of reducing quotations to the briefest space consistent with keeping the integrity of their authors' thoughts, and also for the purpose of clarity, use has been made of three dots, thus . . ., to denote elision of words or phrases not essential to the meaning in the present connection, or otherwise redundant. Sometimes, more than one elision is made in a quotation. In some such cases, in order to avoid awkwardness of typographical appearance and impediment to the reader's quickness of grasp, only one set of dots is used. In this book, therefore, the appearance of three dots (. . .) in the body of a quotation signifies that one or more words or phrases have been deleted, always, of course, with care not to alter the meaning. Occasionally, to achieve clarity, the order of the sentences in a quotation is changed. In such cases attention is called to the fact in a foot-note.

President and see the whole field. After the most careful thought, after the most earnest effort as to what you desired and thought best, I have come, irrevocably, to the decision that I shall appoint you to the Supreme Court in the vacancy caused by Judge Shiras' resignation. This is one of the cases where the President, if he is fit for his position, must take the responsibility.

Again was perturbance of Taft's spirit; again was family council; again was decision to decline the elevation which, from Taft's standpoint, would interrupt his obligation to the Filipinos, and from Mrs. Taft's would take him out of the current of the more active career that might lead to the Presidency. Taft, pondering just how much "irrevocableness" lay behind the "old mans" and "old fellows" that Roosevelt used to temper his command as a superior with his affection as a friend, wrote a pleading, apologetic protest: "Recognize soldier's duty to obey orders," he cabled. "If your judgment is unshaken I bow to it." But he gave at length his reasons for not wishing to bow. "I presume on our personal friendship, even in the face of your letter, to make one more appeal, in which I lay aside wholly my strong personal disinclination to leave work of intense interest half-done. Circumstances have convinced these people, controlled largely by personal feelings, that I am their friend and stand for a policy of confidence in them and belief in their future and extension of self-government. Withdrawal will, I fear, give impression that change of policy is intended. . . . I feel it my duty to say this."

Roosevelt, impressed less by the soldierly acquiescence than by the personal reluctance, and sincerely desiring that Taft as his long-time personal friend should have whatever he preferred — though puzzled at Taft's repeated refusal of a place which because of their intimate friendship in the past he knew Taft prized — Roosevelt let Taft have his way. "All right," he cabled, "stay where you are. I shall appoint someone else to the Court."

A year passed, during which Taft made solid progress, despite discouraging difficulties, in establishing an orderly government for his wards. Then, in the Fall of 1903, he received another summons from Roosevelt to larger duties at Washington, which he accepted. Roosevelt's new offer was not to a justiceship on the Supreme Court but to the Cabinet post Elihu Root was relinquishing to return to the practice of law. The office of Secretary of War, having charge of the Philippines, would permit Taft to continue to keep a benevolent hand upon their destinies. To Mrs. Taft, the War portfolio "was much more pleasing than the offer of the Supreme Court appointment, because it was in line with the kind of work I wanted my husband to do, the kind of career I wanted for him and expected him to have, so I was glad there were few excuses for refusing to accept it open to him."[12]

On February 1, 1904, Taft took the oath of office as Secretary of War in Roosevelt's Cabinet.

[12] "Recollections," Mrs. William H. Taft.

MEMORABLE YEARS

Partial Picture of the United States During a Period When the People Felt All Was Well, Because Roosevelt Was in the White House and Because Whenever He Journeyed from Washington He Left Taft "Sitting On the Lid."

TAFT was more than Secretary of War. Wherever a tension needed the solvent of good-will, or friction the oil of benevolence; wherever suspicion needed the antidote of frankness, or wounded pride the disinfectant of a hearty laugh — there Taft was sent. He was given prodigious tasks, and the greater the pressure that Roosevelt put upon him, the more effectively he worked. It is difficult to phrase what Taft was to the Roosevelt administration, and to the country. It occurs to one to borrow a term from business, and say Taft was America's "trouble-shooter" — but that implies high-pressure explosiveness, and also ruthlessness sometimes, and Taft was neither explosive nor ruthless. It was Roosevelt who was under high pressure always and explosive often; Taft was his jovial, never-excited, considerate, smiling associate, partly subordinate, partly partner. When Cuba's groping first steps in self-government faltered, Taft was sent to repeat what he had done in the Philippines, his success causing Roosevelt to write in a private letter,[1] "Taft . . . has handled the situation marvelously." When construction of the Panama Canal was almost halted, partly through the ineptitude of an engineer in charge, who forehandedly took a coffin to the Isthmus with him — with obvious results to the morale

[1] To Henry Cabot Lodge, October 1, 1906.

of the workers — Taft, explosive for once, "bawled him out," took hold himself, and reorganized the work — he made seven journeys to the Isthmus in seven years.[2] When trouble arose over land-holdings in the Philippines by some friars of the Catholic Church — a delicate matter fraught with possibilities of religious rancor — Taft went to Rome[3] and negotiated a settlement that ultimately left everybody satisfied — Vatican, friars, and Filipinos; American Catholics and American Protestants alike. It was fortunate that Taft's 354 pounds of jovial

THE PEACE-MAKER

From "The Post" (Cincinnati).

A cartoonist's joke about Taft's weight, published after Taft, as his country's "trouble-shooter," had stopped a revolution in Cuba in 1906.

flesh did not interfere with a natural enjoyment of travel, for his journeys to run down his country's troubles carried him literally around the world.[4] At Tokio, he calmed the waters troubled by California's proscription of Japanese from public schools and from owning land. At Manila, he assisted in opening the first Filipino legislative assembly. In China, by negotiations with the government, he got rid of a boycott against American goods. His official routine, said the New York *Sun*, began with

2 Some of Taft's trips to Panama were taken after he became President.

3 Taft's journey to Rome took place while he was Governor-General of the Philippines.

4 Twice; once while Governor-General of the Philippines and again while Secretary of War.

"grabbing a time-table and throwing a change of clothing into a traveling-bag"; his success consisted of "making two laughs echo where one groan was heard before." All of which inspired a tribute in newspaper verse, widely quoted:

> Pattern for all beneath the sun,
> To Taft award the palm and bun!
> They told him what they wanted done —
> He done it.

The country liked Taft. They made infinite jests about his fatness — and no one heard or repeated the

"Mr. Taft, you're really not near so fat as they say you are."

jokes with greater savor than Taft himself. Making a speech he would pause, with an effect of suspense, just long enough to intensify the audience's attention; then throughout the immense torso and up into the broad features would run little tremors and heavings, rising to a climax in a rumbling chuckle as infectious as only a fat man could achieve, and Taft would tell a story in which the point was, as he would say in an engaging falsetto, "on me." While he was in the Philippines, disturbing reports about his health caused Secretary of War Root to send a cabled inquiry. Taft cabled back that he was perfectly all right — he had just finished a twenty-five-mile horseback ride and was feeling fine. Root read that, smiled, and sent off another cable of solicitude: "How is horse?" Justice Brewer of the Supreme Court said that "Taft is

the politest man in Washington; the other day he gave
up his seat in a street-car to three ladies." All the jokes
that have been made about fat men since Shakespeare
invented Falstaff were brought from their ancient clos-
ets and stretched to fit Taft's ample form. New ones
emanated from Taft himself. A lady calling on him in
the interest of her son's career in the army, had received
the assurance she wished, and, departing, said, as the
highest feminine conception of showing appreciation:
"Mr. Taft, you're really not near so fat as they say you
are."

He was fat, but he had the frame that carries weight
with an effect of majesty, of the sort that primitive men,
and even modern men in the average, like to see in their
kings and leaders. "He looks," said Arthur Brisbane at
this time, "like an American bison, a gentle, kind one."
People thought of Taft's tonnage as they think of the
Leviathan,[5] something that makes for substance and dependability and does not interfere with efficiency. Confidence and affection attended him everywhere. He was
regarded as good medicine; at once a tonic and seda-
tive, good for the national nerves. Old-fashioned people liked to think of him as a man who probably said
his prayers. Frederick Palmer called Taft's laugh "one
of our great American institutions":[6]

It is good to see Big Bill Taft enter a room after a number
of other men. He reminds you of a great battleship following
the smaller vessels, coming into port with her brass bright,
and plowing deep. You feel that when a giant is so amiable it
would be impolite not to agree with him; and, moreover, it
would be unwise, considering that the power of the United
States is behind him. Foreigners have observed that he looked

[5] This comparison will be instantly understood by readers belonging to the
generation during which this history is written. To readers of future generations it may be desirable to explain that the *Leviathan* was, during the 1920's,
the largest ship in the world.
[6] *Current Literature,* June, 1907.

like the United States personified, whatever they mean by that. With his smile and his inflexible purpose he has managed to keep the gun covers on when a smaller man might have had to take them off. Besides, he does give the impression that if he did begin firing it would be in broadsides to the bitter end; and that helps in any negotiation.

As Taft liked to travel and as his tasks took him to every corner of the country, he was seen in the flesh by probably as many people as Roosevelt. He had a natural liking for people and a human understanding of democracy — in a sense different from political understanding, which Taft did not have at all.[7] By preference he did his travelling in an ordinary lower berth, reading his newspaper in the smoking compartment, joining in conversations with his fellow passengers — in all respects he liked to share the common lot. Entering the dining-car of a morning, his face had the rosiness of the dawn, his bearing the heartiness of a giant refreshed. The cheeriness of his greeting to the conductor and the waiter, and to the friend or acquaintance that any average dining-car gathering was sure to contain, had the effect of diffusing good cheer, infecting the whole car with a sense of well-being, a feeling that all was well with the world. The people associated him with his chief, Roosevelt, and felt that with two such at the helm, the country was well cared for.

II

As the people loved Taft, so did Roosevelt. Whenever Roosevelt mentioned Taft's name it was with an expression of pleasure on his own countenance, a pleasure that was more than mere smiling affection. Roose-

7 "Taft, although one of the most lovable men ever in American life, has absolutely no genius for politics whatever. His bump of politics is a deep hole." — Oscar King Davis, in "Released for Publication." "Taft the politician [was] the honest greenhorn at the poker table." — Charles Willis Thompson, in "Presidents I've Known and Two Near-Presidents."

velt had regard for Taft's stability and serenity. In Cabinet meetings, or at gatherings of friends, to say "Isn't that so, Will?" or "Don't you think so, Will?"

From a photograph by Underwood & Underwood.

Secretary of War Taft on one of his trips to the Far East (S. S. *Manchuria*). The young woman in front of him is Alice, daughter of President Roosevelt; upon her left (reader's right) is Nicholas Longworth, whom she later married.

was Roosevelt's way of getting what he regarded as the most convincing buttressing of his own opinions — an attitude never modified by the fact that at evening gatherings in the White House study, the question would sometimes wake Taft from a nap. Nor was Roosevelt ever disturbed when occasionally, in the midst of one of his eager disquisitions to a group about Irish sagas or the coloration of zebras, there came from the easy chair in which Taft rested an audible sign of preoccupation with restoration from the day's more serious labors. Roosevelt would only beam the more, like a mother pleased to see a child at peace. One felt that that Brobdingnagian frame, because of the labor it performed, was entitled to take rest where it could. To contemplate the giant relaxed was a pleasure that gave one the feeling that everything must be all right.

The very ease that Taft had in Roosevelt's presence, his immunity from infection by the latter's eager energy, helped to increase Roosevelt's estimate of the soundness and surefootedness of his judgment. Far from resenting Taft's placid, good-humored indifference to some of Roosevelt's more recondite enthusiasms, Roosevelt valued him the more for it. Instinctively, Roosevelt seemed to sense that Taft's imperturbability was a needed and valuable corrective to his own impetuosity. Taft privately thought of himself as holding on to Roosevelt's coat-tails to prevent him from going too fast — but publicly always said that whatever Roosevelt did was Heaven's law. Conversely, Roosevelt publicly accepted Taft's benediction as proof that he was right — but privately told friends that sometimes he had to restrain Taft from letting his loyalty carry him too far, from being, in the furtherance of Roosevelt's policies, more Roosevelt than Roosevelt himself.[8]

Once Taft resigned. It was while Roosevelt was run-

---

[8] "Taft was an open, and sometimes almost extreme, supporter of the Roosevelt policies, and it was not unknown among Washington correspondents who were on terms of confidence at the White House that Roosevelt sometimes wished his Secretary of War were not quite so unrestrained in his utterances." — Oscar King Davis, in "Released for Publication."

ning for re-election in 1904. Taft, making speeches meant to help Roosevelt, had unfortunately chosen the tobacco-growing State of Connecticut as the place to deliver a speech favoring a lower tariff on tobacco from his beloved Philippines. Connecticut farmers, irritated, complained to Connecticut Republican politicians. Connecticut politicians transmitted the complaint to Republican National Chairman Cortelyou. Cortelyou transmitted the complaint to Roosevelt — with a suggestion that it might be as well if Taft would defer his speeches about Philippine tobacco until after the election. Roosevelt, perfunctorily, wrote across the correspondence "Respectfully referred to the Secretary of War [Taft]." Taft, deeply moved, closed his office door, denied himself to visitors and spent laborious hours writing out a letter of resignation in long-hand. Roosevelt in two minutes sent the resignation back to Taft, with three words and an initialled signature scribbled across the corner: "Dear Will. Fiddledeedee. T. R."

Roosevelt loved Taft and admired him, extravagantly — admired him to a degree that almost reached a kind of generous envy. "You know," Roosevelt once said to Archie Butt,[9] "I think Taft has the most lovable personality I have ever come in contact with. I almost envy a man possessing a personality like Taft's. People are always prepossessed by it. One loves him at first sight. He has nothing to overcome when he meets people. I realize that I have always got to overcome a little something before I get to the heart of people." And Roosevelt, with a characteristic screwing up of his features that always preceded something humorous, added, "No one could accuse *me* of having a charming personality."

In scores of such private conversations and public statements Roosevelt expressed his pleasure about Taft

---

[9] "The Letters of Archie Butt."

with his habitual "corking" and "bully." Not only his
affection, but the regard he had for Taft's ability, and
his gratitude for Taft's services. "If only there were
three of you," wrote Roosevelt in a letter to Taft, "then
I would have one of you on the Supreme Court, one of

From "The Plain Dealer" (Cleveland).

President Roosevelt (on his way to Texas): "Oh, things will be all right in
Washington. I have left Taft sitting on the lid."

you as Secretary of War, and one of you permanently
Governor of the Philippines." Leaving Washington[10]
for a long trip to a Rough Rider reunion at San Antonio, Texas, and a swing around the circle, Roosevelt
told the newspaper correspondents: "Oh, things will be
all right; I have left Taft sitting on the lid" — a passage which, considering Taft's weight, was one of the
most fruitful of the many opportunities that Roosevelt's
pungent phrases presented to cartoonists. Once, in a letter[11] to Henry Cabot Lodge, Roosevelt recited his current troubles — riots in Chicago, discrimination against

10 April, 1905.
11 May 15, 1905, "Correspondence of Roosevelt and Lodge."

the Japanese in California, the hard job of making peace between Japan and Russia, trouble with England over Newfoundland fisheries, the difficulty of getting a railroad rate bill through Congress — but concluded, as if with a sigh that implied confidence to face all troubles, "Taft has been the greatest comfort to me." In another letter to Lodge, he told of picking a successor to John Hay as Secretary of State, and of hesitating between Elihu Root and Taft — "for Taft, as you know, is very close to me." Deciding upon Root (because thus he would have both Root and Taft about him) he said, "Taft is a big fellow; he urged me to bring Root into the Cabinet." In public and formal testimonials Roosevelt combed the dictionary for superlatives: in "courage," "capacity," "inflexible uprightness," "disinterestedness," "wide acquaintance with governmental problems and identification of himself with the urgent needs of the social and governmental work of the day, Taft stands preeminent." In an article in *The Outlook*, Roosevelt quoted a friend as saying, and on his own account indorsed the statement, that there was only one man in the United States who combined all the qualities that would make a first-rate President with all those which would make a first-class Chief Justice, "and that man is William H. Taft."

III

While Roosevelt mentioned both the Presidency and the Supreme Court, his persistent instinct, expressing itself largely subconsciously, over a period of years, told him the Court was the post to which he should urge Taft. Early in 1906, by the retirement of Justice Brown, Roosevelt had another opportunity to make an offer, his third. Taft's declination, like his previous ones, was accompanied by such obvious trouble of mind that Roosevelt chose to regard the interview as not ending the matter, and on March 15, 1906, wrote Taft a long letter. That private letter to a friend and associate, as much as anything Roosevelt ever wrote or any act for which he received world-wide applause, reflected his finest qualities. He divorced himself completely from his own desires. Rather, one should say that Roosevelt, when acting in a matter that affected Taft's fortunes, had no desires of his own. Instinctively, without self-consciousness, out of spontaneous affection for a friend, he put himself in the friend's place. He pictured all the alternatives, recited all the arguments, poured out reasons pro and con. More than a President writing to a member of his Cabinet, more even than one friend writing to another, it was like a wise father writing to a son. In this paternal quality of Roosevelt's letter one recognizes, as one reads it to-day, the judgment that caused Roosevelt three times to press the Court upon Taft, and the affection which led him to wish that Taft should have whichever career would most appeal to him. Roosevelt wrote of the apparent confusion in Taft's own attempt to pilot himself through intricacies of duty, inclination and interest, and continued:

My dear Will, it is preeminently a matter in which no other man can take the responsibility of deciding for you what is best for you to do. . . . In each case it is the man himself who is to lead his life after having decided one way or the other. No one can lead that life for him, and neither he nor any one else can afford to have any one else make the decision.[12]

Then Roosevelt turned to the public aspects of the case, the problems ahead of the country, which the Supreme Court must face, problems arising out of "the dull, purblind folly of very rich men, their greed and

[12] "Theodore Roosevelt and His Time," Joseph Bucklin Bishop,

arrogance"; the "corruption in business and politics" that had produced an "unhealthy condition of excitement and irritation in the public mind." It was those problems in part that caused Roosevelt to have a preference, caused him to wish Taft to go on the Court. "In such a contest you could do very much if you were on the Bench. . . ."

But Roosevelt would press neither his own interest, nor his own judgment. "You know what your soul turns to better than I can," he said. He brought up the argument against taking the Justiceship which he felt might be having weight with Taft, the fact that Taft by going on the Court might foreclose any chance for the Presidency:

It is not a light thing to cast aside the chance of the Presidency, even though, of course, it is a chance, however a good one. It would be a very foolish thing for you to get it into your thoughts, so that your sweet and fine nature would be warped and you would become bitter and sour, as Henry Clay became; and, thank Heaven, this is impossible. But it is well to remember that the shadow of the Presidency falls on no man twice, save in most exceptional circumstances.

Now, my dear Will, there is the situation as I see it. It is a hard choice to make, and you yourself have to make it. You have two alternatives before you, each with uncertain possibilities, and you cannot feel sure that whichever you take you will not afterward feel that it would have been better if you had taken the other.

And Roosevelt concluded, again in the spirit of a wise father putting upon the shoulders of an adolescent son the responsibility for making an important decision affecting himself: "I feel sure that you should decide in accordance with the promptings of your own liking, of your own belief as to where you can render the service which most appeals to you, as well as that which you feel is most beneficial to the nation. No one can with wisdom advise you."

Taft's alternatives were: to go on the Supreme Bench where he could remain for life and have a reasonable expectation of perhaps becoming Chief; or to remain Secretary of War. The latter course had two advantages: he would be able to continue to look after the Filipinos (over whom the War Department had jurisdiction), and he would be open to accept the Presidency if it should come to him.

With this confusing equation of chances and values, Taft wrestled for a full three months and a half. In his hesitancy, he asked Roosevelt to call together a little informal council of his friends, consisting of Secretary of State Root, Attorney-General Moody, and Secretary of Commerce Oscar Straus, together with Taft and Roosevelt. The council thought Taft ought to accept the place on the Supreme Bench. Taft, still troubled, said he would write to his brother Charles in Cincinnati.[13] He took the problem away with him on his summer vacation, and from Murray Bay, Canada, wrote Roosevelt on July 30, 1906, that his decision was to decline the place on the Supreme Court, to remain Secretary of War. He put it on the ground that was his own convincing motive: "Circumstances seem to me to have imposed something in the nature of a trust to me personally" to look after the Filipinos. He realized that many would say he was refusing the certainty of the Court for the chance of the Presidency, and that "I must face and bear this misconstruction of what I do." But he was confident that Roosevelt would "credit my reasons as I give them to you, and will believe me when I say that I would much prefer to go on the Supreme Bench for life than to run for the Presidency."[14] Roosevelt did credit Taft's reasons. That Taft preferred the Court was com-

---

[13] "As I Knew Them," Henry L. Stoddard.
[14] "Theodore Roosevelt and His Time," Joseph Bucklin Bishop.

mon knowledge to his intimates. "Never," wrote Mrs. Taft, "did he cease to regard a Supreme Court appointment as vastly more desirable than the Presidency."[15]

If Taft "would much prefer to go on the Supreme Bench than to run for the Presidency," why did he not take his heart's desire when Roosevelt tendered it? The reason Taft gave now and on the two preceding occasions, was that he felt a "trust to me personally to look after the Filipinos," which he could not do, directly, if he went on the Supreme Court. That is the only reason that was within Taft. There was another reason outside him but close to him. Taft had given a clew to it when he said he would write to his brother. Taft, as is often the case with men of high ability, modestly rated his prospects less than his relatives and friends who estimated them more accurately. Taft's brothers, men who were leaders in the several fields in which they functioned, together with his wife, a vital personality deeply ambitious for her husband, believed Taft was capable of filling the Presidency, believed it was possible the Presidency might come to him, and steadily influenced him to hold himself open for it.[16]

Out of that conflict between his heart's desire and the worthy ambition of those close and dear to him, Taft, in the fall of 1906, made a formal statement, its unusual wording and almost backward-leaning spirit reflecting the innate hesitancy of a fine and able man en-

[15] "Recollections," Mrs. William H. Taft.

[16] "Taft is still undecided [about accepting Roosevelt's tender of a place on the Supreme Court]. Friends say he is almost certain to take Justiceship. He is coming here today to confer with his brothers, who have the Presidency in mind for him." — Head-line, New York *Sun*, March 14, 1906.

"It has always been my feeling that the presidential ambition was much more a family matter than a personal one with Mr. Taft, and that family influence was the factor which determined him to make the race for the Presidency instead of taking the place on the Supreme Court to which President Roosevelt stood ready to appoint him." — Oscar King Davis, in "Released for Publication."

"The subject of my husband's appointment to the Supreme Court cropped up

tering a world, politics, that was essentially foreign to him, and a little dismaying:

For the purpose of relieving the burden imposed by recent publications on some of my friends among the Washington newspaper correspondents of putting further inquiry to me, I wish to say that my ambition is not political; that I am not seeking the Presidential nomination; . . . but that I am not foolish enough to say that in the improbable event that the opportunity to run for the great office of President were to come to me, I should decline it, for this would not be true.

Upon this formal announcement of Taft's candidacy, Roosevelt did not commit himself. On the contrary, some time later he said to Mrs. Taft that he might "feel it to be my duty to be for Hughes."[17]

Mrs. Taft reported the remark to Taft, who wrote to Roosevelt in a spirit almost of relief and hope: "If you do you may be sure you will awaken no sense of disappointment on my part. . . . You know what my feeling has been in respect to the Presidency." Roosevelt, replying to Taft, said he had merely meant that Hughes might have so much popular sentiment behind him that there would be no course open but to support him.[18]

---

with what seemed to me annoying frequency." — "Recollections," Mrs. William Howard Taft.

"From the day that the elder brother [Charles] saw the gift of Will for making friends and for dictating in an easy way a legal analysis of a bundle of documents, that younger brother has been a hobby surpassing all the old masters. He has always been trying to show Will the road to opportunity, knowing that once Will was started he could do the traveling himself. When McKinley wanted to send the younger brother to the Philippines, Will was all for declining. He wanted to remain on the bench. Charles P. argued far into the night in favor of going. . . ." — *Collier's,* June 20, 1908.

[17] In "As I Knew Them," Henry L. Stoddard says that about May, 1908, "shortly before the convention, Roosevelt said to William R. Willcox: 'I said to Mrs. Taft less than a year ago that as much as I thought of Will, it might be that I would feel it my duty to be for Hughes.'" This conversation has been verified by Mr. Willcox to the author of the present history.

[18] "Recollections," Mrs. William H. Taft.

3

AN AMERICAN DYNASTY

Which Was Brief and Ended Tragically, but Was Important While It Lasted, and During the Latter Part of It, Very Spectacular. The "Insurance Scandals." Quarrels Among Men in High Places. Together with Something About Fathers and Sons, and About Some Captains of Finance, and About America as It Was in the Year 1905, and About One Who Departed from the American Scene to Dwell in Europe.

THERE had come to New York City in 1850, from the paternal village store in the foot-hills of the Catskill Mountains, a youth of sixteen named Henry Baldwin Hyde. He worked seven years for the Mutual Life Insurance Company of New York, learned the business thoroughly, became discontented with what he considered the cramping conservatism of the company's methods, and irritated the officials with suggestions for introducing what would have been called, half a century later, "pep." Failing in that, the youth asked one of his superiors to help him found a company of his own. For

Henry Baldwin Hyde, founder of the Equitable Life Assurance Society.

this unworthy ambition he was discharged on a Saturday night, and on Monday morning rented a vacant second-floor room directly above the office of his recent employer, and hung out a sign thirty feet long, THE

EQUITABLE LIFE ASSURANCE SOCIETY OF THE UNITED STATES — the sign dwarfing and obscuring that of the Mutual Life below. He borrowed a desk and some chairs, and "in order to make everything agreeable and cheerful for visitors, I purchased a box of cigars and placed them in a convenient position on the mantelpiece." Thus equipped, and with a little money he induced acquaintances to invest, this enterprising youth crossed swords with his recent employer and nineteen other competing companies. He lived frugally, paid himself a salary of $1,500 a year, worked desperately, scrutinized every penny of expense, kept a growing staff of clerks and agents at concert pitch, told subordinates that he must have "results, not futile endeavors," turned sharp corners at high speed, was intolerant of any devotion to the business that was less than his own, was hard and inflexible toward the easy-going, took what he needed when he needed it and let his lawyers look after the details, held that "to blunder is a crime"; maintained, on Sundays, a connection "with the Fifth Avenue Presbyterian Church, one of the most prominent congregations in the city . . . where he made the acquaintance of a number of men of substance and high standing, some of whom became stockholders and directors of the Equitable Society."[1] He paid claims a little earlier than other companies, invented new devices and inserted new allurements in his policies, got rid of inconvenient restrictions in the insurance law, erected an ornate head-office building, founded branches in the larger cities, pioneered in sending American life insurance methods to Europe, erected fourteen branch office buildings, five in American cities, two in Paris, one in Mexico, one in South America, and one each in the cities of Berlin, Vienna, Madrid, and Melbourne and Sydney,

[1] "Henry Baldwin Hyde," printed privately by the Directors of the Equitable Society, 1899.

Australia — and, after forty years, on May 2, 1899, died of overwork, leaving a life-insurance company that was one of the three largest in the world. Whereupon the directors of his company resolved that "in testimony

From a photograph © Brown Bros.

The Fifth Avenue Presbyterian Church at 55th Street.

of our recognition of the great and noble work accomplished . . . a portrait statue of Mr. Hyde, designed by a competent sculptor, executed in the best manner, and composed of appropriate materials, be erected to his memory in the Grand Central Hall of the ground floor of the Equitable Building"; and further that "a committee be appointed to supervise the preparation of a historical sketch of the life of Mr. Hyde." Which historical sketch, printed de luxe at the De Vinne Press, and containing 244 wide-margined, large-typed pages of adulatory appreciation, slumbers forgotten on the shelves of the Congressional Library — the binding, on the sides, still its original color, royal purple; the back, exposed to the light, faded to a grayish mauve.

II

That was that. Mr. Hyde, in his less preoccupied moments, reared also a son, whom he named James Hazen Hyde; raised the boy as strictly as he managed the insurance company, so strictly that the youth was awkward, countrified, causing his mates in the Harvard Class of 1898 to associate his long hair with hayseeds and to put a touch of amiable derision in their use of his foster-name "Caleb." Within a year after graduating, the youth, twenty-three years of age, became, by the elder Hyde's death, custodian of a billion dollars of life insurance, caretaker of the savings of six hundred thousand policyholders; became, as symbolized by the vignette which his father had ordered to embellish the heading of policy contracts, "protector of the widow and orphan," to the number of three million; became autocrat[2] over an organization involving the fortunes of several thousand employees, and master of four hundred million dollars of assets with all their ramifications of power and prestige. He became a director in forty-six corporations, as incidents to his control of the life-insurance company, and as gestures of ingratiation from

[2] The elder Hyde left a majority of the shares of the Equitable, 502 out of a total of 1,000, to young Hyde, in trust until he should reach the age of thirty, and thereafter outright. Control of a majority of the stock carried absolute control of the Society; policyholders had no voice.

financiers who wished his good-will, or, more accurately,
wished the good-will of the four hundred million dollars, or, more accurately yet, wished lucrative access to
the four hundred millions. He became a director of the
Union Pacific and thirteen
other leading railroads and
traction companies; of nineteen banks and trust companies in New York City, Boston, Philadelphia, Pittsburgh,
San Francisco and points between; of the Western Union
Telegraph Company, the
Westinghouse Electric Company, and some thirteen other
industrial corporations.

Vice-President Hyde of the Equitable, as *Puck* saw him.

With these directorates and
other attributes and perquisites of power festooned about
his slender shoulders, the
young man ceased to be called
"Caleb." He ceased to be
Caleb. In his transformation he swung to an extreme
which expressed itself in addiction to things æsthetic,
and French. He had his erstwhile "hayseed" hair cut
by a French barber in the vogue of Paris, raised a
beard and kept it trimmed in the French manner, imported his clothes from Paris, wore the queer-looking
"stovepipe" silk hat of France in his Sunday walks on
Fifth Avenue, spent a part of each year in France, made
himself patron of an *Alliance Française* at Harvard and
a French literary colony in New York, achieved perfection in pronouncing the French *eu*, and liked to show it;
decorated his conversation with *bon mots* in the French
tongue, to the annoyed mystification of some of his less

cosmopolitan associates in the Equitable; was made by
the French Government an officer of the *Legion d'Hon-
neur;* entertained a great French actress, Mme. Réjane,
at a costume ball in New York, at which one detail of
the entertainment was a
classic play in French;
gave, with Senator Chaun-
cey M. Depew as a joint
host, a similar entertainment and dinner (of five
hundred plates at a cost of
twelve thousand dollars)
to the French Ambassa-
dor, M. Jules Cambon;
brought François Guillot
from F r a n c e to take
c h a r g e of his stables,
brought a French chef to
cook at an inn at which he
was accustomed to stop on
his four-in-hand coaching
trips. For his c o u n t r y
house, he had a "châ-
teau" on L o n g I s l a n d,
with an office in the sta-

Madame Réjane.

ble, "a room," said a French journalist whom he entertained, M. Jules Huret of the Paris *Figaro,* "full
of telephones and electric bells, furnished with fine
carpets, old mahogany furniture, sporting photographs
and prints, coaching trophies and hunting horns; next
to his office is the kitchen, which permits him and his
guests to come when the whim seizes them and have
supper in the stables more freely and gaily than in the
château; I remember a very festive supper that we had
there with the thermometer outside fifteen above zero,

where ladies donned old postillion hats or bull-fighter bonnets and blew hunting horns while everybody danced the cake walk." From his town house to his office in the Equitable Building, his daily journey was a pageant:

Countess de Roguemont and Mr. James Hazen Hyde at Bradley-Martin Ball (1897).

he drove "jauntily down town in his private hansom cab, a bunch of violets nodding at the side of the horse's head, another bunch nodding from the coachman's hat, and a third bunch breathing incense from the button-hole of the young man himself."[3] The New York *World*, contemplating the spectacle of the gilded,

[3] New York *World*, April 2, 1905.

scented youth sitting in the high places of four hundred million dollars, reflected, reasonably, that "Dumas' riotous, turbulent imagination never conceived of such a situation."

Reams of such publicity streamed in young Hyde's wake — it had been his hard-headed father's boast that he could walk every street in New York and never be recognized.

This newspaper picture of Hyde as a spectacular dilettante was accepted by the public without making allowance for the overemphasis of a press which, figuratively no less than literally, tends to portray everything in all-white or all-black. Hyde was flamboyant, but not a wastrel. He was "quite without vicious tastes or tendencies." The connotations which the America of that day tended to associate with things French did not, in Hyde's case, exist. Friends who knew him well said that on his annual pilgrimages to Paris he eschewed the paths of the excitement-seekers and sought instead the company of French statesmen, authors, artists. These and his other French associations were meant no more for his own pleasure and showiness than for the benefit of the Equitable. Knowing, and sharing, the Gallic temperament, its volubility, its love of the dramatic and graceful, Hyde believed that his attentions to the French, and the conspicuousness of them, would advance grandiose plans he had for the Equitable in France.[4] When as a result the business of the Equitable in the United States suffered from the obtuseness of provincial American ideas about disbursement of life-insurance funds and about how the head of a life-insurance com-

[4] France was considering legislation which would have restrained American insurance companies in that country. Young Hyde believed, and according to contemporary standards was justified in believing, that his attentions to the French might overcome this restraint.

pany should comport himself, that disappointing outcome could fairly be called merely the case of a good
impulse whose fruits did not turn out as expected, an
incident neither uncommon nor unforgivable in a young
man of twenty-eight.

If it pleased Hyde's sense of self-importance to take
three secretaries with him on his trips to Europe, nevertheless he was able to say, "my records will show they
have not wasted their time." If it pleased his flair for
grandiosity to have four separate offices, each elaborately
furnished, scattered among the institutions from which
he drew salaries, nevertheless it comported with his conception of a *grand seigneur* of high finance that during
his work-day hours he should be found in one or another
of them, busy, according to his lights.

So quaintly exquisite a youth strolling jauntily in the
Wall Street jungle, was Little Red Riding Hood to the
wolves, and likewise game for the hunters and trappers,
the netters, the ginners, the allurers; prey for the pitfalls and precipices. Assiduously the promoters and captains of industry, the bankers and financial figures of
high and low degree, applied themselves to inducting
the young elegant (blithely unaware of the rôle he was
filling) into the mazes of high finance; flattering him
with seats on the directorates of the banks, railroads, and
corporations they controlled; alluring him with hints
that, through their political "pull," they could make
him Ambassador to France; explaining to him, or playing in his sight, like city sophisticates at a country fair,
esoteric games they knew, chicaneries of financial
sleight-of-hand, played with paraphernalia of figure-
head directors, underwritings, syndicates, interlocking
directorates, fictitious loans for millions made in the
names of office-boys and clerks. With leering winks

they let him see, in the existing practices of the big insurance companies, the possibilities of remunerative manipulation inherent in the dual capacity of one who is at
the same time a director of an insurance company and
also a stockholder in trust companies and banks — how

James Hazen Hyde.

the enormous funds of the
insurance company could be
deposited in the trust companies and banks of which
he was a stockholder, with
agreeable profits accruing to
the stockholder in his individual capacity; and other
intricate transactions, in
which, in effect, the same
man fills the rôles of both
buyer and seller, and is
thereby enabled to achieve
his profits without such sordid haggling as would be
distasteful to an æsthetic
soul. Adroitly they tempted
young Hyde with participations in underwriting syndicates, an intricacy in high finance which, in a way that
the young man did not quite understand, yielded agreeable remuneration to the individual participators —
while the insurance-company treasury provided the
money that sustained the transaction. Patiently, art-
fully, hungrily, they pursued the usufructs of that four
hundred millions in the Equitable treasury, wove snares
for its cock-sure young custodian.[5]

[5] An especially well-informed writer, in *The World's Work* for March, 1906,
put it thus: "The seduction of James Hazen Hyde could not have taken place
without his consent; but it is not at all likely that he was conscious of the in-
sidious process by which he came to use the assets of the company almost as if
they were his own property." In hearings before the New York State Insurance
Department, in 1905, James W. Alexander, an official of the Equitable, said:

Presently there was alarm for the safety of the Equitable. Intrenched within the Society was a family, the Alexanders, who had a hereditary concern for the young heir and his patrimony. The Alexanders had been associated with the Equitable and officers of it from its founding; they had been among those "men of substance and high standing" whose acquaintance the elder Hyde had made in his early days at the Fifth Avenue Presbyterian Church, where one of the Alexanders was pastor. They were always spoken of as "an old Princeton family," the grandfather having been a professor in that institution, and they had a clear title to a place in what was known and accepted as the "old New York aristocracy." Two Alexanders had been enrolled by the elder Hyde as the first names on the original directorate of the Equitable in 1859; and as the Equitable grew, the Alexanders grew with it, both in wealth and in the number of them that attached themselves to the Equitable treasury. They became stockholders and partners in banks, trust companies, law and brokerage firms which made profits out of transactions with the Equitable —

"Mr. Hyde has thrust himself forward as the Equitable . . . and put himself in an attitude with all these big promoting and banking interests around town as one of themselves. I have always regarded it as a menace that a young man of twenty-eight years of age, open to flattery and fond of prominence, should be so intimate with these great magnates of Wall Street."

James W. Alexander, quoted above, was young Hyde's severest critic, with a motive for making the case against him as severe as possible. To the author of this history, writing twenty-five years after the event, Hyde's chief faults seem to have been flamboyancy and egotism, qualities often associated with youth in any walk of life. The record does not show that young Hyde ever had an evil impulse, and shows he had many good ones. All the emphasis of the day was on Hyde's faults; there was little consideration for his misfortune, which was that he was born into a business and a milieu to which his temperament was grotesquely ill adapted; he should have been born into a dukedom in the France of Louis XIV, when his bearing, his manners, his tout ensemble would have been perfect in their timeliness, and his ethics would have been nearly two centuries in advance of the time.

Most of the other characters in the Equitable drama seem less odious to the historian than they were made out by the journalists and other critics of the day. The Equitable scandal was one of those moral revolutions in which usages long accepted come into collision with new standards.

practising for nearly half a century what might be called a mild parasitism upon the Society, in a quite respectable way, strictly within the permitted conventions of the day and to such a comparatively harmless degree as the hard-headed elder Hyde would permit. By the time the senior Hyde died and the son came into his inheritance, three Alexanders were directors of the Equitable, four were stockholders, seven drew salaries as officers or employees of it, and seven drew incomes from banks, trust companies or firms affiliated with it — it was estimated[6] (with newspaper exaggeration) that the total salaries, fees, commissions, retainers, perquisites, and emoluments drawn by the Alexanders from the Equitable, directly or indirectly, was above a million dollars a year.

It would be seriously unfair and inaccurate to picture the Alexanders merely as self-interested limpets clinging to the perquisites and power going with the young heir's person. In the step they now took, they were moved, without doubt, by a wish to safeguard their own remunerative relation to the Equitable, but their forty-six years of association with the Hyde dynasty gave them an additional and more elevated motive. One of them, head of the clan, James W. Alexander, had been made by the elder Hyde a trustee of the younger Hyde's estate until he should reach the age of thirty. In the spirit of that relation of temporary regency, the Alexanders conceived of themselves in a rôle which they would have described, in the Covenanter circles where they had their Sabbath-day being, as "saving the young man from himself," and rescuing the Equitable, its assets and reputation, from exploitation by an outside group of financiers and promoters antagonistic to them, with whom young Hyde had affiliated himself. Moreover, Hyde, in 1905,

---

[6] By the New York *World*, May 3, 1905.

was within two years of being thirty, when Alexander's trusteeship would cease and the young heir would become absolute master of his inheritance, sole autocrat of the Equitable. Already Hyde had shown distaste for the tutelage of the Alexanders, irritation over their criticism of his social éclat, resentment against their nepotic favor to their relatives, disapproval of their management of the Equitable. Hyde indeed had said[7] "that he intended to change it [the Alexanders' management] and that his desire was to surround himself with independent men." Already he had brought into the directorate of the Equitable a newly arrived Napoleon of railroads, Edward H. Harriman, and Harriman had said he "did not think

Photograph by Rockwood, New York. Courtesy of the New York "World."

James W. Alexander.

that the [Alexanders'] method of management of the Equitable was the right one."

In short, the Alexanders saw, in the influence of rival financiers over the orchidaic young prince, imminent danger to their own emoluments as well as catastrophic menace to the Equitable.[8] Acting upon this medley of

---

[7] To Edward H. Harriman, in 1901. Testimony before the Armstrong Investigating Committee.

[8] Several persons familiar with these events as they took place, who have read the proofs of these chapters, express strongly the conviction that James W. Alexander was moved solely by concern for the Equitable, not by self-interest. An authority who had a better opportunity to arrive at correct judgment than almost any other person writes: "In his fight with Hyde, James W. Alexander impressed me as acting from motives above any thought of personal gain; in

motives, the Alexanders, in February, 1905, drew up, together with other high officials[9] of the Society, a protest in which they demanded that Hyde surrender the control he enjoyed as owner of a majority of the stock, and that the society be "mutualized," that is, that the right to elect the directors be taken from Hyde and given to the policyholders. This demand for abdication the chief of the Alexanders delivered to Hyde in person, with allegations that some of the transactions of Hyde and his new friends had been seriously questionable. The action, while sensational in the extreme, was kept, for a while, prudently within the walls of high finance, for everybody concerned realized, with terrified apprehension, the disaster that would fall upon all if the state of affairs within the Equitable should become known to the policyholders and the public.

Young Hyde was stunned — not, however, because of any feeling of guilt. The charges of financial wrong-

that contest over the control of the Equitable I think that he was really trying to protect the interest of the policy-holders which he believed to be in jeopardy."

William C. Redfield, later one of the "reform" trustees who were put in charge of the Equitable, writes: "I have always understood that Mr. James W. Alexander died of a broken heart; among the 'reform' trustees the feeling was that he had been a victim of forces which his own conscience had set in motion."

Bainbridge Colby writes: "The determination of Mr. James W. Alexander to make a stand for the rescue of the Society from the situation which had grown up around the younger Mr. Hyde was reached very deliberately and under a compelling sense of duty. . . . He realized that he entered upon this bitter controversy at the disadvantage of a man who had [himself] been part and parcel of the Society's history, and that he would be unable to disengage himself from various transactions in which he had really played a secondary rôle and yet, in the presence of hostile criticism, an implicating one. He was truly alarmed at conditions that had grown up and that demanded correction. He was an old gentleman at the time, being soon to retire; he shrank from a fight but steeled himself for it."

[9] Bainbridge Colby writes: "The demand that Mr. Hyde should . . . relinquish his position was signed by every executive official of the Society, forty or more in number, with a single exception who was in reality a personal attaché and factotum for young Mr. Hyde. Every signer of the paper put his position and his salary at hazard and I think no body of men ever took a course in the line of their duty with a clearer realization that they were acting against their personal interests."

doing awakened in him no sense of self-conscious blame; rather they amazed him. He had not initiated these practices, nor been active in the execution of them; he had merely, in a taken-for-granted way, followed customs he had found in full flower when first he stretched his spat-clad feet beneath the directors' table. Had he not gone into these operations with the beaming approval of, and in partnership with, fellow directors of the Equitable, men whose names were synonyms for business competence, personal integrity, public honor? As for the syndicates, had not the Alexanders themselves, respected churchmen, participated in them? Had he not himself heard his father's life-long friend, Director-Senator Depew, pillar of respectability and paragon of wisdom, approve and expatiate upon the desirability to the Society of having its interests mingled with the private interests of its officials?

So far as Hyde's conscience was concerned, he could fight back. But there was another quality in him, which crisis brought to the front. He had genuine respect, almost veneration, for the memory of his father, and for the institution his father had founded and builded. Like the French king, and in a more worthy sense, Hyde would have said, "L'Equitable, c'est moi." He loved the Equitable, and a fight by him would injure it. Moreover, beneath his youthful irritation against the chaperonage of the Alexanders he had a real regard for them and for the other older officials of the Society whom his father had left in temporary guardianship over him. Their formally expressed judgment that his actions had been hurtful to the Society shocked him into self-questioning. Deeply hurt, sincerely moved to give heed to his father's associates, reluctant to make a fight for personal power that would do damage to the Equitable and to his father's memory — Hyde proposed a compromise, in which control would be divided between stockholders and policyholders.

But if Hyde was hesitant to fight, the financiers who were profiting by making use of him had no such scruples. They, grim realists, saw the situation as it was, saw that the ousting of Hyde would be the ousting of them. It was a contest between, on the one hand, the Alexanders and the banks and corporations with which they were affiliated, and, on the other hand, the banking interests with whom Hyde was intimate, those whom Alexander, in his charges against Hyde, described as "these great magnates of Wall Street . . . these big promoting and banking interests." They realized that if the Equitable were mutualized, as the Alexanders proposed, the result would be that the Alexanders themselves, being officers of the Society, would be able, through the Society's agents all over the country, to corral the votes of the policyholders, would be able to perpetuate themselves in power and keep control of the Equitable funds. The prize — one of the country's three largest reservoirs of funds available for security flotations, for railroad mergers and trusts, and for other forms of promotion and exploitation — the prize was too great to be lost without a struggle. The fight for control of the Equitable, in short, was a major battle in a bigger war, the biggest[10] war there was in the banking and railroad world.

[10] The motive for Edward H. Harriman and his banking connections to keep their access to the Equitable was the stronger since Harriman's rival, J. P. Morgan, had similar access to another insurance company, the New York Life. "So long as the spoils of the policy holders were apportioned among these great banking firms and the banking firms worked in harmony, there was tranquility and peace — the good feeling that comes from profitable secrecy and popular ignorance. But this harmony did not last. The beginning of the present [insurance] exposure was as long ago as the railroad fight between Messrs. Harriman and Morgan for the control of the Northwestern transcontinental railroad companies. [See "Our Times," Vol. II, Ch. 18.] The possible owners of great rail-

The moment that Alexander's demand for Hyde's resignation precipitated struggle, the fifty-two pillars of financial society who composed the board of directors of the Equitable resolved themselves into warring groups, not at all as a line-up of Alexander men and Hyde men, and decidedly not as Equitable men (except in a few cases), but in accordance with their several financial, railroad, and other affiliations. Almost as quickly as a chemical solution succumbs to an acid precipitate, the directorate of the Equitable became Harriman men, Hill men, Morgan men, representatives of this railroad or that, of one banking group or another, each faction the trustees not of the Equitable but rather of the bank or railroad or other institution it represented, with the Equitable playing only the part of a prize fiercely fought for.[11]

In the phase into which the Equitable battle now passed, young Hyde became a piece in the game, with which and over which the rival financiers contended. Him the factions successively cajoled and intimidated.

---

road systems were the few men who had the ability to invest unattached capital. Banks and trust companies could not safely part with much cash without feeling certain that the depositors would not demand it back. This assurance could be given only by the life insurance officials whose investments could be securely left for long times and whose irresponsible millions could thus be put where they would do the most 'good' for their manipulators." — "Q. P.," in "Life Insurance Corruption," *World's Work*, March, 1906.

[11] One who was a director of the Equitable at the time of the 1905 fight read, in 1929, the proofs of this chapter, and wrote me, with some sadness, about the "men of 'light and leading,' presidents of railroad systems, heads of trust companies, trustees of universities, quite of the 'pillar of society' type, who became instantly responsive to outside orders and sought only to promote and safeguard the particular interest that was closest to them. In very few instances was that particular interest the interest of the Equitable Society, of which they were trustees. Instead, therefore, of the Board room becoming a place for the calm consideration of measures calculated to conserve and promote the interest of the Equitable, it became an arena in which the trustees of the Equitable showed that they were trustees of everything else first, and of the Equitable, last. The stakes were vast and tempting. If one group despaired of landing control it might at least upset the efforts of a competing group."

He was pushed and pulled, hustled and jostled. When his troubles were thickest upon him, four separate interests tried to press him into selling the Equitable to them; and when one of them, Harriman, heard that another, Thomas F. Ryan, was about to get it, he, Harriman, threatened Ryan with reprisals, financial and political, unless Ryan would let him have a half-interest in it.[12] In the din of reproach, solicitation, and blame with which young Hyde was now surrounded, he lost confidence in his own position, doubted the wisdom and good faith of many of his associates. His former overweening self-confidence became a quagmire of self-doubt. In the end, after much public humiliation, he sold the institution which was his patrimony to a lone wolf for $2,500,000,[13] and removed himself to his beloved Paris, whence he never returned.

Photograph by Davis & Sanford.
Courtesy of New York "World."

Thomas F. Ryan.

[12] Ryan so testified. Harriman denied that his approach to Ryan had the color of intimidation and declared that his motive had been to keep control of the Equitable in the "proper hands."

[13] For this sum paid to young Hyde, the purchaser, Thomas F. Ryan, received 502 shares, a majority of the Equitable stock, on which his total direct and legitimate income was limited by the company's charter to $7 a share, in all $3,514 yearly. Pungently did the New York *World* ask "Why? What is the real motive?" An answer is to be found in some words of the legislative committee which subsequently investigated the Equitable: "The stock must be regarded as affording enormous collateral advantages to those interested in financial operations."

The Equitable's charter stipulated that all profits except 7 per cent on the $100,000 of stock should belong to the policyholders.

There for the next quarter-century he lived, a voluntary expatriate, in semi-retired munificence in an old palace on the Rue Adolphe Yvon. As the years went on, echoes of him came back across the ocean in occasional despatches sent by newspaper correspondents old enough to remember that Hyde had once been a conspicuous figure in American life. One such casual allusion mentioned him as "an epicure of the younger French School, which includes such distinguished names as Marcel Fouquier, the Duc de Morny, Santos-Dumont and, if you please, our own James Hazen Hyde, who has nothing less than a 'poached peach à la James Hazen Hyde' named for him at Durand's, in Paris; the peach is poached like an egg, and then has kirsch poured over it and ignited; this completes its cooking and the burnt kirsch provides the sauce."[14]

One wonders if ever there came to him nostalgic yearnings for the land of his birth, homely feelings such as come to even the most exalted — atavistic dreams of the quiet little community of his fathers in the Catskills . . . frosty October nights in the lamplit country store and the cracker-barrel discussions about the stove . . . the gently contoured hills, hauntingly sad on sunny autumn days . . . the poignant realism to a boy of the legends of Sleepy Hollow and of Rip Van Winkle bowling with the gnomes . . . memories of the Harvard Yard in spring, the grass bright green, burgeoning elms, rich young voices singing on the steps of Holworthy, wistaria blooming exotically in prim gardens around ancient New England homes on Brattle Street . . . his early happy years with the Equitable — the beelike buzz of down-town New York . . . stenographers at lunchtime strolling arm in arm among the tombs in Trinity Church-

[14] From a Paris letter in the Philadelphia *Public Ledger*, December, 1929.

yard . . . the scents of spices and coffee drifting up through the April air from the South Street wharves to his office on the tenth floor of the Equitable Building.

One wonders if, during the years of his exile, there ever passed flickeringly across his mind, like the projection of a time-worn movie film, jagged images of such car-window glimpses as he might have had, on occasional trips in his private car, of the America west of the Hudson River; or thoughts about an America of which he had been prevented from becoming a part by his misfortune of being, by birth and temperament, too far removed from the common lot: sunny

Old Equitable Life Building.

Indiana farmhouses . . . sycamore-shaded villages, their main street hitching-posts crowded with horses on a Saturday afternoon, tobacco-chewing rustics taking their ease on baggage-trucks at the "depot" . . . grinning Italian section-hands greeting the passing train with a cheerful wave of the hat . . . glimpses of women and girls at croquet on the lawns of small-town cottages . . . lush green cornfields of Illinois, smiling after a summer shower . . . "Old Man River, rolling lazy to the sea" . . . tramps boiling coffee in the shade of a water-tank

. . . straw stacks silhouetted against the salmon-and-orange sunset of the Nebraska prairies . . . little one-street Rocky Mountain villages, still close to their pioneer stage, with chap-clad cowboys and an occasional Indian on horseback watching the "Limited" go by . . .

© *Brown Bros.*

Statue of Henry Baldwin Hyde in the ruins of the Equitable Building, following the fire.

the lonely desert . . . mist from the Pacific blowing in through the Golden Gate . . . miles on miles of spruce-clad mountains in Oregon and Washington . . . herds of cattle spread over Montana's fenceless grazing-lands . . . the pioneer sod-houses dotting the lonely Dakota prairies . . . the green-painted trains of the Great Northern Railroad winding slowly into the Twin Cities with a suggestion of having come from a country of cold and wilderness . . . the hurrying crowds of Michigan Avenue in Chicago . . . the sand-dunes along the southern shore of Lake Michigan . . . Pittsburgh at night with its flaring furnaces . . . the elation of journey's end, with the New York City sky-line seen from the Jersey City ferry.

If ever there came to Hyde any of these memories which, to others of his generation, made the America of the early 1900's poignant and dear — doubtless they were, to him, but the light shadows of summer clouds on the broad surface of his contentment with the land of his adoption, where, in the Bois or at the Opera, his pointed mustaches and Rue de la Paix clothes caused him to be mistaken, by titillated tourists from the States, for a "typical Parisian."

How quickly effected, and how complete, was young Hyde's effacement from the American scene, is pictured bleakly in that cold barometer of relative importance in American life, "Who's Who" — which, before the Equitable revolution ended his régime, devoted 47 lines to the cataloguing of his corporation directorates, clubs, and other distinctions — and in 1908 dismissed him in ten words, with its formula for an epitaph to a "has-been"; "Hyde, James Hazen, capitalist; see Who's Who in America, 1906–7."

That was that. By the seventh year after the father's death, the only Hyde in the Equitable Company or building was that statue of the founder of the brief dynasty, in the Grand Central Hall "executed in the best manner and composed of appropriate materials." *Sic transit gloria.*

4

MELODRAMA IN HIGH PLACES

Which Caused the Newspapers of the Day to Recall Some
Ancient Figures, and Some Exalted Phrases, Such as "Colossus," "Hercules," and "Augean Stables." A Man with a
"Rock-crusher Mind" Makes Some Breaches in the Cita-
dels of High Finance, and Thereby Causes Himself to Become an Important Figure in American Public Life, Destined to Remain So for Many Years. Hughes Emerges.

AFTER the fight of the rival packs over the Equitable
had gone on for some time, but still was kept safely
within the temples and be-
hind the altars of high finance, the fighters, too preoccupied to be sufficiently
vigilant, became, in turn,
the quarry for a stalker of
another breed. The pointers
and setters of the New York
World, sniffing the noisome
air drifting up Park Row
from Wall Street, felt their
nostrils and ears agreeably
titillated by scents and sounds
of wolves at war over prey.
The hounds of the press,
slinking, soft-footed and
tense, through circuitous
canyons, brought back mor-

From a photograph © Brown Bros.
Joseph Pulitzer, publisher of *The
World.*

sels of rumor about scandal in the very highest financial
circles of New York, of charges and counter-charges, of
rival committees wrangling, of the pot calling the kettle black, of violent quarrels, of bitter invectives hurled

across the mahogany tables in closed directors' rooms, of
one of the most prominent financiers in the country excited to a point where he could express his emotion only
by shrill yelps, "Wow! Wow! Wow!"[1] — some one,
extenuating, said Mr. Harriman's expression was not that
at all; it was "You! You! You!"

The stories of corruption on the most sacred altars of
high finance seemed incredible to *The World's* owner,
Joseph Pulitzer, who suspected his hounds of over-
zeal, but characteristically let them have their head.
Presently, the public read an amazing series of editorials.
To give the cumulative effect of timed blows they were
numbered 1, 2, 3, 4, etc. With the driving force of
repetition, all had the same heading, "Equitable Corruption," accompanied by an effective device of irony, the
dictionary definition of the word "equitable" printed under the caption of each editorial. The earlier ones were
guarded, vague, mere generalizations, "most astounding,
far-reaching financial scandal known to the history of
the United States," and the like. Presently, however, the
factions fighting over the Equitable reached that degree
of passion in which each was willing to let the public
know the worst — about the other; and the public
learned that some of the richest men in New York were
charging some of the other richest men in New York
with looting the Equitable Life Assurance Society.
"There must be Publicity!" shrieked *The World*, much
in the dark itself as yet. "Purging, Punishment and full
Restitution! . . . Open the books! Let the policyholders know what has been done in secret with the money

---

[1] One of Mr. Harriman's fellow directors, reading the proofs of this chapter
in 1929, recalled a sequel: After Mr. Harriman had uttered his last "wow," a
painful silence fell. All present realized that the great man had delivered himself of a sentiment that was a little obscure but very deep and intense. The
stillness was broken by Judge Cohen, who had a suave mode of speech. Turning
to Mr. Harriman, he said: "Mr. Harriman, I must confess that that is an aspect
of the situation which had quite escaped my attention."

saved for protection of widows and orphans. Let in the light! . . . There should be full publicity through a legislative investigation. Investigate, gentlemen of the Legislature!"

The gentlemen of the legislature (called into session,

From a photograph © by Underwood & Underwood.

Charles Evans Hughes, in 1905, during his investigation of the insurance companies.

most reluctantly, by Governor Francis W. Higgins, who said "nothing is to be gained by it") appointed a committee to investigate not only the Equitable but all the big life-insurance companies. The chairman[2] of the committee set about finding a lawyer to conduct the inquisition, a lawyer who must be able, of course, but who

[2] William W. Armstrong, of Rochester.

also must be comparatively young and not too far up toward the top of the bar — no law firm with long-established corporation connections could afford to attack anything so sacrosanct as the great insurance companies and their banking affiliations. The chairman, in his search, called on the editor of the New York *Press*, and the editor of *The Press* telephoned the manager of *The World*, saying, "You are more interested in this than I am; can you think of anybody?" The manager of *The World*, recalling a comparatively young lawyer who had done well in an investigation of gas matters, said: "What's the matter with Charley Hughes?" The suggestion coincided with recommendations made by many others, and with the judgment of Governor Higgins.

For Charles E. Hughes, at the age of forty-three, fate seemed to have little in store. As a child he had seemed, so said the newspaper sketches that now introduced him to the public, "unfitted for the natural animalism of boys, the roughing and scuffling and romping" (odd, considering that in later life virility was the most conspicuous of his qualities). He had written, at the age of thirteen, an essay on the "Limitations of the Human Mind." He had graduated from Brown University in 1881 and from the law school of Columbia University in 1884; had begun practice in New York City, but after seven years, when he was twenty-nine, had "found himself so worn with work that he determined upon a rest, and got it by accepting a chair in Cornell University for two years." In 1893, at the age of thirty-one, he had resumed practice in New York City.

One would have checked Mr. Hughes off as a man a little too delicate in body, too refined in mind, for the pace of legal work in the metropolis. Now, however, Hughes emerged upon the American scene as a Hercules

about to clean the insurance stables, in cartoons that overemphasized virile whiskers and big white teeth, and in
newspaper sketches which overemphasized Puritan aus-
terity, and emphasized, but did not overemphasize —

From a photograph by Brown Bros.
Charles Evans Hughes in 1908.

because it would be difficult to exaggerate this quality of
Hughes — intellectual sinew. The whiskers, being not
so dressily trimmed or tended as to look worldly, and being accompanied by mild blue eyes and studious manner, conveyed a clerical or academic suggestion, which
the newspapers bore out by recalling that his father had
been a Baptist clergyman, that as a youth he had him-

self been intended for the church, and that he had spent a period of his youth teaching Greek and higher mathematics at a country academy at Delhi, N. Y. The big teeth, in his case, struck one as not primarily for alimentary purposes, but rather for biting into hard facts, like a mental rock-crusher. Hughes had the Puritan streak that the papers imputed to him — later they called him Charles the Baptist, a "twentieth-century roundhead," and also, incongruously, the "Baptist Pope." That was a caricature's implication of a piety that did not exist in fact; his was an intellectual moralism; he believed in God but believed equally that God was on the side of the facts. The mind of Charles E. Hughes, focussed upon the facts of life insurance and finance, grasping the actuarial intricacies of insurance as a science, following the deliberately devised complexities of secret financial manipulations, was such an ideal relation of man to task as to enable him measurably to live up to the newspaper phrase "mental colossus."

For the duration of fifty-seven public hearings of the legislative investigating committee, from September 6 to December 30, 1905, Hughes put upon the witness-stand a parade of the plumed élite of New York finance, politics, and society. Under the cold questioning of Hughes, "great reputations became great notorieties." His incisive, tenacious, unhurried methods made such an impression on the personalities of finance and insurance that some, terrified at the prospect of being subjected to his even-voiced questioning, unobtrusively departed for destinations unknown, while others found reasons of health for temporary retirement; one of the most conspicuous went to a sanitarium. The distinguished lawyers whose highly recompensed arts were counted on to guide their clients safely through the reefs, found themselves engaged in a hopeless struggle against an intelligence that penetrated their every subtlety, made wreckage of their most carefully erected defenses, and reduced them generally to the intellectual and moral level of "amateur-night" performers. Even that synthesis of the legal erudition and urban adroitness of the New York bar, Samuel Untermyer, could on one occasion of acute discomfiture find no more lucidly concatenated combination of words to express his state of mind than "I think it is in a very disorderly and disorderly way."[3]

"Disorderly" was exactly what the Hughes investigation was not. Nothing dominated by the mind of Charles E. Hughes could by any possibility be disorderly. Without ever heckling a witness, permitting every sweating financier to make such explanation or excuse as he could improvise; without seeming to be a cross-examiner at all, as unemotionally as a teacher finding a mild enthusiasm in leading a child to concede the irrefutable verities of mathematics, with no violence of gesture or words, in a voice that was only saved by its virile timbre from being a monotone, Hughes by the sheer clarity and power of his mind made every newspaper reader understand what had gone on. As undramatic himself as an adding-machine, he brought out such a series of dramatic revelations as had the effect, on the public, of a tumbling cascade of sensations.

Hughes showed

That the cost, $12,000, of that banquet to French Ambassador Cambon had been paid from the Equitable treasury, as expense for advertising — which in fact it was, though not the sort to make the best impression on the policyholders whose money was thus used. Hyde, in a stumbling, though quite sincere, defense said "It

[3] Hearings, New York legislative investigating committee, vol. II.

was given for business reasons. . . . We wanted to have the Ambassador favorably impressed with this Society; not that I wanted to get the Legion of Honor, as I got the Legion of Honor two years before."[4]

Hughes showed

That the twenty-seven-year-old Hyde drew yearly salaries of $100,000 from the Equitable Life Assurance Society, $12,000 from the affiliated Equitable Trust Company, $12,500 from the affiliated Mercantile Trust Company, and $2,500 from the affiliated Commercial Trust Company — an aggregate of $127,000 yearly.

Hughes showed

That the president of the Mutual Life Insurance Company of New York, holding "practically irresponsible power"[5] through "an autocracy, maintained almost without challenge,"[5] drew a salary of $150,000 a year; that the president's son, Robert H. McCurdy, drew commissions to an amount not clear but apparently upward of a hundred thousand dollars a year, partly as superintendent of the foreign department and partly as partner in a favored agency which was allowed "special and exorbitant rates of commission which were not justifiable from any point of view";[6] that the president's son-in-law, Louis A. Thebaud, also a partner in the fa-

[4] Hyde, explaining that the Society was trying to overcome French legislation adverse to American life-insurance companies, added: "We devoted a great deal of time to entertaining these people and then we engaged in a press campaign there [in France] which undoubtedly had a great deal of effect in the modification made to the proposed law. . . . It is not very likely that a man of my youth and not very large fortune, would be very likely to give a dinner to five hundred people. . . . That dinner was used a great deal here, and particularly abroad, to advertise the Equitable and to show the great tribute paid to France and the French people who have a little different psychology from ours and are very much flattered by such a dinner."

[5] Hughes's Report. For the sake of clarity and condensation I have used, in this chapter, the phrase "Hughes's Report" for the report made by the legislative committee of which Hughes was counsel. The document, officially, is "Report of the Joint Committee of the Senate and Assembly of the State of New York Appointed to Investigate the Affairs of Life-Insurance Companies."

[6] Hughes's Report.

vored firm, drew, in 1904, $147,687.74. "Relatives,"
Hughes's Report added, "have been conspicuously favored."[7]

The nepotism and the huge salaries and the paying of
personal expenses and personal servants out of the insurance companies' treasuries was, as respects the amounts
involved, relatively no greater than office-boy till-tap-
ping on an insurance-company scale. The weighty of-
fenses lay in those speculative and underwriting uses
made of the insurance companies' treasuries by their directors and officials, summed up by an officer of the
Equitable, who said the companies were managed, not
as institutions conducting a life-insurance business but as
"financial annexes to Wall Street interests."

Hughes showed

That the Equitable, during eleven months of 1904,
kept in various trust companies and banks an average
balance of $36,272,725 (9.15 per cent of its total as-
sets) on deposit as idle funds drawing only 2 or 3 per
cent interest. "The obvious purpose of these deposits,"
said Hughes's Report, "was to assist the [trust] companies . . . whose prosperity was also of concern to individual officers."[8] To conceal the excessive size of these
deposits, it was the custom of the Society's officers, as the
end of each year approached and annual statements must
be made public, to make pro forma loans for a few days
to the firm of Kuhn, Loeb & Co.; in one year, 1904, the
amount of the pro forma loan was $10,250,000.

Hughes showed

That in 1902 the New York Life subscribed to $4,-
000,000 of bonds of the International Mercantile Marine, a flotation by J. P. Morgan & Co., $800,000 of
which was concealed by a bookkeeping manipulation;
Hughes's Report stated: "It is plain that there was no

---

[7] Hughes's Report, p. 8.   [8] Hughes's Report, p. 128.

bona-fide sale and that the whole purpose of the transaction was to conceal the extent of the [insurance] company's interest in the . . . syndicate. The interest was closed out in 1904 at a loss of $80,000 to the Company."[9]

Hughes showed

That a firm of which Jacob Schiff was a member, Kuhn, Loeb & Co., sold to the Equitable, of which Mr. Schiff was a director, securities to the value of $49,-704,408 during five and a half years[10] — the State Insurance Law (Section 36) provided that any director of an insurance company who profited by "selling or aiding in the sale of any stocks or securities to or by such corporation shall forfeit his position . . . and be disqualified from thereafter holding any such office in any insurance corporation."[11]

Hughes showed

That the New York Life, in order to conceal its ownership of stocks, so as to be able to say in its annual report that "the Company does not invest in stocks of any kind," and thereby evade a stipulation of the Prussian Government, made fictitious loans through its affiliated New York Security and Trust Company to a bond clerk, in the sum of $1,857,000, and a colored messenger, in the sum of $1,150,000.[12]

These transactions, selected here because of their comparative simplicity, to illustrate the chicaneries that went on in the insurance and banking fraternity, were less offensive ethically, and less costly to the insurance com-

[9] Hughes's Report, p. 69. [10] From February, 1900, to August, 1905.

[11] A competent authority, having read the proofs of these chapters, says that this and similar cases of the sale of securities to an insurance company by a firm having directors in common with the insurance company, while a technical offense, were not ethically offensive provided the securities were sound and the price fair.

[12] Hughes's Report, p. 67.

panies' treasuries, than the syndicate operations. These the public could not follow, but they understood quite well the implications of the newspaper head-lines which recorded Hughes's unravelling. The head-lines in turn gave inspiration to the wits of the editorial pages and of the comic press. *Puck*,[13] in "Little Sums For Policy-holders," asked:

The tenth Vice-President of a big Insurance company buys one thousand shares of stock at 84. If the stock goes up ten points, how much will he win? If it goes down ten points, how much will *you* lose?

Three directors are coming back from Europe to explain things. The first returns on a five-day steamer. The second, on a tramp steamer. The third man falls overboard. Which man has the most foresight?

Puck printed a parody of an application for insurance, the questions to be answered, not by a prospective policy-holder but by the president of the insurance company:

What is your name, salary, and rake-off?

Have you any predisposition, either hereditary or acquired, to any constitutional diseases, such as lying, speculatitis, grafting, grand or petit larceny?

How many relatives have you on the company's payroll at salaries above $25,000?

Have you ever had any of the following diseases:

Paralysis of conscience?	Surplusitis? If operated upon,
Shortness of memory?	state particulars.
Itching palm?	Perquisitis? How many at-
Acute or chronic nepotism?	tacks?
That guilty feeling?	Enlargement of the wallet?

Have you any conscientious scruples against perjury?

Do you know anything about the insurance business? If so, what?

More romantic and picaresque than the financial scandals, and hardly less costly to the policyholders, was the alliance of the companies with both political parties in the nation and in the States (according to location and

13 October 18, 1905.

relative capacity to return financial favors), the wide-spread web of political espionage which the companies threw over Washington and over the capitals of every State and territory, as well as Canada. "The three companies divided the country, outside of New York and a few other states, so as to avoid a waste of effort, each looking after legislation [as well as politics] in its chosen district, and bearing its appropriate part of the total expense."[14] It was a major agency in that "invisible government," that interlocking of politics and big business with which the public had become familiar through President Roosevelt's attacks upon it.

The expense, enormous, which sustained this web of espionage and the miscellaneous lobbying, was carried on the books of the life-insurance companies under the color of two accounts, both deceptive and both meant to deceive.

Hughes showed

That the Mutual Life Insurance Company of New York disbursed in one year, 1904, $364,254.95 as "legal expenses." The quotation-marks are the legislative committee's and are designed to convey the committee's conviction, elsewhere made explicit, that "the [legal] expenses were far in excess of the amounts required for legitimate purposes."[15] Sums running as high as a hundred thousand dollars a year were paid out without record of the recipient or of the services — "there was no reason for this practice save to conceal the purpose for which the monies were used."[16]

Hughes showed

That for "legal expenses" the New York Life Insurance Company disbursed in ten years to and through Andrew J. Hamilton, "who had supervision of matters

[14] Hughes's Report, p. 19. [15] Hughes's Report, p. 12.
[16] Hughes's Report, p. 12,

of legislation and taxation throughout the country,"[17] the sum of $1,312,197.64. This was "in addition to all the ordinary outlays in connection with suits or legal proceedings of the work of the legal department of the company."[18] The president of the New York Life, John A.

Courtesy of the New York "World."
President of the New York Life Insurance Company on the witness stand during the investigation, November 27, 1905.

McCall, explained that it "was essential to [the] successful prosecution [of Hamilton's work] that all his transactions should be regarded as confidential and that no accounting should be required."[19]

To conceal the disbursements to and through Hamilton, the New York Life, among other elaborate devices, carried, in a trust company affiliated with it, a syndicate participation in the flotation of the United States Steel Corporation, and "out of a portion of [the] profits, . . .

[17] Hughes's Report, p. 45.   [18] Hughes's Report, p. 46.
[19] Additional sums were given Hamilton by the Mutual of New York and the Equitable, under the system of joint management of lobbying.

certain notes of Hamilton's were taken care of."[20] The Equitable kept an account with its allied Mercantile Trust Company "to facilitate disbursements which would not bear disclosure."[21] The moneys thus spent were designated by the newspapers "the yellow dog fund."

Hamilton, when the investigation began, was among the considerable number of persons who, as the committee put it, "was in Europe . . . and has remained without this jurisdiction; evidence has been furnished to the committee that the absence has been due to illness."[22] Under pressure from the committee and stimulated by the jeering in the newspapers, a higher official of the New York Life went to Europe to persuade Hamilton either to come back or to send an accounting of the $1,-312,197.64. Hamilton, remaining himself in Paris, sent a statement, not accompanied, however, by checks or check-stubs, Hamilton explaining "that they would disclose nothing, payments by check not having been favored, and the accounts having been disbursed in cash or its equivalent."[23] Hamilton, trying, one presumes, to place his expenditures in the light most favorable to himself, said they included Congressional revenue matters, other matters before Congress and before the legislatures of every State, and also the territories, and Canada, "ill-advised legislative bills which it was deemed proper to oppose . . . matters for the real estate department, investment and securities, agency affairs, the routing of newspaper blackmailers, legal licenses, insurance department action, state codification and revision of insurance laws, of various litigations, many matters of highly confidential character."[24]

Hughes showed

That additional to "legal expenses" so called, the

[20] Hughes's Report, p. 73.   [21] Hughes's Report, p. 122.
[22] Hughes's Report, p. 47.   [23] Hughes's Report, p. 49.
[24] Hughes's Report, p. 49.

other channel through which the companies carried on surreptitious expenditures was the "supply department," designed, in its legitimate aspect, to do the purchasing of printing, stationery, and postage. Under that heading — very inclusive as it turned out — the Mutual reported as expenses for 1904 the extraordinary sum of $1,324,833.76, the New York Life $851,284.66, the Equitable $772,645.50. The Mutual, in connection with the Equitable, maintained at the capital of New York, Albany, a house — promptly designated by newspapers the "House of Mirth" — under the care of the head of the Mutual's "supply department," Andrew C. Fields; and through him and his agents a close watch was kept upon the legislature. The nature of Fields's work is indicated by general instructions, sent him by an official of the Equitable at the opening of the legislature of 1903 (and again in 1904) which read: "We will be interested in all banking and insurance measures, taxation schemes, and bills affecting particularly the following interests: safe deposit companies, banks, trust companies, street railways . . . public places of amusement, etc."[25] These general instructions were followed up with specific directions about individual bills: In the files of the Equitable the committee found scores of letters and telegrams to Fields at Albany, of which one is sufficiently typical:

Memorandum for Mr. F.:   Feb. 21, 1898.
    Assembly Bill, Introductory 709, introduced by Mr. Sullivan, should be killed.
                     (Signed) T. D. J.[26]

More extensive investigation of Fields and his "House of Mirth" was prevented by a remarkable simultaneous-

---

[25] In this quotation from the Hughes Committee's Report, p. 17, the instructions for the two years 1903 and 1904 are combined.
[26] Hughes's Report, p. 14.

ness of absences. Fields "left for parts unknown soon after the committee began its hearings and it has not been able to procure his testimony."[27] L. W. Lawrence, through whom the Mutual's "supply department" did much of its purchasing, also joined the hegira: "since these matters attracted public attention, it has been impossible to serve Lawrence with a subpœna."[28] Similarly, the comptroller of the Equitable, Thomas D. Jordan (who was the Equitable's liaison with the Mutual's "supply department"), became, after the investigation, one of those "whose whereabouts the committee has been unable to ascertain although it has made diligent effort to do so."[29]

Hughes showed

That four large insurance companies — the New York Life, the Mutual, the Equitable, and the Prudential — made contributions to the Republican National Committee during Presidential campaigns, totalling, in 1896, $21,000; in 1900, $80,000; in 1904, $148,-702.50 — expenditures the propriety of which was stoutly defended by some of the companies' officials, especially by George W. Perkins, as meant "to assist in the maintenance of a proper monetary standard."[30] Hughes's Report observed that "the payments have not been disclosed by satisfactory entries upon the books of the company, and apparently every effort has been made to conceal them."[31]

Hughes showed

That the Mutual Life contributed from time to time $10,000 to the New York State Republican Committee. Senator Platt, head of the organization and United

---

[27] Hughes's Report, p. 13.   [28] Hughes's Report, p. 21.
[29] Hughes's Report, p. 13.
[30] Sound money was not an issue in 1904. In 1900, Byran was the Democratic candidate, though his old silver issue was obsolete.
[31] Hughes's Report, p. 59.

States Senator, "testified that it was supposed that an advantage would be derived [by the insurance company, its officials and their allied financial and business interests] through his [Platt's] relation to the state committee and that he would be ready to respond to an appeal for assistance in case hostile measures were threatened; in short, that the use of the contributed moneys, in the election of candidates to office would place them under more or less of an implied obligation."[32] Hughes's Report observed that "it is apparent that contributions by insurance companies for use in state campaigns were made with the idea that they would be protected in matters of legislation."

Hughes showed

That Chauncey M. Depew received from the Equitable annual retainers of $20,000, beginning about 1888, and continued to receive them after he became United States Senator. Mr. Depew testified "that his services consisted of advising the late Mr. Hyde in regard to matters of investment, settlement of controversies and troublesome questions of various sorts."[33] In his Report Hughes commented: "The testimony as to the services is very general, and it does not appear that outside of those which the Society was fairly entitled to receive from him as a director, the services were such as to warrant the payments made."[34] In shocked surprise at this detail of Hughes's revelations, a member of the New York State Senate, Edgar Truman Brackett, introduced[35] a resolution saying "The people of the state and nation have been staggered by the relations shown to have existed for years between the Equitable Life Assurance Society and Chauncey M. Depew, one of the senators of the state in the United States Congress. . . . Re-

---

[32] Hughes's Report, pp. 20, 21.   [33] Hughes's Report, p. 105.
[34] Hughes's Report, p. 106.
[35] January 3, 1906, reported in the New York *Sun*, January 4.

solved that Chauncey M. Depew be and hereby is requested to forthwith resign." The resolution was not
adopted. Mr. Depew did not resign. The New York
World[36] reprinted an interview Depew had given six
years before on "Why It Pays to Be Honest."

Hughes showed

That another United States Senator, Democratic, David B. Hill, received from the Equitable annual retainers of $5,000 (for one year, 1900, $7,500). Ironically
Hughes's Report said: "It does not appear what services
were rendered by Mr. Hill, who became a United States
Senator in 1892, and whose retainer, it seems, began in
1895."[37] The Hughes Report added, "in justice to Senator Hill," that "when the committee desired his testimony he was too ill to appear, and there was not sufficient time to take his testimony by deposition as requested."

Hughes showed

That "large sums have also been expended in the attempt to influence public opinion through the press by
the insertion of so-called 'reading notices,' that is to say
by disguised advertising and by payments to newspaper
correspondents and news writers for presumably similar
services. Even during the hearings of the committee
colored statements of its proceedings, intended to place
the officers of the company in a favorable light, were
sent out by the Mutual to numerous papers throughout
the country and published at a cost of one dollar a line."[38]

Hughes's investigation ended December 30, 1905.
The following week the New York State Legislature met.
By April 28, 1906, it completed a programme of legis-
lation which reformed the life-insurance business. The

[36] December 1, 1905.   [37] Hughes's Report, p. 106.
[38] Hughes's Report, pp. 21, 22.

new laws provided machinery for mutualizing stock companies and for enabling policyholders in mutual companies to elect directors; required the companies to dispose of speculative securities within five years and forbade them to hold stock in banks, trust companies, or other corporations; forbade participation in syndicates; limited salaries, commissions and other expenses, and put an annual limit on the amount of new business a company could write; prohibited officers and agents from holding pecuniary interests in transactions with their companies; required vouchers for all expenditures of a hundred dollars or more; opened the courts to suits by policyholders against the companies; prescribed standardized forms of policies; provided that a policyholder, unable or unwilling to continue payment of premiums, should nevertheless receive a policy representing an appropriate ratio to the amount of premiums already paid; prohibited insurance companies (and other corporations) from making contributions to political campaign funds; required that all legislative agents (lobbyists) be registered with the names of their employers and the purposes of their employment.

As a result of Hughes's investigation, two vice-presidents of one company and the president and two vice-presidents of another were indicted. All the presidents and most of the other high officials of the three big companies resigned or were forced out. The members of the finance committee of the New York Life Insurance Company who had sanctioned contributions to political campaign committees paid back to the company $148,-000 out of their own pockets, fifteen men giving about $10,000 each. James Hazen Hyde reimbursed the Equitable for the expenses of the dinner to the French Ambassador and for other expenditures deemed unjustifiable. The president of the New York Life, "after making a brief defense of his management and justifying it with so much earnestness that the conviction was forced upon most people that he had really erred more in the head than in the heart, first gave up all that he had in restitution and then died of a broken heart."

Far more to the country's advantage than penitence and restitution by life-insurance officials, more broadly important than reform in insurance practice, was the introduction into American public life of a new and potent figure. Hughes, while the investigation he conducted was still under way, was nominated as Republican candidate for Mayor of New York, but refused to run. The following year, 1906, he was nominated for Governor, ran against William R. Hearst, was elected on November 4, 1906, by a vote of 749,002 to 691,105, and on January 1, 1907, took office. Immediately he initiated a vigorous administration of the office of Governor and a programme of reform legislation. Distinctly he was a Presidential possibility, whose growing momentum justified Roosevelt in telling Mrs. William H. Taft that he might "feel it to be my duty to be for Hughes."

5

ROOSEVELT'S POWER

Which Arose in Large Part from His Valor as a Fighter, and to Some Degree from Particular Arts of Combat That He Practised, and from the Agreeable Excitement That Accompanied His Fighting — Causing the Public to Feel, as It Was Put by a New York Policeman Who Had Served Under Him, "The Fun of Him! There Was Such Fun in Being Led by Him!" Including Allusions to Certain Inventions, Whereby Cartoons Became a Polemic Feature of Newspapers; and Whereby Magazines Became Forums of Public Discussion, Media of the Literature of Exposure.

THE assumption, generally accepted, that Roosevelt's successor would be whomever he should name, attributed to him a power greater than most heads of States have possessed. And it is simple history to say that the relation Roosevelt had to America at this time, the power he was able to wield, the prestige he enjoyed, the affection he received, the contentment of the people with him — their more than contentment, their zesty pleasure in him — composed the lot of an exceptionally fortunate monarch during a particularly happy period of his reign. The basis of it was the fights Roosevelt made against organized wealth — the sum of which was that he had, in the plain sight of the common man, presented spectacle after spectacle in which business, capital, corporate power, took off its hat in the presence of the symbol and spokesman of government.

Some serious folk, thinking this triumph was the whole of the attraction Roosevelt had for the people, wrote exalted tributes in which they pictured him as St. George slaying the dragon. But that kind of service, if it stood alone, would have made Roosevelt not a king, but rather an austere Cromwell destroying kings. The battles Roosevelt fought, had they been waged by a La-Follette or a Bryan, or even a Grover Cleveland, might

From a photograph by Underwood & Underwood.
President Roosevelt at Inspiration Point, Yosemite, April, 1903.

have had the sombre sourness of a Puritanical crusade. What brought to Roosevelt the affection that few kings have had, and gave gay delight to the people, was, in addition to his valiance in high affairs, certain qualities of his temperament, facets of his scintillating personality, not all of which need be enumerated at this place, but which included his methods of combat, and the agreeable excitement that accompanied them: the din, the alarums, the thunderclaps of his denunciations, the lightning strokes of his epithets, his occasional ruthlessness of attack, his grinning acceptance of occasional setbacks the quickness of his rally, the adroitness of his parry; the vibrations he emitted, like a master tuning-fork, setting the whole atmosphere of the country a-tingle; "the fun of him," as one of his New York police captains remarked after his death — "It was not only that he was a great man, but, oh, there was such fun in being led by him." So that if Roosevelt's victories were those of St. George, his activity in combat, if one may use a far-fetched figure, was that of St. Vitus — except that no warrior nor statesman, and indeed no musician or artisan, ever wasted less energy in lost motion than did Roosevelt. His every gesture counted, his every blow went to the mark, or started there, and if he had to retreat, he knew — to the surprised dismay of those who thought they had him beaten, the precise moment when he could turn. Roosevelt in battle — which was Roosevelt most of the time — was a huge personality endowed with energy almost abnormal, directed by an acute intelligence, lightened by a grinning humor, engaged in incessant action. The spectacle, occupying the biggest head-lines in the daily newspapers, gave to the life of that day a zest and stimulus and gaiety such that average Americans who lived through the period carried it as a golden memory, and, in their elder years, recalled it as the ancient forty-niners remembered California, sighing "there'll never be another Roosevelt," and telling their grandchildren that once they saw a giant. *Anni memorabiles!*

Roosevelt's fighting was so much a part of the life of the period, was so tied up to the newspapers, so geared into popular literature, and even to the pulpit (which already had begun to turn from formal religion toward civic affairs), as to constitute, for the average man, not merely the high spectacle of the Presidency in the ordinary sense, but almost the whole of the passing show, the public's principal interest. It caused the people to take delight in Roosevelt as President, to wish nothing better than that he should go on being President, and to be willing, if Roosevelt himself would not run, to accept whomever Roosevelt might choose.

II

Roosevelt in his political battles used many arts. He neglected no old manœuvre, and devised several new ones, of which the characteristic was that they were carried out before the public eye, making of the average man always an excited spectator, usually an ardent partisan.

Roosevelt used the newspapers, not in the older furtive manner of holding out offices and perquisites to editors, nor by the direct way (which the railroads and other great corporations to some extent practised) of establishing alliances with newspaper owners, or identity of interest with them. Roosevelt had another method, largely original with him, and as novel in political warfare as aviation in martial combat. Roosevelt's method was looked upon by his Old Guard adversaries somewhat as old-school military men looked upon the first use of gas — they knew no continuously effective way of getting help from newspapers except directly, by appeal to the editor or business office, usually the latter.

Roosevelt asked no favors from the newspapers. He did not request their attention, he commanded it. "Roosevelt," said a critic[1] of him, "has the knack of do-

[1] J. W. Bennett, in "Roosevelt and the Republic."

ing things, and doing them noisily, clamorously; while he is in the neighborhood the public can no more look the other way than the small boy can turn his head away from a circus parade followed by a steam calliope."

From a photograph by Underwood & Underwood.
Speaking at Boise City, Idaho, May 28, 1903.

And an editor who printed some of Roosevelt's outgivings reluctantly — but printed them — explained that Roosevelt had a way of "slapping the public on the back with a 'bright idea.'"

The heart of Roosevelt's method was to inspire headlines. He was the first public man to realize and adapt himself to the relative ebbing of the power of the editorial compared to the news despatch and the cartoon, the first to have a technic for getting the advantage of the head-line. Probably Presidents before him had known the thing that Roosevelt meant when he said, "The White House is a bully pulpit," but no President before him or after used the White House so frequently or effectively for pulpiteering and other forms of promotion of his policies and purposes. More than any other President he understood that everything coming out of the White House is news, and turned that fact to his advantage. He was the earliest American public man to grasp the syllogism that on Sunday all normal business and most other activities are suspended; that Sunday is followed by Monday; and that, therefore, the columns of the Monday papers present the minimum of competition for public attention — whence many of the public statements, epithets and maledictions with which Roosevelt conducted his fights were timed to explode in the pages of the Monday morning newspapers.

During each of Roosevelt's several crusades he conducted a barrage of newspaper head-lines deliberately designed to stir up public sentiment for his cause and for him, and even more directly to incite public odium for his

Let me
be your
Teddy Bear?

Post-card of 1907. During Roosevelt's Presidency the "Teddy Bear" was, to older people, a symbol of the President's fun-loving and playful qualities, and, to children, a welcome and beloved addition to the menagerie of toyland — no doll family was complete without its snow-white, awkward, laughter-provoking bear.

adversaries. To the head-lines and news despatches that he especially devised and timed for the direct purpose of promoting the matter he had in hand were added the despatches that arose spontaneously from his multifarious collateral activities, the investigations he ordered, the indictments he incited, the prosecutions he pursued, the denunciations he uttered. The whole composed a veritable onslaught of anti-trust, anti-railroad, anti-boss ammunition, and created in the minds of average Americans an imperious demand for the measure Roosevelt advocated, with the result that, for example, the debate on the railroad rate bill in the Senate in 1906 was, as Senator Dolliver of Iowa put it, "only a counterpart of the larger discussion that has gone on throughout the country in city and village and township alike."

III

Cartoons, Roosevelt inspired as the morning sun awakens life. At any gusty word from him, cartoons filled the air like autumn leaves in a high wind. The cartoon, as a method of political combat, was not new; but until the 1890's it had been confined to weekly periodicals, and was handicapped therefore by some remoteness from instant timeliness; the process of reproduction had involved time-consuming tooling on wooden blocks by hand-working engravers. About the time Roosevelt became an important figure in American life, there had been invented a photo-engraving process which permitted the making of a chemically etched zinc block within a few minutes after completion of the artist's pen-drawing. Thus the daily newspapers were enabled to use cartoons freely, thus cartoonists were able to make their drawings within an hour of receipt of the current news, and thus the newspapers were able to present them to the public a few hours later.

Into this new development, Roosevelt, with his incessant activity, fitted like a Heaven-devised engine. A cartoonist, going to his office in the late afternoon, need hardly worry about finding a topic for his cartoon; Roosevelt would have been sure to have done something or said something. Some essential quality in Roosevelt's temperament and in his characteristic actions was kin

"I am the State!" *Puck* and some of Roosevelt's other critics felt or pretended that they felt alarms lest he should constitute himself Theodore I, King of America.

to the spirit in which cartoons had to be made, lent itself to the nervous tension that was a condition of the cartoonist's art. Upon the inspiration of a phrase from him, cartoonists' pencils swung to paper like a needle to the North, their crayons cavorting like kittens in an ecstasy over catnip. His teeth, grim in contest or grinning in triumph, were Heaven-made for the caricaturist's art, and likewise his thick-lensed glasses, happily adapted to portraying glaring looks — his whole physical make-up, as well as his temperament, ideal for both the subject and the spirit of the cartoonists' technic.

Roosevelt, in a quite academic address about international relations, said: "Speak softly — but carry a big stick," and a myriad cartoons pictured him as a mighty fighter swinging a hundred variations of a war-club against the dragon railroads. He said "strenuous life," and a thousand pencils drew him riding at top speed in pursuit of some malefactor of great wealth. He said "the spear that knows no brother," and in a hundred newspapers, harassed amassers of money shrank from a spear held in Roosevelt's burly fist. He said "square deal" and cowering figures with dollar-marks upon their fore-

Lowry in "The Chronicle" (Chicago).

His favorite author. This cartoon of a farmer reading one of Roosevelt's messages was a favorite with the latter, who had it framed and hung above the mantel of his study.

heads and labelled "trusts" listened to doom from an avenging god that had big teeth and wore glasses. He demanded regulation of the railroads, and the newspapers blossomed with pictorial melodrama, in which the railroads played the rôle of villain, their sprawling lines on the map lending themselves to depiction as "the octopus"; a railroad-train adapting itself to portrayal as an angrily twisting snake or dragon with the separate cars labelled "rebates" or with the names of the other sins charged against the railroads; a railroad-train emerging from a tunnel lending itself to the suggestion of a maddened wild animal at the mouth of his den, while Roosevelt — always in the rôle of hero — facing the dragon, provided the kind of dramatic action the cartoonists loved to picture. In scores of drawings by W. H. Walker, the innocent child "Common People" was rescued by Roosevelt from the villain "Trusts." He announced a hunting trip to Colorado, and a thousand mountain-lions or grizzly bears — biologically extraordinary because they had dollar-marks upon their skins — together with vultures, coyotes, rattlesnakes and other manner of varmints, labelled "railroads" or "trusts," fled in terror before a figure who held a pistol in one hand, a lariat in the other, and a knife in his gleaming teeth. He started a house-cleaning in one government department or another, and the press flowered with pictures of Roosevelt as the "Old Dutch Cleanser," his strenuous broom an adaptation of the "big stick." He announced his mediation between Japan and Russia, and the mace with which he conducted the peace conference was the "big stick" not too completely concealed by festooned olive-branches — suggesting that any divagation by Roosevelt into pursuit of peace was merely a temporary departure from his native, permanent, and preferred function of hitting heads. He said "parlor socialist," and even the left wing of his own reforms scurried beneath the base-board to escape the blinding light that glared through the thick lenses of Roosevelt strenuous in satire. At the end of a fight he said "delighted," and on a hundred million newspaper pages, pleased teeth purred "dee-lighted" over some conquest of a trust.

Nine times out of ten the cartoon was Roosevelt in

combat; always, almost without exception, it was Roosevelt in action. From having lived through the period and from having searched the files during the preparation of this history, I venture to say that not among the

L. D. Bradley in the Chicago "Daily News."
Roosevelt "rough-riding" the world.

literally myriads of Roosevelt cartoons are half a dozen in which he sleeps, or even rests. Once, seeking to symbolize his retirement from the Presidency, I worked for days with an artist[2] to devise a picture in which Roosevelt, his labors over, should enjoy repose. We gave it up. The thing could not be done, was contrary no less to art than to nature. Even when he died, the cartoon that was universally accepted as appropriate and that

[2] E. W. Kemble.

became an American classic was the one in which Jay N. Darling of the Des Moines, Iowa, *Register*, pictured him on horseback, waving the gallant farewell of an unconquerable spirit to those left behind as he started unafraid upon the long trail.

IV

Roosevelt realized the power inherent in the popular magazines, and took pains to keep in touch with the editors and writers of them, young men, as a rule, as ardent as himself. By reading the periodicals diligently, and by more intimate contacts, he knew the personnels of their staffs, knew the individual traits and biases of the writers, knew even the office politics of the periodicals as adequately as he followed the internal politics of his own party committees. If there was in a magazine office an owner, editor, or writer unsympathetic to his policies, Roosevelt took especial pains to maintain a balancing friendliness with others of the staff, doing it all with the habitual directness and casual boldness of his spirit. If a magazine printed an article with which he disagreed, he would write a letter to the author or editor, or have a talk with him, in which he would express his dissent with the forcefulness that was customary with him, a letter in which belligerency and graciousness were so mingled as to seem to say, "You can print this if you want to and we will fight it out before the public; or you can come to see me in fair friendliness and I will give you the facts that will enable you to see the light."[3] The more direct acquaintance of the

[3] Not alone with American, but with European writers as well, Roosevelt carried on a correspondence designed to get a presentation of his ideas, acts, and policies that was in accord with his own view of them. Archibald R. Colquhoun, an Englishman, writing in *The Fortnightly Review*, May 2, 1910, remembered

writer of this history with Roosevelt began with a not wholly approving editorial allusion I had written about one of Roosevelt's judicial appointments, which drew

from Roosevelt a letter of eleven typewritten pages, with many inter-lineations, in which he reviewed every one of the judicial appoint-ments he had made in the six years of his Pres-idency, detailing, as to each, the considerations that had determined the selection. If a new au-thor wrote something helpful to one of Roose-velt's fights, or other-wise interesting to him, the writer was likely, soon, to glow at a White House luncheon, at which his experience was apt to be that de-scribed by one such au-thor:[4] "You go into Roosevelt's presence, you feel his eyes upon

From "The Gazette-Times" (Pittsburgh).

This cartoon typifies the conception great masses of the people had of Roosevelt during his Presidency.

you, you listen to him, and you go home and wring the personality out of your clothes."

It would be inaccurate historically, and unfair to

that "even with the Atlantic between us, he could not read one of my books with-out dashing off first one and then another letter to me, pointing out what he be-lieved to be misconception on my part. 'You haven't got it quite right on page so-and-so. I wish you'd call round and see Taft.' That sort of a reader is a treat to any author."

4 Richard Washburn Child.

Roosevelt, to imply that his cultivation of magazine writers was merely a cold technic for advancing his causes. His relations with authors, while they were of advantage to him, were a spontaneous incident of the enormous range of his interest in varied kinds of human beings. Roosevelt was interested in, and therefore had the power of stimulating every sort of writer and artist, poets like Edwin Arlington Robinson and Bliss Carman, novelists like Owen Wister and Kathleen Norris, historians like James Ford Rhodes and the English Trevelyan, naturalists like John Muir and John Burroughs, artists like Saint-Gaudens and Frederic Remington.

All these — artists, writers, poets, and sculptors — were stimulated by Roosevelt to new endeavor. And not only they. Everybody in America, in every sort of career, from teachers and naturalists to cowboys and prize-fighters, seemed to derive from Roosevelt in the White House a lift toward higher functioning. Partly the wide-spread stimulus arose from the number of representatives of diverse lines of work or art with whom Roosevelt had contact — during no Presidency did the White House visiting list contain so many names, or reflect interest in so wide a gamut of human activity. Partly the increased elation with which nearly everybody in America went to his job in the morning arose from awareness of the obvious delight that Roosevelt had in his own job. Partly the stimulus Roosevelt radiated to the average man arose from consciousness that Roosevelt was making the fight for the common man, for the preservation of individuality against the irking chains of organization, corporate power.

Writers, functioning at joyous speed upon ignition from the emanations of Roosevelt's personality, kept the

First he chops down a few trees.

Then takes a cross-country canter.

And a twenty-minute brisk walk,

After which he gives the children a wheel-barrow ride.

He then rests for a moment

By which time he is ready for breakfast.

Cartoons always emphasized Roosevelt in action. This one is by John T. McCutcheon of the Chicago *Tribune*.

pages of the popular magazines glowing with support of Roosevelt's crusades. The friendly writers who took inspiration direct from him were sometimes called, jeeringly, Roosevelt's "fair-haired boys." A wider group who took their inspiration from many sources, and who as frequently inspired Roosevelt as they were inspired by him, came to be recognized as a definite school of writing, sometimes called the "literature of exposure," which historically has a fairly important place in both the letters and the politics of the early part of this century. "Exposure," said a careful writer[5] in *The Atlantic Monthly* for August, 1907, "forms the typical current literature of our daily life. . . . They expose in countless pages the sordid and depressing rottenness of our politics; the hopeless apathy of our good citizens; the remorseless corruption of our great financiers and business men, who are bribing our legislatures, swindling the public with fraudulent stock schemes, adulterating our food, speculating with trust funds, combining in great monopolies to oppress and destroy small competitors. They show us our social sore spots, like the three cheerful friends of Job. They show us the growth of business 'graft,' the gangrene of personal dishonesty among an honorable people, the oppressing increase in the number of bribe-takers and bribe-givers. They tell us of the riotous extravagance of the rich, and the growth of poverty. Titus Oates and his plot live again in the amazing historian of modern finance. The achievement of the constructive elements of society has been neglected to give space to these spicy stories of graft and greed."

The media for these jeremiads consisted chiefly of low-priced magazines, made possible by innovations in the art of printing — glazed paper made from wood-

[5] George W. Alger.

pulp, much cheaper than rag-paper, and an advance in photography followed by improvement in the art of printing photographs. The inexpensiveness, accompanied by attractiveness, thus made possible was first[6] utilized to print, at a price of ten or fifteen cents, magazines which aimed at entertainment alone, and achieved it, in typical cases, by liberal extravagance with photographs accompanying casually improvised articles about actresses or queens, or persons deemed socially important. Then the greatest magazine genius America has ever known, Samuel S. McClure, created a fifteen-cent magazine which, in its influence upon public opinion, was hardly less important than Roosevelt himself, and of which

Samuel S. McClure, founder of the school of literature of exposure.

Roosevelt took advantage — it was thought, indeed, by an English critic[7] that "the historian of the future may determine how much of the 'uplift' that distinguished the Roosevelt administration was due to the influence of the McClure type of magazine; we cannot, at this distance of time, see things quite in proportion; but it seems to me certain that Mr. McClure both paved the way for President Roosevelt and potently furthered the movements with which his name will always be identified."

---

6 The earliest magazines, of the type here described, selling at ten and fifteen cents, and achieving thereby a large circulation, were *Munsey's* (Frank A.) and an early phase of *The Cosmopolitan* as conducted by John Brisben Walker.

7 William Archer.

McClure,[8] without particularly intending to, as a spontaneous expression of his personality, achieved a union of what is interesting and what is important, by commissioning writers with a background of scholarship and mental habits of accuracy and thoroughness, such as Miss Ida M. Tarbell, to make clear to the understanding of the average man the intricacies and chicaneries which lie in the area where business comes in contact with politics. Miss Tarbell's "History of the Standard Oil Company," starting in *McClure's* during 1902, followed, in the same magazine, by Lincoln Steffens's "Enemies of the Republic"[9] and Ray Stannard Baker's "The Railroad on Trial," presently inspired other writers to follow, other magazine publishers to imitate. By the time Roosevelt's crusades were under way there was "a group of some half-dozen periodicals of extraordinarily vital and stimulating quality, which must be reckoned among the most valuable literary assets of the American people; there is nothing quite like them in the literature of the world — no periodicals which combine such width of popular appeal with such seriousness of aim and thoroughness of workmanship."[10]

The energy of the "exposure" writers in uncovering corporate and political iniquity, together with President Roosevelt's official activity toward the same end, caused "Mr. Hennessy" to remark to "Mr. Dooley," the Archey Road saloon-keeper, that "it looks to me as though this country was going to the divil." Whereupon Mr. Dooley reassured him with remarks which included

---

[8] McClure, with the passing of the particular vogue of letters that he created, was forgotten by a generation that satisfied its zest with newer forms of entertainment; but posterity will always have the picture of him, "his feverish fertility of ideas, his irrepressible energy, and his sanguine imagination," in characters which Robert Louis Stevenson built upon him in "The Wreckers," and William Dean Howells in "A Hazard of New Fortunes."

[9] Even better known was Steffens's "Shame of the Cities."

[10] The quotation is from William Archer in the British *Fortnightly Review.*

critical disquisition upon the changes that had occurred in American periodical literature.

Put down that magazine, Hinnissy! Now d'ye feel betther? I thought so. But I can sympathize with ye. I've been readin' thim meself. Time was when I seldom throubled thim. But wanst in a while some home-farin' wandhrer wud jettison wan in me place, an I'd frequently glance through it and find it in me lap when I woke up. The magazines in thim days was very ca'ming to the mind. Angabel an' Alfonso dashin' f'r a marriage licence. Prom'nent lady authoresses makin' pomes at the moon. Now an' thin a scrap over whether Shakespear was enthered in his own name or was a ringer, with the long-shot players always agin' Shakespeare. But no wan hurt. Th' idee ye got fr'm these here publications was that life was wan glad sweet song. They were good readin'. I liked thim th' way I like a bottle iv white pop now an' thin.

But now whin I pick me fav-rite magazine off th' flure, what do I find? Ivrything has gone wrong. Th' wurruld is little betther thin a convict's camp. Angabel an' Alfonso ar-re about to get married whin it is discovered that she has a husband in Ioway an' he has a wife in Wisconsin. All th' pomes be th' lady authoresses that used to begin: "Oh, moon, how fair!" now begin: "Oh, Ogden Armour,[11] how awful!" Read th' horrible disclosures about th' way Jawn C. Higgins got th' right to build a bay-window on his barber-shop at iliven forty-two Kosciusko Avnoo, South Bennington, Arkansaw. Read Wash'n'ton Bliffens's[12] dhreadful assault on th' board iv education iv Baraboo. Read Idarem[13] on John D.; she's a lady, but she's got th' punch. Graft ivrywhere. "Graft in th' Insurance Comp'nies," "Graft in Congress." "Graft be an Old Grafter," "Graft in Its Relations to th' Higher Life," be Dock Eliot;[14] "Th' Homeeric Legend an' Graft; Its Cause an' Effect; Are They th' Same? Yes and No," be Norman Slapgood.[15]

An' so it goes, Hinnissy, till I'm that blue, discouraged, an' broken-hearted I cud go to th' edge iv th' wurruld an' jump off. It's a wicked, wicked, horrible, place, an' this here counthry is about th' toughest spot in it. I don't thrust anny man anny more. I niver did much, but now if I hear th' stealthy step iv me dearest frind at th' dure I lock th' cash dhrawer. I used to be nervous about burglars, but now I'm afraid iv a night call

11 The reference is to the Beef Trust and tainted meat scandals, which caused Roosevelt to demand that Congress enact a "pure food" bill.
12 Lincoln Steffens.   13 Ida M. Tarbell.
14 Charles W. Eliot, president of Harvard University.
15 Norman Hapgood.

fr'm th' prisidint iv th' First National Bank. It's slowly killin'
me, Hinnissy — or it wud if I thought about it.

Do I think it's all as bad as that? Well, Hinnissy, now that
ye ask me, an' seein' that Chris'mas is comin' on, I've got to
tell ye that this country, while wan iv th' worst in th' wurruld,
is about as good as th' next if it ain't a shade betther. But
we're wan iv th' gr-reatest people in th' wurruld to clean
house, an' th' way we like best to clean th' house is to burn it
down. With this here nation iv ours somebody scents something wrong with th' scales at th' grocery-store an' whips out
his gun, another man turns in a fire alarm, a third fellow sets
fire to th' Presbyterian Church, a vigilance comity is formed
an' hangs ivry foorth man; an' havin' started with Rockyfellar,
who's tough an' don't mind bein' lynched, they fin'ally wind
up with desthroyin' me because th' steam laundhry has sint
me home somebody else's collars. Th' throuble with this house
is that it is occypied entirely be human bein's. If 'twas a vacant house, it cud aisily be kept clean.

An' there ye ar-re, Hinnissy. Th' noise ye hear is not th'
first gun iv a rivolution. It's on'y th' people iv th' United
States batin' a carpet. What were those shots? That's th'
housekeeper killin' a couple iv cockroaches with a Hotchkiss
gun. Who is that yellin'? That's our ol' frind High Fi-nance
bein' compelled to take his annual bath.

In the compulsory lavation that Roosevelt adminis-
tered to High Finance, the writers of exposure provided
at once much of the discovery of pollution, much of the
soap for the cleansing, and much of the applause for the
performance. Despite "Mr. Hennessy's" pessimism and
"Mr. Dooley's" satire, the average man got from it both
satisfaction and fun.

v

After the literature of exposure had enjoyed its remarkable vogue for some five or six years, it passed into
a phase that not only impaired the value of it to Roosevelt and his reforms, but gave concern to him in his rôle
of watchful guardian of the nation's good.

The public appetite for exposure continued eager as

ever. Because of that, inevitably, as always, promoters arose to commercialize it, imitators to cheapen it and to offer the public a decidedly inferior brand. Magazines very different from the originating *McClure's* stridently adopted exposure as a specialty; writers very distant in background and method from Miss Ida M. Tarbell hurried to the market with wares for which the description "inferior" would be eulogistic. A sensational stock-market operator, Thomas W. Lawson, who had been a handy man for captains of industry in some of their more sordid adventures, wrote the secrets he had shared with them, under the heading, "Frenzied Finance," and added a new name "the System" to the phrases of odium, with which were designated the interlocking chicaneries of big business. That Lawson's motive might have been something less than conscientious scholarship is suggested by the contract

Courtesy of the New York "World."

Thomas W. Lawson, of Boston, who turned, for a brief period, from the practice of "Frenzied Finance" to the exposure of it.

he made with a theretofore obscure magazine, *Everybody's,* in which he asked for no compensation, stipulating only that the publishers should spend at least $50,000 in advertising the articles, to which Lawson on his own account added at least five times the sum,[16] with the result that the circulation of *Everybody's Magazine* multiplied in a year from less than 150,000

[16] Professor C. C. Regier in *The Historical Outlook,* January, 1924.

to more than five times that. What Lawson may have lacked in experience as a writer, or in conformity to conventional standards in his own decidedly bizarre business practices, he made up in a most extraordinary vividness of characterization, which caused crowds to

ONE LAST WORD

If it should happen that my reports arrive to-day and you should read them in my to-morrow's advertisement, with the word "Buy," I will advise the purchase of Nevada-Utah only up to 20 for the present. This will not mean that I advise buying orders to be limited at 20, as I advise that under no circumstances should any one buy at over five points above the closing to-night. That is, if Nevada-Utah closes to-night at 10, see to it that your broker is instructed to-night to buy at not over 15 to-morrow— if my advertisement says "Buy." If, after the excitement of the first two hours has subsided—I predict a new "Wildest two hours in stocks," with transactions of 200,000 to 300,000 shares for the day—the price is still above 15, I will advise further as to price limit in my advertisement of the following day.

THOMAS W. LAWSON

A section of a Lawson advertisement in one of his many stock manipulation campaigns.

clamor at news-stands for the monthly instalments of *Everybody's* — the crowds including the financiers whom Lawson exposed, eager to end the suspense in which during thirty days of every month they wondered what ghastly secret of the underworld of high finance Lawson would tell next. There was plenty of fact in Lawson's narrative; the evidence was intrinsic and was also to be found in collateral exposures of an official sort; but Lawson's facts were so mingled with fantastic emanations from his extraordinarily ebullient personality, and Lawson's own performances in the field of stock speculation were so inconsistent with the rôle of soldier for the common good, as to cause newspapers justly to belittle him. The public became satiated — by the end of four years of it, Lawson felt called upon, as in 1908 he went back to his stock speculation, to turn his extraordinary powers of vituperation upon the ungrateful public themselves, calling them "gelatine-spined shrimps," "saffron-blooded apes."[17]

William R. Hearst, expanding from daily newspapers into periodicals, bought the *Cosmopolitan Maga-*

William R. Hearst.

zine, and announced, in the month in which Roosevelt's railroad rate bill was launched in the Senate, February, 1906, a series of exposures which, he told the world, would be "the most vascular and virile" thus far printed.

[17] "Why I Gave Up the Fight,"*Everybody's Magazine*, February, 1908. Lawson's vociferous disgust was perhaps due no more to the public's failure to follow his exalted advice about the purification of public morals, than to its prudent restraint about accepting his luridly advertised "tips": "Buy Amalgamated. Buy it quick. It's on its way to 150. Buy it. Buy it quick"; and, "I repeat, I reiterate, I advise unqualifiedly, as President of Trinity and as an individual, I advise unqualifiedly the purchase of Trinity at any figure below 65."

Condescendingly, Mr. Hearst's announcement said of his predecessors: "Well-meaning and amazingly industrious persons writing without inspiration . . . have been able to pile before magazine readers indiscriminate masses of arid facts." From such prosaic tedium Mr. Hearst promised to steer clear; his exposures would be "by the masterly hand of David Graham Phillips."

Phillips was a novelist. In the articles he wrote for Hearst, which he called "The Treason of the Senate," he demonstrated that in senses more subtle than the obvious one, fiction may be far from fact. He was unfamiliar with his material and with the background of the picture he purported to paint. Instead of the austere setting down of fact, which had been the very essence of the literature of exposure, and which had carried conviction to the reader, Phillips substituted tawdry literary epithets, "the Senate's craftily convenient worship of the Mumbo-Jumbo mask and mantle of its own high respectability." For the stark citation of documents that had given convincing force to Miss Tarbell's exposures of railroad rebates, Phillips substituted — sure sign, in a writer, of haste and paucity of fact — lavish exclamation-points. "The treason of the Senate! . . . Thomas Collier Platt! Chauncey Mitchell Depew! . . . Revolution indeed!" And the rhetorical question, "Did the people send him to the Senate? No!" Transposition of a member of the House of Representatives (Sibley of Pennsylvania) into membership in the Senate Committee on Finance in order to buttress proof of a point against Aldrich, was but a minor inexactitude among the factors that made Phillips's articles unconvincing. The inaccuracy and hysteria of Phillips and others gave a justified opening to a Senator, Henry Cabot Lodge, to defend the body against "some of our irresponsible magazine writers whose only thought was to turn a penny by meeting what seemed a momentary demand for a sensational statement."

Another writer of novels who turned to the current vogue of exposure, Upton Sinclair, put his revelations into the form of fiction, adding heart interest, a love-affair, and the other ingredients of standard romance, to the setting of "dirty work" in the Chicago stock-yards. Fiction as a medium for exposing wrong and facilitating reform had been used in the past, frequently and effectively: Harriet Beecher Stowe's "Uncle Tom's Cabin"; Charles Reade's "Foul Play," in which he exposed some iniquities of English shipping and facilitated the reforms wrought by Samuel Plimsoll and the "Plimsoll Mark"; "Hard Cash," by the same author, which exposed abuses in private lunatic asylums. But the literature of exposure during the early years of the present century in America was on a basis that was the exact opposite of fiction; it had a definite technic of its own, of which the essential detail was austere, restrained, underemphasized statement of bald fact. It was not fiction. Sinclair's "Jungle," coming directly to Roosevelt's attention because of his interest in the pure food bill pending before Congress, brought home to Roosevelt the fact that the literature of exposure,[18] in its later phases, had got partly into the hands of a different class of writers.

[18] One effect of the vogue of exposure literature was to give rise, in England and elsewhere abroad, to a corresponding literature of disapproval of life as lived in the United States. Since exposures that will be tolerated and even welcomed so long as they are kept within the family, tend to become irritating when made the occasion of fingers of scorn pointed from outside, there arose in America a disposition to look upon the literary exposers as undesirable.

When European magazines and newspapers showed self-righteous horror about America, Mr. Dooley explained to Mr. Hennessy:

"We use sthrong disinfectants here. A Frinchman or an Englishman cleans house by sprinklin' th' walls with cologne; we chop a hole in th' flure an' pour in a kag iv chloride iv lime. Both are good ways. It depinds on how long ye intind to live in th' house. . . . But I want to say to thim neighbors iv ours, who're peekin' in an' makin' remarks about th' amount iv rubbish, that over in our part iv th' wurruld we don't sweep things undher th' sofa. Let thim put that in their pipes an' smoke it. We come home at night an' find that th' dure

It was part of Roosevelt's art of winning the decision before the court of public opinion to dissociate himself from the more extreme among his own partisans and followers — from what he himself later called the "lunatic fringe" that rushes into the comet's tail of every reform movement. This course he followed now. Not forgetful of the help the responsible writers of exposure were to him, to the railroad rate bill, and to many other good causes, he took care that his rebuke should apply only to the irresponsible ones. The time and the occasion for his rebuke were determined by his reading "with great indignation a certain magazine," containing a loose diatribe, just before a private dinner of the Gridiron Club on March 17, 1906. At the dinner, Roosevelt took as the theme for his speech a passage from Bunyan's "Pilgrim's Progress":

the Man with the Muckrake, the man who could look no way but downward with the muckrake in his hand; who was offered a celestial crown for his muckrake but who would neither look up nor regard the crown he was offered but continued to rake to himself the filth of the floor.

Although the speech, following Gridiron Club tradition, was not published, gossip about Roosevelt's allusion got around. In the amount of comment he heard, he realized the potentiality in the chance inspiration that had led him to revive Bunyan's generally forgotten fig-

---

has been left open an' a few mosquitoes or life-insurance prisidints have got in, an' we say: 'This is turr'ble; we must get rid iv these here pests.' An' we take an axe to thim. We destroy a lot iv furniture an' kill th' canary bird, th' cat, th' cuckoo clock, an' a lot iv other harmless insects, but we'll fin'lly land th' mosquitoes. If an Englishman found mosquitoes in his house he'd first thry to kill thim, an' whin he didn't succeed he'd say: 'What pleasant little humming-bur-rds they ar-re; life wud be very lonesome without thim.' An' he'd domesticate thim, larn thim to sing 'Gawd Save th' King,' an' call his house Mosquito Lodge. If these here inthrestin' life-insurance scandals had come up in Merry ol' England we'd niver hear iv thim, because all th' boys wud be in th' House iv Lords be this time, an' Lord Tontine wud sit hard on anny scheme to have thim searched be a lawyer fr'm Brooklyn."

ure of speech. With Roosevelt, to recognize opportunity was to put both arms around it, quickly and firmly. Determining to expand his Gridiron Club speech,

From a photograph by Underwood & Underwood.
T. R. at Asheville, N. C., September, 1902.

and make it public, he first took care to reassure some
disquieted writers who felt themselves to be unmerited
victims of the generalization Roosevelt had built upon
Bunyan's allegory. To one of the most accurate and con-

scientious of the writers of exposure literature, Ray
Stannard Baker, Roosevelt wrote: "People so persistent-
ly misunderstand what I said that I want to have it reported in full. You understand it. I want to let in
light and air but I do not want to let in sewer gas. If a
room is fetid and the windows are bolted, I am perfectly
willing to knock out the windows, but I would not knock
a hole in the drain pipe."

Roosevelt found his opportunity for having the
speech "reported in full," and with carefully designed
additions, in an engagement he had to dedicate the cor-
ner-stone of the House of Representatives Office Building, Washington, April 14, 1906. Characteristically
he used his balanced form of speech, devoting one portion of his address to one of the most radical attacks on
big business that he had yet uttered, including some of
the most provocative phrases — a proposal that "fortunes swollen beyond all healthy limits" should be subjected to a "progressive tax" in order to "put it beyond
the power of the owner of one of these enormous fortunes to hand over more than a certain amount to any
one individual. . . . No amount of charity in spending such fortunes," he added, with the effect of an ugly
look at Mr. Rockefeller, "in any way compensates for
misconduct in making them."

Then, within the speech as a whole, he balanced even
more carefully his allusions to the exposure writers:

I hail as a benefactor every writer or speaker, every man
who, on platform or in book, magazine or newspaper, with
merciless severity, makes such attack, provided always that he
in his turn remember that the attack is of use only if it is absolutely truthful.

But

The effort to make financial or political profit out of the
destruction of character can only result in public calamity.

Gross and reckless assaults on character, whether on the stump or in newspaper, magazine, or book, create a morbid and vicious public sentiment.[19]

In the outburst of comment on the speech, the conservative portion of the press ignored — though they could not ignore for long — Roosevelt's detonant phrase about "swollen fortunes." Gleefully they fastened the name "muckraker" on each and all, good and bad, among the writers in behalf of reform. The New York *Sun* wrote their requiem — somewhat prematurely, and from a too limited point of view: "It was a great day while it lasted, but it became too hot; the muckrakers worked merrily for a time in their own bright sunshine, and an unthinking populace applauded their performance; now there are few to do them reverence." Quickly the word "muckraker" blazed through other head-lines; quickly the newspaper versifiers took it up:

"What's all that noise that shakes the ground?" said Lawson-
        on-Parade.
"It's Teddy Roosevelt's muck-rake speech," a pale reformer
        said. . . .
"They're exposin' the exposers; it would make your hair turn
        gray
To reflect on what will come when they expose each exposé.

With equal promptness, and equal glee — and with a good deal of generosity, considering the circumstances — all the writers of exposure accepted the epithet that was meant for some of them, and in the eyes of most of the public "muckraker" became a term of approval.

[19] Taft, then Secretary of War, indorsing, as commonly, his chief's sentiments — out-Roosevelting Roosevelt — delivered a speech at New Haven which the New York *Sun* epitomized in its head-lines, April 25, 1906:

TAFT SCORES MUCKRAKERS. NO JUSTIFICATION FOR THEIR WORK IN WASHINGTON. THEIR OWN EXCESS OF DENUNCIATION HAS DEFEATED THEIR AIM.

"His nature was so forceful, and yet his character so built up of the magnified virtues and failings of mankind, that by his very resemblance to the ordinary soldier, his conformity to the type of the average citizen, he won an absolute ascendancy over the minds of normal men. It touched the vanity of every individual that a man, by the exercise of brains and faculties no greater than his own, was become lord of half the world. It was no prodigious intellectual genius who ruled the earth with incomprehensible ability but a burly, virile, simple, brave, vulgar[1] man. . . . Antony was not a genius; he was a gigantic commonplace." — Arthur Weigall, writing of Mark Antony in "Life and Times of Cleopatra."

"The most glorious exploits do not furnish us with the clearest discoveries of virtue or vice in men; sometimes a matter of less moment, an expression or a jest, informs us better of their characters and inclinations than the most famous sieges, the greatest armaments, or the bloodiest battles whatsoever." — Plutarch.

---

[1] Weigall is using the word "vulgar" in an older sense, meaning ordinary, similar to the average, partaking of the common. Mark Anthony may or may not have been vulgar in the modern sense also; the present author does not know. In any event, Roosevelt was not vulgar in the modern sense. He never, for example, used profanity; a man with his rich fecundity in the invention of epithets which damned by the aptness of their specific application to the objects at which they were aimed, did not need to fall back upon the trite maledictions of ordinary profanity.

6

"TEDDY"

"The Scrapes He Gets Into, the Scrapes He Gets Out Of;
the Things He Attempts, the Things He Accomplishes, the
Things He Demolishes; His Appointments and His Disap-
pointments; the Rebukes That He Administers and Those
He Receives; His Assumptions, Presumptions, Omnisciencies and Deficiencies, Make Up a Daily Tale Which Those
of Us Who Survive His Tenure of the Presidential Office
Will Doubtless Miss, as We Might Miss Some Property of
the Atmosphere We Breathe." — *Life*, December 27, 1906.

"The Scrapes He Gets Into"

In the early part of December, 1906, an editor of the
Boston *Herald*, visiting Washington for a few days of

"Teddy." "At times he seemed almost
like an impish boy."

direct contact with na-
tional politics, dined with
Senator Foraker of Ohio,
and heard a fragment of
behind-the-scenes infor-
mation. Several Senators,
Foraker said, had received
copies of a confidential
document from Bellamy
Storer, explaining the
causes for Storer's abrupt
withdrawal, eight months
before, from his post as
American Ambassador to
Austria-Hungary. The
document, Foraker stated,
contained sensational letters that had passed between
Storer and Roosevelt, and also between Mrs. Storer and
Roosevelt dealing with matters of high public and international importance.

The editor transmitted his information to his Washington correspondent, Ernest G. Walker, and Walker hurried to his most intimate acquaintance in the Senate, William P. Frye of Maine. Frye declined to give up the pamphlet, and Walker, after similar failure with other sources, took into partnership in his search a correspondent of the Chicago *Tribune*. The latter went to the venerable Senator from Illinois, Shelby M. Cullom, who said yes, he had a copy — it was lying on his desk at the moment. "Uncle Shelby" felt he could not be in the position of giving the document to a newspaperman, but, he told the correspondent, he apprehended that in a few minutes he would be obliged to leave his office for a brief interval; if upon his return he found that anything had been taken from his desk it was possible he might not notice the loss — certainly he would not feel called upon to make any fuss about it.

When the two newspaper correspondents got possession of the document it was late in the afternoon of December 7. Hurriedly, with the help of officials of the Western Union, they arranged for extra telegraph service to their respective home offices; by midnight the bulk of the eleven thousand words of the document were in type in the offices of *The Herald* in Boston and *The Tribune* in Chicago. In those two cities the following morning, and in every other city and town the succeeding morning, America saw blazing head-lines:

Assail Roosevelt with Own Letters[1]

Sensational Attack on President by Former Ambassador

Question of Veracity Raised Over Attempts to Secure Red Hat for Archbishop Ireland

Ex-Diplomat Says that When He Called on the Pope He Did So at Express Request [of Roosevelt]

[1] From head-lines on first page Chicago *Tribune,* December 8, 1906.

Beneath, readers saw seven columns of compact type, not sufficiently coherent to convey, to the average person, a clear story — but decidedly intriguing in their connotations of high sensation: Letters by Roosevelt beginning "Dear Bellamy" and "Dear Maria," and, from the other side, "Dear Theodore." Phrases in Roosevelt's letters, "Oh warmest of friends and staunchest of supporters." Other phrases, in letters from both sides, dealing with *haute politique*, both ecclesiastical and secular, "promotion to the Cardinalate" . . . "personal favor to the President."

Bellamy Storer.

. . . "Methodist clergymen who are political prohibitionists and [who] denounce the President because he will not encourage drunkenness in the army by putting down the canteen." . . . "Participation in French politics." . . . French "anti-Republican intrigue." . . . "Marriage of Victor Bonaparte with a member of the Orleans family." Cities and places mentioned in an atmosphere that, to the average American, seemed distant and associated with world affairs, Rome, Madrid, Vienna, Paris, the Vatican, Cairo, Luxor. Allusions to personages of two continents, Secretary of State Root, Secretary of War Taft, Mark Hanna, M. Jusserand, Princess Alexandrine Windisch-Graetz. Allusions to churchmen — never, probably, did there appear in a single issue of any American newspaper, nor possibly in a whole year of issues, so many names of dignitaries of the Catholic Church: Pope Leo

XIII, Pope Pius X, Cardinal Merry del Val, Cardinal Rampolla, Cardinal Satolli, Archbishop Ireland, Archbishop Farley, Archbishop Corrigan, the Archbishop of Havana, the Archbishop of Manila, Bishop O'Gorman, Monsignor O'Connell. . . .

Clearly the letters between President Roosevelt and the Storers dealt with matters of high import, though to what effect could not be exactly gathered from the first instalment of the revelations. It was certain, however, that Roosevelt had got into another scrape.

As the comedy developed through days of thunderous outgivings from the private letter-files of both sides, the roster of the dramatis personæ, stated in order of the characters' nearness (now erstwhile) to Roosevelt, began with Mrs. Bellamy (Maria) Storer. Mrs. Storer had a place in an order of society which at that time, and in the oldest of our large midwestern cities, carried the prestige suggested by the newspaper phrase "people of wealth and social importance." Her daughter had married a European and bore a title, Marquise de Chambrun; her nephew, Nicholas Longworth, of similar station in the old Cincinnati aristocracy, was the husband of President Roosevelt's eldest daughter. With the sense of obligation that went with the social position Mrs. Storer occupied, and in the spirit in which, at that time, the obligation was frequently carried out, she was an active patron of the Cincinnati Art Museum, founder of the Rookwood Pottery, contributor of money as well as personal devotion to the establishment of training-schools for nurses, generous giver of money and energy to church work and other good causes.

Mrs. Storer had ambition for herself, and two vicarious ambitions. One was for her husband, Bellamy Storer, who, according to common contemporary judgment, did not seem to have a capacity to hold on to high stations in proportion to his wife's enthusiasm and diplomacy in manœuvring him into them. That he was personally of fine c h a r a c t e r, everybody agreed; President McKinley described him as "noble-hearted . . . the most unselfish man I ever knew"; William Howard Taft spoke of him as "high-minded." He had, wrote another, "the power to inspire fellow men with really tender affection." Storer's capabilities, however, seem not to have been as exceptional as his character was attractive. A magazine writer, at a time when Storer had got himself into troublous embarrassments, characterized him, possibly with undue acerbity, as "a dilettante, a dabbler in the arts and graces, but a man without striking force." He had served two terms in Congress,[2] and then, because of an inattention to the Cincinnati Republican magnate, "Boss" Cox, was dropped. He was appointed by President McKinley to be Assistant Secretary of State, but Senator Foraker prevented his confirmation by the Senate; when McKinley asked Foraker if he would consent to Storer's appointment to a foreign post, Foraker said, "Certainly, the foreigner the better." Upon that not very flattering propulsion, Storer became Minister to Belgium in 1897, and, in 1899, to Spain.

Mrs. Bellamy Storer.

The Storers had become acquainted with Roosevelt

[2] 1891 to 1895.

during the latter's residence in Washington in the early 1890's, when he was Civil Service Commissioner and Storer a Congressman. The two families became devoted to each other, became Bellamy and Theodore, Maria and Edith. The Washington home of each was a second home to the other; when Roosevelt had a larger dinner-party to give than his modest dining-room would accommodate, he had it in the ampler house of the wealthy Storers. The Storers, when Roosevelt became Vice-President, offered him their house in Washington rent-free, and Roosevelt, though his sense of taste led him to decline, replied that "Edith and I were so touched by your note and your absolutely characteristic offer. . . . What trumps you two blessed people are." To Storer on another occasion Roosevelt wrote: "your dear wife, whom we feel to be, like yourself, among the few very staunchest friends we ever had," and, "Dear Old Fellow: You cannot be a bit fonder of us than we are of you." The two families were, as Storer later wrote, "on terms of close and affectionate personal intimacy." When they were separated, they exchanged, "frequently, letters written on both sides with the greatest unreserve on both private and public matters." To Mrs. Storer Roosevelt wrote: "Your letters are so delightful that we keep every one."

This intimacy Mrs. Storer felt justified in drawing upon to advance her ambition for her husband. When fate, through the assassination of McKinley, made Roosevelt President, Mrs. Storer, within eight days, wrote Roosevelt urging that her husband be given a Cabinet position — "please give him either the Navy or War. . . . I pray that Bellamy, who so richly deserves it, shall have a chance for honorable service at home to his country."

All the cartoonists stressed Roosevelt's aliveness.

Roosevelt patiently explained that he did not expect immediately to make any changes in his Cabinet. "My dear Maria," he wrote, "you need never be afraid of asking anything; if it is in my power to grant it, I shall do so. . . . Bellamy was right about its being needless to write me in order to keep him in mind; I think of both of you all the time and have gone over several times possible plans." As for giving Storer the War Department, Roosevelt pleaded that he really could not get along without Root: "Secretary of War Root is one of the very strongest men in our whole party. . . . His advice is invaluable not merely in reference to his own department but in reference to all branches of the service. It would be a public calamity to have him leave the Cabinet now. If he went out, it may be that after carefully looking over the matter I should conclude that Bellamy was the man for the purpose. . . . I do not believe that Secretary Long intends to leave the Navy. In this department I am sure without further thought that Bellamy would be admirable. . . ."

Failing the Cabinet, temporarily as she believed, Mrs. Storer wrote Roosevelt, on October 17, 1901, asking for an ambassadorship, "suggesting London or Paris as fit places for her husband and stating that [the incumbents] Mr. Choate and General Porter, were not proper persons to be ambassadors." "I received," said Roosevelt later, "many letters of the general tenor of those mentioned." When announcement was made of the approaching nuptials of King Alfonso of Spain, Mrs. Storer wrote: "Please, please send us to Madrid as special envoys to the wedding; it would be very appropriate and I would love it." Mrs. Storer's letters became so importunate that Roosevelt's affection for a petted friend was touched almost with a little impatience: "She has written me," he said to a friend of hers, "an awful letter, she allows me no time; try, I beg of you, to calm her."

Energetically Mrs. Storer urged her friends to see Roosevelt in behalf of getting her husband made an ambassador, discussed ways of bringing about a vacancy in order to make a place for him. "I must, I suppose," said Roosevelt to a mutual friend, "poison off one of our ambassadors, but which one to experiment upon first I do not know; but Bellamy is safe in my hands, only let him give me time, the best at my disposal will be his."

Finally, after more than a year of such pressure, Roosevelt, in October, 1902, appointed Storer Ambassador to Austria-Hungary.

With zeal no less great, Mrs. Storer used her standing with Roosevelt to promote the second of her ambitions, the advancement of a prelate of the church to which she was a convert and to which in turn she had converted her husband, Archbishop Ireland of the Catholic diocese of St. Paul. Him Mrs. Storer wanted Rome to make a Cardinal. That the elevation was deserved and would in all respects be appropriate, that it would be pleasing to Americans of all creeds, and that for certain definite reasons it would be useful to the American Government, was the opinion of leading men in the United States, non-Catholics no less than Catholics. Archbishop Ireland had a unique hold on American thought and sentiment; he had been chaplain of a famous Minnesota regiment in the Civil War, his urbanity and charm made him a sought-after figure in public gatherings of all sorts, his standing and ability caused him to be invited, and his good-will led him to participate, in worthy movements of all kinds. A book he had written, "The Church and Modern Society," had won high esteem. The place he had in national life is suggested by the honorary degree, LL.D., that Yale University gave him in 1901. To the America of that day he was, in some aspects, what Cardinal Newman had been to England half a century before. People were accustomed to asso-

ciate the phrase "Americanism" with him. President R o o s e v e l t on one occasion wrote of "the Archbishop's efforts to act in his ecclesiastical office so as to meet the highest demands of American citizenship," and on another occasion of "the high plane of American patriotism which the Archbishop p u b l i c l y and definitely advocated." Ireland was known, in his communications with the Vatican, to stand up for the American point of view, and to i m p r e s s upon the

Courtesy of the New York "World."
Archbishop Ireland, of St. Paul.

Church authorities the importance of American public opinion. Without being "modern" in any sense even faintly approaching lack of orthodoxy, he was looked upon as reflecting American liberal thought as distinguished from the thought, denominated reactionary, that was ascribed to some European princes of the Church, especially in Spain.

The relation of Spain as an officially Catholic country, to the Vatican, and the influence of Spanish churchmen at Rome, had come to be a matter of concern to the United States during our war against Spain and afterward. The Consistorial Secretary of the Vatican, later Papal Secretary of State, Cardinal Merry del Val, was a Spaniard — "anything American set him in a rage." Archbishop Ireland had approved America's making the war, had conducted funeral services in Washington for a Cuban general, Calixto García, whom he referred to as a "patriot," and had taken the position, after we acquired the Philippines, that the Spanish head of the Church in the Islands should be supplanted by an American. He had been helpful to President McKinley throughout the war, and equally helpful as an intermediary with the Vatican in the subsequent negotiations made necessary by the ownership of immense lands in the Philippines vested in orders of Catholic friars. Ireland's attitude, indeed, had been so unequivocally and consistently American as to cost him the friendship of some European churchmen[3] whose sympathies had been with Catholic Spain in the war. He wrote, a little sadly, in a letter to a friend in 1903: "The Friar Cardinals . . . — once friends of mine — are now opposed to me. They blame me for the attitude of the administration towards the Friars of the Philippines; they say I could have changed that attitude; they even say I am the chief cause of it. Cardinal Rampolla is a mystery. He talked so much friendship — and yet did so little."

Archbishop Ireland had been helpful also to the Republican party, had publicly sided with the Republican and "sound-money" forces, and against Bryan and "free silver" in the Presidential campaign of 1896. His action had made it easy for groups of Catholic voters, theretofore commonly Democratic, to unite with the Republican party. In the campaign of 1900 he had given an interview having the effect of averting a drift of Catholics back to the Democrats. On two subsequent occasions he gave out interviews designed to assure

[3] Mrs. Storer, in a letter to Roosevelt, spoke of "the Pope being angry with Archbishop Ireland for not stopping the war with Spain."

American Catholics of the propriety and good-will of the American Government's management of the Philippines. The Archbishop was able to say, in a letter to a friend: "[President] McKinley realizes . . . the services I have rendered him."[4]

In short, Mrs. Storer's ardent desire that Archbishop Ireland be made a Cardinal coincided with the sympathetic attitude toward him of the American people, and with the desires of American public men; such an elevation would put an end to whatever feeling existed in America that the Church had leaned toward Spain in the war of 1898, and would make the management of future matters in the Philippines more easy.

That the American Government should make a formal request, however, or that any man high in American official life should make such request in any way that committed his office, would have run counter to our diplomatic traditions, and would have entailed possibilities of criticism that no man in American political life cared to court. And it was just this that Mrs. Storer, in her zeal, wanted Roosevelt to do.

In March, 1899, Mrs. Storer twice wrote Roosevelt, then Governor of New York, asking him to send her a cablegram which she could use at Rome to promote the Archbishop's elevation; and Mr. Storer in a third letter asked Roosevelt to, in addition, see President McKinley and urge upon McKinley that he should aid in having Archbishop Ireland made a Cardinal.[5] Roosevelt replied: "I have written to the President [McKinley] stating my belief that it would be a most fortunate thing for this country, and I believe an especially fortunate thing for

[4] Ireland to Bellamy Storer, December 20, 1900.

[5] Roosevelt, six years later, said in a public statement: "When they [the Storers] first wrote to me on the subject, I was Governor of New York. Not being President myself, and not having thought out with clearness the exact situation, I asked President McKinley whether he could properly do anything to help

the Catholics of this country if Archbishop Ireland could be made a cardinal. I feel this precisely because of what may be done in the Philippines and in other tropic islands. I am strongly of opinion that the uplifting of the people on these tropic islands must come chiefly through making them better Catholics and better citizens, and that on the one hand we shall have to guard against the reactionary Catholics who would oppose the correction of abuses in the ecclesiastical arrangement of the Islands, and on the other hand guard against any Protestant fanaticism which will give trouble anyhow, and which may be fanned into a dangerous flame if the above mentioned Catholic reactionaries are put into control. . . . On every account I should feel that the election of Archbishop Ireland to the Cardinalate would be a most fortunate thing for us in the United States, Catholics and non-Catholics alike."

Roosevelt said he did not like to send the cablegram Mrs. Storer had requested, because he did not quite see "where it would end if I began to interfere directly in the election of a cardinal; if I make a request or express a desire in such a form as to make them [sic] seem like requests, I inevitably put myself under certain obligations and I do not quite know what these obligations are. Of course I feel that I am not justified in interfering in any way, directly or indirectly, with matters in the Vatican, but it is only fair, in response to your letter, that I should write you fully and frankly of my great appreciation of Archbishop Ireland."

Roosevelt was willing that the Vatican should be told, in an informal way, of his conviction that it would be a

Archbishop Ireland. He responded that it was not a matter with which he could with propriety interfere, although he expressed himself as having the same high opinion of the Archbishop that I had. I had a further conversation with the President on the subject, either just before or just after my election as Vice-President, in which he stated what he felt was the proper position."

most fortunate thing for America if Archbishop Ireland could be made a Cardinal, and of his communication of this belief to President McKinley. "While I
would not like," he said, "to have this letter [to Mrs.
Storer] published, you are most welcome to show it to
any one you see fit."[6]

Mrs. Storer showed Roosevelt's letter to various persons in Rome, whence gossip trickled back to Washington to the effect that Roosevelt had urged that Archbishop Ireland be made a Cardinal, and, more dangerous
yet in American politics, had made slighting allusions to
"Protestant fanaticism" and had expressed an opinion
which could be construed as a conviction on his part that
wholesale proselyting by Protestant missionaries in the
Philippines should not be encouraged. In the meantime, Roosevelt had taken on a status of direct official
responsibility for the nation and for the Republican
party; he had been elected Vice-President on the ticket
with McKinley. To Roosevelt came two members of
the McKinley administration, disturbed by the rumors
from Rome, who told him his letter to Mrs. Storer had
been indiscreet, and might, if it should become public,
cause embarrassment. Roosevelt wrote Mrs. Storer:
"My desire is so great to help you whenever you ask it
that I did what I ought not to have done in writing that
letter. I mean by 'what I ought not to have done,' having a just and proper regard for the effect (should it by
any chance get out) upon the political fortunes of those
associated with me, for a letter such as this, which contains what every thoughtful and fair-minded man will
agree with, can nevertheless in a campaign be twisted.
. . . Can you reclaim any copy of my letter, if any has
been sent anywhere?"

[6] The quotations from Roosevelt are from two letters written to Mrs. Storer
and one to Mr. Storer, March 23 and March 27, 1900, and April 30, 1900.

A year later, Roosevelt having now become President himself, echoes about his letter continued to come to him from Rome, and on January 16, 1902, he wrote to Storer: "Will you ask Maria again if there is any letter of mine to her or a copy of any letter which, so far as

From "The Tribune" (Chicago).
All ready for the fireworks.

she is aware, is in the hands of any one else? It is stated with the utmost insistence that [Cardinal] Rampolla has one."

Mrs. Storer at once communicated with Cardinal Rampolla and he had the copy returned to her. She so informed Roosevelt, and Roosevelt wrote her to keep it.

Up to this point, Roosevelt was blaming no one but himself. The Storers had done no more than he had given them permission to do, and he had no reproach for them — though he may have had moments of wishing they had not made the request to which he had acceded, may have unconsciously classified them as not having the discretion that persons must have if they are to be on intimate terms with a President of the United States. In any event, he had his warning about writing letters containing allusions to promoting an archbishop to be a cardinal. Roosevelt never wrote another letter to either of the Storers about the Cardinalate that could make him any embarrassment. He did, however, have conversations with them, and out of conflicting interpretations of these conversations arose vast trouble.

In the summer of 1903, the Storers, returning to the United States from their post in Vienna, visited Roosevelt at Oyster Bay. There were, of course, conversations, including allusions to Archbishop Ireland and the Cardinalate. After one of the conversations, Storer made a memorandum. Storer returned to Europe and on December 2, 1903, had an audience with Pope Pius X, to whom Storer delivered the memorandum purporting to be an oral message from Roosevelt to the Pope:

He (the President) said to me, and he authorized me to say to your Holiness that the Archbishop of St. Paul is his personal friend and that he possesses all his confidence as prelate and as citizen; that he desires emphatically for Mgr. Ireland all the honors of the church and that he will see with the greatest pleasure and satisfaction the elevation of Mgr. Ireland to the Cardinalate.

An alert newspaper correspondent at Rome, representing the Scripps news-gathering association, learned of Storer's call at the Vatican and sent to America a despatch saying in effect that Storer visited the Vatican in the interest of Monsignor Ireland, and spoke there for the President.

Roosevelt, upon seeing the newspaper article, wrote to Storer: "What has occurred shows clearly that it is hopeless for you to expect that people will appreciate the difference between what you as an American Catholic in your private capacity say, and what you, as an American Ambassador, say. . . . I must ask you while you are in the United States service to take no part either directly or indirectly in such a matter as this and hereafter to repeat to no man what I have said to you concerning the subject of the article." Roosevelt repeated that he had the heartiest admiration for Archbishop Ireland, and would be delighted to see him made cardinal, just as he had been delighted to see Bishop Lawrence made the Episcopal bishop of Massachusetts, and just as he had been delighted about various Methodist friends of his who had been made bishops. "But as President it is none of my business to interfere for or against the advancement of any man in any church; and as it is impossible to differentiate between what I say in my individual capacity from what I say as President — at least in the popular mind and apparently also in the Roman mind — I must request you not to quote me in any way or shape hereafter."

Storer, with rather fatuous incapacity to recognize an imperative order, replied to Roosevelt with defense of what he had done, and an appeal to Roosevelt to see the value of it. Storer put it on the ground of the good of the Republican party. "Do not shut your eyes," Storer wrote to Roosevelt, "to the danger which for five years I have been trying to head off from the Republican party and its candidates." The "danger" was that Catholic voters, having switched in 1896 from a long allegiance to the Democrats in order to vote for McKinley and against Bryan and free silver, might turn back to their older allegiance. This danger, Storer believed, he could avert if he could persuade the Vatican to confer a cardinal's hat upon Archbishop Ireland, who was known to have Republican leanings. "I hope," Storer wrote to Roosevelt, "I am not the only one who is tired of my church possessing a hierarchy which is (so far as it knows politics) by a very large majority in principle opposed to us politically." He named the several prominent Catholic prelates in America who had Democratic associations, he pointed out that Archbishop Ireland was the outstanding Catholic prelate who was a Republican, and he said that, for himself, he was "straining every nerve to have the great Republican influence in my church recognized as standing of equal value in the eyes of the spiritual authority of the Church [at Rome]."

Roosevelt replied in a way that markedly ignored Storer's self-justification: "While I am President and you are Ambassador, neither of us in his public relation is to act as Catholic or Protestant, Jew or Gentile. . . . I shall ask you not to quote me to any person in any shape or way in connection with any affair of the Catholic Church; and yourself not to take action of any kind which will give ground for the belief that you, as an American ambassador, are striving to interfere in the affairs of the Church."

Storer, finally recognizing a rebuke (and being in difficulties with the State Department over an error of judgment in another matter), tendered his resignation as Ambassador to Vienna. Roosevelt replied, January 19, 1904: "Dear Bellamy: I have your letter. It is absolutely all right; we will treat the incident as closed. Nothing would persuade me to accept your resignation, old fellow."

Apparently everything was serene. In the summer of 1904, the Storers, during a visit they paid to America, were again guests at the White House. The intimacy of the two families was undisturbed.

Meantime the enterprise upon which the Storers had set their hearts was prospering and finally, early in 1904, seemed certain of success. Assurance to this effect came to Mrs. Storer from her intimate friend, Princess Alexandrine Windisch-Graetz, a long-time confidential friend of the Pope, having "known him for years in Venice when he was Patriarch." The Princess Alexandrine wrote Mrs. Storer that she had had a private audience with the Holy Father, that she had spoken to his Holiness about Archbishop Ireland and the Storers' wish that he be made

Archbishop (later Cardinal) Farley, of New York.

a Cardinal, and that the Pope had answered: "Ho studiato la causa; sara fatto."[7]

This joyful news Mrs. Storer immediately wrote to Ireland, who replied: "I congratulate you very heartily upon the good news. . . . You, above all others, deserve to be congratulated, for the success which is now reliably announced is due to you — to your ceaseless planning and working, and to the intelligence characterizing your planning and working. Take all the credit to yourself — yourself, of course, including my dear Bellamy. It was most fitting that the first news of the success should have come to me from you. I shall not waste

[7] "I have studied the matter; it will be done."

words to thank you: you know full well that I am grateful to you." In high good spirits the Archbishop concluded his letter with a promise not to speak to any one of the great good fortune that was now to crown his career. He anticipated a little innocent fun: "I wish to enjoy the surprise it will cause to many, who are believing they have nothing to fear from me. Here in New York some hopes run high [for another American aspirant for a red hat, Archbishop Farley] — altho it is confidentially admitted, no ground has been given to them in any positive, defined manner."[8]

The Pope's "sara fatto!" brought a lull in the activities of the Storers in Monsignor Ireland's behalf. They had won. The Pope had said it would be done, and now all that remained for them to do was to possess their souls in patience until the Consistory to name new cardinals should be called. No change in the situation occurred throughout the rest of 1904. During the winter announcement was made that the Consistory would be held December 13, 1905. Month succeeded month, uneventfully except for sporadic and seemingly ineffectual efforts on the part of friends of Archbishop Farley, to which the Storers gave little heed. Thus the situation continued almost up to the end of November, 1905, when to Mrs. Storer at the Embassy in Vienna came news that shocked her. From her friend, Princess Windisch-Graetz at Rome, came a letter saying that Vatican gossip had it that no American would be among the new cardinals. From another source information reached Mrs. Storer that Cardinal Merry del Val had made the almost incredible statement that President Roosevelt had recommended the promotion of Archbishop Farley to the Cardinalate. Cardinal Merry del Val was said to have remarked also, with a logic that could not be gain-

[8] "In Memoriam Bellamy Storer."

said, that if Roosevelt was backing both Farley and Ireland he could not care very greatly about either. Since only four cardinals were to be named, it was not possible that two of them should be Americans.

Mrs. Storer, panic-stricken over imminent calamity to her hopes, began a fever of letter-writing. She wrote to William Howard Taft, she wrote to Cardinal Merry del Val, she wrote to Princess Alexandrine Windisch-Graetz, she wrote to Archbishop Keane, and — after all that had passed — she wrote to Roosevelt.

In order that Roosevelt should be sure to get her letter she sent it in care of Mrs. Roosevelt, who — considerate wife of an impetuous husband — treated it (so Roosevelt subsequently wrote to Mrs. Storer) "as she sometimes has treated other letters that you have sent her to deliver to me when she knew that the receipt would merely make me indignant or puzzle me; that is, she did not give it to me."[9]

Taft, however, showed Roosevelt the letter he had received, and in Roosevelt's anger over that, Mrs. Roosevelt showed her husband the letter that Mrs. Storer had written to him directly. It was a remarkable letter. Mrs. Storer recited the rumors she had heard about the approaching Consistory and the apparent likelihood that Archbishop Ireland would not be made a cardinal; she recited, as if in confident expectation of praise for it, the energetic last-ditch efforts she was making; she even enclosed to Roosevelt copies of the letters she had written to Cardinal Rampolla and others, and Cardinal Rampolla's reply, which, though couched in the most elegant phrases of Vatican diplomacy, plainly indicated — to others, at least, who read the letter, if not to Mrs. Storer — that she had been "unwarrantedly officious in

[9] Roosevelt to Mrs. Storer, December 11, 1905.

matters with which properly you have no concern."[10]
Finally, and astonishingly, considering all that had
passed, Mrs. Storer made a request of Roosevelt which
seemed to imply that a Papal Consistory must be much
like a Republican National Convention, and that Roosevelt must have as much weight with one as with the
other. She asked Roosevelt to send her a cablegram that
she might deliver to the Pope in person! Naïvely, she
added, "You can trust me, really."

Roosevelt blew up. On December 11, 1905, he
wrote two letters and put them in the same envelope.
One, to Mr. Storer, said: "I am very sorry to write the
enclosed letter to Mrs. Storer, which I shall ask you to
read and then hand to her. . . . I am deeply attached
to both of you, but it is evident that I cannot longer delay using the plainest kind of language."

In the letter he enclosed to Mrs. Storer, Roosevelt
used very plain language indeed:

I have continually been hearing [he wrote] of your having
written one man or the other about such matters. I find you
are alluded to by members of the diplomatic body in Washington as the "American ambassadress to Rome." Information
of this kind has repeatedly been brought to Secretary [of
State] Root. Root's feeling about the case is stronger than I
care to put in words. . . . You actually propose that I should
use you to go to Rome to take part in what I must call an ecclesiastical intrigue — and drag the United States government
into it. Such a proposal is simply astounding.

If you cannot make up your mind absolutely to alter your
conduct in this regard while your husband is in the diplomatic
service, to refrain absolutely from taking any further part in
any matter of ecclesiastical politics at the Vatican and to refuse
to write or speak to any one (whether laymen or ecclesiastics,
at home or abroad), as you have been writing and speaking in
this cardinal's hat matter, then Bellamy cannot with propriety continue to remain ambassador of the United States.

[10] The words quoted are Roosevelt's interpretation of the spirit of Cardinal
Rampolla's reply to Mrs. Storer.

I must ask you to give me this positive promise in writing if Bellamy is to continue in the service; and if you even unintentionally violate it, I shall have to ask for Bellamy's resignation; for I can no longer afford to have the chance of scandal being brought on the entire American diplomatic service and on the American government itself by such indiscreet and ill-advised action as yours has been.

The Storers did not reply. Indignant, humiliated, hurt to the point of sickness, Storer went to Egypt. There he received from Roosevelt a brief and peremptory demand, in which Roosevelt referred to his two unanswered letters, and said: "Both letters called for answers; I should like to have these answers as early as is convenient."

A month later, Storer still not having answered, he received from Roosevelt a succinct telegram in which Roosevelt called attention to his previous letters and to his failure to receive a reply, and ended: "I request your resignation as ambassador." On March 7, 1906, Storer wrote to Secretary of State Root: "In obedience to the peremptory telegram of the President just received . . . I have the honor to tender my resignation."

Storer's resignation was publicly announced as a matter of course. There was some shrewd newspaper surmise that it had some relation to Mrs. Storer's activities in Roman ecclesiastical circles, but the facts and the letters remained securely within the high secrets of the State Department and the sanctity of President Roosevelt's private letter-files until, eight months later, the Storers embodied their side of it in the confidential pamphlet which they sent to Senators and other officials, and which the two newspaper correspondents found and published.

Roosevelt, on the morning of the publication, sent for the two correspondents, not to reproach them — he

accepted their unravelling of the confidential Storer
document as part of the game — but merely to admit,
with a boyish grin, the contretemps that had fallen upon
him; and to inspire them to print on their own authority, as they did the following day, December 9, 1906:

Some of the President's friends doubt the wisdom of his
noticing the pamphlet in any way. Much will depend on the
effect of the publication of the letters on the country. If he
does make a statement he will not spare the feelings of anybody,
as the President is confident that his actions and his motives
are alike entirely honest. . . . The President has kept every
scrap of paper he ever received from Storer or Mrs. Storer,
together with good press copies of what he wrote to them. It
is claimed there are damaging assertions in the letters Mr. and
Mrs. Storer wrote to the President and that the publication
of these letters will somewhat change the aspect of the case.

That afternoon Roosevelt played a smashing game of
tennis on the White House lawn; in the evening he participated in the fun-making of the semi-annual Gridiron dinner. The following day, Sunday, December 9,
he gave out, and the newspapers on Monday, December
10, printed, a second seven-column instalment[11] of the
Storer comedy, this one headed:

ROOSEVELT BRANDS STORER A LIAR

PRESIDENT WRITES RED HOT ANSWER TO ATTACK BY DISMISSED
DIPLOMAT.
WOMAN INTRIGUER BLAMED.
MRS. STORER REVEALED AS INVETERATE MEDDLER, WIRE-
PULLER AND BACKBITER.[12]

[11] Roosevelt, when he concluded it was necessary to make all the Storer cor-
respondence public, had the mass of letters on his desk. Senator Henry Cabot
Lodge was in the room.
"It is too bad," said Lodge, perturbed, "that all this must be made public."
"It is too bad," assented Roosevelt, and his teeth snapped. With a frown on
his face he began turning over sheet after sheet. "It is too bad," he repeated.
Then something caught his eye. The frown receded before gleaming teeth. "But
some of this is delicious," he almost shouted. — Arthur Wallace Dunn, "From
Harrison to Harding."
[12] Chicago *Tribune*, December 10, 1906.

Roosevelt, in the part of his reply that was apologia, said that he had "submitted to conduct from Mr. and Mrs. Storer to which I would have submitted from no other ambassador and his wife"; he had been moved by a "certain chivalric feeling that I ought to do what I could to help them and be as patient as possible with them," because "Mrs. Storer insisted to me often that their change of creed had proved a deadly blow to her husband's career, and that they were suffering for conscience's sake."

In the part of his reply that was counter-attack he described one of Storer's assertions as "not only an untruth but an absurd untruth," one of his actions as "peculiarly ungentlemanly," and another as "simply dishonorable," and his conduct as a whole as "peculiar perfidy."

In justification before public opinion of his actions Roosevelt said: "I explained repeatedly that my friendship and admiration for Archbishop Ireland (which is like my friendship and admiration for Bishop Lawrence of the Episcopal church and Bishop Cranston of the Methodist church, like my friendship and admiration for many clergymen of many denominations — Baptists, Lutherans, Congregationalists, Presbyterians and others) would make me pleased to see any good fortune attend him, or any churchman like him, of any creed; but that I could not interfere for his promotion, or, indeed, in any way in the ecclesiastical affairs of any church."

As the story "burst upon an unprepared world, and ran its lurid course like a newspaper serial of diplomatic intrigue," there was, of course, much discussion, and infinite jest. "Dear Maria" became a phrase to provoke a smile wherever two Americans came together, a symbol for an indiscreet letter, for any partisan whose zeal outran his wisdom, or for the disruption of any friendship too beautiful to endure. Congress, wary of talking much about any controversy that had religious implications, chortled less than it did about most of Roosevelt's other scrapes. Newspapers chastised Mrs. Storer as a "gushing intriguer,"[13] Roosevelt as a writer of "incredibly reckless letters";[13] they pointed morals about the undesirability of the "eternal feminine in politics and diplomacy,"[14] and rendered solemn judgments about whether Roosevelt had or had not sought to "influence the Vatican in the choice of Cardinals."[15] Possibly the comment that was most kin to the spirit in which the average American looked upon the episode was that of the Philadelphia *North American*, which treated the incident as occasion for a dissertation upon the Catholic Church, celibacy, and matrimony in all its aspects: "Many persons criticize the Roman Church for insisting upon sacerdotal celibacy. But the rulers of the church are far-sighted; they know human nature; they have, no doubt, in the flown centuries, considered the awful possibility [of] a Mrs. Bellamy Storer. . . . Considerate married men of long experience will surely find reason for regarding Bellamy with mournful commiseration."

For one of the persons involved there was universal sympathy. Archbishop Ireland was clearly an innocent and to-be-pitied victim — to him the situation which newspapers epitomized as "the 'Dear Maria' incident" was no comedy. Utterly without fault on his part, the impact of unfortuitous accident overbalanced the deserts that Ireland's fine character had built up through

---

[13] New York *Evening Post*.   [14] Cleveland *Plain Dealer*.
[15] Springfield *Republican*.

years of exalted achievement. He was "so far away
from a red hat that it might almost as well be resting

From a photograph by Clinedinst.
One of Roosevelt's favorite photographs.

on the North Pole." With the conviction taught by his
faith that God's will is best, he may have recalled from
the stores of his scholarship the words of Cardinal
Woolsey in "King Henry VIII," and may have accepted

the forestalling of his ambition as meant by Providence to avert perils that might attend the fulfilment of it. With the resignation that was part of his faith, he took, from 1906 on, less and less part in public or secular affairs, and made an outlet for his imagination, talent, and vitality in the building of a great cathedral at St. Paul. By the time it was ready to be consecrated, America was engaged in another war that made the Spanish War seem long ago and very small; and the Archbishop, an old man, was saying prayers for the repose of the souls of lads killed in battle, some of them children of parents whom he as a young priest had christened and confirmed in the prairie villages of his early career. He died two months before the Armistice.

As for Mrs. Storer, she, too, turned to faith and good works. During the Great War she and her husband organized and directed for the Vatican at Rome one of the most poignantly appealing of the institutions that grew up for the alleviation of war, a bureau of inquiry for missing soldiers, to answer the enormous number of letters from distracted wives and mothers who appealed to the Pope to help find their loved ones, whether dead or prisoners. In 1922 she saw her husband die at Paris, after being more than two years "paralyzed and almost speechless." A year later, in 1923, Mrs. Storer, now seventy-six years old — her husband gone, Ireland gone, Roosevelt gone — looked about her upon the changed world into which she had survived, found it to be "a rampant and indecent modern society where religion is derided and manners are extinct," and decided to withdraw from it to her faith, her charities and her memories. Upon the man who had been her friend and later her chastiser, she passed the judgment of age and tolerance:

"As I look back, I can see that the peculiar fascination of Theodore Roosevelt for us all lay in the fact that he was like a child, with a child's spontaneous outbursts of affection, of fun and of anger, and with the busy

The Long Long Trail

From "The Herald-Tribune," New York.

J. N. (Ding) Darling's cartoon at the time of Roosevelt's death.

brain and fancy of a child. As President he was still a child. In anger, like a child, he was rash and inconsiderate. Power and ambition did him harm when he became angry or excited; they led him into misstatements and misunderstandings. When he hurled 'winged words' from his extraordinary vituperative vocabulary at some of his special *bêtes noires*, he laughed at his own absurdities. . . . It was characteristic of him that when [one of his] tempests simmered down he forgot all about it. Sometimes, also, he completely changed his views of men and things after years of bitterness and dislike."[16] Mrs. Storer, concluding, spoke of Roosevelt forgivingly as "our dead friend," expressed faith "that his soul, purified by suffering in this earthly purgatory, went upward into light," and repeated for him the Catholic Church's prayer for departed souls, "Requiem æternam dona ei, Domine, et Lux perpetua luceat ei."[17]

II

"The Scrapes He Gets Out Of"

On his fourth day in the Presidency, Roosevelt, in an hour's talk with the Washington correspondent of the New York *Evening Post*,[18] revealed as much of his plans for his administration as he had had time to make. The correspondent, in one of those "indirect discourse" despatches that sometimes follow confidential talks between Presidents and newspapermen, emphasized an ambition close to Roosevelt's heart, one that he was especially eager to achieve. Roosevelt wanted to "see the South back in full communion" with the rest of the nation. Whenever a Republican administration was in power at Washington — and with the exception of Cleveland's two terms there had been none but Republican administrations since before the Civil War — the

[16] From "In Memoriam Bellamy Storer." The passage here printed is condensed, and some sentences are transposed.

[17] "Eternal rest grant him, O Lord, and let light perpetual shine upon him."

[18] Francis E. Leupp.

South, partly from its own choice and partly from discrimination against it, remained "standing on the outside." This Roosevelt deplored. He wanted to see the South as much at home in Washington under all conditions, as the North and West, and he "would take

Courtesy American Press Assn.

Theodore Roosevelt and Booker T. Washington at Tuskegee, Ala., October 24, 1905.

great pride" in bringing about this final step of reconciliation. In the carrying out of his purpose, he told the correspondent, he would, in making appointments to office in Southern States, take sympathetic account of the South's peculiar problems and its point of view. Naturally, as a party man, Roosevelt would feel obliged to give preference to Republicans over Democrats, but "if it came to a question between an unfit Republican and a fit Democrat," he would "not hesitate a moment to choose the Democrat."

Had Roosevelt been timid, or expedient; had his good impulses been limited by political caution, his advanced policy toward the South could have stopped with the recognition of Democrats. But Roosevelt's restlessly adventurous mind proposed to deal with the South's great incubus, the intermeshed social and political problems associated with the presence of negroes in large numbers. The negro in the South, Roosevelt said, "must take his chances like the rest; if he be a man who has earned the respect of his white neighbors . . . he has nothing to fear from President Roosevelt because of his color." At the same time, a negro who has failed to live up to this standard "will have no favor because he is black or because he is a Republican. By this measure [the respect of his white neighbors] every negro who aspires to office will be tested."

"The standard of personal character and civic virtue which the President will set up for the negro's emulation" — so he told the correspondent — "is best embodied in Booker T. Washington."[19]

It was a statesmanlike wish, to heal the forty-year sore of sectionalism, to show the South that a Republican administration could have the same attitude toward it as toward other sections. For this aim, Roosevelt had, besides the ordinary motive of patriotism, the not overlooked one of doing a service to the Republican party. In addition, Roosevelt had toward the South a personal relation which at once partly inspired his purpose and equipped him to carry it out: His mother had been a Southerner, from Georgia; two of his mother's brothers had fought on the Confederate side in the Civil War, and his father, rather than bear arms against his wife's family, had refrained from enlisting with the Union

[19] The quotations are of Leupp's words, describing Roosevelt's intentions.

troops, had confined himself to the Civil War equivalent of Red Cross work.

This personal equipment for reconciling the South and getting its confidence was coupled with another. Roosevelt, having come to the Presidency from the Vice-Presidency through the assassination of McKinley, was under no obligation to Republican leaders. He could ignore Southern Republican leaders, a class composed largely of persons whom the South still called "carpet-baggers," who kept open the old sores of the reconstruction era by cultivating negro constituencies, by grabbing Federal appointments for themselves, and by practising odious discrimination against the Democrats that composed the great bulk of the whites and the most respected portion. Similarly, Roosevelt was independent of those Northern Republican leaders who still "waved the bloody shirt," still talked about "force bills" to surround Southern polling-places with Federal troops so that negroes might be enabled and encouraged to vote.

Roosevelt, in short, had a fine national purpose and was peculiarly adapted to carry it out; success would shorten one of the less pleasing chapters of American history. He began by making appointments that electrified the South with hope of a new day, of a place in the nation's councils comparable to what it had had before the Civil War. Incredulously at first, and then warmly, the South applauded. From the best papers in the North and from thoughtful persons everywhere, came praise. Roosevelt was not a man to have grandiose visions about his place in history, but it is not surprising that there came to him[20] his earliest glimpse of what every President sometimes thinks about if he has any imagination at all, the realization that he has got hold of something with which to "mark his administration

[20] According to his friend, Francis E. Leupp.

in history." Roosevelt consciously set the political regeneration of the South as the first of his ambitions.

Then, suddenly, on October 18, 1901, only five weeks
after taking office, his whole policy toward the South
encountered devastating contretemps. Unexpectedly, he
stubbed his toe — stubbed it
in a manner and with a dis-
astrousness that, to a man
less buoyant than Roosevelt,
might have brought perma-
nent discouragement.

Booker T. Washington.

Roosevelt had settled
upon Booker Washington as
the best type of negro, one
to encourage and to set up
as an example. Washington,
born in slavery, had climbed
to a leadership of his people which at the time ex-
pressed itself in headship
of a great negro industrial
school, Tuskegee Institute, in Alabama. That Washington was the outstanding negro everybody agreed; indeed, he was an outstanding member of the human family, by the tests of any race. By his methods and example he stimulated the negro to better things, and did not
offend whites. All his counsel to his race was that they
should not seek social equality, but forget it; that they
should strive to gain the respect and good opinion of the
whites by industry, thrift, self-discipline, wholesome
family life — just the homely virtues that appealed to
Roosevelt. Roosevelt decided he would appoint to office
occasionally negroes recommended by Washington, or
of Washington's kind,

With this purpose in mind, and wishing at once to encourage Washington and to get his advice, Roosevelt summoned him to the White House. Washington, undoubtedly seeing in the invitation an aspect which must have escaped Roosevelt's attention, took pains to make his visit inconspicuous. His precautions, as respects his own actions, were successful. But for a trivial detail of White House routine, the custom of entering the names of visitors in a book, Washington might have come and gone with the unobtrusiveness he aimed at successfully achieved. It happened that a reporter for the Washington *Post*, looking over the day's guest-list, saw Washington's name, thought of it vaguely as well known, the sort of public or semi-public name that a reporter should mention, and wrote the kind of item he would have written about any other distinguished visitor. The managing editor of *The Post* either must not have read the item or must have been as unaware as his reporter of just who Booker Washington was; the item appeared next morning in an obscure position near the bottom of an inside page: "Booker T. Washington, of Tuskegee, Alabama, dined with the President last evening."

Despite the meagreness of the item, and its inconspicuousness among the routine news, its significance was realized by the Washington correspondents of Southern newspapers. Their despatches next day led to a fuming of head-line and editorial writers that inspired one of Roosevelt's less known but characteristically vivid phrases, "torrential journalism."

"White men of the South," shrieked the New Orleans *Times-Democrat*, "how do you like it?" "White women of the South, how do YOU like it?" The Memphis *Scimitar*, prevented by the immensity of its indignation from practising the keen-edged deftness suggested by its name, grabbed the biggest brick in sight; Roosevelt, *The Scimitar* said, committed "the most damnable outrage ever perpetrated by any citizen of the United States when he invited a nigger to dine with him at the White House." The Richmond *Times* went to grotesque

L. C. Gregg in the Atlanta "Constitution."

An amusing book, "My Negro Policy"! A Southern cartoon inspired by resentment at Roosevelt's having Booker Washington as a table guest.

lengths in imputing to Roosevelt ideas that no sane person could believe ever entered his head: "It means the President is willing that negroes shall mingle freely with whites in the social circle — that white women may receive attentions from negro men; it means that there is no racial reason in his opinion why whites and blacks may not marry and intermarry, why the Anglo-

Saxon may not mix negro blood with his blood." The Raleigh, N. C., *Post* jeered in rhyme:

> Booker Washington holds the boards —
> The President dines a nigger.
> Precedents are cast aside —[21]
> Put aside with vigor;
> Black and white sit side by side,
> As Roosevelt dines a nigger.

The most savage exhibition was a hand-bill — it was suppressed, soon after its issue, by local Southern Democrats who revolted against its violence — which represented Roosevelt and his wife at table, Roosevelt's face wearing a broad smile of delight, while Mrs. Roosevelt assiduously pressed dainties upon a hideous black savage seated between them. These were some of the expressions that were printed. In violence they fell short of the anonymous letters that came to the White House, many serving notice that for the rest of his term Roosevelt and all members of his family had better not set foot in the South.

Not all the Southern press was so excited and violent in expression — though all had strong feeling. The Memphis *Commercial-Appeal*, while it applied an ugly adjective to Roosevelt, made a reasonable statement of the Southern point of view:

> The negro ... is entitled to his rights under the law, and the men who stand for white supremacy are the strongest advocates of granting him these rights. Beyond that they will not go. The example of President or potentate cannot change their views. Their reasons are good and sufficient. If some coarse-fibred man cannot understand them, it is not the concern of the Southern people.

[21] Roosevelt was not the first President to entertain a colored man in the White House. Grover Cleveland invited Frederick Douglass and his white wife to a Congressional reception.

The New Orleans *Times-Democrat* put the mischief of Roosevelt's example, from its standpoint, in a sentence: "When Mr. Roosevelt sits down to dinner with a negro, he declares that the negro is the social equal of the White Man." Similarly, the New Orleans *States* expressed a fear for the effect on the negro mind, an apprehension of "revivifying a most dangerous problem, one that has brought untold evil upon the whole country in the past, but which it was hoped, and believed, had been removed by the firmness and wisdom of the South." It was this aspect of the episode, the interpretation that ignorant negroes might take from it, that Senator Benjamin ("Pitchfork") Tillman had in mind when he was quoted as saying: "The action of President Roosevelt in entertaining that nigger will necessitate our killing a thousand niggers in the South before they will learn their place again."[22]

The sincerity of the Southern press was as great as its words were violent; nevertheless, Southern editors were cool enough to be shrewd. They recognized that chance

[22] Violence of criticism in the South provoked violence of reprisal in the North. To Tillman's outburst, *Life* of New York replied: "Tillman is a brute, and what he says ought not to be of much importance, except as it illustrates himself and his qualifications to be a Senator of the United States. But if he spoke the words attributed to him he ought to be in jail, where he would make a suitable companion for Emma Goldman, who ought to be there also, and for the same offense — inciting murder."

A more equable comment, from the Northern point of view, on the rage shown by the South over the Washington incident, was published in the New York *World*, October 20, 1901:

"An American named Washington, one of the most learned, most eloquent, most brilliant men of the day, the President of a college, is asked to dinner by President Roosevelt. And because the pigment of his skin is some shades darker than that of others, a large part of the United States is convulsed with shame and rage. The man is a negro. Therefore in eating with him the President is charged with having insulted the South. This man may cast a ballot but he may not break bread. He may represent us in the Senate Chamber, but he may not 'join us at the breakfast table.' He may preach our Gospel, but not be our guest; enlighten our minds, but not entertain our bodies; die for us, but not dine with us. Truly Liberty must smile at such broad-minded logic, such enlightened tolerance. Or should she weep?"

had given them the means to combat Roosevelt's purpose to make the South Republican, or bi-partisan; and they grasped it, eagerly. They had needed it long before Roosevelt announced his purpose. As early as 1896 the unity of the South for Democracy had been

Reynolds in the Tacoma "Ledger."

Chorus — "There is no South, there is no North, there is no East or West."
  The South, disaffected since the Civil War, was encouraged by Roosevelt to resume its historic place in the political life of the Union. The cartoonist has here successfully depicted the pleasure of the entire country at the success of one of Roosevelt's overtures to the South.

shaken by the "free-silver" platform that Bryan forced upon the party; many of the best men in the South, their conservatism shocked by Bryan's radical heresies, had helped to form the Gold Democratic party, and had voted for its candidates, failing, for the first time in their lives, to vote the regular Democratic ticket. As the menace of free silver waned, and the Gold Democratic party died for lack of reason to exist, these conservative Southern Democrats, having gone through an experience of temporary separation from their traditional faith, were susceptible to permanent departure. Much of the South, much of the best of it was fallow for the Republican plough and for Roosevelt's project.

Now, Roosevelt, through the Booker Washington incident, had given the Democratic press of the South material to repel the Republican invader. Cleverly they made the most of it, phrasing their comment in just the terms which seemed to say finis to Roosevelt's ambition, which served notice on Roosevelt that he could never recover his lost prestige. "The President's action," said the New Orleans *States*, "was a studied insult, adopted at the outset of his administration for the purpose of showing his contempt for the sentiments and prejudices of this section." The Richmond, Va., *Times* touched the chord of sorrow that an elderly person may feel for an erring nephew: "At one stroke, and by one act, Mr. Roosevelt has destroyed the kindly, warm regard and personal affection for him which were growing up fast in the South." "Rooseveltism," said one editor who felt the addition of "ism" to a name carries a special quality of odium — "Rooseveltism means nigger supremacy as surely as Grantism did." The Memphis *Scimitar* told the President that "he has rudely shattered any expectation that may have arisen from his announced intention to make the Republican party in the South respectable; he has closed the door to any accessions of Southern white men to the Republican ranks." "No self-respecting white man," Governor Candler of Georgia was reported as saying, "can ally himself with the President after what has occurred."

Roosevelt's hope of bringing the South to comity with

the North, and to tolerance of the Republican party and of himself — that quickly became, for the moment, one with *die Ewigkeit*. By the Booker Washington incident, the negro became as securely a reason for the South remaining solidly Democratic as at any time since the Civil War.

The historian of, say, five hundred years from now, who will look back from the standpoint of whatever is then the status of this one of America's problems; who will be so far from the occasion and so unfamiliar with the spirit of the time as to necessitate inquiry to discover what it was all about — such a historian will find in the newspapers little but the yells and the fury; will search almost in vain for any temperate statement of the reasons for the South's attitude and the understandable expediency that was involved. Almost nowhere will he find a simple statement that in portions of the South where negroes equalled or outnumbered the whites, the maintaining of separation of the races[23] was a constant and conscious concern — as it was not in the North where the number of negroes in proportion to the whites presented no serious problem; and that, worst of all, ignorant negroes in the South, who had always accepted social separation as a matter of course, might now, because a negro had dined with a President of the United States, aspire to social equality as a matter of right.

[23] Roosevelt's dinner to Booker Washington aroused resentment not only in the South but everywhere in the world where the white race is in contact with the yellow or the black. Robert Lincoln O'Brien, editor of the Boston, Mass., *Herald,* wrote me: "When I went around the world in 1903 I found that the biggest single factor in Roosevelt's life, about which the British Colonials and others knew most, was his lunching Booker Washington. I found considerable exaggeration in the minds of those to whom it had reached. One very good Scotchman at Hong Kong said: 'I hear that your President believes in breaking down all the barriers between the races.' "

Over it all "Mr. Dooley" threw the emollient of humor. He described, in one of his Sunday newspaper dissertations, the circumstances under which Roosevelt had given the invitation, bringing out, in this part of his discourse, an irony that will be utterly lost to later generations, not familiar, perhaps, with the part Roosevelt had played in the Cuban War — a part it was not his nature to minimize. Roosevelt did not make any secret, exactly, of his estimate of the charge up San Juan Hill as the most satisfying experience of his life, and would not have disagreed too violently with any one who argued that it had high rank in the contemporary history of the world:

They'd been talkin' over th' race problem an' th' future iv th' naygro an' th' Cubian war, an' findin' Booker T. was inthrested in important public subjects like th' Cubian war, th' Prisidint ast him to come up to th' White House an' ate dinner an' have a good long talk about th' Cubian war.

The colored man's manners, Mr. Dooley felt sure, had been unexceptionable:

Fr'm all I can learn, he hung his hat on th' rack an' used proper discrimination between th' knife an' th' fork, an' ast f'r nawthin' that had to be sint out f'r. An inventory iv th' spoons afther his departure showed that he had used gintlemanly resthraint.

Mr. Dooley admitted that he too had a racial prejudice:

I don't mind sayin' that I'd rather ate with a coon thin have wan wait on me. I'd sooner he'd handle his own food thin mine. F'r me, if anny thumb must be in th' gravy, lave it be white if ye please.

But Mr. Dooley realized that with himself as with the President, it was not a matter of what he would prefer. With both it was a matter of consulting self-interest, in his case, business, in the President's, politics:

I think th' Prisidint's place is a good dale like mine. . . . If Fate, as Hogan says, had condimned me to start in business on th' Levee, I'd sarve th' black man that put down th' money as quick as I wud the white. I feel I wudden't, but I know I wud. But bein' that I'm up here in this Cowcasyan neighborhood, I spurn th' dark coin. They'se very little iv it annyhow, an' if anny iv me proud customers was f'r to see an unshackled slave lanin' agin this bar, it'd go hard with him an' with me. If it wint th' rounds that Dooley was handin' out rayfrishment to th' colored popylation, I might as well change in me license. So be th' President. They'se nawthin' wrong in him havin' me frind Booker T. up to dinner. If me an' th' Prisidint was in a private station, d'ye mind, we cud f'rget th' color iv th' good man. But I — an' th' Prisidint — is public sarvants, an' manny iv our customers have onrais'nable prejoodices. . . . 'Tis not me that speaks, Hinnissy, 'tis the job.

Into his discourse Mr. Dooley brought just that shade of the deeper touch that raised him above the rank of humorist and made him a philosopher and a seer:

At the conclusion iv th' festivities Booker T. wint away, lavin' his illusthrees frind standin' on th' top iv San Joon Hill. Th' ghost iv th' other Wash'ton didn't appear to break a soop tureen over his head. P'raps where George is he has to assocyate with many mimbers of th' Booker branch on terms iv akequality. I don't suppose they have partitions up in th' other wurruld like th' kind they have in th' cars down South. They can't be anny Jim Crow Hivin. I wondher how they keep up race supreemacy? Maybe they get on without it.

About the political consequences, as to the prospect that the incident was "goin' to be th' roonation iv Prisidint Tiddy's chances in th' South," Mr. Dooley thought:

Thousan's iv men who wudden't have voted f'r him undher anny circumstances has declared that undher no circumstances wud they vote f'r him now. He's lost near ivry State in th' South. Th' gran' ol' commonwealth iv Texas has deserted th' banner iv th' Republican party, an' Mississippi will cast her unanimous counted vote again him. Unless he can get support fr'm Matsachoosetts or some other State where th' people don't care anything about th' naygur excipt to dislike him, he'll be beat sure. . . . Mane-time we hear that th' white man in Alabama that voted f'r Rosenfelt las' year has come out again him. Th' tide has turned.

Roosevelt himself made no public utterance. In private conversation he showed no anger, except toward the more violent part of the Southern press. To Senator Lodge he wrote: "[It] was to me so much a matter of course that I regarded its sole importance as consisting in the view it gave one of the continued existence of that combination of Bourbon intellect and intolerant truculence of spirit, through much of the South, which brought on the Civil War. If these creatures had any sense they would understand that they can't bluff me. They can't even make me abandon my policy of appointing decent men to office in their own localities."[24]

For those who rallied him about the wreck of his hopes to reconcile the South to the Republican party, and those who said "I told you so," he had only the "sheepish grin" which his sister Mrs. Douglas Robinson mentions, his frequent expression in moments of discomfiture.

For once he declined a challenge, shrugged his shoulders under a shower of epithets, chose not to match violence with violence. What had happened caused no diminution in his zeal to conciliate the South; and he knew that to reply to his detractors, however unjust their attacks, would only jeopardize his permanent purpose.

The policy of restraint which Roosevelt imposed upon himself under provoking circumstances was supplemented by careful adherence throughout his entire Presidency to his attitude of warm friendliness toward the South. In literal fulfilment of his programme he appointed to important posts several Southern Demo-

[24] October 28, 1901. "Selections from the Correspondence of Theodore Roosevelt and Henry Cabot Lodge."

crats, among them Confederate officers beloved by the South, or sons or other relatives of them. To other offices, chiefly postmasterships, he appointed carefully picked colored men; and had the satisfaction of seeing these appointments, in most instances, regarded with ap-

From a photograph © Underwood & Underwood.
Roosevelt addressing an audience of colored school children, 1902.

proval by the whites of the communities where they were made; on the occasions when the appointment of a colored office-holder was criticised or resisted, Roosevelt stood firm. Gradually the South came to understand that Roosevelt was following a definite policy, a policy that was revolutionary in its contrast to what had been the practice of previous Republican administrations in the South — the bartering of patronage in return for support by Southern delegates in Republican national Presidential nominating conventions.

As part of his determination to have the South understand him, Roosevelt made more journeys into that section than any other President before or since. On his earlier trips crowds gathered, drawn by curiosity; later, under the spell of Roosevelt's personality, they came to be able to cheer, spontaneously, and with the generous heartiness that was the South's characteristic. They forgot what Republicanism meant to them, they forgot Booker Washington, they forgot the Civil War. On Southern trips that Roosevelt made in 1905, hours before his train was due to arrive people assembled by hundreds and thousands, packing the streets about the railroad-stations in the cities and congesting the roads leading to country tank-stops. On his arrival, even before they caught sight of him, they would break into the noisy tribute that humanity in the mass always renders to a great leader. The roar of greeting they gave him was not a semi-tone less enthusiastic and affectionate than the receptions he got in the West and the North. He was their President, their "Teddy." At San Antonio, where he went in April, 1905, to attend a Rough Riders' reunion, the adjective repeated over and over by the newspapers describing his welcome was "riotous." "I never saw such a reception," a Southerner[25] writes me, "as Roosevelt got in Richmond in October, 1905."

The editor[26] who in October, 1901, had proclaimed that "no future act of his can remove the self-imprinted stigma," was proved wrong by the editor[27] who in Jan-

[25] Stewart Bryan, publisher of the *News Leader* of Richmond.
[26] Of the Memphis *Commercial Appeal*.
[27] Of the New Orleans *Times-Democrat*.

uary, 1905, wrote: "The differences between the President and the South have been adjusted most satisfactorily. Mr. Roosevelt has spoken in a friendly spirit, and has shown that he is not hostile to the South. He did not confine himself merely to words. . . . It is not to be wondered at that the South should entertain a new opinion of Roosevelt."

Most concrete of all, when in 1904 Roosevelt was a candidate for a new term he received more votes in the South than any previous Republican candidate; by carrying Missouri he made a sensational breach in the Democratic solid South.[28]

[28] A baffling detail of the writing of this chapter was the inability of the author to determine with complete certainty whether the meal destined to become famous was a dinner served in the evening, or a midday luncheon. The item in the Wasnington *Post,* which is the nearest we have to a contemporary record, reads "dined last evening." That could have been a reporter's inference; but "dined" is supported not only by the best evidence, but by a majority of all the evidence. Practically all of the contemporary newspaper clippings in Roosevelt's scrap-books refer to the meal as a "dinner." Nevertheless, friends of Roosevelt and authors who wrote contemporary books about him say "luncheon" almost as frequently as "dinner." Two authors who purport to quote Roosevelt's own words, Harry Thurston Peck in "Twenty Years of the Republic," and Arthur Wallace Dunn in "From Harrison to Harding," both represent Roosevelt as saying it was luncheon. On the other hand, Charles G. Washburn (classmate of Roosevelt, Harvard, 1880), author of "Theodore Roosevelt, the Logic of His Career," quotes Roosevelt as saying it was dinner. A colored servant at the White House, James E. Amos, who helped serve the meal and later wrote a book about "Roosevelt, Hero to His Valet," says it was luncheon. William Roscoe Thayer, in "Theodore Roosevelt," and ex-Senator from Ohio Joseph Benson Foraker, in "Notes of a Busy Life," say it was a luncheon; while William Draper Lewis, in "The Life of Theodore Roosevelt" and Francis E. Leupp, in "Roosevelt the Man," say it was dinner.

Equally opposed are the accounts with respect to a more significant aspect of the episode — whether Roosevelt, some time in advance, deliberately sent Washington an invitation to a meal at the White House; or whether, on an occasion when Washington had called at the White House, Roosevelt impulsively said, in effect, "Stay to dinner (or lunch)." Here, again, authors who purport to quote Roosevelt represent him as giving varying versions. William Roscoe Thayer, in "Theodore Roosevelt," says: "It happened that on the day appointed for a meeting, Washington reached the White House just before luncheon time and that as they had not finished their conference, Roosevelt asked him to stay for luncheon. Washington hesitated politely. Roosevelt insisted."

Arthur Wallace Dunn, in "From Harrison to Harding," says that Roosevelt told him: "I'll tell you how it happened. The man was here talking with me when luncheon was announced, and I told him to come in and have lunch with me while we continued our talk. That was all there was to it." Harry Thurston

III

"The Rebukes He Administers"

In 1903, a newly appointed Washington correspondent of the Chicago *Evening Post* was taken by a friend
to the White House and introduced to the President.
Roosevelt heard his name, Edward B. Clark, repeated
it, and asked Clark if he was the author of a monograph
on a Southeastern bird "with a name" — Roosevelt had
forgotten it — "as long as the moral law." Clark replied that ten years before he had published an article

Peck, in "Twenty Years of the Republic," relates a version said to have been
told by Roosevelt to a friend: "When luncheon-time came around, my first
thought was to invite him to stay and lunch with me. Immediately it flashed
across my mind that this would make no end of trouble. But I asked myself:
'Are you afraid to do it?' and I answered, 'No!' And so I invited him to come
in to luncheon."

All the foregoing versions picture the invitation to a meal as being an unpre-
meditated incident of a call; and two of the versions quote Roosevelt as saying
it was that. Yet a peculiarly convincing authority represents the invitation to
a dinner as having been sent to Washington in advance; Joseph Bucklin Bishop,
the more or less official biographer of Roosevelt ("Theodore Roosevelt and His
Time"), says: "I had been spending a day and a night with him [Roosevelt] in
the White House, and on the morning of the 18th he asked me if I could not stay
over another night, saying that Booker Washington was coming to dinner, and
he would like to have me meet him."

Booker Washington himself, in "My Larger Education," says that the invitation came to him while stopping at the home of a friend in the District of Columbia, but does not say whether it was to take a meal, or merely to call.

There were, needless to say, several apocryphal versions: A Republican candidate for Congress in one of the few Southern districts where it was worth while
for a Republican to run, managed to overcome the effect of the Booker Washington incident by giving an improvised — and original — account of the details
in his campaign speeches. He would tell his mountaineer audiences: "Roosevelt
said to Booker, 'You must be hungry by this time. Go around to the back door
and tell Mandy to give you something to eat. You do not have to go away from
here to get something to eat. Mandy will give you the best in the house. Just
go around to the side door there, and tell her I told you to.'"

There is one version that makes no contribution to the effort to achieve historical accuracy about the Booker Washington incident, but which, for that very
reason largely, has appealing interest. This account, with immaterial variations, was still current in the South in the year [1928] in which this chapter is written: The late Rufus N. Rhodes, publisher of the Birmingham,
Ala., *News,* had a relation of mutual respect and friendship with Booker T.
Washington. Rhodes, soon after the incident, asked Washington to tell him

about the "prothonotary warbler." "That's the one," said Roosevelt, delighted, "come on into my office and let's get outdoors for a while." For three-quarters of an hour the two enjoyed a talk that was, to two office-confined prisoners, a partial substitute for a trip to the woods.

During this and many other conversations the two had in the course of three years following, Roosevelt spoke of a concern he felt about a school of so-called "nature" writers who at the time were in high vogue. These were the contemporaries, or followers, or imitators[29] of an author-artist of sound merit, Ernest Thompson Seton, who

---

exactly what had occurred. Washington (according to this version) said he had called on Roosevelt and had happened to remain over the luncheon hour. It was the President's custom to have luncheon served to him in his office, and always a separate tray was brought for any one who was there. This was done on the present occasion.

That version, I am quite certain, is incorrect, for it was not Roosevelt's custom to have his luncheon served in this way; he invariably (I never saw or heard of an exception) walked the few yards to his own dining-room. Yet I am almost equally confident that Washington may have told this version; it would have been like the man Washington was, first gentleman of his race, to tell a version, which, even though it involved the invention of some material details, would do the least harm to the white man, the President who was his friend.

The variations in the versions of the Booker Washington incident — variations that include conflict between accounts given at different times by Roosevelt himself, as well as among accounts given by his intimate friends and the several painstaking biographers of him — is dwelt upon here partly for purposes collateral to the main theme of the narrative. They illustrate how events which monopolize the attention of the country for the proverbial nine days quickly pass into the hazy ambient of legend. More important, they suggest the difficulty of being accurate about history — indeed, they provoke disturbing doubt about just how much of error there may be in all history. True, the Booker Washington incident was a comparatively trivial detail; but what is characteristic about the detail may be characteristic about the picture. The present history is written while many of the actors and witnesses of the events described are still alive. That method has at once advantages and difficulties, not all the tally of which is pertinent here. That this method includes access to a larger quantity of evidence than in the case of history written generations after the event, would seem to be obvious. Yet it is impossible to be certain, either from the memories of living witnesses (all confident, though conflicting), or from available records, whether a certain famous meal was a lunch or a dinner, and what were the circumstances leading up to it.

[29] Doctor Long complains that this passage contains an implication that he was "an imitator of Thompson-Seton" and adds, "I was fairly well-known as a naturalist before Seton was ever heard of."

had started the school with his charming "Wild Animals I Have Known,"[30] and poignant "Trail of the Sand Hill Stag,"[31] both widely read and appreciated.

Seton had been official naturalist to the government of Manitoba, had written and illustrated a scientific work, "Art Anatomy of Animals," and had made the animal illustrations for the Century Dictionary. As artist, naturalist, and man, Seton was entirely admirable and praiseworthy. Roosevelt thought well of Seton, sensed the innate honesty of his mind, and found enjoyment in his books. However, Roosevelt's regard for all science was as unsmilingly concerned with the literal as that of a German professor, and he could not but feel a sense of disapproval of Seton's fictionizing in a branch of natural science in which Roosevelt himself, the most versatile American of his day, occupied the rôle of high priest, being a recognized authority on several species of American mammals and birds.

But if Roosevelt was gentle in his allusion to Seton he was savage toward others of the nature fictionists. These writers, he told Clark, not only lacked the great fund of knowledge which Seton possessed as a result of years of careful observation and study, but in addition they were much less restrained than Seton in their imputations of qualities of mind to animals and birds. The chief characteristic of the writings of the new school was their supplementing of attainable (and in Seton's case attained) accuracy of observation about the appearance and ways of wild things, with narration and description, necessarily speculative and assumptive, based on their presumed emotions and powers of reason. What they did in some cases was to take the framework of the conventional short story, with its plot and climax, hu-

[30] 1898.

[31] 1899. Among other books by Seton were "The Biography of a Grizzly" (1900) and "Lives of the Hunted" (1901).

mor or tragedy, and weave about it romances in which birds and animals played the rôles of villain and hero.

Some of the writers who arose in the wake of Seton's vogue went far beyond him in their imputation of emotions, sentiments, altruisms, and intellectual processes to the animals they wrote about. Though they described themselves as "realists" and in their books emphasized the attribute of authenticity, their choice of nature as the subject of their writings came perhaps less out of long and intimate experience with the wild than out of infection from the existing vogue. Their writings shared the current popularity of the type; indeed, some of the books containing the less of responsible scholarship sold in larger quantities than the more austerely accurate ones; certain of the more imaginative ones were put out at low prices for use in schools. As a result, children were getting notions about natural history more sentimental than exact, were indeed being subjected to a detail of education that might lessen their regard for exactness in all respects — and Roosevelt was stirred up about it. He would, he told Clark, "get after those fellows," but for the fact that he was President — a consideration not often permitted by Roosevelt to restrain him when he felt like saying something that he regarded as needing to be said.

In further talks over a period of three years, Roosevelt poured out to Clark his increasing annoyance. One night in the early part of 1907, Clark repeated his familiar urge, "Why don't you get after them?" and Roosevelt reached the detonating point of his irritation, saying "I think I will." That was all Clark needed; that night he wrote out from memory, in the form of a statement dictated to him by Roosevelt, his recollections of what Roosevelt had been saying.

Roosevelt read the manuscript, found it satisfactory,

but not an adequately complete expression of his indignation, and, taking some White House stationery, added about a third more with his own hand. Clark took the manuscript to *Everybody's Magazine*, which gave it to the country in its June, 1907, number, under the title, "Roosevelt on the Nature-Fakirs."[32]

Jack London.

Roosevelt began with a safeguarding distinction. "If the stories of these writers were written in the spirit that inspired Kipling's 'Jungle Book,'" he said, "we should know that we were getting the very essence of fable, and we should be content. . . . If those stories were written as fables, published as fables, and put in children's hands as fables, all would be well and good. But when such fables are written by a make-believe 'realist,' the matter assumes an entirely different complexion. There is no more reason why children should be taught a false natural history than a false physical geography. Giving these books to children for the purpose of teaching them the facts of natural history — why, it's an outrage."

Roosevelt indicted Jack London, whose story (in "White Fang") of a bulldog putting up a prolonged fight against a great northern wolf was, Roosevelt said,

[32] Altered, in subsequent popular use of the phrase, to "Nature-Fakers." While the word was universally attributed to Roosevelt, and while it was Roosevelt who gave currency to the idea, it was Clark who coined the word, in the "Fakir" form.

"the very sublimity of absurdity — in such a fight the chance for the dog would be only one in a thousand; that kind of realism is a closet product." He indicted Charles G. D. Roberts, whose story "On the Night Trail" about a lynx taking the aggressive against eight wolves was "utterly ridiculous — the lynx in that story would stand no more chance than a house-cat in a fight with eight bull-terriers." He indicted, very mildly, Ernest Thompson Seton, who "has made interesting observations of fact, and much of his fiction has a real value; but he should make it clear that it is fiction, and not fact."[33]

But "the worst of these nature-writing offenders," Roosevelt said, "is William J. Long." Long was the nature-writer whose books were published largely for school-children, and who, therefore, had excited Roosevelt's particular indignation. In the preface to his "Wayeeses the White Wolf," Long had written — and Roosevelt now quoted — a certificate of authenticity: "Every incident in this wolf's life, from his grass-hopper hunting to . . . the meeting of wolf and children on the storm-swept barrens, is minutely true to fact, and is based squarely on my own observation and that of my Indians."[34] Toward Long, Roosevelt was savage.

Long was a clergyman of the Congregational Church, a graduate of Harvard and of Andover Theological Seminary, who wrote books about nature, mainly for use in schools, such as "Ways of Woodfolk,"[35] "Beasts of the

[33] The mention of Seton was less an indictment than an off-hand allusion. Roosevelt had regard for Seton. Seton was careful in his prefaces and otherwise to make the reader understand what part of his books was fiction. Seton's standing as a naturalist was assured. He received in 1927 the John Burroughs medal for the most valuable contribution to natural history, and in 1928 the Elliot medal awarded by the National Academy of Sciences.

[34] In another book, Long had said, "Every smallest incident is as true as careful and accurate observation can make it."

[35] 1899.

Field,"[36] "Fowls of the Air,"[37] "Secrets of the Woods,"[38] and, many years later, "How Animals Talk."[39]

Long's "true to fact" narrative, Roosevelt charged, "is filled with the wildest improbabilities and not a few mathematical impossibilities." Long, in one of his stories, had represented a wolf as killing a bull caribou with "a quick snap under the stag's chest just behind the fore-legs where the heart lay." Roosevelt, with as much earnestness as if he were conducting a correspondence with a foreign nation on a *casus belli*, undertook to disprove this alleged feat. He disproved it by anatomy: Doctor Long's wolf would have been obliged "either to turn a somerset — or pretty near it — or else get his head upside down under the fore-legs of the [caribou], a sufficiently difficult performance." He disproved it by the laws of mechanics: "The wolf's jaws would not gape right." He disproved it by natural history: "Nothing except a shark or an alligator will attempt to kill by a bite behind the shoulders." He disproved it by his own experience: "I have seen scores of animals that have been killed by wolves; the killing or crippling bites were always in the throat, flank or ham." He disproved it by expert testimony: "Mr. George Shiras, who has seen not scores but hundreds of such carcasses, tells me that the death wounds or disabling wounds were invariably in the throat or the flank except when the animal was hamstrung." Finally, Roosevelt disproved it by mathematics: "Let Mr. Long measure the length of a wolf's fang, and then measure what the length would have to be to do the thing he describes. . . . No wolf's teeth are long enough; it would need the tusks of a walrus." The feat was "impossible of performance by any land carnivore since the death of the last sabre-tooth tiger." Roosevelt suggested that Doctor Long, as a "parallel perform-

[36] 1901.   [37] 1901.   [38] 1901.   [39] 1919.

ance," should "hang a grape-fruit in the middle of a keg of flour and then see whether a big dog could bite through the keg into the grape-fruit."

"It is grotesque," said Roosevelt, "to claim literal truthfulness for such a tissue of absurdities. . . . He

Courtesy of the New York "World."

Rev. Doctor Wm. J. Long.

[Long] must produce eye-witness and affidavits. I simply don't believe the thing occurred. I don't believe for a minute that some of these men who are putting the word 'truth' prominently in their prefaces know the heart of the wild things."

Long, in his quiet New England home, peacefully hatching more of his brain-children, was as startled as the gentlest of his own forest-creatures; he must have felt like a dove[40] shot at by an elephant gun. Some of his immediate protests were a little breathless, like the scared bleatings of a panic-stricken doe. Flutteringly he said that "a man named Roosevelt has gone out of his way to make a violent attack upon me"; it was "not worth a gentleman's consideration"; it was "personal and venomous in spirit, while its literary style was the poorest of the poor." In one sentence that conveyed a particularly convincing good faith, Long said he had "no desire for a controversy" with a President of the United States upon the war-path.

As the phrase "nature-faker" went blazing through newspaper head-line and cartoon, as reporters hounded Long in his peaceful Connecticut home, he set about systematically defending himself. Out of Stamford came a newspaper despatch[41] saying that "Dr. William J. Long has received an affidavit with which he expects to prove his story of the white wolf killing a caribou by a bite through the chest." "The affidavit" — so the despatch said, with a connotation of presumably special convincingness, "is that of a full-blooded Sioux Indian who is studying theology."[42]

In Long's further defense of himself, and in the carefully prepared "open letter" he wrote to Roosevelt, he

[40] The description of Doctor Long's reaction to Roosevelt's attack aims only to picture the impression the events made as they emerged before the public eye, as recalled by the author of this history and as they now read in the newspaper files. It is not intended to imply that Doctor Long personally had qualities either dove-like or doe-like; on the contrary, his reply to Roosevelt, as described elsewhere in this chapter, shows he was a first-class fighting man. Unconsciously, perhaps, one reads into Doctor Long's personality the qualities of gentleness he attributes to some of the wild creatures in his book. In 1930, after reading a proof of this chapter, Doctor Long wrote the author: "I have faced death a few times and danger many times, and so far as I can remember I have never once been fluttered or scared by any man or beast."

[41] New York *Tribune*, June 2, 1907.

[42] Doctor Long writes: "Since in Roosevelt's article he had demanded 'eye-witnesses and affidavits,' I sent him and later published, more than twenty affidavits, with the addresses of men who had witnessed what he denounced as impossible. To this he [Roosevelt] made no acknowledgment whatever."

showed that his ability as a writer was not limited to the sentimental recording of nature stories — that he could, in defense of his literary children, be as belligerent as one of his own wolves, and more effectively deadly because more coldly deliberate; that he could, indeed,

Roosevelt on a bear hunt in Colorado in 1905 with the dog "Skip," who liked riding on horseback.

achieve literary and controversial dignity of a high order.

"Who is he [Roosevelt] to write, 'I don't believe that some of these nature-writers know the heart of the wild things'? As to that, I find after carefully reading two of his [Roosevelt's] big books, that every time Mr. Roosevelt gets near the heart of a wild thing he invariably puts a bullet through it."

From a careful survey of Roosevelt's books about his own hunting exploits, Long counted "a full thousand hearts which he has known thus intimately." Long assembled and quoted several of the more gory of Roosevelt's accounts of his exultation upon shooting a wild animal. The massing of the incidents had an effect of slaughter, arousing almost an emotion of abhorrence, as Long meant it should. "There is," said Long, "a keener pleasure than to walk up to a noble animal dead in the cool shade of the evergreen, his glad life gone, his symmetry distorted in the death-struggle, his beautiful brown coat all clotted and blood-stained, and his soft eyes glazing rapidly as if to hide the reproach that is in them. There is a greater pleasure and wisdom than all this; but you will never know what they are. The bloody endings over which you gloat bring little 'self-satisfaction' to a thoughtful man who has seen the last look in the eyes of a stricken deer, and who remembers that even this small life has its mystery, like our own. You are not a sportsman, though you have slain your thousands; you are not a naturalist, though you have measured hides and horns; you do not and you can not understand 'the hearts of the wild things,' though you have made a grievous quantity of them bleed."

Long's counter-attack was, to much of the public, convincing. As the newspaper discussion ran through the summer, it was a question whether Roosevelt had made Long seem as ridiculous in the rôle of nature-faker as Long had made Roosevelt seem insensitive in the rôle of animal-killer; whether, in the public eye, Long was more odious for sentimentalizing animals than Roosevelt for shooting them. Long, in short, raised an issue which put a weapon into the hands of persons unsympathetic to Roosevelt on various grounds. A few years later, *Life*, on an occasion when Roosevelt received from a French society an award for merit as a naturalist, said: "Scientific societies do not, as a rule, bestow medals upon just that kind of naturalist; the medal should have gone to Mr. Armour[43] of Chicago—his record as an animal-killer puts Mr. Roosevelt in the children's class." Another habitual critic of Roosevelt, the New York *Sun*, took pleasure in reprinting some verse from the British Humanitarian League:

> Hail, blustering statesman, butcher of big game,
> Less President than Prince in pride of will,
> Whose pastime is the princely sport, to kill,
> Whose murderous feats unnumbered fools acclaim!
> On all things big thy braggart thoughts are bent —
> To strip the lordliest lion of his skin,
> The bulkiest trophies of the chase to win —
> Big bag, big story, big advertisement!...

Roosevelt's naturalist friends, upon the initiative of Edward W. Nelson of the United States Biological Survey, got up a symposium[44] in support of Roosevelt and in indorsement of his attack on the nature-fakers. Long having said that Roosevelt was no naturalist, the naturalists replied that he was.[45] And they added, pungently, that the Reverend Doctor Long was not, decidedly.

Edward W. Nelson, introducing a new phrase into the controversy, called Long and those like him "animal novelists." Frederic A. Lucas, curator-in-chief of the Museums of Brooklyn Institute, substituted for "nature-fakers" the less harsh "nature-humanizers." John Burroughs (in a newspaper interview) introduced yet another phrase, "yellow journalism of the woods," and said it was "high time these Munchausen yarns about our

---

[43] The reference is to the head of a great packing plant at Chicago, which daily slaughtered thousands of cattle.

[44] Published in *Everybody's Magazine* for September, 1907.

[45] C. Hart Merriam, chief of the United States Biological Survey, wrote: "Theodore Roosevelt is the world's authority on the big game mammals of America. His writings are fuller and his observations more complete and accurate than those of any other man."

wild animals were exposed by an authoritative source."
William T. Hornaday, director of the New York Zoological Park, said that Doctor Long "has left 'Sinbad
the Sailor' and Baron Munchausen far behind him."
Barton W. Evermann, head scientist in the United States

From "The North American" (Philadelphia.)
Leading the simple life in Colorado. A lively cartoon inspired by Roosevelt's
hunting trip to Colorado in 1905.

Bureau of Fisheries, said that "the salmon Dr. Long
saw [in the act of carefully selecting a rock from which
to leap over a waterfall] must indeed have been an exceptional and remarkable salmon; we are glad Dr. Long
saw it for if we had seen it we should not have believed
it." (Roosevelt said "this feat was about as probable as
that the fish should use a step-ladder.") George Shiras,
3d, outstanding photographer of wild animals in their
natural background, thought that the reverend author
of "true" nature stories, "having abandoned his degree
of D.D.[46] should have conferred upon him the new one
of P.P. —Patron Prevaricator — of the Ancient Or-

[46] Long was not a "D.D."; his doctorate was in philosophy, "Ph.D."

der of Ananias." The productions of all the nature-fakers, Shiras said, were "frenzied fiction, as rare as it is raw."

From the books and magazine writings of all the accused "fakers," during the controversy, their more incredible stories were picked out for ridicule: a mother eagle that caught her nestling on her back by flying under it when it tumbled out of the nest; a porcupine who rolled among apples and speared them, and then went home and shook them off in his den; a woodcock who made a mud cast for its broken leg ("it seems a pity," said Roosevelt, "not to have added that it made itself a crutch to use while the splint was on"); a bullfrog jumping from the water and catching a barn-swallow by the wing; a rabbit that stole the overalls of an Indian guide from under his head while he slept, and nibbled them for the taste of the salt; a caribou cemetery in Northern Labrador where the animals went to die; a pet toad with a taste for music, individual, and elevated — "quiet hymns he seemed to like, for he always kept as still as a worshipper, but rag-time he detested."

A few such stories really fitted the word that Roosevelt applied to them; they were "grotesque." Yet readers and editorial critics who were stirred by the controversy to read Long's books sensed the gentleness of his temperament, his real love for wild life, his wish to cause children to love it as he did; and they felt that Roosevelt's attack had been unnecessarily shrill. They concluded that the stories and the authors of them, — as well as the music-loving toad, the surgical woodcock, the acrobatic salmon, the rabbit with an appetite for salty overalls — were game rather small for a President of the United States who had slain bears in their dens and beaten giants in politics.

After the battle had raged through three months of newspaper head-line, cartoon, editorial, and quip, Roosevelt returned[47] to it, in a temper that suggested consciousness of having stirred up a hornet's nest more capable of counter-attack than he had anticipated. In his original onslaught he had been an irritated naturalist reading a pulpit lecture from the elevation of the White House; now he was a combatant aware that the battle was going not too well for him and angrily determined to take himself out of the mêlée with a devastating broadside. He condemned, wholesale, not only the nature-fakers, but all who could doubt his assertions about them, or fail to share his indignation. "Real outdoor naturalists," he said, "real observers of nature" feel a "half-indignant, half-amused contempt, both for the men who invented preposterous fiction about wild animals and for the credulous stay-at-homes who accepted such fiction as fact." The nature-fakers "show neither knowledge of nature nor love of truth"; they are "an object of derision to every scientist worthy of the name, to every real lover of the wilderness, to every faunal naturalist, to every true hunter or nature-lover." Drawing upon his armory of equivalents for the "short and ugly word," Roosevelt used for this occasion "deliberate invention," "deliberate perversion of fact," "deliberate . . . reckless untruth." In high-pitched phrases he repeated that Doctor Long[48] was "the most reckless and least respon-

---

[47] In *Everybody's Magazine,* September, 1907.

[48] The author of this history, in accordance with his custom, sent proofs of this chapter to persons still living who were participants in the events, among others to Doctor Long. Some passages from Doctor Long's comments are printed as foot-notes elsewhere; his summing up of exceptions taken by him reads:

"By quoting other men, who either never read my books or else deliberately misrepresented them, you represent me as seeing, for example, a salmon select the rock from which he will jump over a fall, or seeing a porcupine spear apples, or seeing something else that no sober man ever saw. Thus you give new legs to an old lie; as you probably know, as well as I know, that a lie once started in print can never be overtaken. . . . I have no doubt that you intend to be fair. You

sible" of the offenders. Examining Long's books again, for further faults upon which to build his own case, Roosevelt found that one of Doctor Long's "story-book wolves" — the quotation is from Roosevelt — "when starving, catches a red squirrel which he takes round as a present to propitiate a bigger wolf." This, Roosevelt disproved by formal testimony from a Newfoundland guide that "there are no squirrels of any kind here." As to the unselfishness attributed to this wolf, and other qualities attributed by other writers to other wolves — "Uncle Remus wolves," Roosevelt called them — he said: "Certain of their wolves appear as gifted with all the philosophy, the self-restraint, and the keen intelligence of, say, Marcus Aurelius, together with the lofty philanthropy of a modern altruist." Roosevelt ended his rebuttal with a declaration that had, under the circumstances, a flavor not reaching the dignity he wished to assert: "No man who has really studied nature in the spirit of seeking the truth, whether he be big or little, can have any controversy with these writers; it would be as absurd as to expect some genuine student of anthropology or archæology to enter into controversy with the clumsy fabricators of the Cardiff giant."

Roosevelt, though his indignation was not abated, entertained for the future a comprehensive willingness to let sleeping nature-fakers lie. When, a year later, Jack

---

fail of your intention because you have written of natural history with a very limited knowledge of the subject, and have written of a man, meaning myself, of whom you plainly know nothing. . . ."

To all of which, the sadly-resigned reply of the brow-beaten author of this history is that if Roosevelt were still living he would probably take as many exceptions to this narration, and as bellicose ones, as Doctor Long has. This history includes accounts of several subjects which in the day of their life, were controversial; the present attempt to write of them without bias after the passage of more than a score of years, has caused many ash-covered embers to glow again, some of which have descended upon the author's unhappy head. Few of these questions have excited such belligerent repercussions as this attempt to tell the nature-faker episode.

London defended himself in an article which *Collier's* described in its caption as "locating the President in the Ananias Club," Roosevelt wrote a five-page personal letter of protest, to one of the editors, emphasizing that he wrote "with the distinct understanding that . . . I have not the slightest intention of entering into a controversy with Jack London, but with *Collier's*, and that of a purely private, not public nature. I would as soon think of discussing seriously with him [Jack London] any social or political reform. But it does seem to me that *Collier's* should be rather careful about admitting such an article into its columns and of giving it such a head-line."[49]

As for Doctor Long, he continued to write books — in 1909, "History of English Literature," and in 1913, "American Literature."[50]

IV

"His Assumptions, Presumptions, Omnisciencies"

"To my mind," wrote an attractively old-world gentleman and scholar, Charles J. Bonaparte, who served Roosevelt as Attorney-General and later described some of his experiences in a magazine article:[51] "His [Roosevelt's] hold on popular favor was strikingly illustrated by the results of his advocacy of 'simplified spelling.' The slightly ludicrous aspect of this official excursion into the fields of lexicography might and probably would have been politically fatal to any ordinary public man; in Mr. Roosevelt's case," wrote Mr. Bonaparte, "the average citizen laughed good-humoredly . . . and con-

---

[49] Letter from Theodore Roosevelt to Mark Sullivan, September 9, 1908.

[50] Doctor Long, after Roosevelt's death, and twelve years after the nature-faker controversy, published more nature books, "How Animals Talk," 1919; "Wood Folk Comedies," 1920; and "Mother Nature," 1923.

[51] *The Century*, March, 1910.

tinued to think of his President with as much respect and as much affection as ever."

A project for simplifying the English language had been conceived during the 1870's at meetings of the American Philological Association, and had been formally launched in 1876 at a gathering which, more consistent than the philologists, called itself a "Convention for Amendment[52] of English Orthografy" — subsequently, and more tersely, as well as more orthodoxly, the Spelling Reform Association; and finally, with increasing c o u r a g e, among other variations, "Simplified Spelling Leag." The movement had been fathered and its progress was furthered by the Professor of the English Language and Comparative

Nicholas Murray Butler, President of Columbia University.

Philology at LaFayette College, Francis A. March,[53] LL.D., L.H.D., and by other learned gentlemen similarly endowed with capital letters after their names, including the Professor of English in Yale University, Thomas R. Lounsbury, LL.D., L.H.D., and the Professor of Dramatic Literature in Columbia University, Brander Matthews, LL.D., Litt.D., and the president of Cornell University, Andrew D. White, LL.D., L.H.D., as well as the president of Leland Stanford University, David Starr

[52] Along with the movement for simplified spelling went a number of movements and suggestions for a new language, the most formidable of which aimed to bring about the adoption of "Esperanto" or "Volapük."

[53] His brother, Peyton Conway March, was a General, and Chief of Staff, in the United States Army during the Great War.

Jordan, LL.D., Ph.D., and the president of Columbia University, Nicholas Murray Butler, whose path across the educational firmament came to be marked by a longer comet's tail of capital letters than that of any other American.[54]

These venerable crusaders against unsounded vowels and other surreptitious recalcitrancies or brazen inconformancies of English orthography assembled arguments and statistics showing the deplorable prevalence of variations in the spelling of English words, and therefore the need, as these laudably intentioned pundits considered, for standardized and simplified forms. There was cited, in a symposium on "Is Simplified Spelling Feasible?" in *The American Anthropologist*,[55] the findings of an official of the United States Pension Office, a person having a curious bent for statistics in an esoteric area of human interest, who had tabulated, in the applications of old soldiers for pensions, 1,690 variations in the spelling of one familiar word, diarrhœa. The statistician did not record, nor did the erudite philologists claim, that any of the spellings had failed to be understood, or that any pension had been refused on the ground of etymological debility; or that there was any demonstrable relation between a soldier's valor in battle or worthiness for a pension, and his capacity to spell the name of an affliction that sometimes besets even the most brave. Intent merely upon the orthographic aspect of the computation, Ainsworth R. Spofford, Librarian of Congress, a scholar who opposed spelling reform, derisively demanded to know: "Is there any phonetic system which could bring about a uniform spelling of that word?"

---

[54] He came to have a peer: Herbert Hoover, who started later than Doctor Butler, had acquired, by the time he became thirty-first President of the United States, 1929, the same number of degrees, twenty-six. Fourteen of Doctor Butler's degrees and nine of Mr. Hoover's were from European Universities.

[55] For March, 1893.

In another area of human affairs, the crusading savants showed that out of 1,972 failures to pass a British Civil Service examination, 1,866 were due to poor spelling, this deplorable result being chargeable, if seen from their humane standpoint, not to the intellectual imperfections of the spellers but to the unnecessary diffi-

Kemble in "Collier's Weekly."

A few shots at the King's English. A "simplified spelling" cartoon.

culty of the task. As an instance, the word "could," they said, "is a markt exampl of unpardonabl spelling; the 'l' is a sheer blunder, the 'ou' has a wrong sound."[56] Much better, they said, reform the recalcitrant word;

[56] Francis A. March, "History of Spelling Reform," 1893.

adopt a simplified spelling which, they suggested, might be either "cud" or "cood" or "kud" or "kood." There were, they pointed out as glaring proof of the need of simplification, at least twenty different ways of spelling the sound of "sh" — as in *sh*ip, *s*ure, *ps*haw, oce*a*n, par*ti*al, man*si*on, and so on. The letter "a," they said, has 8 uses, "e" has 8, "i" has 7, "o" has 12, "u" has 9 and "y" 3; "so that the singl vowels hav, collectively, 47 uses, giving an average of $7\frac{5}{6}$ apiece."[57] Similarly, they continued, "twenty-one consonants have 70 uses, averaging $3\frac{1}{3}$ apiece." From which it followed "that the word 'scissors' may be speld 58,365,440 different ways and stil hav analogies justifying each combination,"[57] of which one of the possible spellings was "schiesourrhce." The word "foolish," one reformer said, choosing an example not having the happiest connotations for the circumstances, "containing only 5 sounds, might be speld in any one of $7 \times 25 \times 11 \times 29 = 613,975$ different ways; one way would be pphoughtluipsh";[58] since *pph* as in sapphire spells *f*, *ough* as in through spells *oo*, *tl* as in hustle spells *l*, *ui* as in build spells *i*, *psh* as in pshaw spells *sh* — therefore pphoughtluipsh spells foolish. "If that is not foolish, what is?"[58]

Get away from this foolishness, the scholars pleaded, and from all similar absurdities, by adopting simplified spelling. They would save for America, they said, putting their plea on an economic basis, "15 per cent of the present expense of tipe-setting and tipe-writing," and would effect corresponding economy in paper and ink. One of the crusaders, a publisher of books named Henry Holt, "made a painstaking calculation of the mony that would have been saved in one year [1900] in the United

[57] W. T. Harris, later U. S. Commissioner of Education, quoted by Francis A. March in "The Spelling Reform," 1893.

[58] This example is taken from "Simplified Spelling Seen as Economic Aid," by Godfrey Dewey, in the New York *Times*, January 16, 1927.

States"[59] if simplified spelling had been in use, and estimated it at $35,000,000. "All books may cost one-sixth less; the Encyclopædia Britannica would make twenty volumes instead of twenty-four, and cost twenty-four dollars less; the newspapers would all save one column in six; one-sixth would be saved in all writing, in the manuscripts of books and periodicals, the records of courts . . . the sermons of preachers, the books of merchants."[60]

To the sum of all this saving would be added an even greater boon, escape from the "appalling and incalculable waste of nervous energy"[61] on the part of teachers in teaching and pupils in learning forms of spelling which the Board deemed undesirable. Two full years — some, conservative, said a year and a half — would be saved in the education of each and every child. "On the basis of actual enrolment and estimated per capita cost, the saving of the fourth grade and one half the third grade would amount to over $220,000,000, while the saving of time devoted to spelling thru the balance of the educational career would amount to $50,000,000 more."[62]

The reformers did not, they said, propose anything "radical" or "revolutionary." They assured the world (in Simplified Spelling Board Circular No. 6, June 25, 1906) that "The Board does not propose to make . . . any change in the spelling of proper names, especially of surnames. That matter is out of its chosen province." Every man would be permitted to continue the spelling of his own name in the way that he had inherited. With naïve self-revelation of the autocrat that lurks in the

[59] "The Case for Simplified Spelling," Simplified Spelling Board, March, 1920.

[60] Commission on Amended Orthografy, report to Pennsylvania Legislature, April 8, 1889.

[61] "The Case for Simplified Spelling," Simplified Spelling Board, March, 1920.

[62] "Simplified Spelling Seen as Economic Aid," Godfrey Dewey, New York *Times,* January 16, 1927.

back of most reformers' minds, they proclaimed their moderation by saying that "geographic names often need regulation but there are [other] societies and boards which take care of this."

To some who rejected their proposals and resented their purposes, they replied with prophetic essays about "Unpopular Causes That Hav Triumft."

Argumentative heat about differences of opinion or of practice in spelling had come into the world as an unhappily contentious consequence of the first compiling of dictionaries, Webster's in America in 1806, and Doctor Johnson's in England in 1755. Previous to Noah Webster's setting up of arbitrary standards in his dictionary (and his spelling-book), and until those standards became familiar, American gentlemen had practised self-determination in spelling with no more liability to reproach than attended their exercise of individual taste or habit in the clothes they wore, the drinks they chose, the political parties they joined, or the denominational gods they followed. They could practise free will in orthography — and could spell it, if they chose, "free wil." George Washington could write "musick"[63] and "expences"[64] without encountering jeers; he could write

---

[63] Washington practised individual self-expression not only in his spelling but in his punctuation, or lack of it:

"We were agreeably surpris'd at y. sight of thirty odd Indians We had some Liquor with us of which we gave them Part it elevating there Spirits put them in y. Humour of Dauncing of whom we had a War Daunce there manner of Dauncing is as follows Viz They clear a Large Circle and make a Great Fire in y. middle they seats themselves around it y. Speaker makes a grand speech telling them in what Manner they are to Daunce after he has finished y. best Dauncer jumps up as one awaked out of a Sleep and runs and Jumps about y. Ring in a most comical Manner he is followed by y. Rest then begins there Musicians to Play ye Musick is a Pot half [full] of Water with a Deer-skin Stretched over it as tight as it can and a goard with some Shott in it to Rattle and a Piece of an horses Tail tied to it to make it look fine y. one keeps Rattling and y. other Drumming all y. while y. others is. Dauncing." — Washington's Diary, March 23, 1748.

[64] Washington's Diary, July 23, 1755.

that he "rid"[65] on horseback; he could write, on August 27,[66] that he "Dind," and on September 4[66] that he "dined," and could alternate the two spellings all through his diary; he could write, in recording a wedding, "maryed,"[67] and describe a frontier bed-covering as a "bairskin";[68] a bed-covering of a different sort

From "The Spokesman-Review" (Spokane), 1906.

Kikt out! A spelling-reform cartoon.

he could describe as a "thread Bear blanket";[69] he could even, by writing "Dogs or Catts,"[68] defy the orthodox spelling of the first word of the soon-to-be-born "primer" for the teaching of elementary spelling. Andrew Jackson suffered no criticism for writing, after his decisive battle in the War of 1812: "I will hold New Orleans in spite of Urop[70] and all hell," and his spelling was as

65 Washington's Diary, September 4, 1769, and in many other entries.
66 1772. Washington's Diary.
67 Washington's Diary, August 31, 1768.
68 Washington's Diary, November, 1749.
69 Washington's Diary, March 15, 1748.
70 Nearly a hundred years later, Roosevelt, defending "Old Hickory's" individuality of orthography, said: "If that doesn't spell Europe, what does it spell?"

well understood, at a time when latitude in spelling was practised and expected, as "Europe" would have been.

Individuality of spelling, respect for personal preference — in short, free will in the field of orthography — was destroyed by the autocracy which the people voluntarily conferred upon the dictionary, an autocracy based on completely perverted understanding of what the function of a dictionary is. The business of dictionaries is not to dictate popular usage, but merely to record it — of which fact the appearance of successive editions is sufficient proof. After the early dictionary had become thoroughly intrenched, after the people had come to think of it as an authority, and after the tendency toward standardization had spread into many fields of American life, we had the strange result: that for a man to practise an individual habit in pronouncing a word was commonly a distinction and a charm, whereas to do so in spelling the same word was an occasion for laughter; in the nineteen hundred and twenties, President Coolidge's oral description of his hilly birthplace as "mount-ins" was regarded as an agreeable whimsicality of pronunciation — had he practised the same divagation from standard in his writing of the word, he would have been laughed at to a degree that would have imperilled his eligibility for the Presidency.

One consequence of the conferring of the prerogative of tyranny upon dictionaries was that any variation from standardized spelling came to be regarded as funny; a laugh was the expected and usual accompaniment of it. The phenomenon gave rise to or facilitated a new school of literature, characteristic of America, consisting of humor achieved or accentuated by deliberately unorthodox[71] spelling. There were three principal exponents of

[71] James Russell Lowell's "Biglow Papers" were not a case of deliberately mangled spelling, but of the faithful transcription of a living dialect. So also was Finley Peter Dunne's "Mister Dooley."

it, Artemus Ward, Petroleum V. Nasby (who gave as his address "Confedrit X Rodes, Kentucky"), and Josh Billings; and these three, together with Major Jack Downey and Seba Smith, supplied most of the humorous popular literature of America from the 1830's to the 1880's. In the writings of all three, especially those of Josh Billings, there was, of course, pith, pungency and some philosophy; but their points would have been regarded merely as rather acid adages — had they not been dressed in the provocative to laughter that was inherent in their deliberately gargoyled spelling. For example, Josh Billings won universal laughter by writing:

It is highly important, when a man makes up his minde tew bekum a raskall, that he shud examine hisself clusly, and see if he ain't better konstructed for a phool.

Subject that to a process no greater than to deprive it of its ragged clothes and dress it in conventional garb — and you have something as austere, as unprovocative of laughter, as a maxim of Epictetus:

It is highly important, when a man decides to be a rascal, that he should examine himself closely, to see if he is not better equipped to be a fool.

Similarly, "This is too much!" is almost the tritest possible phrase for indignation or reproach; but it made all America laugh when Artemus Ward wrote it "This is 2 mutch."

Artemus Ward, Josh Billings and their fellow artisans in comic spelling supplied most of the popular humor for America during three generations; one effect of the long vogue of their humor, and of the introduction of dictionaries, was that all variations from dictionary spelling were seen as one of two things, deliberate humor or illiteracy.

Orthography had become standardized; and the aim of the crusaders for spelling reform was to simplify the dictionary standards.

In 1906 the scholars in the movement were joined by one whose sparseness of academic background was more than offset, for this purpose, by his generosity and his money; one who was a go-getter for results, as well as a great giver of the fruits of his getting, a retired iron-master named Andrew Carnegie. Carnegie, having been forced by poverty to end his own schooling at the age of eleven, carried throughout the remainder of his life, as one of his most conspicuous qualities, a likable enthusiasm and reverence for learning and for men whose careers and distinctions were in the world of letters. His regard for education, he expressed, after he became wealthy, in a lavishness of benefaction to institutions associated with learning which made him, at that time, the greatest[72] giver in the world.

To the Spelling Reform Association, Carnegie gave, for the purpose of greater energy in propaganda, $10,-000 a year (later increased to $25,000; the total was $250,000). Together with the money, he conferred shrewd counsel about changing the name of the association from one containing the word "Reform" to the less prejudice-provoking "Simplified Spelling Board," and about other devices for carrying on the publicity campaign which, the Board believed, would carry their movement to success. "What is needed," said Professor Matthews, "is to focus attention on this important subject, and to arouse a lively interest in it."

In the expansion of propaganda that followed Carnegie's gift, the attention of President Roosevelt was ar-

[72] At this time (about 1906) John D. Rockefeller was only just getting into the stride of his giving.

rested. He, infected, addressed, on August 27, 1906, a letter to the Public Printer, ordering him, "Please hereafter direct that in all government publications of the Executive Departments the 300 words enumerated in [enclosed] Circular No. 5 [of the Simplified Spelling Board] shall be spelled as therein set forth. If anyone asks the reason for the action, refer him to Circulars 3, 4 and 6 as issued by the Simplified Spelling Board."

In his ardor as a convert, Roosevelt forgot his astuteness as a politician, and accompanied his official action with a defense of it:

Resistance to simplified spelling, Roosevelt wrote, is "made in entire ignorance. . . . It is not an attack on the language of Shakespeare and Milton, because it is in some instances a going-back to the forms they used, and in others merely the extension of changes which, as regards other words, have taken place since their time." He did not have, he said, "the slightest intention to do anything revolutionary or initiate any far-reaching policy. The purpose simply is for the government, instead of lagging behind popular sentiment, to advance abreast of it and at the same time abreast of the views of the ablest and most practical educators of our time, as well as of the most profound scholars. . . . It is merely an attempt to cast what slight weight can properly be cast on the side of the popular forces which are endeavoring to make our spelling a little less foolish and fantastic."

The changes that Roosevelt ordered were not, for the most part, extreme; fully 90 per cent of them were already to be found, as optional or alternative spellings, in the standard dictionaries. "Honour" was to become "honor," "parlour" to become "parlor"; and a like dropping of a "u" was to result in "labor," "rumor," "humor," "color," "odor," and the like. "Axe" was to drop its final "e"; and similar, so to speak, decapitation of the caudal "e" was to result, somewhat woefully, in "wo" and "good-by." By a more extreme decaudation, "programme" was to become "program"; "omelette" to become "omelet"; "coquette" to become, barbarously, "coquet"; "catalogue" to become "catalog"; "decalogue" to be shortened to "decalog."

In several familiar American words a French strain was to be harshly eliminated by reversing the order of two letters: "centre" to become "center," "sabre" to become "saber," "fibre" to become "fiber," "theatre" to become "theater," "accoutre" to become "accouter." Similarly the French was to be ironed out of "cheque" by making it "check" and out of "barque" by making it "bark," and out of "comptroller" by making it "controller." All memory of Greece was to be squeezed out of "drachm," which was to become "dram." "Æon" was to be shortened to "eon."

By a harsh violence which seemed puritanically to disapprove the prolongation of sentimental experiences, "kissed" was to be "kist," "caressed" to become "carest," "clasped" to become "claspt," "pressed" to become "prest," "blushed" to become "blusht," "winked" to become "winkt," "blessed" to become "blest." Several double g's were condemned: "waggon" was to become "wagon," and "faggot" to become "fagot." "Judgement" was to lose the unsounded "e" in its middle, and likewise "lodgement."

The double "r" which suggested the sound that was meant by "purr" was to be shortened, horribly, to "pur." The diphthong "ph" was to be supplanted by "f" as in "sulfurous." Several other diphthongs were to be ruthlessly divorced, "phœnix" becoming "phenix," and "mediæval" becoming "medieval" and "subpœna" becoming "subpena." The spelling that described a Chinaman's tonsorial pride was to suffer the same demeaning as the queue itself, being bobbed, and otherwise starkly altered, to "cue." In several words "s" was to become "z" and thus make "artizan" and "surprize" and "compromize" and "raze" and "legalize" and "idolize" and "catechize" — though "catechism" was permitted to keep the sanctuary of its hallowed form. The old "gaol" was sentenced to a fiat obsolescence, and only "jail" was authorized; "y" was to become "i" so as to make "dike" and "gipsy." The soft "c" was to become "s" so as to make "defense" and "license."

"Cough" was left undisturbed, but the same word when preceded by a convulsion of the gullet, was to become "hiccup." With similar illogic, "fill" was left with its full complement of "l's," and likewise "dull"; elsewhere, however, the double "l" was condemned, so as to change "fulfill" to "fulfil" and "instill" to "instil," and "distill" to "distil," and "fullness" to "fulness," and "dullness" to "dulness." "Woollen" lost one of its "l's" and "skillful" became "skilful." "Instead" was left undisturbed, but "steadfast" lost an "a," becoming "stedfast." "Whiskey" became "whisky." "Mamma" lost one of its interior "m's."

Among all the changes, some that struck the eye as repellent were the changing of the final "ed" to "t" — "clipped" being clipped to "clipt," and "lopped" being lopped to "lopt," and "clapped" to "clapt," and "dashed" to "dasht," and "drooped" to "droopt," and "dropped" to "dropt," and "fixed" to "fixt." The melodious, three-syllabled "accursed," which had lent itself to rhythm since Shakespeare's day, was to become "accurst."

Of all the changes that Roosevelt ordered, the ones that most struck the eye with an effect of something missing were "tho" for "though," and "thoro" for "thorough," and — worst of all — "through" mangled and amputated to "thru."

A movement which, though led by many of the country's most eminent scholars, had not got so far, in forty years of effort, as even to chop the final "e" from "axe," now became, because Theodore Roosevelt wrote an official letter about it, the most talked about topic of the day, a nation-wide sensation. More than nation-wide — because England was concerned, gravely. In London, the uprising in America against the King's English aroused disquiet almost as acute as had the uprising against His Majesty's collectors of revenue upon tea in Boston a hundred and thirty years before. There were angry allusions to the "President's American" as a usurper of the "King's English." The London *Times* — speaking for the senior partner in the legacy of English speech and the joint responsibility for sympathetic custodianship of its traditions — regretted that the sudden step was "inconsiderate" and "unconcerted," feeling that the President ought to have consulted the British Government in a matter so important to the country of the mother tongue, and so important also to the amicable relations of the two nations, since a separate language developing in America under the impetuous promotion of so energetic a President might lead to cleavage of sentiment and interest. *The St. James Gazette*, less urbane than *The Times*, exclaimed: "Here is the language of eighty million people suddenly altered by a mere administrative ukase! Could any other ruler on earth do this thing? . . . Could the Czar . . . or even the Kaiser?" The British press as a whole, said a London despatch to the New York *Times*, "replies to Mr. Roosevelt with an outburst of ridicule." It was, indeed, more mordant than ridicule, more directly invective. England, said the

London correspondent of the New York *Times*, "characterizes [Roosevelt] as whimsical, silly, headstrong and despotic."

These clanging repercussions from England were comparatively unnoticed in the din of controversy that arose at home. Roosevelt's order to the Public Printer had applied to "government publications of the Executive Departments." But how much did that include? And how about other public documents? Would the Supreme Court permit their august decisions to be printed in a spelling different from that which their predecessors had used? Would Congress, unfond of Roosevelt anyhow, permit its deliberations to be demeaned by such barbarities as "tho" and "thru"? Even as to the executive departments, directly under the President, would learned men in the government service submit to be told by Mr. Roosevelt that they must spell the documents they wrote in an orthography offensive to their learning, taste and traditions? "The President," said the New York *Times* in an editorial entitled *Super Grammaticam*, "is above grammar or above dictionaries; of course he can himself misspell words and possibly can order the Public Printer to follow copy; but can he order every member of the cabinet, including such a fastidious scholar as Secretary Root, to forbear from correcting vile and glaring misprints?" In the diligence with which answers were sought to these and similar questions, one Washington correspondent discovered authoritatively, and assured an anxious country, especially the bankers, that the President "has no power to change" the spelling on currency, that species in the technical sense would not become "mony," that a paper dollar would not become a "silvr sertifikit." The responsible Treasury official, having carefully looked up the

statute creating his office, found that he was "Comptroller of the Treasury" and "Comptroller he would continue to be — not 'Controller.' "

Such authorities of institutions of learning as had not
committed themselves to the movement were anxiously
queried by the newspapers. President Eliot of Harvard
said: "I suppose that President Roosevelt has a right to
write his message in any style of orthography to which
he may incline"; the reporter observed that the Harvard president had a twinkle in his eye. Goldwin Smith,
a distinguished scholar, formerly honorary professor of
history at Cornell University, emitted disapproval so
stern as to be shrill. Arthur T. Hadley, president of
Yale, asked to be excused. The professor of psychology
at Harvard, Hugo Münsterberg, wrote (in *McClure's
Magazine* for September, 1906) about "The Psycholog-
ical Objection to Systematic Simplification." Woodrow
Wilson of Princeton had already expressed disapproba-
tion of the new system. Andrew S. Draper, New York
State Commissioner of Education, "did not believe that
the State Educational Department should tell the people
how they must spell." Governor Higgins of New York
declined, eloquently, to discuss the matter. Cincinnati
school officials disagreed. The superintendent of schools
at Washington said he would allow the students to choose
for themselves.

One newspaper, the Worcester, Mass., *Telegram*,
tried the new spelling — for one day. But the New
York *Evening Post* declared that this was one of the occasions when "that pioneer phonetic speller Artemus
Ward would have said 'This is 2 mutch.' " And the
New York *Times*, speaking for itself and, it believed,
for newspapers generally, declared: "Every newspaper,
we assume, will take the kindly view that the President's
heterographical freaks are misprints and will correct

them into English according to accepted standards. . . .
The press, we think, can be trusted to render entirely
nugatory this arrogant and outrageous attempt to disturb
the natural evolution of the English language." The
New York *Morning Telegraph* combined terse criticism
of Roosevelt with succinct counsel: "He is in wrong and
he'd better back out at the first opportunity."

The opposition ranged from furious denunciation of
Roosevelt and Carnegie, to subtle satire at the expense
of their proposal. "What may he not do next?" asked
an appalled contributor to the Rochester *Post-Express*.
"It is a scheme financed by Carnegie, backed by certain
large publishing interests and designed to carry out an
immense project for jobbery in reprinting dictionaries
and school books." Critics less suspicious and more
urbane dwelled upon the undesirability of taking away
from venerated English words the letters and forms that
were the insignia of their origins, and of depriving others of sentimental or traditional associations that were
inherent in their familiar spelling. It was argued, not
too seriously, that to spell the word for a gallant gentleman "bo," would, in the eyes of the lady most concerned, take away some of the grace and charm and ele-
gance implied by "beau"; that a bunch of flowers, if
spelled "bo-ka," might continue to smell as sweet, yet
would have lost some of the fine aroma that goes with
"bouquet"; that a "quadril" on a dancing-floor would
have lost some of the grace that goes with "quadrille";
that "gazelle" is more stimulating to poetic phantasy
than "gazel" is to "fantasy"; that "lustre" loses some of
its sheen when it becomes "luster."

It was conceded, however, that "laf" might seem a
little more provocative of mirth than "laugh."

Some of the more delicate arguments dwelled upon
the analogy between superfluous letters at the end of a

word, such as the "te" at the end of "coquette," and, on the other hand, the outward extremity of the tail of a dog. Neither has any practical usefulness, both can be decaudated without doing fatal damage. Yet the tail of a dog, like the vocabulary of a man, is useful to the possessor as a means of expressing his emotions. To abbreviate a dog's tail, or otherwise simplify it, would correspondingly constrict the dog's capacity to express his feelings, might even reduce his whole range of emotion. A Newfoundland, if his tail should be shortened, obviously could not express his joy over seeing his master with so sweeping a gesture of happy emotion; a setter or a pointer, scenting game and calling his master's attention by the rigidity of his pose, could not achieve so conspicuous a stoniness if his tail were shortened.

Other disputants, admitting (with a wink) the advantages of the proposed change, said that it did not go far enough, that it should be done all at once, and not by any such graduation as 300 words at a time. If you decide, they said, to shorten a dog's tail, it had best be done not by sandpapering the end and reducing the length minutely each day, which would make the tail sore and spoil the temper of the dog much more than to cut it off once for all and bandage the stub.

Many opponents, less discursive, merely quoted Josh Billings, saying that for them the old-time spelling, like the old-time religion, was "good enuf." Disputants not endowed with the materials or the disposition for refined ratiocination on this point, just said "I don't like it," and clasped the older spelling with the accentuated devotion of one who comes to the rescue of an assailed friend. There was, indeed, a recognizable body of angry emotion. By the time Roosevelt's order had been in effect ten weeks, *Life*[73] was able to observe:

[73] November 15, 1906.

"Is not the zeal of the simplified spellers outrunning their discretion? When they converted President Roosevelt and got the executive machinery of our Government to work in the interest of their improved orthography, they made a great many citizens mad. It was justly considered an impertinence for the President to meddle officially with American spelling."

For the newspaper wits, it was, of course, a field day. Instantly, Andrew Carnegie became "Andru Karnegi." As for Roosevelt, the Baltimore *Sun* asked: "How will he spell his own name? Will he make it 'Rusevelt' or will he get down to the fact and spell it 'Butt-in-sky'?" Henry Watterson in the Louisville *Courier-Journal* wrote it "Rucevelt," adding, subtly, "the first silabel riming with goose." Mr. Watterson observed that

Nuthing escapes Mr. Rucevelt. No subject is tu hi fr him to takl, nor tu lo for him tu notis. He makes tretis without the consent of the Senit. He inforces such laws as meet his approval, and fales to se those that du not soot him. He now assales the English langgwidg, constitutes himself a sort of French Academy, and will reform the spelling in a way tu soot himself.

The newspaper poets, punsters and paragraphers, to whom Roosevelt had always been stimulus and inspiration, could now be grateful to him for making their labors easy, because, of all varieties of quip, the least laborious of accomplishment is that which can be produced by use of the mechanism for which Roosevelt now provided timeliness. The oldest classics in the language, quotations from the Bible and from Shakespeare, could be justified as copy for the day's newspaper by the mere device of translating them into Roosevelt orthography. The range of the possible puns in the English language was increased to the degree that Roosevelt had brought about double spellings for 300 words; and the simplification that Roosevelt prescribed for 300 words, could be extended, by comic license, to every word in the language. In short, Roosevelt, as often before, opened up new pastures of wit, and gave timeliness to old ones. Newspaper artisans of humor, rushing to the now aging volumes of Artemus Ward, resurrected what was, perhaps, the most delicious paragraph he ever produced:

Some kind person has sent me Chawcer's poems. Mr. C. had talent, but he couldn't spel. No man has a right to be a lit'rary man onless he knows how to spel. It is a pity that Chawcer, who had geneyus, was so unedicated. He's the wus speller I know of.

Puck, among some later repercussions of the episode, combined a joke in the simple spelling formula with characteristic comment about a phase of the times:

No it is not strictly true that the nave of a church is simplified spelling for the pillar of a church when he's doing business outside.

After Roosevelt's order had called public attention to one group of orthographic eccentricities,[74] the newspaper poets could wander at will through the dictionary to pluck others. Of the mechanical verse thus easily achieved, one of the more ingenious specimens was

When the English tongue we speak
Why is "break" not rhymed with "freak"?
Will you tell me why it's true

[74] In the innumerable bits of verse devised to illustrate the eccentricities of English spelling, one of the most apt was printed on a menu of the Lake Placid Club and "publisht" in a quarterly periodical issued jointly by Simplified Spelling Society, Simplified Spelling Board, and Spelling Reform Association, September–December, 1925:

THE GO–GEBTOR.

A merchant addressing a debtor
Remarked in the course of his lebtor
That he chose to suppose
A man knose what he ose,
And the sooner he pays it the bebtor.

We say "sew," but likewise "few"? . . .
"Beard" sounds not the same as "heard";
"Cord" is different from "word";
"Cow" is cow, but "low" is low;[75] . . .

Verse so trite that not even the humblest poetaster
would have put it on paper, now became printable by
the device of spelling it as Josh Billings would have
done. Wallace Irwin, beginning an ode to spring with

O jentil Spring, O jentil Spring! . . .
O prity burds, O warbling burdz!
What soro hav u now?

threw up his hands with a plaintive regret:

Grate Scot! I kannot spel the wurdz
That sizzle 'neath my brow
Sins A. Karnaygy spoyld the rulz,
We ust to hav in gramar skulz.[76]

Further examples one forbears to reproduce. To a degree greater, even, than is the case with all newspaper
quip and verse, their adequacy for the day's newspaper
was accompanied by inadequacy for the era's history.

That the quantity of the parodying, punning, dispu-
tation and other forms of commotion was disadvan-
tageous to the cause of simplified spelling, everybody
recognized. An official of the Simplified Spelling Board,
Brander Matthews, having declared some time before
that "what is needed is to focus attention . . . to arouse
a lively interest," now said, somewhat defensively, that
Roosevelt had not consulted him about issuing his order
to the Public Printer. Another official of the board,

---

[75] *Literary Digest,* December 4, 1909; reprinted from *The Church Review.*
[76] "Random Rhymes and Odd Numbers," Wallace Irwin.

Doctor Charles P. Scott, Secretary, observing Roosevelt's unconscious capacity for evoking spontaneous commotion, observed, with truth, "I do believe that if President Roosevelt declared that it would be wise to annex the planet Mars to the United States, the papers would immediately proceed to print columns about it."

Professor Brander Matthews of Columbia.

Roosevelt's order had been given to the Public Printer on August 27. Congress and the Supreme Court were on vacation. The Court was the first to resume sittings. The Chief Justice called the attention of the Solicitor-General to the action of the head of the executive branch of the government, and stated that "in quoting to the Court any [citation from previous decisions] the use of simplified spelling was not a literal quotation."[77] Pointedly the Court continued to hand down its decisions in the old spelling.

Not enough for Congress, however, was indirect reproof nor silent pursuit of its own way. When it assembled on December 3, Roosevelt sent his annual message in the new spelling. The provocation was superfluous. Promptly the House of Representatives, through a committee, called the Public Printer on the carpet. With the manner familiar in a prosecutor cross-examining a cowering witness, Representative Bingham of Pennsyl-

[77] Representative Bingham of Pennsylvania, describing the attitude taken by the Court, in the House, December 10, 1906.

vania asked the Printer "Is there any statute that gives the President authority in any way to change the spelling — have you looked into that?"[78] The committee made the Printer admit that the innovation, giving rise in effect to a dual system, would result in extra expense, because of confusion to typesetters and the need of extra vigilance on the part of proof-readers. Representative Livingston arrived at an estimate that the 113 "simplified" words in the President's annual message to Congress had cost $760.

Expense, however, was the least of the reasons Congress had for taking notice. They put their action on grounds that were broader, if not necessarily higher. The truth was they didn't like Roosevelt. For five years he had been making them do what they didn't want, steadily taking public confidence away from them and to himself, repeatedly making forays across the no-man's-land that lies between the executive and legislative branches of the government, steadily absorbing for the executive, prerogatives and prestige that the legislative wanted for itself. Now, Congress felt, they had caught him in an attempted exercise of power in which, their observation of the popular reaction told them, public opinion would not support him. Congress proposed to "give the President a jolt."

Congressman Sullivan of Massachusetts shrewdly drew in a current criticism which said that Roosevelt would like to be a king: "If the President of the United States has authority by imperial ukase to change the spelling of three hundred words, it follows that he has authority to change 30,000 words, or every word of the language. The result may be that a new court language may be established by Executive decree for the new American Empire. We got along very well with the cus-

[78] *Congressional Record,* December 10, 1906.

tomary form of the English language until the reign of the present Ruler." (The timorous Public Printer was careful to spell ruler with a capital "R.") "Tell me," Sullivan demanded, "by what right the President can enforce his idea of spelling upon the public official whom we call the Public Printer, and whose salary is paid out of the Treasury of the United States."

Courtesy of the Washington "Star."

Summer, 1908. Archie Roosevelt and White House policeman. The helmet worn was practically the same in all cities at that time. The visored cap has taken its place.

"Before very long," said Democratic Representative Champ Clark of Missouri, "the people of the United States are going to insist on having a President who will attend strictly to his constitutional functions and expend his energies only on subjects of great pith and moment." Clark, when his mind was not on rebuking Roosevelt, was not seriously unsympathetic to the merit of simplified spelling. He was "willing to go the whole hog" but not willing to "take 300 words out of the 120,000 and pester ourselves and everybody else with this new-fangled orthography." Representative Grosvenor of Ohio cited a statute of Edward III, enacted in 1632, decree-

ing that "all pleas . . . within the realm shall be
pleaded . . . answered, debated and judged in the English tongue." That statute, Grosvenor said, fixes "the
English language as the language of England, from
which, as I claim, we inherit the language that we have
in this country. . . . The English language is the law
of the people of the United States. He who seeks to
change that language in an official document," said Grosvenor, with the effect of an ugly look at Roosevelt, "will
be compelled to change existing law."

Too anxious to wait for an opportunity to legislate
specifically upon Roosevelt's order, Congress attached to
the first appropriation measure a rider decreeing that

In printing documents authorized by law or ordered by
Congress, the Government printing office shall follow the rules
of orthography established by Webster's or other generally accepted dictionaries of the English language.

To Roosevelt's aid, with a defense more sly than sincere, came Representative Shackleford of Missouri, with
a proposed variation of the rider, according to which
the Public Printer should follow "the language in which
the document is written." "In other words," said the
Missouri Congressman, with a wit in which the point
lay in the closing clause, "let every man enjoy his fancy
in spelling, from the President of the United States up
to a Member [of the House]." With sincere even
though tepid defense of Roosevelt, Representative Oscar Underwood of Alabama pointed out that Congress
"is denying the President the right to spell his message
to Congress any way he pleases." Not so, said Representative Lacey of Iowa: "He can spell it any way he wants
to, but when Congress prints it we should print it in the
usual and accepted orthography."

More robustly to Roosevelt's defense came Representative De Armond of Missouri: "I hope," he said, "that

the Committee on Appropriations will see whether there can be found something else upon which . . . they can exercise their power and zeal. I wish the gentlemen of that committee, when they desire to say anything about the Executive in reference to this matter of spelling, would get into a direct discussion with the Executive upon the subject, and not resort to an expedient which is not as bold or open as the Executive order, by hiding a little bit of a provision in a large appropriation bill, which they think the Executive dare not veto on account of the necessity for the appropriations carried. [Laughter.] Just go and meet the President in the open — and you will find him there!"

That the House would deliver an official rebuke was certain. The only question was about the form. To the proposed "rider," objection was made, in the form of a point of order, on the ground that under the rules of the House no "provision changing existing law" may be enacted as a part of any general appropriation bill. Upon this point of order, the House wrangled for most of four days.

As a way out of the fog of quibbling, Representative Bingham of Pennsylvania suggested another statutory form for reaching Roosevelt: "No money appropriated in this act shall be used in connection with the printing of documents authorized by law . . . unless the same shall conform to the orthography recognized and used by generally accepted dictionaries of the English language."

In that form, the rebuke was enacted, by a vote of 142 yeas to 24 noes. The following day, the rebuke was put in an even more direct form, which placed a prohibition upon Roosevelt specifically:

Resolved: That it is the sense of the House of Representatives that hereafter, in printing reports, documents or other publications authorized by law, ordered by Congress or either branch thereof, or emanating from the Executive departments, their bureaus or branches, and independent offices of the government, the Government Printing Office should observe and adhere to the standard of orthography prescribed in generally accepted dictionaries of the English language.

By this time, Roosevelt's partisans — what few there were — knew they were beaten. "I recognize," said Congressman Gillett[79] of Massachusetts, "that this House prefers the spelling now approved by the dictionaries. . . . I am obviously in the minority. I bow to the will of the majority and approve the adoption of this resolution."

It was agreed to, without a dissenting vote.

On the same day, Roosevelt formally withdrew his order to the Public Printer.

From a photograph © Underwood & Underwood.

Roosevelt at a cowboy breakfast at Hugo, Colo., May 4, 1903.

Roosevelt said he did not wish to have spelling reform overshadow matters of great importance; the Providence (R. I.) *Bulletin* said the same thing the other way round: "President Roosevelt is a lucky man; this Cuban business gives him a fine opportunity to let go the tail of the simplified spelling bear."

To an official of the Simplified Spelling Board[80] who

---

[79] Later Speaker; later Senator.　　　　[80] Brander Matthews.

regretted his surrender, Roosevelt wrote: "I could not by fighting have kept the new spelling in, and it was evidently worse than useless to go into an undignified contest when I was beaten. Do you know that the one word as to which I thought the new spelling was wrong — thru — was more responsible than anything else for our discomfiture? But I am mighty glad I did the thing anyhow. In my own correspondence I shall continue using the new spelling."

7

THE RAILROAD RATE FIGHT

The Climax of Roosevelt's Crusade for Economic Reforms and a Classic Example of How a Strong, Resourceful President Can Force an Unwilling Senate to Do His Will. A Struggle that Called for Every Weapon in Roosevelt's Armory. Story of the Subjection of the Railroads to Regulation by the Federal Government. Including Charges of Inveracity Exchanged by Statesmen in Exalted Stations. Together with Other Episodes Piquant or Explosive.

THE railroads, in the beginning, were subject to but one legal limitation upon the rates they could charge, an ancient restraint originally devised to apply to carters and draymen and very inadequate for such organized instrumentalities of transportation as railroads came to be. The railroads were, under the ancient common[1] law, "common carriers." As common carriers, the railroads were required (1) to render their services to all who sought them, without discrimination; and (2) to exact only reasonable charges. The remedies for the public under the common law were confined to suits in courts; the remedies were (1) to tender a reasonable amount in payment and recover damages for any loss sustained because the service was not supplied after such tender; or (2) to pay under protest the charge demanded and recover by suit any amount in excess of a reasonable charge.

In addition to this restraint common to all railroads, some were limited, by stipulations in their original charters, as to maximum rates they could charge.

[1] "Common law" is distinguished from statute or enacted law. Common law is the fundamental, the so-to-speak "taken for granted" law, which does not depend upon enactment but exists and has force in the absence of enactment. The common law grew up in England, prevailed in the American colonies, and became the basis of all American law (except in Louisiana, where the basis is the French "Napoleonic Code").

I

With these exceptions — not important under the conditions of the nineteenth century, and not material to the present history of the development of statutory regulation — the railroads[2] in their early days were, with regard to the rates they could charge for transportation, as immune from regulation by government as any other owner of private property; they were wholly free from statutory regulation, wholly free from administrative supervision by government; they were, in their power to fix arbitrarily the price of what they sold (transportation), on the same footing with mill-owners, farmers, merchants, ship-owners, physicians, and other producers

[2] Throughout this chapter, the word "railroads" (as well as "railways") is used in two interchangeable meanings, sometimes as the name for the physical railroad, sometimes as the name for the corporate owner of it. The practice is common in all discussions of the subject, and will not, I think, confuse the reader. It cannot readily be avoided except by adopting phraseologies that would seem awkward and circumlocutious.

Actually, both terms are misleading, in the use made of them often in history and quite generally in other forms of writing. The two terms are used in this chapter as an almost indispensable convenience for describing some broad movements and general conditions. But railroads, whether in the physical sense or the corporate sense, do not "do" things. Much of the muddled thinking in the world arises out of the assumption that corporations (or other groups of persons) can have purposes, or can think, or can exercise other sorts of intellectual process. What actually goes on, in the case of a railroad, or any other corporation or group, is that some individual or other becomes dominant; the dominance may be achieved through personality, or intelligence, or money, or persuasiveness upon his fellows; it may come about through the gravitation, toward one individual having strong convictions, of other individuals having similar convictions. With dominance achieved, the individual directs the corporation toward ends that appeal to him, with such concessions as he may be obliged to make to conditions, or to other men. The ends an individual may have are as various as the differences between man and man. They may be dictated by ambition, or by appetite for money, or by jealousy of other men; by self-interest or by altruism. The end may be dictated by a combination of motives. During the period covered by this chapter, the Great Northern Railway, for example, reflected the will of James J. Hill; the Union Pacific, that of Edward H. Harriman. What each did with the railroad he controlled was prompted by a combination of motives. Hill can be presumed to have had the motive of making exceptional profits for himself and for those who invested their money with him. But it is equally certain that Hill took pleasure in the function of turning virgin prairies into farms occupied by prosperous families. To some degree, Hill may have been motivated by a sense of rivalry with Harriman.

of goods or sellers of services; each had in this respect the same status with respect to government, the broad legend common to all being, "A man can do what he will with his own." The practice, with the railroads, as

A railroad right-of-way — a bit of the roadbed of the Old Portage Railroad, near Gallitzin, Pa., showing stone sleepers which proved not to be practical.

expressed in a phrase of the day, was to "charge all the traffic will bear."

As respects this immunity from regulation, railroads were on the same basis as other forms of private property. But railroads had a right, a privilege, that other forms of private property had not. Railroads had the right called "eminent domain."

The possession by the railroads of this special right was the reason for the raising of a question about their immunity from government interference with the price at which they sold their services. And the raising of this question is the beginning of the history of railroad rate regulation.[3]

II

For their rights-of-way, early railroad builders needed narrow strips of land which had to be acquired, in most cases, through purchase.[4] Usually the owner was willing to sell, or even, if he believed the presence of the railroad would be an advantage, to donate the necessary strip of land. But there were occasions when an owner, seeing his opportunity to hold up the railroad, demanded an exorbitant price. And other occasions when a farmer, moved by his affection for the land that was almost a part of himself, or instinctively fearful of the disruption which the railroad would bring to his familiar and beloved ways of life, or suspicious about the city strangers who would be brought to his door, or solicitous for the safety and peace of mind of his cattle and horses that would be terrified by the engine's noise and endangered by its speed, was flatly unwilling to sell at all.

When such cases arose, the railroads went to the courts, called attention to their right of eminent domain (granted to them in their charters), and pleaded that the courts, in accordance with that ancient doctrine, should condemn the land, bestow title upon them, and fix the amount of compensation to be paid. The courts always granted the plea (unless there was some defect in the railroad's charter, or other technical legal objection).

Eminent domain traditionally had been a principle as-

---

[3] By "government regulation," as used in this chapter, is meant regulation of the sort that came to be practised by the Federal Government after 1887, and by some States about the same period. Regulation in this sense is not to be confused with an early form of limitation on rates practised by some of the older eastern States, which, in some of the original charters they granted for the building of railroads, inserted stipulations about maximum rates.

[4] This was commonly the method in the East. In the West, great quantities of land were frequently granted to the railroads by the Federal Government, or by the States.

sociated chiefly with a *public service*, granted to forms of property affected with the special attribute of performing a public service. Eminent domain could only be conferred by government; it was a grant by government of a portion of its own prerogative; it was analo-

Courtesy Stevens Institute of Technology.

Probably the first locomotive in America driven by steam upon a track. Colonel John Stevens in 1826 invented a multitubular boiler and experimented on his own tracks in Hoboken, near the present Lackawanna terminal.

gous to the three supreme controls which government exercises over private property: the police power, taxation, and expropriation or destruction during wartime.

Only upon the representation by the railroad promoters that their lines would perform a public service, did legislatures grant, and courts apply, the doctrine of eminent domain for the railroads' benefit.

Without the privilege of eminent domain, the railroads could not have been built — but it was the possession of this privilege that ultimately led to their subjection to public control of their rates. It was the spectacle of railroads exercising the right of eminent domain that caused the public to reason that if the railroads had this extraordinary privilege, it ought to be accompanied by an analogous right on the part of the public.[5]

III

The idea took concrete form and came to a head in the Midwest.[6] There "hard-headed old pioneers from New England and Northern Europe who thought as they plowed" reasoned that "the railroad was only another form of highway." Holding this conviction, and feeling that they and their communities were wronged by some rates that the railroads dictated, the farmers formed the "Patrons of Husbandry," popularly known as the "Grangers." The aim of the Grangers was to secure legislation which would give the State governments the right to regulate rates, which would deprive the rail-

[5] I merely assert that in the historical development of the idea of regulation of railroad rates, there was a relation between that idea and the possession by railroads of the right of eminent domain. Particularly was this true in the quarter where the demand for rate regulation became most potent and ultimately most successful, among the farmers of the "Granger States." I do not assert that the relation is inevitably logical, though many do so assert, and their position is tenable. To the contrary, a very able and scholarly railroad man who has read this chapter in one of its drafts, Mr. Leonor Fresnel Loree, president of the Delaware and Hudson Railroad, points out that many enterprises are given the power of eminent domain which are not subjected to regulation of their rates or prices; for example, in some States, the power of eminent domain is given, under some conditions, to mining enterprises, milling, irrigation. At the same time, rate regulation has frequently been imposed upon trades or enterprises that do not possess eminent domain, for example, draymen, ferries, innkeepers, wharfingers.

[6] In narrating the phase of railroad rate regulation with which this chapter deals, I take, as a starting-place, the Midwest, because it was there that the particular movement arose that went on directly to the enactment of Federal regulation. But any choice of one starting-point in what is essentially a flowing stream of history, though inherently unavoidable, results inevitably in danger of false emphasis. The idea of government regulation of railroad rates existed sporadically in New England and New York during the earliest decades of the railroads' existence; and more or less organized efforts to achieve regulation arose in various parts of the country before the Granger movement began. Geographically, the place of genesis of the ultimately successful movement for regulation of railroad rates was Texas. See foot-note on page 198.

roads of their power to make such arbitrary rates as they chose.[7]

This demand the railroads resisted with as much self-righteous defiance as if they were ordinary owners of private property against whom injustice was being attempted. To defend themselves they became more active in politics than before. As it was put by Robert M. LaFollette, the railroads "saw that they must either accept control by the State, or control the State." This statement is historically accurate, and logical; a further statement by LaFollette is colored to some degree by his mordant anti-railroad bias, "They adopted the latter course; they began right there to corrupt . . . all the States of the Middle West."[8]

Presently, in four midwestern States,[9] the anti-railroad movement won in the local legislatures, and then in the courts, the right of the State to regulate a part, but only a part, of transportation. The portion of transportation that a State could regulate was the portion that was intrastate, transportation in which the shipment or journey began and ended within the same State.

But this was of small avail, for the bulk of railroad transportation is *inter*state, that is, begins in one State

[7] This conclusion, that the railroads did not fit into the general category of private property but belonged in a special classification — that they were identical, as respects ownership, with other forms of private property, yet differentiated in their relation to the State — was a mile-post in American history. It would be difficult to overstate its importance and significance. There was little precedent for it in history. It was remarkable in that it had its origin and its greatest momentum, principally, among American farmers, traditionally the most conservative of conservatives, and less among the industrialists and merchants of small cities and towns who, more even than the farmers, suffered under the arbitrary and often vicious exercise by the railroad managers of the power of dispensing or withholding prosperity through their rate schedules. It was significant in that it revealed the capacity of the American democracy to analyze and define a complicated economic ill and to prescribe for it a political cure which, while not damaging to the concept (always tenaciously held in America) of the sanctity of private property, nevertheless was adapted to correct the conditions the country suffered from.

[8] "A Personal Narrative of Political Experiences," Robert M. LaFollette.

[9] Wisconsin, Minnesota, Iowa, and Illinois.

and ends in another. Some States, notably Illinois, attempted to regulate this interstate portion of railroad transportation. The railroads fled to the sanctuary of the Federal courts. The Supreme Court (in the case of Wabash Railroad versus Illinois, 118 U. S. 557) declared that "a statute of a State intended to regulate . . . transportation from one State to another is not within the class of legislation which the States may enact, *in the absence of legislation by Congress.*"[10]

In the absence of legislation by Congress, interstate transportation could not be regulated. Congress had the power to enact such legislation, had the "power to regulate commerce . . . among the several States,"[11] but, aside from two unimportant laws had never exercised the power during more than forty years following the building of the first American railroad.[12] "Bills were introduced . . . and laid aside; some investigations were made. But it all came to naught."

IV

About the time the effort of Illinois to regulate interstate rates was thwarted by the Supreme Court's decision, the representative of Illinois in the United States Senate was Shelby M. Cullom. Cullom,[13] taking account of

---

[10] Italics are the author's.   [11] Constitution, Article I, Section 8.
[12] Jonathan P. Dolliver, United States Senator from Iowa.
[13] Cullom, in the autobiography ("Fifty Years of Public Service") he wrote a quarter-century later, pictured himself as a pioneer, and his advocacy of railroad rate regulation as a high determination inspired by crusader zeal: "I then and there determined [to] make it one of my great aims in the Senate to secure enactment of a Federal statute regulating interstate commerce." That was a case of memory seeing the past, not as it actually was, but with the mellowing glamour of time. Cullom, in temperament and by habit, was as far as possible from being a crusader or a pioneer. Cullom was, to use the word in its better sense, a politician of politicians, superlatively secretive in his methods, cautious in his expressions of opinion. What Cullom did was to take account of an irresistible public demand. His writing a bill for rate regulation and the passage of it by a Senate of whom a majority were reluctant, was — in part at least — a

his State's determination to achieve regulation, and of the agitation attending it, had introduced in the Senate a bill providing for regulation by the Federal Government. "Never . . . was a bill," Senators remarked during the ensuing debate, "which would inevitably affect, directly or remotely, so great financial and industrial interests." The decision of the Supreme Court forever ending the hope of the States (as States) to regulate interstate commerce was handed down October 4, 1886; four months later, February 4, 1887, Cullom's bill for regulation by the Federal Government came to a final vote in the Senate. It was passed, as a direct result of the agitation attending the Supreme Court's decision.

V

By the Interstate Commerce Law of 1887 was created a new instrumentality of government, without precedent in our Federal institutions, the Interstate Commerce Commission. To the Commission, Congress delegated to a limited degree the power of Congress to control the railroads, in particular its power to regulate rates. At the time, public sentiment echoed the exalted opinion which Congress itself held about the reforms the bill would work. The occasion was hailed as an historic landmark.

As respects assertion by Congress of its power to regu-

---

case of allaying public unrest with a moderate bill in order to stem demand for a drastic one. The Cullom bill was introduced in the Senate as a substitute for a bill that had already passed the House, of which the author was John H. Reagan, of Texas.

It was Reagan who was the really important pioneer in the fight for Federal regulation of railroad rates. Reagan, a Democrat, had a remarkable career and deserves more attention than history has accorded him. He served as a Representative in Congress for ten years preceding the Civil War, then became Postmaster-General of the Confederate States, returned to Congress as a Representative in 1875 and entered the Senate in 1887. Reagan, while in the House in the 1870's and early 1880's, introduced and pressed several bills providing for railroad rate regulation, two of which passed the House but failed in the Senate. It was after pressure of these bills by Reagan and the Democrats that Cullom wrote, and a Republican Senate passed a bill less drastic than Reagan's.

late rates, the act of 1887 was a landmark; from that assertion Congress never receded. As respects the creation of a new instrumentality of Federal government, the Interstate Commerce Commission, that was likewise a landmark and likewise remained permanent. But as

Senator Shelby M. Cullom.

respects the powers given the Commission through which it could function, as respects the controls which the Commission was authorized to exercise over the railroads, most of these were in time destroyed, neutralized, or weakened.

The railroads, far from submitting docilely to the yoke of Federal regulation, entered upon a long siege of legal attacks upon the new law, questioning the constitutionality of the whole of it and of each of its parts. In court after court, railroad lawyers argued, in part, that the railroads were citizens of the individual States that had given them their charters, and that therefore they were amenable only to the States, and not to the Federal Government. This was the reverse of their previous plea — used when the railroads were defending themselves against State regulation — that they were "citizens of the United States" in the sense defined in the Fourteenth Amendment to the Federal Constitution,[14] and that therefore the States could not regulate their interstate rates. This nimble scurrying of the rail-

[14] "No State shall make . . . any law which shall abridge the privileges or immunities of citizens [interpreted by the courts to include corporations] of the United States." — Constitution, Article XIV, Sec. 1.

roads from the shelter of their United States citizenship to the shelter of their State citizenship suggested an epigrammatic indictment — like every epigram, not containing the whole of the truth, and maiming what part it does contain — which pictured them as playing hide-and-seek with the public in that twilight zone, that no-man's-land, which lies between State sovereignty and Federal sovereignty.

From "The World-Herald" (Omaha).

Twenty-five years of interpretation by the courts left the Interstate Commerce Commission with but shreds of its original powers.

In their attacks upon the new law, the railroads were in large part victorious.[15] Their success, it was charged, was due no more to the plausibility of their contentions, or the talent of their lawyers, than to their influence with the courts, an influence so powerful by 1904 that it was described in inflammatory words by a member of the Interstate Commerce Commission, Charles A. Prouty. Commissioner Prouty's violent charge must be read in the light of his temperament, which was ardent, and his political philosophy, which was somewhere between

---

[15] In the Maximum Freight Rate decision the Supreme Court in 1897 decided that the Interstate Commerce Commission had no mandatory power to fix rates; and in the same year, in the Alabama Midland case, the Court interpreted the long-and-short-haul clause in such a way that it became ineffective.

independent and radical: "The railroads own many of our courts and other public bodies. Not because they have of necessity bought them by the expenditure of money; they have a different way of doing things. They see to it that the right men, the men of friendly inclinations, are elected." He added, in bitter emphasis upon the impotence to which court decisions had reduced his own office, supposed to regulate the railroads, "If the Interstate Commerce Commission were worth buying, the railroads would try to buy it. . . . The only reason they have not tried to purchase the Commission is that this body is valueless in its ability to correct railroad abuses."[16]

Hand in hand with the process by which the railroads overcame the Interstate Commerce Act of 1887, they guarded themselves against future legislation.[17] Railroad

[16] Interview in the Chicago *Record-Herald*, December 31, 1904. I quote Commissioner Prouty's statement because it expressed an emotion that was a part of the life of the time. That the statement was not judicial, and was emotional, shows on its face. I have neither read nor heard of any case of a Federal judge of any rank who was accused of having been bribed directly or indirectly by a railroad. When Commissioner Prouty says the railroads, through their power in politics, saw to it that judges of "friendly inclinations are elected," he necessarily cannot mean Federal judges, because no Federal judge is elected, all are appointed. As respects all courts, Commissioner Prouty's statement would be no less true, and would perhaps more accurately fit the facts, if instead of his phrase, "friendly inclinations," we use the phrase "conservative temperament" or "conservative habit of mind." What Commissioner Prouty says about the railroads "buying" the Interstate Commerce Commission, calls for the same understanding, that Prouty is speaking emotionally and figuratively, not literally. In the forty-three years of history that the Interstate Commerce Commission has had, there has been no charge of bribery or attempted "buying" by the railroads. The chairman of the Commission in 1929, Ernest I. Lewis, was able to say, "The reputation of the Commission has never been clouded by scandal." That the railroads sometimes sought, through their influence in politics, to bring about the appointment of commissioners sympathetic to the railroad point of view, may be taken for granted. They could not have been successful always, nor even often. The Commission has contained few men who were conspicuous for favoring the railroad point of view; it has contained several who were conspicuous for an attitude of sternness toward the railroads. (The reader will of course distinguish between the Interstate Commerce Commission and the Interstate Commerce Committee of the Senate. As to the latter, the statement of Senator Cullom that it was habitually "packed" with Senators likely to do no great harm to the railroads, accords with the common judgment.)

[17] "The [railroad men of the early period] did not hesitate to dominate gov-

lawyers and other representatives of railroad interests in the various States made themselves political bosses, or allied themselves with existing bosses. The bosses elected pliant legislatures, the legislatures sent to Washington Senators satisfactory to the railroads, in some cases lawyers who stepped from — if they did step wholly from — the office of railroad counsel to take their seats in the Senate. In the Senate, the railroads completed their chain of power by seeing to it that members favorable to them were placed upon the Interstate Commerce Committee. "The railroads had firmly determined to stop any further railroad regulation."[18]

The combined result of the success of the railroads' attacks in the courts upon the 1887 law, and of their prevention of the passage of new legislation by Congress, was a condition which the Interstate Commerce Commission formally described in its annual report for 1897: "Under the law as now interpreted, there is today and there can be no effective regulation of interstate carriers." As Roosevelt more tersely put it in his autobiography: "The law . . . was a dead letter."[19]

VI

The Pass, Its Potency and Its Passing

One of the means by which railroads prevented regulation of their rates or other legislation undesired by

ernment where they could." — Ernest I. Lewis, Chairman of the Interstate Commerce Commission, April 10, 1930.

[18] "The railroads had been very active in securing a change of the personnel of the Committee on Interstate Commerce, and men had been elected to the Senate and placed on that Committee whose sympathies were in favor of very conservative regulation, if any regulation at all." — Senator Shelby M. Cullom, explaining the defeat of a railroad rate bill in 1899.

[19] The emphasis which this chapter puts upon evils practised by the railroads tends to obscure most unjustly their really remarkable excellence in the function they performed. "In their management of their railroads," said a French observer, Pierre Leroy Beaulieu, in 1906, "the Americans have displayed at once the greatest ingenuity and the most remarkable faculty for organization, suc-

them was the pass.[20] "In the Pennsylvania State Senate, the representative of the Pennsylvania Railroad had a desk in the front row, alongside the secretary of the Senate; his business was to record requisitions and issue passes daily [i. e., "trip" passes for constituents — every member of the Senate had his own "annual" as a matter of course]; he was probably the most popular and important individual on the floor of the Senate, and participated in all its activities except the roll-calls. The same condition prevailed in other legislative bodies throughout the country."[21]

The pass was not only the railroads' buttress against legislation; it was their shield, in some cases, against unfavorable action by courts and unfriendly mention by newspapers. The system was intricate and practically universal.

In each State, as the 1st of every January approached, the railroads sent annual passes to the Governor and all State officials, to all the members of the legislature and, especially, to the heads and leaders of the two party organizations; in every community they delivered passes to the county or municipal officials, to the local officials of the two party organizations, to the newspaper editors, to practically every person in a position to influence either legislation, court decision, administrative action, or public opinion. If ever any one to whom a pass was tendered refused it, the case was apt to be that of an unusual temperament, or a most extraordinary conscience.

---

ceeding in reducing freight rates to an average of six mills per ton-mile, an average found in no European country, and but a third of the American average itself thirty years ago." — "The United States in the Twentieth Century."

[20] Analogous to the railroad pass were the telegraph frank, a perquisite cf the politically powerful, which permitted the sending of unlimited numbers of telegrams without payment; and the express frank. For an account of an express frank that had important political consequences, see page 218.

[21] Quoted from a letter written the author by a man long familiar with Pennsylvania politics, who has read the proofs of this chapter.

Far from being seen as a bribe or an impropriety, or a thing to conceal, the pass was regarded more nearly as an honor. Everywhere, to "flash a pass" on the railroad conductor was a gesture of distinction, of a sort — a sign of having arrived at some degree of power. To pay railroad fare was a mark of failure to emerge from the

The most inclusive railroad pass ever issued — to "Brigham Young and Family."

herd. "Men of high degree who would look with horror upon a direct bribe were as eager for passes as a dipsomaniac for drink."

Annual passes were but the beginning. Immediately below the top caste of the social system that carried "annuals," was an order composed of those who, by direct application or by negotiation through superiors, could get "trip passes." The ability of a member of the legislature, or any other political leader, to get trip passes for his constituents or partisans, was perhaps the most potent form of patronage he had. Any important political boss, such as Quay of Pennsylvania, could command trip passes by the thousand for the accommodation of such delegates as would support him in a State convention, and such hundreds of henchmen as would cheer him

from the galleries or chant his name in parades. "A political boss who has obtained and used for the purpose
of debauching his followers a bushel or more of passes

Front and reverse of the type of complimentary pass used on the Pennsylvania
Railroad until 1905, when the practice was discontinued.

is not likely to be indifferent to the expressed wish of the
railroad company for some new kind of crook in legislation, or the suppression of bills which ought not to
be suppressed. Thus the railroad company corrupted the

boss, and the boss added a new taint of putridity to the ancient corruption of the railroad company; and, both together, they put depravity into politics and filled the land with knavery. There is really no exaggeration in the assertion that no single influence proceeding from one source and operating in one direction has done so much to poison the very fountains of political life as the railroad free pass."[22]

The protest against political bosses that came to be called the Progressive movement had many roots, and its beginnings were too multifarious to be stated within a paragraph. But any fair outline of the sources and the history of that movement would list, as one important contribution, the part played by the pass in building up the boss system.

In every State, the railroads had legitimate need of a lawyer at the State capital or in some cases at the principal large city, supplemented by a local lawyer in each county seat, for the purposes, originally blameless, of looking after damage suits, taxation, and the like. These lawyers had power to requisition passes, often, likewise, for legitimate purposes—a farmer whose cow[23] had been killed by the engine would accept more readily a pass that would cost the railroad theoretically nothing, than the fifty or a hundred dollars that would be so much sub-

---

[22] From an editorial in the Philadelphia *North American,* 1905; paraphrased.

[23] A whole category of indigenous American humor grew up about the cow and the "cow-catcher," the latter being the vividly descriptive name of the locomotive's equivalent for what, in an automobile, is called, with equal vividness, the fender. No live cow of a farmer was ever so valuable, so blue-blooded, so good a milker, as the one killed on the railroad right-of-way. A cow that had been unsuccessful in disputing possession of the track with an oncoming locomotive automatically multiplied in value. In the farmer's claim for damages she took on all the bovine perfections and lost what earthly defects had been hers. There were reputed cases of hard-bitten old husbandmen who managed to lose six or eight cows in this way a year — the accidents usually occurring on moonless nights and the victims being, it was suspected by the worldly, worn out or sick stock.

There was likewise a category of native American humor that dealt with

tracted from the railroad treasury. Railroad lawyers thus equipped became persons of consequence, in politics as well as in the courts. Other corporations, following the

From the Philadelphia "Record."

A cartoonist's satire at the expense of the much maligned "Railroad Senators."

shrewd lead of the railroads, retained them, for purposes both political and legal; and thus their influence grew. Presently, in many States, the counsel or other representative of the railroad interests was the political boss of the State, and the local county representative was the

---

passes. A famous story, used by many an after-dinner speaker who wished to deal wittily with any character whose presence was less desired than his absence, was attributed to Chauncey M. Depew. Depew was head of the New York Central Railroad, and at the same time the road's ambassador to the world of legislation and politics. In that dual capacity he was at once the most magnificent bestower of passes in all history, and at the same time the most shrewdly discriminating. Upon being solicited for a round-trip pass to Chicago by one whose usefulness in New York City politics had been superseded by adeptness in importunity, Depew replied that he could not give the return trip — but would be most happy to facilitate a one-way trip to — Chicago or to any more distant point.

political boss of the county, and the whole was a vast pyramid of compact power, its base resting upon railroad passes, its peak at the very dome of the National Capitol.

One railroad, the Pennsylvania, had long been lavish with passes to Senators and Representatives in Congress; and also to Washington newspapermen, for whom it provided each year, in addition to ordinary passes, a free vacation of several days at a seaside hotel. "So far as I am concerned," said one Washington correspondent of that time, "if the Pennsylvania Railroad wants the Capitol Rotunda for a roundhouse they can have it."[24]

The Pennsylvania, during the prevalence of its lavishness with passes, had its station and some of its trackage in Washington on land owned by the government. When a new union station was projected, Congress co-operated handsomely with an appropriation of $1,500,-000. Whether Congress was amiably open-handed with the railroad in return for favors in the form of passes to individual Senators and Representatives, need not be asserted. That such was the case was, at that time, a common assumption,[25] an assumption less than fair to the railroad. At any time, in any case of the passage of legislation favorable to railroads, it was a question whether legislators were making payment for their passes — or

[24] A little later, when several Eastern roads abolished passes, the bereft beneficiaries of the railroads' former largesse were grievously provoked. Having been accustomed always to travel free, they found difficulty in achieving mental adjustment to the new order. To continue to travel free they would make their journeyings by roundabout routes on lines which continued to give passes. One trip of legend, perhaps more storied than authentic, from Washington to New York City, was said to have been made via St. Louis.

[25] There was legitimate justification for the appropriation by Congress of $1,500,000 to help build the Union Station, to serve not only the Pennsylvania but all railroads entering Washington. The station was conceived as, in part, a worthy ornament of the nation's capital, toward the construction of which the government could properly contribute; the station is in fact one of the loveliest buildings in America. Part of the government's contribution was for the elimination of grade crossings, which, in all cities, is regarded as a proper object of government contributi n.

whether, in their mental attitude, they insisted upon passes as the price of not being unfair to the railroads. It is a fact that many railroads, particularly after 1900, were a reluctant and coerced party to the exchange of passes for legislative indulgences and immunities.[26]

This pass, made of gold, was issued by the builder of the road to his daughter. Another on the same road was of solid silver. They suggest the glamour that went with power in the railroad world and with the giving and receiving of passes, until the custom was discontinued in 1906.

By the early 1900's the whole pass system had become distasteful to the railroads. Railroad managers came to doubt whether the friendship of those who received passes balanced the animosity of those who were denied them. Also, the practice had acquired such dimensions that some trains did not carry enough paying passengers to defray their costs — President Cassatt of the Pennsylvania produced figures to show that the passes issued in a year made a difference of a million dollars in the gross earnings of his road. Furthermore, the railroads

[26] Leonor Fresnel Loree, president of the Delaware & Hudson Railroad, comments shrewdly, and accurately : Passes "came to be regarded as normal perquisites of public office and business prominence. Long before 1906 they had ceased to be the occasion for gratitude, much less for reciprocal favors. It had become possible to offend by refusing them. In other words, passes had become much like the schoolboy's definition of salt, which he said, 'is something that spoils potatoes by not putting it on.'"

had long been under fire for giving rebates to favored shippers, and now the giving of passes had come to be regarded as another public grievance. In intervals when those who disapproved of passes got temporary control of legislatures or town councils, legislation was passed adverse to the railroads, some of it attempting occasionally to forbid or limit the giving of passes to public officials.

Finally, some railroads, convinced that the pass had become more a liability than an asset, decided to get rid of it. The directors of the Pennsylvania, on December 13, 1905, resolved "that the issue of passes and free tickets of all kinds be discontinued from and after 1st January next."[27] Like action was taken a day later by the Philadelphia and Reading, the Central Railroad of New Jersey, and the New York Central. Later and slowly, the movement spread to some other roads.[28]

Whether the voluntary abolition of passes by some railroads was a wise gesture toward placating public opinion, or whether it was an imprudent surrender of their chief defense against undesired legislation, became, in the light of some subsequent happenings, a controverted question.

That it was the latter was the sad belief of a cynical spokesman, the editor[29] of *The Wall Street Journal*, who, writing in 1925, said that the abolition of passes

[27] There were exceptions, in favor of "directors and their wives and children living under their roofs . . . as well as officers and employees and members of their families living with them and dependent upon them."

[28] Not all the roads discontinued passes voluntarily; complete passing of the pass came only by Federal statute, in June, 1906.

[29] William Peter Hamilton. Hamilton deplored the assent by the railroads to the abolition of passes as an unwisdom, uneconomical either in the political sense or the financial one. The passes, he thought, were not really a material expense to the railroads, because most of the " 'deadheads' would have stayed at home if they had not received their transportation for nothing; it is highly improbable that any railroad ever ran an extra train, or even an extra coach, to accommodate holders of passes. . . . It was corrupting or not, according as you look at it, but the ban on passes was, upon the whole, the most expensive enforcement of a somewhat pharisaical virtue this country has ever seen."

"was in its consequences perhaps the most devastating blow our railroads ever sustained. . . . Its provocative effect, its deadly force [is] obvious to anybody who knows the influences which control American politics." "Without a single exception," this financial editor said (with a superlativeness of terms that suggests some danger to truth), "without distinction of creed, or color, the hand of every politician was turned against the railroads." Citing statistics to prove his assertion, this authority pointed out that after the abolition of passes, "new [State] regulatory commissions were created in about thirty States, while the others brought their powers up to what might, without temper or offense, be called the persecution level. In the prohibition of passes, virtue was its own — and only — reward."

That judgment is rather too confident to be certainly sound. The movement toward regulation of rates, State as well as Federal, had too strong a momentum by 1906 to be entirely headed off, though its rapidity may have been accelerated by the abolition of passes.

That there was a relation of cause and effect between the abolition of passes and the proposal for regulation of railroad rates by the Federal Government was occasionally asserted at the time; it was epitomized by the New York *Sun*, January 8, 1906, in a head-line:

MAY RETALIATE ON RAILROADS
CONGRESSMEN HURT BY THE CUTTING OFF OF PASSES

It is of record that within a month after the railroads began to abolish passes, in December, 1905, began also the climactic fight in Congress for a law to regulate railroad rates. The coincidence will not bear portrayal as isolated cause and effect. Abolition of passes undoubtedly — to express it accurately — took away from some members of Congress (and from politicians everywhere) a sense of obligation to the railroads. But this fact should not be given more than contributory weight. More important was the action of Theodore Roosevelt, who about the same time threw himself wholeheartedly into the fight for Federal rate regulation.

VII

LaFollette

The actions of men who exercised their ambitions and talents in the building and managing of railroads created opportunity for other men, who exercised other ambitions and other talents in the world of politics. Thus there arose, especially in the Midwest, certain political leaders violently antagonistic to the railroads, whose anti-railroad agitation, spreading east and west and south, infected most of the country. One among these stood out, not necessarily because of his greater wisdom, more because of certain personal qualities.

Robert M. LaFollette by birth had the temperament of a dramatic tragedian. By the circumstances of his youth he acquired a sense of resentment against cosmos that made him a crusader. Because of the conditions of his time and place, he took the railroads as the object of his crusading zeal. His anti-railroad bias came early. "As a boy on the farm," he wrote,[30] "I heard and felt this [anti-railroad] movement . . . swirling about me; and I felt the indignation which it expressed in such a way that I suppose I have never fully lost the effect of that early impression."

The French in LaFollette's blood that made him instinctively dramatic might have been contented by his winning of intercollegiate contests with his orations on

[30] "A Personal Narrative of Political Experiences," Robert M. LaFollette.

"Iago" and by his early lecturing on "Hamlet," as sufficient satisfaction to the urge for self-expression that was
strong in him. But if we were to carry the symbolism
about inherited characteristics farther, we might say

that the French in him,
happening to be Huguenot,
caused him to have a high
susceptibility to infection
from "causes," an almost
overready disposition to dissent from whatever was accepted and orthodox, eco-
nomically or politically,
and an almost perverse bent
toward visualizing himself
in the rôle of martyr. With
this emotional and moral
equipment, he found his
medium for functioning
ready and present in the political and economic practices of the railroads.

The Senator from Wisconsin.

LaFollette was born June
14, 1855, on a farm near
Primrose, Wis., in a two-room log cabin. In his later
life he had a drawing made of his cabin birthplace,
which he used in his campaign literature when running
for office, satisfying thus a political instinct which led
him to capitalize early poverty, and expressing a personal quality that caused him to take an almost mor-
bidly luxurious pleasure in the endurance of hardship,
in the recollection of it, and in the public parading of
it. At the University of Wisconsin, as a "scrub," an outsider, a non-fraternity man, he endured experiences of a
sort that most boys quickly forgive and ultimately for-

get, but which in LaFollette's case left memories that, forty years later, flowed acidly out of his pen as he wrote his autobiography, causing him to recall and record his "overmastering sense of anger and wrong and injustice." For his early education he paid the price of hard sacrifice and gained — as those do who survive — the reward of a stiffened will-power. The inconspicuousness of his stature, mocking his passion for distinction, he overcame somewhat by adopting the "pompadour"[31] style of arranging his hair, which he retained until he died. When he came to the Senate, acting on the advice of a friend, he abandoned the "slouchiness" of attire that had been one of his studied arts for appealing to a rural constituency, and thereafter, until the end of his days, was the most carefully dressed man in whatever forums he functioned in.[32]

A dog-eared copy of Henry George's "Progress and Poverty," loaned to LaFollette by a philosophical blacksmith neighbor, stimulated the youth's grim zest for combat against injustice. At the University of Wisconsin he got the grounding in economics and government that later enabled him to make vivid to farmer audiences the intricacies of the effects of railroad rates on their own fortunes; no public man of his day equalled him in the energy with which he dug into economic data or in the skill with which he made statistics support and

[31] When Bob LaFollette with defiant glare
Leaps forth to smite the foemen of his land,
Five feet he soars into the zenith and
Six inches farther soars his fretful hair.
Of his fierce clay there was not much to spare
When stingy nature framed him . . .
A capsule statesman with a whirlwind's way.
—From a sonnet by George Fitch.

[32] Albert J. Beveridge, Senator from Indiana, told me that when LaFollette came to the Senate, Beveridge, already a Senator for six years and having a concern at once for the Senate's dignity and LaFollette's fortunes, went privately to the latter and addressed to him Chesterfieldian advice, beginning, "Robert, you are now a Senator of the United States; dress the part."

confirm his theories. A chance reading of one of Robert Ingersoll's speeches, followed by going to hear every lecture of that great rebel against orthodoxy that he could get to, and the reading of every word Ingersoll published, "entranced" LaFollette, left him with "tears streaming down my face" and inspired him to perfect his own arts of emotional oratory and to emulate Ingersoll's dogma of protest.[33]

By the time LaFollette could vote he had a rare equipment for insurgent leadership. Immediately after leaving college he ran for District Attorney of Dane County; resented the implication of inferiority when farmers asked him "Ain't you over-young?"; resented more the insult of the local boss, outpost of the railroad political machine, who told him, "You are fooling away your time"; was elected by 93 votes; suffered a breakdown at the end of each term of court, and when "too weak to walk I had myself rolled in a blanket and driven to the court-house."

In 1884, he won the Republican nomination and then the election to Congress, against the opposition and conniving of the local party boss. In 1886, he won again, and in 1888 yet again, but in 1890 suffered a defeat that engendered in him a "bitter emotion," and caused him — with curious misunderstanding of his own nature — to decide to give up his political career and be content with a private lawyer's life of dull briefing and court-

[33] Robert Ingersoll was familiar to the America of that generation in two rôles, as an unbeliever who aggressively attacked all churches, and as a political orator whose ornateness satisfied the taste of the 1870's and 1880's. In the latter rôle, he gave currency to a famous characterization of James G. Blaine:

"Our country, crowned with the vast and marvellous achievements of its first century, asks for a man worthy of the past, and prophetic of her future; asks for a man who has the audacity of genius; asks for a man who is the grandest combination of heart, conscience, and brain beneath her flag — such a man is James G. Blaine. . . . Like an armed warrior, like a plumed knight, James G. Blaine marched down the halls of the American Congress and threw his shining lance full and fair against the brazen foreheads of the defamers of his country and the maligners of his honor."

house wrangling. Fate hurriedly sent an agent in the shape of a reigning head of the State's railroad political machine who, according to LaFollette's subsequent story, tried to bribe him to influence his brother-in-law,

From a photograph © by G. V. Buck, Washington.
Senator Robert M. LaFollette of Wisconsin.

a judge, in the matter of a decision. It was a queer blind-spot in an experienced political boss which would let him imagine that LaFollette would prefer a few hundred dollars to the luxury of the impassioned indignation with which LaFollette spurned the bribe, denounced the briber, made the story public, and used the episode as the spring-board for a spectacular re-entry into politics.

By about 1895 LaFollette was set in the intellectual, moral, and emotional mould that determined his rôle in national politics. In whatever stand he took on any issue, he was always dramatic and heroic, ever the crusader against wrong, eternally the champion of the under-dog (whom he dramatized as wholly virtuous and always right). He visualized himself, and insisted that his followers regard him, as the faithful servant of the people, the chosen of fate to lead moral causes — most of the moral causes of the time and place being embraced in one, opposition to the railroads. Three times he ran for Governor, making the issues mainly regulation of the railroads, heavier taxation upon them, abolition of the passes with which they kept their political power — and a proposal for a novel "direct primary," which should supplant the convention system and thereby render impotent the political bosses.

In LaFollette's second campaign for Governor he had the advantage of an episode that made vivid one of his issues. The local agent of the United States Express Company at Madison, the State capital, infected with resentment against railroad practices to a point where he forgot his obligation to keep his employer's secrets, revealed that LaFollette's opponent, the sitting Governor, Edward Scofield, in the course of a lavish gubernatorial indulgence in passes and franks, had shipped from his home in Oconto, on express frank No. 2,169:

> 2 boxes, 2 barrels; January 7, 1897.
> 3 barrels, 1 box; January 8, 1897.
> 2 boxes, 200 pounds; January 9, 1897.
> 2 barrels, 2 boxes, 1000 pounds; January 11, 1897.

And, finally,

> 1 cow (crated); January 13, 1897.

It was not against the law, and most decidedly it was

not contrary to the accepted usage of politicians — but it was against, so to speak, the average man's equilibrium of sedateness, and gave rise to that powerful weapon of politics, ridicule. "Scofield's cow" became famous, the best-known animal of any species from Kenosha to Menomonie. Her likeness, beaming ruminatively from the first pages of newspapers, outdid in vote-getting effectiveness LaFollette's own grim countenance upon his campaign banners; but, unfortunately, her political potency, the greatest ever achieved by any bovine, was sterilized, so LaFollette alleged,[34] by his opponents' distribution of $8,300 among the delegates to the convention on the night before the balloting on candidates. Her memory lingered, however. Two years later, in 1900, when LaFollette, with a pertinacity that was part of his unyielding grimness, again sought the governorship, he was elected by the largest majority in Wisconsin history.

As Governor, LaFollette, after years of denunciation of the boss system, was himself the boss of Wisconsin. He was a boss of a new and utterly different type, who worked always in the interest of the common man as he saw it, who discarded the sordid methods of the older type — and yet a boss, autocratic, imperious, peremptory, practising toward his apostles a dictatorial insistence upon obedience such as no boss of the older type would ever have dared attempt. Whoever opposed him, whoever disagreed with him, became, *ipso facto*, one with Lucifer. Whoever, having once been with him, thereafter failed to give 100 per cent allegiance to every one of LaFollette's courses, by that fact became guilty certainly of sedition and presumably of corruption, and was exiled and pursued with a ruthlessness even greater than LaFollette practised against his avowed enemies. He was all grimness. It is doubtful if LaFollette, in

[34] "A Personal Narrative of Political Experiences," Robert M. LaFollette.

his mature life, ever threw back his head and laughed, heartily. The streak in him that made the wearing of a hair shirt a pleasure, that made of martyrdom a luxury, he expressed by reciting often, as his favorite poem:

> Out of the night that covers me,
> Black as the pit from pole to pole,
> I thank whatever gods there be
> For my unconquered soul.[35]

LaFollette's governorship was one long controversy. He harried a legislature that was at first reluctant and tricky into enacting heavier taxation upon the railroads,[36] an inheritance tax, a graduated income tax, a direct primary law, a railroad regulation bill that "provided for a commission with power not only to fix rates but to control service and to make a complete physical valuation of all the railroad property in the State; it was more sweeping than any legislation enacted by any State up to that time."[37]

But much more than by his official acts as Governor, and in a territory that extended far beyond the boundaries

---

[35] This is as LaFollette recited it and as he printed it in his autobiography. Actually, the last two lines of Henley's verse read:

> I thank whatever gods *may* be,
> For my *unconquerable* soul.

[36] While LaFollette, in his campaign attacks upon the railroads, was bitter, the legislation which he fathered while Governor of Wisconsin was comparatively temperate. At that time LaFollette realized, and guided himself by the realization, that fair dealing with the railroads was necessary for the prosperity of the State. His extreme radicalism with respect to the railroads came after he was in the Senate, and was caused, in the judgment of the writer, supported by the judgment of some of LaFollette's intimates, by the relation he adopted toward Roosevelt. LaFollette hated Roosevelt, primarily because Roosevelt took the leadership of an issue that LaFollette had made. LaFollette would follow no leader, must at all times be the leader himself. It was not difficult for LaFollette to make himself believe that he must go farther than Roosevelt, must repudiate Roosevelt's leadership, must even decry Roosevelt's leadership as too conservative, to the end that LaFollette himself might be the leader of the Progressive cause. But for Roosevelt, LaFollette, perhaps, would not have been more radical in the Senate than he was in Wisconsin, which is the same as to say that but for Roosevelt, LaFollette might have had some chance to become President.

[37] "A Personal Narrative of Political Experiences," Robert M. LaFollette.

of Wisconsin, LaFollette by his campaigns, by the paper
The State that he and his friends conducted, and by literally thousands of campaign speeches, as well as lyceum
and Chautauqua lectures that he delivered up and down
the country — LaFollette, with the aid of other leaders, gave to the old Granger anti-railroad movement a
momentum that by 1906 had reached the proportions
and the characteristics of what politicians call — at once
a vivid description and an acknowledgment of readiness
to run for shelter — a "prairie-fire."

As one brand flung off by the now nation-wide conflagration, LaFollette himself was elected to the United
States Senate, where he took his seat on January 4, 1906.
In the Senate the Republican "stand-patters" who were
then in control, bestowed on the young David, with a
humor not entirely discreet, the chairmanship of the
"Committee to Investigate the Condition of the Potomac
River Front (Select)," which in all its history "had
never had a bill referred to it, and had never held a meeting." His committee-room, so he dourly told his constituents through his weekly periodical and in a chapter
of his autobiography (which, with his love of dramatiz-
ing himself as a martyr, he called "Alone in the Senate"), "was reached by going down into the sub-cellar of
the Capitol, along a dark winding passage lighted by
dim skylights which leaked badly, to a room carved out
of the terrace on the west side of the Capitol." Actually,
LaFollette's committee-room was more desirable than
those assigned to other new Senators.[38]

[38] LaFollette arrived in the Senate January 4, 1906, about a month after the
session began. Another Senator, who had arrived at the opening early in the
preceding December, read LaFollette's description of his committee-room here
quoted, and wrote (to the author of this history): "No! LaFollette had an
outside room fronting the west and overlooking the grass and tree covered
grounds. For this better room, LaFollette was indebted to his colleague, Senator Spooner, who detested LaFollette but held this room for him although it
was coveted by new Senators already sworn in, who had been given rooms in
the basement of the Capitol, or over at the Senate Annex, the Senate office-
building not then being in existence."

LaFollette's arrival in the Senate coincided, almost to the exact day, with the introduction of the (Hepburn) railroad rate bill in the House, and with Roosevelt's determination to drive that bill through Congress. LaFollette was too new in the Senate, and also too mordantly radical, to have much hand in shaping that legislation. Indeed, his incapacity to co-operate with other men, his suspicion against all men whose notions did not coincide identically with his, made LaFollette a handicap rather than a help to Roosevelt — the time came when LaFollette deliberately embarrassed Roosevelt. But the prairie-fire of anti-railroad feeling that LaFollette had been building in the Midwest over a period of ten years, was one of the causes of the public demand for rate regulation that Roosevelt took up. It was also one of the principal agencies that Roosevelt had to aid him in the fight.

VIII

Roosevelt, becoming President by accident, through the assassination of McKinley in September, 1901, found himself head of a party that had not, nationally, taken notice of the country's anti-railroad sentiment, a party, indeed, that, except locally in a few States, was sympathetic to the whole nexus of conservative interests of which the railroads composed the principal element. It was the Democratic party that had taken the anti-railroad side, had, in its platforms of 1896 and 1900, demanded and promised relief from railroad inequities. Roosevelt almost immediately began a series of steps with respect to railroads and other corporate business interests, which in their entirety composed one of the historically most important aspects of the Roosevelt era, the gradual separation of the Republican party from the conservative point of view, its ultimate complete identification, by the time Roosevelt's Presidency ended, with a point of view which the political thought of the time denominated "Progressive."[39]

Within three months after his accession to the Presidency, Roosevelt, in his first message to Congress, December, 1901, proposed relief from one specific railroad inequity, the granting by railroads of rebates to favored shippers.[40] This, Congress, a little over a year later, enacted.[41] In 1904 and 1905, Roosevelt, in several speeches in various parts of the country, laid down a policy of broad and effective regulation of railroad rates. Upon the assembling of Congress in December, 1905, he demanded in his message "some scheme to secure to . . . the government supervision and regulation of the rates charged by the railroads."

Characteristically, as an accurate expression of his fundamental and rarely interrupted avoidance of radicalism, Roosevelt surrounded and cushioned and balanced his demand with safeguarding assurances: "I should emphatically protest against improperly radical or hasty action. I do not believe in the government interfering with private business any more than is necessary. Let me most earnestly say that these recommendations are not made in any spirit of hostility to the railroads. On ethical grounds, on grounds of right, such hostility would be intolerable; and on grounds of mere

[39] In the process, Roosevelt, on many occasions, was in a position laying him open to charges made by Bryan, good-humoredly even if a little ruefully, that he was stealing the Democrats' property.

[40] The practice was commonly so described; actually, it was quite as often a case of the railroads yielding unwillingly to demands by large shippers for favorable rates. More than any railroad, or all of them, the agency most responsible for rebates on an enormous scale had been Andrew Carnegie, who used the immensity of the shipments he controlled as a leverage to exact concessions from the railroads.

[41] The Elkins Act, 1903.

national self-interest we must remember . . . a multitude of small investors, a multitude of railway employees, wage-workers, the public as a whole. This legislation should be enacted in a spirit as remote as possible from hysteria and rancor."

Roosevelt's proposal indeed could be regarded as having the purpose of protecting the railroads, and the institution of private property, by warding off demands for more drastic action. "In my judgment," he said, taking account of a type of radical sentiment that Bryan was shortly to propose, "public ownership of railroads is highly undesirable and would probably in this country entail far-reaching disaster."

For his reasonableness, Roosevelt, as is often the fate of one who takes the middle of the road, received bricks from both sides. His action was denounced by LaFollette and other spokesmen of anti-railroad sentiment, as a weak expedient, an odious compromise. From the side of the railroads and their allied interests, Roosevelt's proposal was attacked as, in the words of their principal spokesman in the Senate, Foraker of Ohio, "contrary to the spirit of our institutions and of such drastic and revolutionary character that . . . the consequences are likely to be most unusual and far-reaching."

The railroads and their allied interests charged that Roosevelt's proposal was an assault upon the rights of private property. Because the railroads so interpreted it, the average man regarded it as a rescue of himself and his interests from what he had come to visualize corporate private property and its practices as being — regarded it as his fight against the head, heart, and all the tentacles of organized wealth. The railroads' network of lines up and down the continent composed the picture of far-flung power which the people had been taught to call the "Octopus";[42] their alliances, through interlocking directorates, with banks, insurance companies and industrial corporations, and the alliance of all these combined with politics, composed what flamed through the political controversy of the time as "The System"; their intrenched advantages, gained and held through their hold on Congress and legislatures, were the "Vested Interests" and, in LaFollette's phrase, "Special Privilege"; their owners, including those who manipulated them, and the bankers who participated, were, in the phrase of the sensational Hearst press, the "Plunderbund."

The sum of which was, that to fight the railroads was to fight, practically without exception, all[43] the organized wealth in the United States. Wealth had, as its spokesmen, generals, and lieutenants much more than half of the Republican membership of the Senate, including nearly all the abler ones and, without exception, all the Senators who held the key places of power on committees. Wealth had also on its side, at the beginning, many Democratic Senators, some because they were, as much as any Republicans, willing servants of power, and others because they clung to the traditional

---

[42] "Octopus" was used sometimes to conjure up radiating railroad lines, sometimes the intricate network of the pipe-lines of the Standard Oil Company.

By some curious law of human nature or of argumentation, while an assailant of the railroads could stir up angry emotion by using "octopus" as an epithet of odium, nevertheless a defender of the railroads could, and Congressman Charles E. Littlefield of Maine often did, get a laugh and win a momentary controversial trick by speaking of a single railroad, or a single corporation, as "one of the octopi."

[43] Exception to this sentence is taken by one of the railroad presidents who has read this chapter. It is true that railroad rate regulation was in the interest of that portion of wealth which was identical with shippers and manufacturers. But on the side of the railroads were the owners of railroad securities, the great private bankers and most of the national banks, the trust companies, the insurance companies, the great express companies which were controlled by the railroads, the capitalists who had much of their wealth in the form of railroad securities. Even some of the greatest shippers were more interested in railroads than in their shipping or manufacturing businesses.

Democratic policy of opposition to concentration of power in the Federal Government.

IX

The bill indorsed by Roosevelt was introduced in the House on January 4, 1906 (by Representative "Pete" Hepburn from a district in Iowa, where anti-railroad feeling was especially strong), in the atmosphere of a universal understanding, proclaimed proudly by friends, resentfully by enemies, that it was a Roosevelt bill — "an administration measure," said one enemy, Senator Foraker of Ohio, with italicized and punctuated emphasis, *"which was to be passed without amendment, just as it was introduced!"*[44]

It was passed by the House — not without amendment but with a committee amendment that made it more drastic. It was passed by a vote of 346 to 7 — a majority which should have been dismaying to the railroads but was not, because the railroads believed and were assured by the New York *Sun:* "The House may go through the form of moulding a hasty measure but . . . the Senate will not; no railway rate bill will be passed by the Fifty-Ninth Congress." The House at that time was the only one of the two bodies elected directly by the people, and was therefore regarded contemptuously by the railroads and conservatives generally as reflecting the mob; while the Senate, being elected by State legislatures,[45] was regarded as a safe city of refuge.

From the House, the bill went to the Senate; in the Senate it went, in the routine way, first to the Committee on Interstate Commerce. There drama began. The Committee was dominated, of course, by the Republicans (since they were the majority party); it was domi-

[44] "Notes of a Busy Life," Joseph Benson Foraker.
[45] Direct election of Senators by the people did not come until 1913.

nated by those particular Republicans who had been put
upon it for the precise purpose of acting as a bulwark
against railroad rate regulation.[46] To that purpose they
now dedicated themselves — with an extraordinary and

From "The Tribune" (Minneapolis).

Trying to block his way. One of the innumerable cartoons printed during
Roosevelt's Presidency which pictured the opposition to Roosevelt's
policies in the unflattering guise of serpents, devil-fish, and the like.

ingenious adaptation of their political and parliamentary
skill to the conditions that confronted them.

Chairman of the Committee was Elkins of West Virginia, a railroad owner and official himself, able in his
personality and powerful in the Republican "Old
Guard." By every rule, precedent, and propriety, if the

[46] "A majority of Senators placed on the Committee on Interstate Commerce
were men whose sympathies were with the railroads." — Senator Shelby M.
Cullom, "Fifty Years of Public Service."

Republicans were going to work in normal harmony
with their own President, it was Chairman Elkins's function to take charge of the bill, to give it his sponsorship
and even his name, to pilot it through the Committee,

and thereafter to steer it
through the Senate. But Elkins disavowed the measure,
thereby making it a nameless
orphan, and, from the official Republican point of
view, a tainted outcast.

Another Republican
member of the Committee
was Aldrich of Rhode Isl-
and. Aldrich came closer
than any other Senator at
that time, or before or since,
to living up to the appella-
tion hurled at him by his
enemies as an epithet and
accepted by his friends as a
compliment, "boss of the

Senator Nelson W. Aldrich of
Rhode Island.

Senate." He was the official floor leader for the Republican majority, chairman of two powerful key committees, Rules and Finance; he wielded such power in
the Republican party as to make his word a fiat to every
orthodox party man. Because of his hold on the key
places of power, his ability, his forceful personality,
and his twenty-five years' experience in the Senate, Aldrich was called by admirers the "manager of the United
States," coming, said one of them, "nearer to filling
that rôle than even the President himself." But titles,
official or unofficial, carried little glamour in Aldrich's
cold eyes. For the power that Aldrich exercised ruthlessly he depended upon the vigor of his leadership, the

discipline he enforced upon the Republican organization, his astuteness as a political strategist, his expertness and experience as a parliamentary tactician.

The making of laws, as an attribute of power, is no more important than the prevention of laws — and to preventing the passage of the rate bill, Aldrich now dedicated himself. The measure having been made an orphan by Elkins, Aldrich now completed its odium by putting upon it an undesired paternity. Aldrich, privately denouncing the bill as "infamous," but publicly taking the high ground that since he and other Republicans did not approve it, they should honorably avoid taking responsibility for it — Aldrich

From "The Inter-Ocean" (Chicago), 1908.
A cartoonist's conception of Senator Tillman in action.

moved and succeeded in passing a resolution which threw it into the sponsorship of the ranking Democrat on the Committee, thereby making the bill a Democratic measure, and putting its fortunes in charge of a Democrat. Not merely a Democrat, but such a Democrat! Tillman, "Pitchfork Ben," of South Carolina! "Pitchfork Ben," arch-enemy, political and personal, of Roosevelt. The opponents of the bill huzzaed their glee; now surely it would be wrecked in the Senate. Upon the railroads and their friends in the Senate, elation and

confidence settled serenely; upon the small group of
Roosevelt Senators pessimism descended — they were
more than half convinced that for that year the battle
had been lost.

Co-operation between a President belonging to one
party and leaders of the other is always difficult, contains at every moment the seeds of the failure that Aldrich planned for. Into such an adventure both participants are reluctant to enter, do so only under the compulsion of necessity, and throughout the negotiations
watch each other suspiciously. Each knows that the
other's permanent tie to his own party is more binding
than the temporary alliance, and each keeps an alert eye
upon the other, aware of the danger, always imminent,
that the other may at any moment make a compromise
within his own party that is more alluring than the bi-
party effort. A Democratic leader in the Senate, co-
operating with a Republican President, is always conscious of the possibility that the latter may use the
Democrats as a lever with which to achieve compromise
with his own party, always apprehensive that the end of
the episode may see the Republicans clasped to each
other's bosoms with a warmth made greater by the temporary estrangement, and always faced with the possibility that in the end his motives may be impugned, his
very honesty be questioned.

In short, such an enterprise as was forced upon Roosevelt and Tillman by Aldrich's manœuvre is inevitably
attended by an atmosphere not favorable to success.[47] It

<hr/>

[47] Roosevelt in his "Autobiography" alluded to this episode: "There were two
or three amusing features in the contest. In the Senate it was referred to a
committee in which the Republican majority was under the control of Senator
Aldrich, who took the lead in opposing the bill. The leading Democrat on the
committee was Senator Tillman of South Carolina, with whom I was not on
good terms. Senator Tillman favored the bill. The Republican majority in the

is so under the best of circumstances — and the present case included circumstances decidedly not the best.

Not only was it grotesque to see a Republican President's pet bill put in charge of a Democrat; not only was it novel and a little ridiculous to see a Republican President obliged to co-operate with a Democratic Senator and to depend on a Democratic minority; in addition Aldrich's trick had a peculiar and subtle flavor.

Everybody knew there was a personal feud between Roosevelt and Tillman, a feud of long standing, that had come to a climax in a sensational affront by Roosevelt to Tillman. The two were antipathetic by temperament, antithetic in every detail of their politics and personal circumstances. As long before as the Presidential campaign of 1896, Roosevelt had described Tillman in a widely circulated magazine article as an "embodied retribution on the South for having failed to educate the cracker, the poor white." He had charged, with a manner of superiority acutely galling to Tillman, that "Mr. Tillman's brother has been frequently elected to Congress on the issue that he never wore an overcoat or an undershirt."[48] After Roosevelt had become President, he invited Tillman, a member of the Naval Committee of the Senate, to a dinner given by Roosevelt to the head of the German Navy, Prince Henry of Prussia, brother of Kaiser Wilhelm; and Tillman had accepted. A few days before the dinner, Tillman had inopportunely engaged in a quarrel on the Senate floor with a fellow Senator, McLaurin, a quarrel in which words had proved

---

committee under Senator Aldrich, when they acted adversely on the bill, turned it over to Senator Tillman, thereby making him its sponsor. The object was to create what it was hoped would be an impossible situation in view of the relations between Senator Tillman and myself. I regarded the action as simply childish."

[48] *Review of Reviews,* September, 1896.

insufficient for adequate expression of the convictions of the disputants. Roosevelt, showing lack of enthusiasm for combat when engaged in on the Senate floor, and by others than himself, had withdrawn his dinner invitation to Tillman. For four years the two had not spoken

Senator "Ben" Tillman.

to each other, but had said much about each other, especially Tillman, whose occasional way of "letting off steam" from an irritated mood on the Senate floor, was to hurl a few savage epithets at Roosevelt in the White House. "The crossing of the big stick and the pitchfork," said the Milwaukee *Sentinel*, in anticipation of a later engagement between the two, "should make a hot and spectacular finish; our fear is that epithet for epithet, tabasco for tabasco, whoop for whoop, Roosevelt will be scolded to a frazzle by the past master in vituperation from the Palmetto State."

By Aldrich's trick, therefore, the railroad bill was given a status such that its enactment could only be achieved by co-operation between the two men, two who not only belonged to opposing parties, who not only had a personal feud, but who were the two men in public life to whom compromise of a feud was temperamentally most difficult; Roosevelt with his berserker belligerence — once he said to the writer of this history: "I suppose I do overdo it, but when I'm mad at a man I want to climb right up his chest"; and Tillman with his fire-eating reputation, his nickname of "Pitchfork," his one blind eye that completed the bellicosity of his overhanging forehead. To these two, with their enmity now made conspicuous by jeering newspapers, the fate of the railroad rate bill was committed.

Roosevelt had many arts for meeting the discomfitures and awkwardnesses that were either the frequent fruit of his own impetuousness or were forced upon him by circumstances untoward or malicious, arts that included sometimes grim silence, sometimes grinning admission of the ridiculousness of his plight, sometimes a shrug of the shoulders that threw off as much of the difficulty as he could and salvaged as much as could be saved from the situation. On this occasion he perforce made the best of it, said he didn't "care a rap" who had charge of the bill or would get the credit for it — he would work with any one for a good end. Tillman said, "I don't propose that this thing shall be turned into a circus with me as the clown," and embarked earnestly about the work of piloting the bill through the Senate.

Roosevelt, after a little, began to wave coyly flirtatious signals toward Tillman through newspaper headlines. He was quoted as saying that Tillman was "an honest man and a hard fighter," and that he, Roosevelt, would be glad to co-operate with anybody who wanted the right kind of rate bill. On February 24, 1906, Roosevelt inspired a newspaper story which, as reported in the New York *Sun*, said: "The President will be ready to see Mr. Tillman if the South Carolina Senator should call at the White House." To this Tillman replied gruffly, also through the indirect channel of a newspaper despatch: "Senator Tillman showed some impatience this evening when asked if he had seen the President. He replied that he had not been to the White House since the bill was committed to his keeping, and saw no necessity for going."

On February 26, 1906, Tillman reported the rate bill out of the Committee on Interstate Commerce, launched it upon the Senate floor — with himself in charge of its destiny, and with practically every important "stand-pat" Republican leader in the Senate opposed, prepared to beat it if they could, and if they could not beat it, to emasculate it.

x

Roosevelt Takes to Head-Lines

Foreclosed from fighting within the Senate, or at least handicapped, Roosevelt used, outside the Senate, the superb art he had of stirring up sentiment through the newspapers.[49] Even before the ultimate battle over the rate bill began, so early as August, 1905, the newspapers, normally recording the activities Roosevelt engaged in, the events and movements he stimulated, reported "Interstate Commerce Commission Begins Investigation of Combinations Between Railroads and Private Car Lines." On December 5, they reported Roosevelt's message to Congress with its demand for legislation to "prevent unreasonable and unjustifiable rates"; on December 11, that "Attorney-General Moody Directs All United States Attorneys to Prosecute All Railroads Shown to be Giving Rebates." As the rate bill fight grew hot, investigations that had been initiated months before by Roosevelt or agencies under him, together

[49] "After three or four months of strenuous fighting here between the contending forces . . . a great hurrah and furore in the papers were made about the Standard Oil Company and its iniquitous methods, and we were told that the exposure of the crimes of that monopoly would help the vote on the rate bill against the railroad view of it." — Senator Tillman, June 29, 1906.

with court actions and miscellaneous movements he had incited, provided from time to time such head-lines as

PROSECUTE RAILROADS NEXT

and

NEW YORK, THURSDAY, JUNE 21, 1906.—*Copyright, 1906, by*

AFTER A RAILROAD PRESIDENT

ROOSEVELT HOPES TO CONVICT ONE OR MORE.

Thinks the Example Thus Set Would Be Wholesome Check on Rebaters—Cassatt and Other Big Railroad Men Not to Appear Before Interstate Commission.

WASHINGTON, June 20.—Big men of the railroad world are not expected to appear at the hearing to be held to-morrow by the Interstate Commerce Commission, which is investigating the relations of the railroads to the coal and oil industries. Advices received here are to the effect that Presidents Cassatt of the Pennsylvania, Newman of the New York Central, Stevens

FOUR YEARS FOR CONGRESSMEN.

Proposed Amendment to the Constitution Fails to Pass the House.

WASHINGTON, June 20.—A new proposition for a constitutional amendment to govern the election of Senators and Representatives in Congress was sprung upon the House of Representatives to-day. Mr. Norris of Nebraska moved to suspend the rules and pass his bill to elect Senators by a direct vote of the people and to extend the term of Representatives to four years. The last part of the bill came as a surprise to the members, who largely opposed it. Mr. Cockran of New York alone of those addressing the House, aside from the proposer spoke in its favor. He advocated it for the reason that under present conditions the House was organized incapacity and disorder, and the principal cause of that was the brevity of the term of the members. Several members asked that opportunity

A Roosevelt-inspired story in the New York *Sun*, one of many of its kind, designed by Roosevelt to aid his purpose of forcing the Railroad Rate bill through Congress against the determined opposition of Senators of his own party.

The cannonade of head-lines took on cumulative frequency — occasionally, indeed, two or more jostled each other on the same front page, the general saturation of the atmosphere causing *Life* to remark, plaintively, that "there are a few solvent and respectable persons left in the country who have not yet been investigated." And moving the New York *Sun* to sardonic jeering:

INVESTIGATIONS

All signs point to a time in the early future when corporate greed shall no longer oppress the down-trodden millions. The corporations are all to be investigated. Mr. Garfield already has the thumb-screws on the Standard Oil and the coal barons. Mr. Moody has the beef trust on the rack and is about to put the elevator companies in the same painful predicament.

This jeering back at Roosevelt by the editorial pages of the New York *Sun* and other conservative[50] newspapers, was part of the enemy's answering cannonade to the machine-gun fire of head-lines that Roosevelt was able to conduct on the first pages of the same papers, which, to be newspapers at all, had to record the news that Roosevelt made.

To a very large degree, the newspaper part of the fight over the rate bill was epitomized as a duel of individuals, between Roosevelt and the New York *Sun*. *The Sun* was the most forceful and brilliant of the conservative papers of the country. Its owner, according to contemporary rumor, had bought the paper with money borrowed from J. P. Morgan, *facile princeps* among the country's railroad bankers and promoters; certainly the relation between *The Sun* and Morgan was close. The opposition of *The Sun* to the railroad rate bill and to most of Roosevelt's policies did not have the air of mere servility to capitalist opinions. It was intelligent, able; and the positions it took were, from the point of view of conservatism, of strict interpretation of the Constitution, tenable.

The Sun began its side of the duel with solemn warning, saying, in the seriousness of a leading editorial on the opening day of the year (January 1, 1906):

The year now begun is likely to be memorable in the eyes of constitutional lawyers and political economists if Congress

---

[50] "Virtually all the most influential newspapers of the country were also opposed to [the railroad rate bill]. The prevailing opinion in press and public was that the measure would never pass the Senate." — "Theodore Roosevelt and His Time," Joseph Bucklin Bishop.

shall sanction the experiment of government rate making for railways which Mr. Roosevelt advocates. The experiment desired by the President is universally condemned by experts.

A few weeks later, when *The Sun's* news pages were obliged to record a belief current in Washington that "because of President Roosevelt's popularity the Hepburn bill would receive practically the unanimous vote of the House" — the editorial page of *The Sun*, a little alarmed, turned to a tone that was partly smug exhortation, partly angry irritation:

Time and the maturest consideration are needed. One would think that this complex and enormous question could be disposed of blithely and off-hand, with no more thought or trouble than is required for the laying of a petition on the clerk's desk. Better go slow than go wrong. . . . We notice that the lawyers are much less enthusiastic than some of the laymen about railway-rate bills. The Constitution is damnably in the way of quick relief reforms and reformers.

At a later stage, when Roosevelt was in the midst of his pressure to pass the bill, when he was facing the worst of the difficulties he encountered — the effort to secure a bill that would "stick" against constitutional attacks, the effort to reconcile the wishes of honest friends of rate regulation, and also to avoid the constitutional pitfalls which seeming friends of the bill were believed to be trying to write into it — under these conditions *The Sun* practised jeering satire. On Tuesday, February 6, 1906, in its leading and double-leaded[51] editorial, *The Sun* described Roosevelt as exhibiting within six days "not one mind, but forty minds on the subject; a dia-

---

[51] The public may not understand that when an editor wants to make a passage appear conspicuous, he writes on his copy the direction, "double-lead," whereupon the printer puts an additional strip of metal between the lines of type, achieving greater space between the lines.

gram of the reported movements of the Chief Magistrate's 'position' on rate regulation since February began would occupy this whole page, and would resemble nothing so much as a temperature chart in a case of intermittent fever, or a profile of the Cordilleras."

Against the pompous fuming of *The Sun's* editorials on its seventh page, Roosevelt returned the sharp rat-tat-tat of the head-lines on its own first page, head-lines *The Sun* was obliged to carry in order to record the news that Roosevelt was making, such as

RAILROADS GET ANOTHER JOLT[52]

— news ammunition that Roosevelt either wrought out of the developments over the rate bill itself or procured through a shrewd or adventitious timing of developments and exposures incident to collateral investigations of railroad and trust evils that he had initiated months before. A report of an investigation of the Standard Oil Company by Roosevelt's Commissioner of Corporations[53] yielded

STANDARD OIL REPORT READY. REVELATIONS MAY CAUSE A SENSATION. DATA WILL BE TURNED OVER TO THE ATTORNEY-GENERAL AND THERE MAY BE PROSECUTIONS.

An investigation of coal-carrying railroads on the Atlantic coast revealed grave scandals in the Pennsylvania. An officer who could influence the purchase of coal for locomotives was by that fact enabled to eke out his salary of $225 a month by gifts from certain coal companies amounting to $50,000 in cash and $11,000 worth of stock; the chief clerk of a superintendent of a division, whose salary had ranged between $30 and $136 a month, had "invested" about $75,000 in stocks of coal

[52] New York *Sun,* March 9, 1906.
[53] James R. Garfield.

companies[54] — the revelations obliging *The Sun's* head-lines to say

In this cannon-fire of head-lines, one of Roosevelt's blasts suffered from a contretemps of nature. On April

From "The Eagle" (Brooklyn, N. Y.)
The fight of his life.

18, 1906, Roosevelt had prepared, and on that day sent to Congress, one of the strongest and most sensational anti-trust messages he ever wrote. He took a portion of

[54] These details are taken from the summary in *The Independent* for June 14, 1906. The investigation was conducted by William A. Glasgow, Jr., for the Interstate Commerce Commission. Judge Glasgow wrote the author of this history, March 18, 1927: "There was one thing accomplished by the investigation which was of great value to the coal industry and to the people of the United States, and that was the forbidding secret apportionment and distribution of coal cars in the coal trade and the discrimination and arbitrary treatment of coal operators by the railroads."

[55] New York *Sun*, May 19, 1906.

his text from a recent decision adverse to the government in one of the courts, and said that the decision came
"measurably near" making the law a farce. He asked,
therefore, for a new and stronger anti-trust law.

This Roosevelt sent to Congress on April 18. But in
the newspaper offices that night, Roosevelt's message
encountered collision with a despatch from California.
When one looked at the papers the following morning
to find the sensational head-lines that such a message inevitably called for, one found instead of Roosevelt-inspired news, the entire first page occupied by a single
story — on which the head-lines were:

EARTHQUAKE LAYS FRISCO IN RUINS[56]

Entire Business District Burned and Hundreds of Lives Lost

MARTIAL LAW IN CITY

The City Hall and all the Great Buildings Reduced to Debris

PEOPLE FLOCK TO THE HILLS

Great Shock Just Before Dawn Starts a Conflagration

BUILDINGS CRUMBLE AT ONCE

— fulfilling a judgment of the newspaper craft which
said that "only an earthquake could drive T. R. off the
first page." Roosevelt, to find his own story, was obliged
to turn to the back pages. The New York *Sun* had it on
page 7.

XI

Roosevelt's Literary Allies

Roosevelt, in marshalling public opinion for the railroad rate bill, had, as always, help from the magazine
[56] New York *Sun*, April 19, 1906.

writers. The literature of exposure in the popular magazines was at full tide, continuing to beat into high fever public sentiment against the railroads, and providing much of the heavy cannonading for Roosevelt's assault. In *McClure's* for March, 1906, Ray Stannard Baker comprehensively reviewed the sins of the railroads, their dominance of politics through packed conventions, their methods of getting newspaper support. *The Outlook*, pulling a valiant oar for the President (who was later to be its Contributing Editor), said, April 7, 1906: "It is a great misfortune that [the Senate] should count among its members a few men who are very gravely and for good reason distrusted by their fellow-citizens; that it includes altogether too many managers of political machines who control the entire political organization of their States; that a small group of Senators stand together too definitely for business in politics — that is to say, for that 'system' of interweaving business and political interests which more than any other single thing has corrupted and lowered the tone of our public life." In *The World's Work* for January, the month in which the railroad rate fight began, Henry Beach Needham, the most devoted of Roosevelt's "fair-haired boys," made a head-on assault against the Senators opposing the bill: "Aldrich, Hale, Frye, Spooner, Gallinger, Penrose, Elkins, Platt, Foraker, Depew and Kean — representatives of corporate business every one . . . [Spooner's] activities in behalf of railroads, which ranged from peddling passes to giving valuable legal opinions on valueless branch lines, first put him in the Senate. For not distantly related reasons comes also Senator Elkins, who with his father-in-law, Henry Gassaway Davis, is heavily interested in railroads. . . . Senator Kean is what Jerseymen call a 'public utility man.' " Aldrich's history, from clerk in fish-market to president of a street-railway combination, was described in terms that stripped some of the glamour from his wealth, some of the prestige from his position as Senate leader. So strongly was antagonism to the Senate stirred by Roosevelt's magazine allies that the very wealthy Senator Elkins, groaning under the harassments to which his wealth and position subjected him, expressed, in a speech before a bankers' association, a plaintive preference for a less exalted station: "Very rich men never whistle, poor men always do; birdsongs are in the hearts of the people."

XII

However resourcefully Roosevelt might use his arts of getting public opinion on his side, all was useless unless he could get a majority in the Senate. That was difficult, under the conditions Republican leader Aldrich had forced upon Roosevelt when he disavowed the bill as a Republican party measure and made it a Democratic one.

The debate consumed more than sixty hectic days.[57] "One of the grandest battles of forensic eloquence witnessed in a generation raged for months. Great lawyers, taking up the narrowest point they could find in the whole controversy, hurled hundreds of thousands of legal missiles at one another. Senators Foraker, Spooner, Knox, Bailey, Rayner, one after another expounded the law and the prophets in extenuation or condemnation of the thing about to be done. So the battle raged until the wind-batteries had literally blown themselves out."[58] Senators who wished to inform themselves adequately on the question were obliged to read five thousand pages of testimony taken in the preliminary hearings, to ana-

[57] The bill was introduced in the Senate, February 26, 1906, the debate began March 12, and the bill came to final roll-call in the Senate May 18.
[58] J. W. Bennet, in "Roosevelt and the Republic."

lyze intricate tables of statistics, to master such complexities as the "long-and-short haul," and to weigh and sift scores of judicial decisions, particularly those bearing on the fine Constitutional hair-line boundary between the right of Congress to regulate railroad rates and the right of the courts to review such rates. The discussion on the Senate floor began with affirmations, trite yet in this case justified, about the deep-reaching significance of the bill — "the most important," affirmed one of its friends, Senator Beveridge of Indiana, "since the Civil War." To which Foraker of Ohio, who disagreed with Beveridge about every aspect of the bill except its importance, added: "Well said." Senator Daniel of Virginia, going back even farther than Beveridge for his comparisons, summarized the philosophy and history of transportation: "Antedating the railroad systems of the world lie six thousand years of history and the countless ages of prehistoric times. . . . Man not only moves his own body by the exercise of his limbs, but also by the subjection of the creatures of the land to his uses; the camel, the ox, the horse, the ass, bear him and his burdens as he ordains."[59]

"I have not time," Senator Daniel said — rather supererogatorally — "to discuss fully the nature of any of these variant and diversified causations that are constant qualities in determining the rates of traffic." Senator McLaurin of Mississippi saw in the bill an opportunity to legislate the country back into simplicity and leisure, proposing an amendment prohibiting, on Sundays, all interstate passenger and freight traffic, and advancing as an argument[60] the Fourth Commandment:

Remember the Sabbath Day, to keep it holy.
Six days shalt thou labor, and do all thy work;

[59] *Congressional Record*, May 1, 1906.
[60] *Congressional Record*, May 16, 1906.

But the seventh day is the Sabbath of the Lord thy God: in it thou shalt not do any work, thou, nor thy son, nor thy daughter, thy manservant, nor thy maidservant, nor thy cattle, nor the stranger that is within thy gates.

There was, of course, during the debate, the usual conjuring up of that terror (ominous to statesmen, but to historians a harmless old friend) "an entering wedge," a first step in Socialism; accompanied, alas, by the usual type of prediction — it would mean, Congressman Sibley of Pennsylvania had said in the Lower House, "government ownership within ten years."

The opposition to the bill was of a kind that, to any one but Roosevelt, would have been dismaying. He had against him practically every important orthodox member of his own party. He had against him Foraker of Ohio, who made 87 speeches, the essence of all of which was outright, thoroughgoing condemnation — "A more unnecessary law, or a more mischief-making law was never placed upon the statute-book.[61] . . . My objection is to the government going into the rate-making business at all.[62] . . . I believe the court review provided in the bill is a cheat, humbug, and fraud."[63]

Roosevelt had against him his own intimate friend, Lodge of Massachusetts, who, living up to his reputation as the "scholar of the Senate," opened his attack upon the measure with a quotation from Coleridge's table-talk in which he cleverly called attention to the part public clamor had in the advocacy of the bill: "I have heard but two arguments of any weight adduced in favor of passing this reform bill, and they are in substance these: 1. 'We will blow your brains out if you don't pass it. 2. We will drag you through a horsepond if you don't pass

---

[61] *Congressional Record,* June 23, 1906.
[62] *Congressional Record,* May 18, 1906.
[63] *Congressional Record,* April 12, 1906.

it.' And there is a good deal of force in both." Roosevelt had against him Knox of Pennsylvania, a former member of his own Cabinet, one of the foremost lawyers in the Senate and in the country, who threw into the balance against the bill the heavy weight of his disapproval on grounds of law and the Constitution, saying: "The framers of this bill have succeeded in producing a measure which permits an administrative body to make orders affecting property rights, gives no right to the owners of the property to test their lawfulness in proceedings to enforce them, and penalizes the owner of the property in the sum of $5000 a day if it seeks a supposed remedy outside of the provisions of the bill by challenging either its constitutionality or the lawfulness of the acts performed under its provisions." Roosevelt had against him Aldrich of Rhode Island, Republican leader of the Senate; Elkins of West Virginia, chairman of the Committee on Interstate Commerce; Spooner of Wisconsin, authoritative as a constitutional lawyer; Crane of Massachusetts, among the shrewdest of the Senate in counsel. In short, Roosevelt had against him every Republican in the Senate whose position and leadership carried weight with the Republican majority.

To combat these, Roosevelt had on his side the Democratic minority, but under what conditions! The minority was small at best, only 33 out of the total of 90. Not all the minority supported the bill — some among the Democrats could be as justly called "railroad Senators" as any of the Republican leaders, and a few of the Democrats, old-time "States'-rights" men, opposed the bill on constitutional grounds. Moreover, co-operation between Roosevelt and the Democrats on whom he had to depend was attended with the cumbersomeness and mutual suspicion that always goes with ephemeral alliance between a President belonging to one party and legislators belonging to the other. Finally, the particular Democrat who had charge of the bill, Tillman, was Roosevelt's bitter personal enemy.

To supplement the Democrats, Roosevelt had a few Republicans, the beginnings of the group, coming chiefly from the Midwest "Granger" States, who years later made much history as "Insurgents" or "Progressive Republicans." One of the ablest of them at the time of the railroad rate fight was Dolliver of Iowa. Another, destined in later years to be outstanding, was LaFollette of Wisconsin; but LaFollette was new in the Senate, and utterly without influence. Besides, because of his ultraradical recalcitrancy of temperament, he could be of little help to Roosevelt; indeed, LaFollette did not want, either on the railroad bill or ever, to be of help to Roosevelt. Further, LaFollette was subject to the unwritten rule of the Senate that a new member must refrain for a term from conspicuousness, and especially from speech-making — a rule which LaFollette contemptuously flouted by making a speech on the rate bill that used up the better part of three daily sessions, and consumed, with its voluminous appendices, 148 pages of *The Congressional Record*. When LaFollette began his impassioned demand for rate regulation, the elderly defenders of Senatorial tradition visited upon him such disapproval as he might infer from their

From a photograph by C. M. Bell, Washington, D. C.

Senator Jonathan P. Dolliver, a "Progressive Republican" from Iowa.

absence from the Senate-chamber, his only listener on the floor being Kean of New Jersey. Kean's presence, it could quite safely be assumed, was due less to any wish to imbibe wisdom at the fount of the young Wisconsin oracle than to fulfil an arrangement with his "Old Guard" associates, by which he was left, a lone sentry, to give the alarm in case an emergency should arise. LaFollette, not at all humbled by the spectacle of the 88 empty seats, cleverly turned the hazing of him into a boomerang which, flying back to the cloak-rooms, sent premonitory shivers up and down many a Senatorial spine. Pausing dramatically in his droning citations of court decisions, LaFollette said:

I cannot be wholly indifferent to the fact that Senators, by their absence at this time, indicate their want of interest in what I may have to say upon this subject. The public is interested. Unless this important question is rightly settled, seats now temporarily vacant may be permanently vacated.[64] [Applause in the galleries.]

LaFollette's ideas about rate regulation were so much more radical than those in the bill as to have little relation of reality to the debate. His attitude, indeed, created cleavage within the little group of Insurgent Republicans who were part of Roosevelt's slender dependence, causing Dolliver to lament that the bill "had to stand fire from two directions, from its enemies and from the scattered tents of its advocates."

Such cleavages among Roosevelt's supporters made his situation almost desperate. They made the passage of a

[64] LaFollette's remark was a prophecy — and LaFollette was a man who took personal pains to make such prophecies come true. After the close of the session, LaFollette, on a Chautauqua tour in nearly all the States from New York to California, made hundreds of speeches of which the substance consisted of data that only a LaFollette could make interesting — the roll-call of the Senate on the amendments he had proposed to the railroad rate bill. Six years later he was able to write, "There were twenty-four 'stand-pat' members of the Senate who are not there today."

carefully considered bill almost an impossibility. When the crux of the fight came, it was about the degree to which the railroads should be permitted to appeal to the courts from rate-fixing actions taken by the Interstate Commerce Commission, and the degree to which the courts should have power to review[65] or set aside the actions of the Commission. The battle became one of "broad court review" versus "narrow court review" — those phrases flamed through Senate oratory and newspaper head-lines.

On this heart of the controversy, the regular Republicans and "railroad Senators" wished a court review so broad as to give the courts the right to overrule practically any act of the Interstate Commerce Commission. They — Aldrich, Foraker and the other regular Republican leaders — wanted a court review by which the courts would in effect take the place of the Commission, a court review so broad as to empower the courts in effect to re-try the case, both as to law and as to facts. That was their preference. If they could not achieve that —

---

[65] Theodore Roosevelt, in his "Autobiography," wrote: "There was another amusing incident. . . . All the wise friends of the effort to secure Governmental control of corporations know that this Government control must be exercised through administrative and not judicial officers if it is to be effective. Everything possible should be done to minimize the chance of appealing from the decisions of the administrative officer to the courts. But it is not possible Constitutionally, and probably would not be desirable anyhow, completely to abolish the appeal. Unwise zealots wished to make the effort totally to abolish the appeal in connection with the Hepburn Bill. Representatives of the special interests wished to extend the appeal to include what it ought not to include. Between stood a number of men whose votes would mean the passage of, or the failure to pass, the bill, and who were not inclined toward either side. Three or four substantially identical amendments were proposed, and we then suddenly found ourselves face to face with an absurd situation. The good men who were willing to go with us but had conservative misgivings about the ultra-radicals would not accept a good amendment if one of the latter proposed it; and the radicals would not accept their own amendment if one of the conservatives proposed it. Each side got so wrought up as to be utterly unable to get matters into proper perspective; each prepared to stand on unimportant trifles; each announced with hysterical emphasis — the reformers just as hysterically as the reactionaries — that the decision as regards each unimportant trifle determined the worth or worthlessness of the measure."

or a reasonably close approximation to that — then they wished, cannily, a review so narrow as to render the bill unconstitutional.

Roosevelt's followers wanted — if their bizarrely diverse objectives can be grouped within one generalization — the narrowest possible court review that would be safely constitutional.[66] Some of them wished to write into the bill a provision specifically limiting the courts in ways that would have turned out to be unconstitutional and would therefore have destroyed the bill. Roosevelt's supporters, in short, extraordinarily variegated at best, some of them almost as hostile to others of them as they were to the "railroad Senators," many of them headstrong by temperament — Roosevelt's supporters, as respects the degree and form of court review, were beset by division, misunderstanding, and misconception. They were divided about the objective aimed at, and about the precise phraseology through which their several objectives could be incorporated into the bill. Not all of them had had legal training; such as had had experience in legislation could have been described, at best, by the phrase in which Tillman described himself, "corn-field lawyer." They could neither themselves write a provision in whose constitutionality they could have confidence, nor fully understand whether provisions written by others would achieve the ends they aimed at. Bewildered, they sat in a fog of phrases, uttered in the long speeches of the constitutional lawyers, about "interlocutory injunctions," "interlocutory injunction upon terms," "suspending orders"; refined

[66] The more reasonable and practical among Roosevelt's followers, or the ones who had sound legal training, such as Long of Kansas, Nelson of Minnesota, and others, wished a court review which would permit the courts to inquire into two, and only two, questions, namely: whether the act of the Commission was within the scope of its authority as conferred by the law; and second, whether the action of the Commission was constitutional, that is, whether a rate fixed by it was so low as to be confiscatory.

distinctions between "jurisdiction" and "judicial power," between "unrestricted review" and "review with limitation"; between suspending an order of the Interstate Commerce Commission, and reversing it; Senator Rayner's distinction, "constitutional court review versus statutory court review"; distinctions between the power of the inferior courts and of the Supreme Court; profound questions about whether Congress, having granted judicial power to circuit and district courts by the act of creating them, can subsequently put limitations upon the scope of their judicial power.

In the maze of such refinements of legalistic ratiocination, Roosevelt's followers were reduced to a condition in which their only guide was to let their opponents do their thinking for them, by voting against whatever draft of court review amendment their opponents proposed. And they lost even that guide when a suspicion got about that the "Railroad Senators" would take advantage of their ignorance and their cleavages by (among other devices) voting for the most radical of the drafts emanating from the anti-railroad Senators, with the shrewd expectation that the Supreme Court would declare it unconstitutional and thereby negative the whole bill.

Rarely was any group of men so sorely in need of leadership as the supporters of the railroad rate bill; sorely was Roosevelt handicapped in supplying it by the fact that the sponsor of the bill, the official pilot of its fortunes in the Senate, was Tillman, his political adversary and personal enemy.

XIII

In this situation, there rushed into Roosevelt's office on a Saturday afternoon in late March one of Roosevelt's "fair-haired boys," Henry Beach Needham, a

magazine writer, slight-built, boyish-looking, mild-eyed
behind horn-rimmed glasses, devoted to Roosevelt and
an ardent wisher for success for the rate bill — one of
those likeable enthusiasts whose laudable impulses sometimes precipitate more than their good intentions contemplate. Needham's acquaintance with everybody in
Washington and his half-gossipy, half-encyclopædic
omniscience about politics, included a fragment of information which now provided him with a bright idea:
he told Roosevelt there was in all the world just one
man who had Tillman's utmost confidence and affection, and was also a Republican — just one man, therefore, who could serve Roosevelt as a liaison with Tillman and the Democrats.

By happy fortune, William E. Chandler shared the
emotion and conviction of stern opposition to the railroads which was common to Roosevelt and Tillman —
a railroad, the Boston and Maine, by its imperious activity in politics, had been responsible for the "ex-" in
Chandler's title, "ex-Senator from New Hampshire";
and for the consequent fact that Chandler, after being
for forty years a trenchant and really important figure
in public life, now cabined remarkable talents in a government sinecure, member of the Spanish-American
Claims Commission.

That Chandler possessed even this small anchorage
to public life was due in part to his curious friendship
with Tillman, who had helped him secure the post. The
intimacy and affection between the lean, acrid New
Englander and the fire-eating South Carolinian was one
of those odd friendships that Washington life sometimes
assembles from far corners of incongruous background.
It would have been unusual under any circumstances,
and in the light of the strikingly contrasting histories of
the two men was extraordinary. Chandler, thirty to

forty years before, had had a hand in the notorious car-
petbagger régime — Southern Democrats call it conspiracy — as an incident of which the vote of Tillman's
South Carolina and other Southern States had been
counted for the Republi-
can Presidential candi-
date, Rutherford B.
Hayes, against Samuel J.
Tilden, thereby depriving
the Democrats of a Presi-
dency to which they felt
entitled.

Courtesy of the New York "World."
Senator William E. Chandler of New
Hampshire.

Whatever the origin or
explanation of the fantastic bond between Chan-
dler and Tillman, it now
provided Needham with
his happy suggestion, and
Roosevelt with the link to
Tillman that he needed to
offset the defection of his
own party leader. Just
what were the words in
which Needham pointed out the opportunity to Roosevelt, is not on record.[67] On their precise form hangs
much of the wrangle about mutual accusations of inveracity that later arose between Roosevelt and Tillman.
If Needham told Roosevelt that Chandler would like to
act as a go-between from Tillman to him, that is one
thing; if Needham merely suggested that Roosevelt send
for Chandler, that is quite different.

In any event Roosevelt, with the grinning vivacity
with which he always seized the very tip of opportunity's forelock, called his secretary into the room and in

[67] Needham died in an airplane accident in France during the Great War.

Needham's presence instructed him to invite Chandler to come to the White House. Needham, delighted with Roosevelt's acceptance of his idea, hurried off to tell Chandler; before he could finish his story a messenger bearing Roosevelt's invitation arrived:

THE WHITE HOUSE

Washington, March 31, 1906.

My dear Senator[68] Chandler: The President requests me to say that he would be glad to have you come to the White House at 8:30 o'clock tonight. Will you please let the bearer know whether you can come?

Very truly yours,

WILLIAM LOEB, JR., Secretary to the President.

Promptly at 8.30 that night Chandler went to the White House and talked with Roosevelt. From the White House he went directly to Tillman.

Chandler told Tillman:

That President Roosevelt wished (through him, Chandler) to get in communication with Tillman as the Democratic Senator in charge of the railroad rate bill; that Roosevelt had said he was in "complete disagreement" with the "Senatorial lawyers," meaning Republican leaders, three of whom he mentioned by name; that Roosevelt believed in the "narrow court review"; that Roosevelt repeatedly stated that he had "reached a final decision"[69] and that "his decision would be unalterable";[69] that Roosevelt "stated carefully and deliberately the basis on which he thought there should be cooperation[69] between the Democrats and himself."

Tillman was "mistrustful and suspicious."[70] "He questioned me [Chandler] closely as to what the President had said."[70] As an experienced politician, Tillman knew

[68] By a convention widely accepted in the world of politics, titles outlast incumbency in the offices they describe.

[69] The quotation is from Tillman's account of the conversation between him and Chandler. — *Congressional Record*, May 12, 1906. Chandler's diary agrees. Many details of the statement were later controverted by Roosevelt.

[70] Chandler's account, *Congressional Record*, May 16, 1906.

the perils of an alliance with a President belonging to
another party, knew the secrecy with which such an arrangement must be managed; he thought also of the
peculiar personal embarrassment inherent in any alliance
between him and Roosevelt; he recalled the bitter
wrong, as he considered it, that Roosevelt had done him,
and the bitter things he had said about Roosevelt. In the
end Tillman concluded to "pocket my pride and lay aside
my just indignation. . . . Having regard for my duty in
charge of a great legislative bill, I decided it to be necessary for me to cooperate and help Theodore Roosevelt
pass a good railroad law."[71]

Tillman's disquiet made him glad to share the responsibility with another Democrat. The following day,
Sunday, April 1, he went to see Senator Joseph W. Bailey
of Texas, and on the same day, reported to Chandler
that "we did not believe there would be any difficulty in
coming to an understanding on the basis proposed by the
President." This message Chandler immediately carried to Roosevelt, and on the next day, Monday, April
2, reported to Tillman Roosevelt's satisfaction with the
arrangement. The alliance was effected. Chandler conferred with Tillman again on Tuesday and again on
Wednesday and yet again on Thursday; repeatedly
Chandler went back and forth between Tillman and
Roosevelt, almost like a shuttlecock — a memorandum
of one evening's activities made by Chandler read:
"April 11, at 9:15 p.m. saw Tillman at Colonial about
railroad rate legislation; at 9:30 at White House saw
President Roosevelt alone upstairs; talked of railroad
rates and many other things for more than an hour, he
was very gracious; at about 10:30 with Tillman until
11:45."

Roosevelt, furthering his co-operation with Tillman,

[71] *Congressional Record*, May 12, 1906.

requested that the Democratic leader confer with one of the Republican leaders, Allison of Iowa, who, on this measure, was disposed to be more conciliatory than the official Republican leader, Aldrich; and Tillman held one brief conference with Allison.

Later, Roosevelt, eagerly promoting his desire to get a court review amendment that would be narrow enough and yet be safely constitutional, arranged for Tillman and Bailey to confer with his own Attorney-General, William H. Moody, asking Chandler to invite the Democrats and himself directing Moody to see them. Moody told the two Democrats "I will send you what I understand to be the kind of [narrow review] amendment we can agree on, and which I think he [Roosevelt] will accept."[72] The following day Moody sent Tillman a typewritten draft. At two subsequent conferences, the two Democratic Senators and the Republican Attorney-General perfected the substance of a "narrow court review" amendment, for which, Tillman told Moody, he "could, I felt sure, get 26 [Democratic] votes and possibly 1 or 2 more . . . and if the President was certain of 20 Republican votes it was a sure thing."[73] Tillman, carefully preserving the original of the draft memorandum that had been sent him by Moody, wrote out a formal "narrow review" amendment, and on May 3 introduced it in the Senate.

The Tillman Amendment read:

If such court shall find that the order was beyond the authority of the Commission or was a violation of the constitutional rights of the carrier it shall issue an injunction against the enforcement thereof: *Provided, however,* That no such injunction shall be issued as a preliminary or interlocutory proceeding.[74]

[72] Tillman's account, *Congressional Record,* May 12, 1906.
[73] *Congressional Record,* May 12, 1906.
[74] *Congressional Record,* May 3, 1906.

Manifestly Roosevelt had a secret agreement with Tillman on a "narrow review" amendment, drafted by his own Attorney-General; clearly there was, for five weeks, from March 31 to May 3, a close liaison between Roosevelt and Tillman, smooth-working, but very dangerous and very necessary to be kept secret.

Tillman's contribution to the joint enterprise of Roosevelt and himself proved to be not enough — he had said on April 16 that he "could get 26 Democratic votes and possibly 1 or 2 more"; on April 18, however, a caucus of the Democrats had shown that Tillman could get only 25 votes.

In this state of facts, Roosevelt, on Friday, May 4, sent a message to the Press Gallery at the Capitol saying he would see the newspapermen[75] at three that afternoon. They came, thirty-six of them. Roosevelt said to them that a court review provision for the rate bill that was satisfactory to him and which he would support had been written. It was known as the Allison Amendment. Allison was a Republican, not less regular than Aldrich, but disposed to compromise, partly because Allison's constituency, Iowa, was strongly anti-railroad, partly because Allison's habitual caution[76] and unemo-

[75] "At the cabinet meeting Friday morning (May 4) it (the Allison Amendment) was not mentioned though Roosevelt had agreed to it. After the cabinet meeting Roosevelt telephoned the Press Gallery that he wanted a group there to come to the White House at three. When they arrived he launched upon an elaborate statement designed to present to the country the idea that the Senate rather than he, had receded in the matter of the much-mooted broad and narrow review. His explanation was quite labored, and after about eight minutes of it, one of his warm admirers, Lindsay of the Kansas City *Star,* interrupted him to ask, 'But, Mr. President, what we want to know is why you surrendered.' This was a body blow and quite took Roosevelt's breath away. But instead of replying he went on to repeat the sort of explanation on which he had set out, continued it for half an hour, and then the Press departed." — From MSS. authorized by Richard Hooker of the Springfield *Republican* and quoted in a biography of Senator Aldrich, by Nathaniel Wright Stephenson.

[76] Allison's caution and his horror of dissension inspired countless stories,

tional temperament enabled him to see when need of compromise arose, partly because Allison's rôle in the Republican Senatorial hierarchy was to supply the oil of conciliation for bruises made by Aldrich's imperious dictatorship. "What a politician and what a smoother he was," wrote Samuel G. Blythe, " — a round, chubby little man, soft-spoken, suave, pervading." It was as conciliator that Allison now came forward with an amendment written less by himself than paraphrased from amendments emanating from both factions, an amendment which conceded much to the Democrats and Western Republicans but at the same time gave to Aldrich and the regular Republicans something in substance and considerable in face-saving form.

The Allison Amendment (subsequently embodied in the law as enacted) read:

Provided, That no injunction, interlocutory order, or decree suspending or restraining the enforcement of an order of the Commission shall be granted except on hearing after not less than five days' notice to the Commission. An appeal may be taken from any interlocutory order or decree granting or continuing an injunction in any suit, but shall lie only to the Supreme Court of the United States: *Provided further*, That the appeal must be taken within thirty days from the entry of such order or decree, and it shall take precedence in the appellate court over all other causes except causes of like character and criminal causes.

---

many of them, doubtless, apocryphal. The New York *Sun* spoke of him as the "distinguished and venerable statesman of the subjunctive mood." Riding in a train, according to one story, he saw a flock of newly sheared sheep in a field. "Those sheep have just been sheared," commented his seat companion. "Looks like it from this side," was Allison's reply. Another story related that Allison and Senator Spooner, on starting to leave the Capitol one day, found it raining. They stood a moment in the shelter of the doorway undecided what to do. "Do you think it will stop?" asked Spooner. "It always has," said Allison, finding for once a subject about which he could speak with positiveness while yet not committing himself to a definite prediction. A famous characterization of him said that if a piano keyboard should be built from Washington to Allison's home in Iowa he could walk over it the entire distance without striking a note.

XIV

Among the newspapermen who listened to Roosevelt's startling announcement of contentment with a form of court review sponsored by a Republican was the Henry Beach Needham who five weeks before had initiated the entente between Roosevelt and the Democrats. Needham, upset, hurried to Chandler. Chandler, agitated, hurried to Tillman. Tillman and Chandler hurried to Bailey. All three dismayed conspirators hurried to Moody. To Moody they told the tale of their abandonment by Roosevelt; they found Moody, according to Tillman, "absolutely innocent of any knowledge of any such purpose on the part of the President."[77]

The co-operation between Roosevelt and Tillman was at an end. For eight days Tillman said nothing, continuing to keep the secret of his negotiations with Roosevelt and their abrupt termination.

XV

There was enough, nevertheless, in the public announcement by Roosevelt of his support of Republican Senator Allison's court review amendment, to create a sensation in the country and an explosion in the Senate. The body of Democratic Senators, while they did not know that Roosevelt had been working secretly with their leader, saw that he was now working openly with a Republican. They were well aware, as the public was, that the Republican Allison's court review amendment differed from the Democratic Tillman's. They knew it differed in wording, and they assumed it must be, in its ultimate working out in the courts, more generous to the railroads. Most of all they knew, as a matter of politics, that any amendment bearing a Republican name,

[77] *Congressional Record,* May 12, 1906.

if incorporated in the bill instead of Tillman's Democratic one, would have the effect of depriving the Democrats of the credit which up to this time they had had. It exasperated them that their leader, after he had piloted the bill through its early perils, was now, when success seemed assured, set aside to give place to a Republican. The Democrats, partly because they really thought so, partly because it was good politics to say so, ignored the fact that Allison was, on the rate bill, a middle-of-the-road Republican, and took the ground that Roosevelt, after being flouted by his own party leaders, had now yielded to them.

Roosevelt hastened to insist he had not yielded. To an anti-railroad organization, the Pennsylvania State Grange, he sent a public telegram saying: "Not only am I standing on my original position. The Allison amendment is only declaratory of what the Hepburn bill must mean. . . . The Hepburn bill with the Allison amendment contains practically exactly (*sic*) what I have both originally and always since asked for."

Nevertheless the Democrats insisted that Roosevelt had compromised — not merely compromised but capitulated. "We understand what all this means," declared Democratic Senator Rayner of Maryland, "we understand that the President . . . has transferred his affections and is now clasping to his bosom, with the fondest and most fervent devotion, the senior Senator from Rhode Island" [Aldrich].[78] The Democratic Senator, aware of Roosevelt's popularity with the public, and careful not to give offense to it, shrewdly pretended to believe that Roosevelt's change had been effected by a ruse practised upon him by the Republican leaders. "I do not say that anyone has set a trap for the

[78] The quotations on this and succeeding pages from Senators Rayner, Bailey, McLaurin, Dolliver and Carter are from *The Congressional Record,* May 11 to 18, 1906.

President of the United States. I would not make a declaration of that kind upon this floor. But I do say, and
I say it again with the greatest respect and deference
to the President, that the President unfortunately is so
constituted that he cannot look at a trap without fooling with the spring. [Laughter.] . . . He kept on
looking at it, and walk-
ing around it, and walk-
ing in and out of it, until
he was caught. [Laugh-
ter.]"

The Democrats kept up
a jeering at Roosevelt as a
"trimmer" and "quitter"
that erupted almost daily
for two weeks. Demo-
cratic Senator Bailey de-
clared that Roosevelt's
"best friends must sin-
cerely deplore that he did
not keep his face set reso-
lutely against every effort
to emasculate this bill."
Bailey did "not pretend to
judge whether he [Roose-
velt] was weary of the conflict and surrendered, as
some men charge, or whether he yielded to the appeals
for party harmony, as other men believe." "But,"
said Bailey, "he will find it difficult to explain to the
American people why it is that he raised their hope
so high and then has fulfilled it in so slight degree."
"I love a brave man," said Bailey a day later, his ire
growing, "I love a fighter, and the President of the
United States is both — on occasions; but he can yield
with as much alacrity as any man who ever went to
battle. Let us have no more talk in the Senate and in

Courtesy of the New York "World."
Senator Joseph Weldon Bailey of
Texas

the country about this 'iron man.' He is clay, and very common clay at that."

Senator Rayner of Maryland chose in several sallies to be facetious. He was not here "for the purpose of abusing the President of the United States." Not at all. He would not "say one word that is either distasteful or improper." But "we have two reviews sent here by the President . . . and both of them in deadly conflict with each other." "The President tells us that these two reviews are one and the same thing, but they are as widely different as it is possible for two divergent propositions to be." Rayner, fecund in wit and words, compared Roosevelt's mind to "an unadjusted kaleidoscope; you have to shake it up frequently before its reflecting surfaces exhibit its beautiful colors and its symmetrical forms, and then, when you have it all adjusted and focused, it sometimes flies off into its original fragments." In a more violent simile, Rayner likened Roosevelt's course to that of "a cometic body that is tearing its way through the solar system without orbit and without circuit, illuminating the horizon in its march of fire, but absolutely oblivious where it came from and absolutely indifferent as to where it is going." In yet another simile Rayner related Roosevelt to the then recent San Francisco earthquake and the eruption of Mt. Pelee: "We are living in an age of natural disturbances, and the President may be somewhat jealous of these volcanic eruptions and earthquakes and does not desire them to have everything to themselves; he wants to get in the game a little himself."

Democratic Senator McLaurin of Mississippi declared: "That [Roosevelt] surrendered there can be no question; hereafter it will be known as 'Roosevelt's surrender' and if it shall ever be set to music it can be sung to the air of 'Bonaparte's Retreat.' " In McLaurin's judgment, not only had Roosevelt surrendered but "when the President surrenders he does not quit fighting; he goes over on the opposite side, swears allegiance to the enemy, and fights those who were his former allies. The President started out as if to be an ally, on rate legislation, of the Democratic Senators; but after a while when it became necessary for him to surrender to those who were his antagonists in this fight, he did not only surrender and quit fighting the common foe, but he went over to the cohorts of discrimination and extortion and commenced to fight those who were formerly, and by his invitation, his allies." As to the reason for the surrender, McLaurin did "not know the motives which prompted him," but sadly opined that the reason was a congenital disposition of Republicans to get together in time for victory and the fruits of victory: "There is always some basic principle that will ultimately get the Republican party together. If my observations . . . are worth anything, that basic principle is the cohesive power of public plunder."

Of course Republican Senators came to Roosevelt's defense. Dolliver of Iowa, one of the small band of progressive Republicans who had been with Roosevelt from the start, apotheosized Roosevelt as "a master of the art of achievement." The President, said Dolliver, "comes out of this fight with every substantive proposition recommended in his message to Congress. There are millions of good people in the United States who will not think less of the President because, without sacrificing any of his personal convictions, he has been able to bring the great political party of which he is the leader to the support of the essential principles for which he stands."

Republican Senator Carter of Montana, an able,

shrewd, genial man of Irish ancestry, expressed his racial sense of humor and titillated his hearers — excepting two — with an informal and benevolently chaffing speech based on a foray he had made into historical research. He had delved into the long legislative records of two of Roosevelt's most vociferous Democratic critics, Bailey of Texas and Rayner of Maryland; and he had found that the only bill about railroads ever introduced by Bailey had been one in the railroads' interest, "introduced by request," to forbid the "scalping" of tickets; and the only one by Rayner had been a bill permitting the railroads to issue "joint interchangeable 5000-mile tickets." With such records on railroad legislation, Senator Carter thought Roosevelt could safely invite comparison. "The statesmen of the country" — thus ironically Carter designated Rayner and Bailey — "have been somewhat delayed in assailing the majestic and supposedly invincible railroad power. No one familiar with President Roosevelt's record upon this railroad rate legislation can justly charge him with either cowardice or shiftiness. There are some who charge that he is too bold and fearless and outspoken, but for the first time it is intimated by the Senators from Texas and Maryland that he is prepared to or did make an abject surrender."

As for the allegation that the present episode was a case of the Republicans composing their party differences and getting together, Carter freely admitted it, even took it to his personal and party bosom, as a matter of pride. "The fact that we get together," Carter said, "is due to a certain clearly-defined basic principle. The people who believe in doing things, who believe in reconciling differences, who believe in results, are on this [the Republican] side of the chamber. The people who enjoy bickerings and continuous strife and ceaseless controversy naturally belong on the other [the Democratic] side. . . . So, in our humble way, we proceed to achieve things and we stand responsible for results when results are attained."

XVI

Something in Carter's impishly unctuous complacence about the adeptness of the Republican party in "reconciling differences" stirred the anger of the man at whose grievous expense and through whose unwilling agency the Republicans had made their latest achievement of unity. It had on Tillman the effect of a personal affront, not to be endured. Something in Carter's "earnest defense and eulogium of the President" stirred Tillman out of the restraint which, for the eight days following Roosevelt's announcement of support of the Allison Amendment, he had put upon his tugging anger. "There will be some surprise," Tillman said, rising in the Senate on May 12, "when I say to the Senate that, through another, the President has conferred with the Senator from South Carolina, who is now speaking. [Laughter.] It is therefore somewhat in the nature of a confession, as well as to give some of the inside history of recent events . . . that I now take the floor."

Tillman's explosion was not, at first, as violent as would have been expected from his temperament. He had rather the air of a man who, in his own judgment, has made a fool of himself, and to whom the more or less expected has occurred; who had embarked on an enterprise recognized in advance by himself to be dangerous, and who now had the consequences upon his head. As he saw it, he, as the leader of one party, had entered into a secret arrangement with a President belonging to the other party, and at the last moment the usual thing had happened — the President had used his bipartisan alliance as the basis of a compromise with his own party. In that mood, half angry and half laughing at himself, Tillman "confessed" to the Senate. It was not his custom, he said, to write out his remarks in advance, but on this occasion "in order that I might be careful to misstate nothing, I have written out my account of my negotiations with the President of the United States."[79]

Among the meticulously cited names, dates, and other details that composed Tillman's apologia, was a declaration that Roosevelt, in one of his talks with Chandler, had imputed odious chicanery to three of the most renowned Senators belonging to his own party, naming Senators Knox, Spooner, and Foraker as "Senatorial lawyers who were trying to injure or defeat the bill by ingenious constitutional arguments."[79]

That was by no means the most vivid of the details Tillman recited, nor the most damaging to Roosevelt. But that particular sentence represented Roosevelt as speaking invidiously about three of the most powerful Senators in his party: Knox, who was his friend and had been a member of his Cabinet; Spooner, who was regarded as the ablest constitutional lawyer among the Republican Senators; and Foraker, who was not only an outstanding Senator but Republican leader of Ohio. In short, the repeating of that sentence by Tillman illustrated the most familiar and deadly of the dangers involved when a President deals with leaders of the opposition party — it was, in the political phrase, "a wedge driven into the Republican party."

Quickly Republican leadership rallied to drive back the wedge. As soon as Tillman finished, Lodge of Massachusetts, Roosevelt's closest personal friend in the Senate, hurried to the stenographers' room for an exact copy of what Tillman had said. Then Lodge spoke by tele-

[79] *Congressional Record,* May 12, 1906.

phone with Roosevelt at the White House. Returning, he secured recognition from the presiding officer and addressed a Senate tense with expectant interest. Tersely, he stated that he had reported to Roosevelt the remarks Tillman had made, and —

> I took down the statement which he [the President] made to me over the telephone and which I will now read to the Senate.... He [Roosevelt] said in reply that the statement which I had read to him, attributed to him by Mr. Chandler, was a deliberate and unqualified falsehood.

This was the first of the casualties, the first of what was destined to be a considerable addition to the membership of the Ananias Club. This earliest victim could be interpreted as either Chandler or Tillman, or — as Roosevelt doubtless would have been glad to have it — both. The newspapers, promoting, as always, the dramatic, chose to designate Tillman, a person with a unique reputation for battle and invective, who could be expected to provide further newspaper copy. The New York *Sun* the following day[80] carried the head-line:

PRESIDENT GIVES TILLMAN THE LIE

Tillman, for a day, did nothing, merely saying, "I am ready . . . to leave the whole question to the thoughtful and honorable men of the country."

Chandler, canny soul, forehanded New Englander, produced a diary, and made a statement which he had Tillman read in the Senate: "I cannot use, toward the Chief Executive of the nation, language like his own. Upon our respective statements I submit the controversy, with confidence, to the judgment of those who know me." With a maliciously subtle allusion to a contemporary sentiment which said Roosevelt thought himself a king, Chandler added that "If the old imperialist days

80 May 13, 1906.

had been *fully* revived at the White House, one whom I considered the best of friends, Senator Lodge, upon demand, would have cut off my head and taken it to President Roosevelt on a charger, and I should have spoken no more. Now, at least, I have left to me the power of speech. But I shall never use it again as a missionary from President Roosevelt to the Democratic Party."

Roosevelt, in an energy of setting himself right, (1) wrote and made public a letter to Senator Allison in which he put the burden of initiating the negotiations on Tillman: "I was asked to see ex-Senator Chandler as representing Senator Tillman";[81] (2) had Attorney-General Moody write a letter to him [Roosevelt] in which Moody said, "There was nothing in the conversations between the [Democratic] Senators and me which in any way bound you to any particular amendment"; and (3) inspired newspaper articles in the Chi-

From "The Journal" (Minneapolis).

"You're another!" In popular thought Roosevelt and his "big stick" were hardly less inseparable than Tillman and his "pitchfork." The split that occurred between Roosevelt and Tillman, after they had worked as a team to get the Railroad Rate Bill passed, is here pictured as a clash between their respective symbols of forcefulness, while Miss Railroad Rate Bill looks on apprehensively.

[81] This letter of Roosevelt was one of a familiar type, about which his daughter Alice and other members of his family "kidded" him, calling them "posterity letters," meaning letters that stated the whole case, from Roosevelt's point of view, for history.

Another of Roosevelt's "posterity letters" about this episode, written to Senator Lodge of Massachusetts, began, "It is just as well to keep a record of what occurred in connection with the Chandler-Bailey-Tillman matter. . . ."

cago *Tribune* and the New York *Tribune,* which exculpated and justified himself. These newspaper despatches put their exculpation of Roosevelt on the ground
that he had been obliged to terminate his negotiations
with the Democrats by his discovery that Tillman
"could not control his own party." Tillman, the despatches said, "could not control the real Democratic
party leader in the Senate, Joe Bailey of Texas." Tillman, the despatches declared, with outrageous affront
to a man dangerous to affront — Tillman was "suspicious of him [Bailey] and said so in so many words.
. . . There is documentary proof of this."[82] Tillman,
according to the exculpatory despatches, "suspected the
Texan [Bailey] . . . of holding secret conferences
with Aldrich"; Tillman "was keeping a close watch on
his Texas friend and would not give him an opportunity
to 'sell out.' "[82] Tillman, so the despatches avowed over
and over in their effort to justify Roosevelt — Tillman
"believed Senator Bailey was treacherous and did not
want a rate bill passed at all, or, if passed, hoped to have
inserted in it some amendment which would be fatal to
its constitutionality."[83]

As justification, before the newspaper public, those
despatches were effective and credible — but extremely
incautious and highly inflammatory. Roosevelt, having

[82] The "documentary proof" was described in the newspaper despatches thus:
". . . That former Senator Chandler wrote to 'a distinguished member of the
administration' that he and Senator Tillman were both suspicious of Senator
Bailey, and that this letter undoubtedly was shown to President Roosevelt himself."

Later, Bailey, in his angry defense of his honor, procured from Chandler
a copy of the memorandum Chandler had sent to the White House. Chandler's
memorandum turned out to be but weak substantiation of the charge against
Bailey's honor. Chandler's memorandum merely said "The game of the railroad senators is to support Bailey's amendment and induce him to agree to
a broad rate review. . . . The principal object is to beat him, meaning Roosevelt."

[83] The quotations are detached sentences from the despatch in the Chicago
Tribune for May 15 and the one in the New York *Tribune* for May 16, 1906.

first angered the most belligerent Southerner in the Senate, Tillman, now, by his effort to exculpate himself, angered the second most belligerent. Bailey was a big,

AS SEEN FROM THE WHITE HOUSE

AS IT LOOKS FROM THE SENATE

Nelson Harding in the Brooklyn "Eagle."

Two points of view!

handsome, proud, rather arrogant Texan, one of the ablest and most forceful men who ever sat in the Senate — and conscious of it; proud of the Senate and jealous for its prestige. Bailey would fight at the drop of a hat, or earlier, and had done so, in spectacular encounters. Bailey could, and readily would, fight with his fists;

or, if the combat were verbal, no man in American public life had better command of the arts of excoriation. The story in the two newspapers was of a sort which would either cause Bailey and Tillman to leap at each other's throat — or both to leap at Roosevelt's throat. Bailey attacked Roosevelt. He had the clerk read the two newspaper stories aloud in the Senate on May 16 and 17. The correspondents who wrote them, said Bailey, were the "two chief cuckoos of the White House [who are] presumed to speak with some degree of authority concerning matters there. . . . Therefore, it seems to me conclusive that this slander proceeds from the White House." Having thus raised the presumption of connivance by Roosevelt with the two correspondents, Bailey now launched out upon a rotund denunciation of all three:

"I hope for the honor of my country it did not proceed from the President himself. I do not know this to be true, and therefore decline to charge that it is true. But, sir, I denounce that statement as an unqualified, a deliberate, and a malicious lie. I denounce that correspondent as an unqualified, deliberate and malicious liar. I denounce the man who furnished him the information on which it was based, or who inspired its publication, as an unqualified, deliberate, and a malicious liar, whoever he may be, and however high the office which he holds."

Thus was registered casualty number two; it happened high up, as one will see who recognizes the innuendo Bailey plainly meant. The casualties were increasing.

In peroration, Bailey delivered, against all slanderers of his honor, a universal bull, postdated, antedated, expost-facto and future estoppel, covering everybody, everywhere, oral slander or printed libel: "Amongst all the accusations that have been made against me, no man ever before imputed to me a lack of candor or charged me with duplicity, and no man ever shall and escape my denunciation. When a man so accuses me, it matters not where I am or who he is, I will write 'liar' across his forehead, so that in future years all men may know him and all honest men may shun him."[84]

Thereupon Tillman arose. He, too, cast a broad insinuation toward the White House. He said: "This correspondent is undoubtedly a muckrake. Into what house the handle goes, or what hand holds that handle, I shall not say; but in the brief time I have had to examine the article, I counted eight distinct and absolute falsehoods in regard to myself. But the one more particularly necessary to mention is that I ever lost faith in the integrity and honor and fair dealing of the Senator from Texas [Mr. Bailey]. There has never been the slightest suspicion on my part of the good faith of the Senator from Texas. . . . Therefore this story, which is concocted now and is being sent abroad by the cuckoos and hirelings of the Republican machine to muddy the waters, is only indicative of the desperate straits to which some people have brought themselves. I do not care to pursue the question further; the country is fully acquainted with the situation." So saying, Tillman inserted some further documents in *The Record*, in order, so he said, that "when future historians come to sift the question who did the lying in this important transaction, they may have all the evidence that I have."

XVII

One of the "future historians" whom Tillman invoked is now functioning, twenty-four years after the

[84] *Congressional Record*, May 17, 1906.

event. (As it happens, I was also on the scene when the
events took place.) However, for either the present
writer or the reader to accept Tillman's challenge and
undertake to pass upon the question of — let us not use
Tillman's harsh word, but say, rather, the relative perfection of recollection of himself and Roosevelt — to
do that would involve the presentation here of collateral
evidence not germane to the larger object of this narrative, which is to tell the story of Roosevelt's fight for
the railroad rate bill. To clarify some of the issues involved, one would need to know whether the magazine-
writer, Needham,[85] on his own initiative, suggested that
Roosevelt send for Chandler, or whether Chandler asked
Needham to make the suggestion. To mention but one
detail that would have to be considered in rendering a
judgment on another of the issues, it may be that Tillman had no suspicion of Bailey, but it may equally well
be that Roosevelt had such a suspicion, even though un-
founded, for Bailey already was beginning to be touched
by the cloud that later put him under the necessity of
fighting for his political life, a suspicion of greater intimacy with railroad and oil interests than was proper,
or at least expedient, for a representative of the Democracy of Texas to have. As for the justification for Roosevelt's termination of his alliance with Tillman, it is a
fact that Tillman could not deliver his party; he had
said he could deliver 26 — it turned out he could count
on only 25, and that was short of enough.

As for the essential point — the rate bill passed, by a
vote of 71 to 3.[86] Of the three adverse votes, one came
from the consistent, unremitting opponent of the bill,
Foraker of Ohio; the others from the two old gentlemen, Democrats, from Alabama, Morgan and Pettus,

[85] See page 252.   [86] May 18, 1906.

venerable men who were as antagonistic to the railroads as Roosevelt himself, but whose old-time interpretation of the Constitution would not permit them to support what they regarded as a trespass by the Federal Government upon the rights of the States.

The bill passed, and passed only because of the driving force that Roosevelt put behind it. Democrat after Democrat so admitted. "I do not believe," conceded Democratic Senator Teller of Colorado, "a bill of this character would have passed the Senate, strongly Republican as it is, and with the support of the Democrats here, if the President had not given life to this enterprise." Even Tillman, moved by the high sense of fairness that went with his strong soul, combined congratulations with humor in two of his late references to the victory:

> The Pitchfork, while on duty on the firing line, to use a military phrase, looking around for the ally, saw the tail of his coat hustling to the rear, and . . . the last seen of him he was sliding on all fours between Father Allison's legs. [Nevertheless] but for the work of Theodore Roosevelt in bringing this matter to the attention of the country, we would not have had any bill at all. . . . Whatever success may come from it will be largely due to him.

Bailey of Texas, also, was able to summon from out of his congeries of irritation a grudging tribute:

> It must not be understood that . . . it is my purpose to withhold from the President of the United States the credit to which he is justly entitled. . . . Without his help even this imperfect and insufficient bill could have never become a law.

There were divers other conclusions, repercussions, judgments, comments, echoes and other sequelæ. *The Independent* averred the victory was "due chiefly to the

men with the muckrake." The leading organ of the
party opposed to Roosevelt, the New York *World*, said:

> Mr. Roosevelt would be more than human if he could con-
> ceal his elation over the achievements of a Congress that has
> evinced almost phonographic fidelity to the wishes of the
> President. . . . Whatever his faults, Mr. Roosevelt has proved
> that he is not dazzled by dollars.

The New York *Sun*, ending its head-line battle with
Roosevelt, hauled down its flag in five words of stark
surrender:[87]

RAILROAD RATE BILL A LAW

— but poured editorial salve on the wounds of the solitary survivor of the opposition, the sole Republican who,
having led in the fight against the bill, alone voted
against it:

THE REPUBLICAN WHO VOTED "NO!"

> The Hon. Joseph Benson Foraker deserves the praise due
> to the man tenacious of his purpose. . . . Blanche, Tray, and
> Sweetheart of the muckrake pack have yapped and snapped
> at "the railroad lawyer," the "friend of the railroads," and so
> on. It has not been a pleasant experience for a proud and a
> sensitive man. . . .

Aldrich said nothing, publicly; but Tillman said, of
Aldrich, "He has come nearer being unhorsed and
thrown in the ditch in this struggle than ever before
since I have been here." As for Elkins, he, less recalcitrant than either Aldrich or Foraker, had surrendered
and gone over to Roosevelt comparatively early in the
fight, giving as an explanation of his conversion, "When
the team is running away, I prefer to be on the seat with
my hands on the lines rather than in front of the runa-
way."

The railroads were sullen — but prudently accepted

[87] June 30, 1906.

the judgment of their lawyers that the law was the law; an Interstate Commerce Commissioner, Franklin K. Lane, wrote in a private letter in February, 1907:[88]

I am conscious each time I ask a question that there is deep resentment in the heart of the railroad official at being compelled to answer; but that he is compelled to, he recognizes. The operating and traffic officials of the railroads are having a very hard time these days with the law departments. They can not understand why the law department advises them to give the information we demand, and I have heard of some most lively conferences in which the counsel of the companies were blackguarded heartily for being cowards, in not fighting the Commission.

XVIII

William Jennings Bryan, feeling, as rather frequently before, that Roosevelt had been committing larceny in the wood-yard where Bryan kept his platform planks, and feeling it desirable to store up a new

From a photograph © by Underwood & Underwood.

Bryan in 1906 in Syria on a round-the-world trip.

railroad issue against the day when he should again have the Democratic nomination for the Presidency, devised a substitute. Bryan, returning from a round-the-world trip in August, 1906, and being welcomed by a mass-meeting at Madison Square Garden, New York, proposed the only issue now left in the railroads, government ownership. In his proposal of it he introduced a bizarre qualifi-

[88] "Letters of Franklin K. Lane."

cation, "the trunk lines [to be] operated by the Federal government, and the local lines by the several state governments. Some have opposed this dual ownership as impracticable, but investigation in Europe [whence Bryan had just returned] has convinced me that it is entirely practicable." Bryan admitted he did "not know that the country is ready for this change; I do not know that a majority of my party favor it." He was quickly to learn. That speech turned into a chilling frost one of the greatest ovations ever prepared for an American statesman after a dramatic return from overseas.[89]

[89] In mentioning some of the men who have had the kindness to read the proofs of this chapter, in one or another of the several drafts through which it has passed, it is desirable to make clear that no view or version of events here expressed is to be taken as necessarily reflecting the views or recollections of any of these generous critics, who include: Leonor Fresnel Loree, president of the Delaware and Hudson Railroad; Ernest I. Lewis, Chairman of the Interstate Commerce Commission; Daniel S. Willard, president of the Baltimore and Ohio Railroad; ex-Senators Chester I. Long of Kansas, Porter J. McCumber of North Dakota, Irvine Lenroot of Wisconsin, Joseph M. Dixon of Montana, John Sharp Williams of Mississippi; ex-Representatives Albert Sidney Burleson of Austin, Texas; Victor Murdock of Wichita, Kan.; William S. Bennet of New York City; James Francis Burke of Pittsburgh, Pa.; John J. Fitzgerald of Brooklyn, N. Y.; Gilbert Holland Montague of New York City; Sam Houston Acheson of Austin, Texas, biographer of Joseph W. Bailey; Herbert Knox Smith of Hartford, Conn., formerly Commissioner of Corporations under President Roosevelt; William Loeb, formerly private secretary to President Roosevelt; Elihu Root, Secretary of State and Secretary of War under Roosevelt.

8

SELECTING A SUCCESSOR

Roosevelt's Position on the Next Presidency. Distinction
Between "Second Term" and "Second Elective Term."
Roosevelt's Preference for Elihu Root. William R. Hearst's
Ambition. Root's Denunciation of Hearst. Popularity of
Charles E. Hughes. The Wadsworths' Opposition to
Hughes. Roosevelt's Attitude Toward Hughes — Respect
Tempered by Condescension. The "John L." Incident.
Turning to Taft as a Candidate.

As Roosevelt looked forward to the next Presidency,
his principal concern was to prevent the renomination of
himself. He had settled his position by his formal statement, issued a few hours after his election in 1904:

A wise custom which limits the President to two terms regards the substance and not the form, and under no circumstances will I be a candidate for or accept another nomination.

From that position, Roosevelt did not waver, though
there was never a day that he was not under pressure,
from force of circumstances and clamor of individuals,
to revoke his decision. One formidable group, determined to renominate him, invented a distinction between
"second term" and "second elective term." They took
the ground that the really wrong thing was not for a
President to renominate himself — but for a President
to interfere with the free will of the people. Declaring
that the will of the people was renomination of Roosevelt, they organized a movement to defy Roosevelt's
wishes. Roosevelt never formally repeated[1] his early

---

[1] Roosevelt said to a newspaper friend: "They want me to keep repeating myself and they don't see that it would make people think I didn't believe myself.
If what I say isn't worth believing when I say it, what additional value would
it have from being repeated? If I were to repeat that statement this afternoon,

public declaration, though occasion to do so arose practically every week — he knew the interpretation put upon protesting too much.   But in letters and statements to friends, frequently in sharp admonitions to them, he declared that renomination of him would be a stain upon his honor.   He kept his hand upon the Republican party machinery until the very hour and minute of the nomination, watchful to prevent any action by what he regarded as his misguided friends.   Elimination of himself was Roosevelt's fixed policy throughout the entire four years.

II

As respects others than himself, Roosevelt's strong preference was Elihu Root.   "I would rather," Roosevelt said to a friend,[2] "see Elihu Root in the White House than any other man now possible.   I would walk on my hands and knees from the White House to the Capitol to see Root made President.   But I know it cannot be done.   He couldn't be elected.   There is too much opposition to him on account of his corporation connections. . . .   Root has always given all that he had to his clients.   What the people do not understand about him is

in two weeks the newspapers would all be clamoring to have me say it again. Then pretty soon I should have to say it every day, and then nobody would believe it." — "Released for Publication," Oscar King Davis.

Though Roosevelt never reiterated his renunciation formally, he made many public allusions to it. On a trip through the West in May and June, 1905, he declared, at Dallas, Texas: "I shall be permanently through with my present position four years hence."   At Omaha, to a representative of *The Bee,* he said: "You are authorized to state that I will not again be a candidate for the office of President of the United States. There are no strings to this statement. I mean it." At a banquet given by the Democratic Iroquois Club at Chicago, when a speaker facetiously nominated him for another term, Roosevelt replied: "In looking at the possibilities of the future, let me add that I have not the least anticipation of Chicago's ever reversing that most complimentary vote which I so deeply appreciated last year, because it will never have the chance."

The precise language of Roosevelt's formal renunciation — "under no circumstances will I be a candidate for or accept another nomination" — became, when he ran again in 1912, a subject of acrimonious dispute about whether it applied to another term after he had been out of office for a period.

2 Oscar K. Davis, "Released for Publication."

that if he were President they would be his clients.   He would be serving the nation with absolute singleness of purpose and with all that intelligence, industry, and fidelity.   Root is really for the public programme that you boys call the 'Roosevelt policies.' "   Roosevelt knew all of Root's qualities, and, knowing all, rated him as what he was, the wisest, the most surefooted, the most far-seeing, on the whole the ablest, American statesman of his day. The public knew the power of Root's mind; Roosevelt knew, also, the essential liberality and idealism of Root's temperament, an idealism that was deprived of conspicuousness only because Root kept it harnessed to practicality and drove the two as a team for the long pull.   Root was humane, tender, almost emotional, essentially more benevolently sympathetic to the average man than some who made political capital out of self-asserted spokesmanship for democracy. This side of Root, however, was not known to the public. To them, he was a "corporation lawyer"; and Roosevelt well knew that in the temper of the day, a man bearing that stigma in the popular mind could not be made President.   Root knew it, too. To a friend who, one day when Root was resting at his boyhood home in the shade of Hamilton College, made him a tender that would have meant a formidable effort for the Presidency, Root replied: "Not for me; the public thinks I am only a corporation lawyer."

If there had been any possibility of Root's getting the Republican nomination, any possibility of Roosevelt's procuring it for him, the chance was impaired when, in 1906, Roosevelt made use of Root to head off the career of one who, in another party and through methods of his own, was seeking the Presidency. A publisher of sensational newspapers, William R. Hearst, pursuing an ambition that recognized no limits, had procured for himself the Democratic nomination for Governor of

New York, and seemed formidably on the way to the White House. Roosevelt, regarding Hearst as dangerous, determined to throw the whole weight of his influence into stopping him before he should win the stepping-stone of the New York governorship. With this purpose Roosevelt sent Root to New York State to speak against Hearst (and for Hughes, who was the Republican nominee). At Utica, Root delivered a denunciation of Hearst that caused a sensation. His arraignment of Hearst had the combined impact of himself and his principal, Roosevelt. Root began by quoting passages from Roosevelt's first message to Congress, delivered after the assassination of McKinley, in which Roosevelt spoke of the assassin as inflamed "by the reckless utterances of those who . . . in the public press appealed to the dark and evil spirits of malice and greed, envy and sullen hatred. The wind is sowed by the men who preach such doctrines, and they cannot escape their share of responsibility for the whirlwind that is reaped. This applies to the deliberate demagogue, to the exploiter of sensationalism." Root continued:

I say by the President's authority that in penning these words, with the horror of President McKinley's murder fresh before him, he had Mr. Hearst specifically in his mind. And I say, by his authority, that what he thought of Mr. Hearst then, he thinks of Mr. Hearst now.[3]

Root's denunciation of Hearst had the effect of recalling some of the public to its angry mood of five years before, when straw similitudes of Hearst had dangled in scores of cities, and his newspapers had been burned in bonfires and boycotted by libraries and business houses, because of the charge that the assassin of McKinley, Czolgocz, had been inflamed to his deed by brutal attacks on McKinley in the Hearst press, a bit of

[3] *Outlook,* November 10, 1906.

verse published in Hearst's New York *Journal* on February 4, 1901:

> The bullet that pierced Goebel's breast
> Cannot be found in all the West;
> Good reason; it is speeding here [to Washington]
> To stretch McKinley on his bier.[4]

Root's speech defeated Hearst[5] for Governor — and put an additional weight of unavailability on Root as a Presidential possibility, for it was certain that Hearst, with his powerful New York press, would make it doubtful whether Root in a Presidential campaign could carry New York State, and therefore, in effect, doubtful whether he could carry the country.

III

There was another Presidential potentiality, to whom Roosevelt might conceivably have turned, or who, even with nothing more from Roosevelt than acquiescence, might have got the nomination. Charles E. Hughes, as a result of his insurance investigation, had become a first-rank figure in public life, second only to Roosevelt as a leader in popular reforms, distinguished above Bryan by his greater exactness of intellect, above La Follette by his greater evenness of temperament, his more judicial attitude of mind.

Hughes was nominated by the Republicans for Governor of New York, was elected, took office January 1, 1907, and with the vigor the public had learned to expect

---

[4] The author of the verse, Ambrose Bierce, after the furor over its alleged association with the murder of McKinley, said that Hearst had not known of the verse until after it was published, and explained that his own intention was merely to warn of the danger of this "particular precedent if unpunished." Goebel was a Governor of Kentucky who had been murdered by a bullet shot through the window of his office.

[5] Not by a great margin. The vote was: Hughes, 749,002; Hearst, 691,105. Hughes was the only one on the Republican ticket who was elected.

of him, energetically initiated a series of reforms. As a
start to reorganizing the State's insurance department he
requested the resignation of its chief, Otto H. Kelsey, an
honest person, one of the better type of politicians, but
quite without qualification to be the head of the insur-

President Taft and Governor Hughes of New York review-
ing the Seventh Regiment of New York at the
Taft inauguration.

ance department as Hughes planned it to be. Kelsey, exhibiting that virtue of office-holders which refuses to
"quit under fire," declined to resign. To force him out
Hughes was obliged to have the consent of the State Senate, and as a result he became involved in a tug-of-war
with much of the Republican "Old Guard" organization
throughout the State.

Among those resisting Hughes in this as well as other
reforms was a Republican clan in western New York,
the Wadsworths, including a henchman named — in-
consequentially except as he became a chip in the ensuing

conflagration — Archie Sanders. Sanders, as it happened, was a Federal office-holder, collector of customs at Rochester, and therefore subject to President Roosevelt at Washington. Under this state of facts, a close friend of Governor Hughes, Fred Stevens, went to Washington and suggested to Roosevelt that he remove Sanders, as a means of reproving the opposition to Hughes's reform programme in New York.

James Wadsworth.

The circumstances of this interview, what Stevens said to Roosevelt and Roosevelt to Stevens, and especially the implications of what each said, became later important and a subject of controversy. It is certain that Stevens, in making his suggestion, acted without authority from Hughes, and even without Hughes's knowledge. It was quite possible, however, for Roosevelt to suppose Stevens was speaking for Hughes. Unquestionably Roosevelt, in adopting Stevens's suggestion and removing Sanders, was moved, in part at least, by the wish to help Hughes. But it is likewise a fact that Roosevelt had a motive of his own. The Wadsworth clan, of which Sanders was a satellite, were bitter enemies of Roosevelt; the head of the clan, James W. Wadsworth, a Congressman, had been Roosevelt's outstanding foe in a fight for pure food and meat inspection, and Wadsworth, after being beaten, had publicly expressed his deliberate judgment that Roosevelt was "a humbug and a faker."

Which of Roosevelt's two motives weighed most with him is immaterial; it is common for every one to have more than one motive for his actions, and no less common unconsciously to emphasize the one most likely to appeal to the public.

Roosevelt's startling demand for the resignation of Sanders was heralded by New York City newspapers[6] as an act by Roosevelt in promotion of Hughes's reform programme. "It is the President's intention," said *The Tribune*, "to strengthen Governor Hughes' stand at every opportunity." At Albany, newspaper correspondents asked Governor Hughes whether he had requested Roosevelt to remove Sanders. Hughes was obliged to say he had not, because that was the fact, and also because in his campaign he had emphasized a pledge that he would not make use of patronage to promote his measures, and that he would deal with appointments and legislation on merit. If it should have been thought that Hughes had arranged with Roosevelt for the expulsion from public office of one of his opponents, he would have been attacked as a hypocrite. Hughes made no formal statement in quotation-marks; but in the familiar formula for inspired information, the New York *Times*[7] said:

It was stated from excellent authority today that Governor Hughes was not consulted . . . and knew nothing about it until it was announced to the public.

Had the newspapers stopped with that, had Hughes's public differentiation of himself from Roosevelt's action been confined to the words he himself inspired, Roosevelt need have taken no great offense — indeed, he would have been in the stronger position of having made

6 April 20, 1907.　　　　7 Sunday, April 21, 1907.

his contribution to Hughes's reform programme voluntarily instead of by request. But there was among the correspondents at Albany one who wrote at length about the episode, and this correspondent was the one who was supposed to be, and actually had been, but now was not, the closest to Hughes, in his particular confidence, and reflecting his most personal attitude. This correspondent's despatches[8] had the effect of implying that Roosevelt's help was a detriment to Hughes, that it was resented by Hughes's friends. In passages, phrases, and head-lines, Roosevelt's demand for the resignation of a Federal office-holder for the purpose of aiding Hughes in his legislative programme was given a color likely to irritate Roosevelt: "Governor Hughes has been more completely embarrassed by the aid of one friend than by the opposition of the whole [State] Senate." Hughes's friends were represented as feeling that Roosevelt's action, "very far from being intended as real support, was a deliberate effort to minimize the governor's achievement by giving the country at large the impression that it was achieved solely by the aid of the President. . . . There is sound basis for believing that the governor felt safe enough as to the outcome of the struggle here to prefer to win alone. It is apparent how distasteful it was to them [Hughes's friends] to have the President interfere. The result [of Roosevelt's action] would be to divide the praise; in any such division the President might expect the lion's share, as a national figure. The President has achieved a splendid position with precious little pains. . . ." Hughes was being made to seem to play "second fiddle" to Roosevelt; Hughes's administration at Albany would become "the shadow of Washington." Roosevelt was pictured as exercising his extraor-

[8] In the New York *Evening Post*, April 22 and 23, 1907. The quotations from the despatches here reproduced are detached sentences.

dinary "political sagacity," as trying to edge himself
under the umbrella of Hughes's popularity: "whatever
strength with the people Hughes possesses . . . now
inures to the benefit of the President, too." On another
count, Roosevelt's use of Federal patronage to influence
legislation was decried as dubious political ethics: "The
questionable method in which the aid came . . . the
descent of the big stick . . . will stir resentment in the
breast of every believer in civil service reform. It is entirely possible that the Governor will repudiate this assistance given through federal patronage." Finally, the
despatches said, in the language most likely to excite
Roosevelt's anger, that he had practised outright duplicity: "The truth is, of course, that the President desired to punish [Congressman] James W. Wadsworth,
Sr., and in order to make a neat cover for this, he announced that it was an action to aid Hughes."

All that, Roosevelt read — and read it on the assumption that it was the "expression of the correspondent and
of the newspaper closest to Hughes," on the assumption
that it was one of those newspaper despatches, of a sort
familiar to every public man, which is written after an
intimate interview with the man reflected. Actually, the
expression was that of the correspondent who in the recent past had been "closest to Hughes," but who had
"broken with him some weeks before and was not now
seeing him."

In the talk that arose about this episode, and the
masses of printed recollections that allude to it, runs an
assumption which grows firmer with time, that Roosevelt
meant to nominate Hughes as his successor, that his help
on this occasion was his opening gesture, and that
Hughes's failure to respond to the gesture (the failure

being made to appear more pointed than it was by Roosevelt's misunderstanding reading of a newspaper account) caused Roosevelt to change his mind. "You can imagine," wrote Henry L. Stoddard, "the effect on Roosevelt; he felt that his friendly offices had been rejected in a most unfriendly way; he expected thanks rather than what he considered a rebuke."[9] "Roosevelt," wrote Oscar King Davis, "backed off and stayed backed off.[10] Hughes could very easily have altered the circumstances so that Roosevelt would have preferred him, and would have exerted his influence to secure the nomination of Hughes."

This assumption is more appetizing to the sense of the dramatic in history than either faithful to the incidents as they happened, or compatible with the human nature of the two men. It was possible that Hughes might have acquired such momentum as to oblige Roosevelt to acquiesce; or that Hughes by a deliberate course of conduct might have made himself Roosevelt's choice. Yet it was hardly in nature for Roosevelt to nominate Hughes. Roosevelt was pre-eminent in a certain field, was the outstanding reformer of the day. If Hughes were to be nominated as the beneficiary of Roosevelt's efforts, he would have had to gravitate into the Roosevelt solar system, taking up his own minor orbit about the gigantic sun that Roosevelt was. Hughes was just a little too big to do that, or else too detached, or too differentiated from Roosevelt in the public mind. On the other hand — at a time when so much of the firmament was monopolized by Roosevelt — Hughes was not quite big enough or radiant enough, or was as yet too new to the public mind, to set up a rival solar system of his own. For whatever reason, Hughes did not become a rival to Roosevelt; he

9 "As I Knew Them."
10 "Released for Publication."

remained an inferior sun, yet not a satellite. In that
rôle, Hughes never excited in Roosevelt any sense of
competition, or other disapproving emotion. Roosevelt's
permanent attitude toward Hughes was one of real
respect, touched with amiable condescension about
Hughes's austere sense of propriety and his lack of eminence in some lines of practical politics in which Roosevelt thought of himself as adept. A true index to Roosevelt's attitude toward Hughes is in a sentence, including the exclamation-mark, in a letter[11] Roosevelt wrote him — Hughes received many from him, all of them friendly — : "Now at the risk of causing a shock to your principles, I desire to say that I would like to make a bet! that you will carry New York by over a hundred thousand. . . ."[12]

John L. Sullivan in 1908.
See foot-note 12.

[11] October 26, 1908; unpublished.

[12] Once, about the time the letter quoted above was written, the author of
this history was a participant in an episode revealing the condescending friendliness of Roosevelt's attitude toward Hughes. I went to the White House and
as I opened the door of the President's office he welcomed me with more than
usual vivacity, arising, I was to learn, from the opportunity my coming gave
him to tell a recent experience that he had enjoyed. Looking up from his desk he
said: "There was a kinsman of yours here to-day." He laughed, leaned over his
desk and wagged his head over a cause of pleasure as yet to me unknown. After
an interval of squeaky laughter he permitted an opening peep into his joke by
saying, "John L. was just here" — those were the days when "John L." was
enough; to have added the "Sullivan" would have seemed a reprehensible affec-
tation of superiority toward a popular hero. "He gave me two cigars," Roosevelt continued, "you can have one of them." "John L." had come to the White
House about a nephew who had entered the navy and by high-spirited disagreement with a detail of discipline had found himself in a position from which

IV

When, finally, Roosevelt put his mind upon selecting his successor — or 'when his attention was called to the necessity of so doing by his secretary, Loeb — he was moved by the axiom of practical politics which says, "You can't beat somebody with nobody." The "somebody" whom Roosevelt, in this case, had to beat was himself. "You should," said Loeb to him one morning, "have a candidate. You are under pledge not to run again. I propose that you make people understand you intend to keep it. Some people believe that a deadlocked convention might force you to disregard it. Others believe you . . . are manipulating things so as to force a deadlock. The air is full of such talk. The way to settle it is to have a candidate."[13]

Roosevelt agreed. "We must have a candidate," he said. "We had better turn to Taft. . . . See Taft and tell him." Loeb told Taft. Taft hurried to thank Roosevelt. "Yes, Will," said Roosevelt. "It's the thing to do."

only high authority could rescue him. "John L." insisted the boy was in the right and was a good lad — he had looked into the circumstances and reviewed his own knowledge of the boy dispassionately and found nothing to condemn, nor any reason for a mental reservation, except such as might lie in the fact that the boy was an amateur musician, had "taken to music," was "John L.'s" phrase of dubiety.

All this Roosevelt told, with writhing enjoyment punctuating each sentence. Then he came to the climax of his delight. It turned out that Roosevelt had no authority in the case — if he had had, we may be sure, he would have turned the naval establishment upside down. But the proper source for the first step in the lad's relief was Governor Charles E. Hughes of New York. "So I gave John L. a letter of introduction to Hughes. Wouldn't you like to see Hughes's whiskers curl when John L. Sullivan walks in on him with a letter of introduction from the President of the United States?"

Roosevelt regarded Hughes as a good man and able, but scholastically remote from the commonalty. Whatever the estimate Roosevelt might make of their respective qualities of statesmanship, Hughes could not give intimate letters of introduction to prize-fighters.

13 "As I Knew Them," H. L. Stoddard. This account of the incident has been verified by the author of this history.

9

AN EMANCIPATION

Narrative of the Healing of Seven Million Afflicted; of a
Happy and Fruitful Union of Science and Philanthropy;
and of a Modest Man Who Worked Patiently Against the
Opposition of Inertia, Made a Great Discovery, Became a
Butt for the Humorists of the World, Was Maligned by
Those Whom He Sought to Help — and Lived to See His
Victory Assured, His Renown Forgotten.

On December 4, 1902, a convention of physicians and
sanitarians[1] at Washington, D. C., listened, with the tolerance of pundits for a neophyte, to an address by a
very youthful appearing man of science, Doctor Charles
Wardell Stiles, described on the programme as Chief of
the Division of Zoology of the United States Public
Health Service. Stiles naturally, since his audience were
specialists in preventive medicine, used the language of
technical men. The physicians present followed him
with understanding, but to one listener, apparently, much
of the lecture might as well have been in Sanskrit. In a
front seat, just below the speaker's platform, sat a rotund, moon-faced young man whose head at short intervals would sink slowly to his breast, while his increasingly heavy breathing approached so close to a snore that
the question whether he would or would not became an
occasion for acute suspense, surpassing, from time to
time, interest in the more formal programme. Whenever
the sleepy auditor mobilized all his resources of attention,
his reviving faculties were again driven into retreat by
such opiatic phrases from Doctor Stiles as "ancylostoma
duodenale" and "uncinariasis americana."

[1] The Sanitary Conference of American Republics.

Doctor Stiles, under the compulsion of a natural law with which public speakers are familiar, found his attention drawn to the spectacle that was a rival to himself. More exactly, Doctor Stiles's mind divided itself into two, half of it concerning itself with the speech

From a photograph by Science Service.
Doctor Charles Wardell Stiles in 1930.

he was making, half turning anxiously to the disturber. With each slow descent of the latter's chin, each resumption of the cumulatively slow breathing of approaching slumber, Doctor Stiles passed through a corresponding cycle of suspense, wondering if this time the snore would really come. Who was he, anyhow? Stiles asked himself; why was he here? why should he be in this audience, embarrassing an earnest young scientist with an exceptionally passionate wish to have the attention of his listeners?

Suddenly, to Stiles's relief, and also to his mystification, the young man shook off his lethargy and began scribbling furiously on a pad. Now, perversely, Stiles's bedevilled mind flashed back and forth from his speech to a new speculation. What had caused the transformation? Had it been something Stiles had said, some solecism or impropriety, perhaps? Stiles had been talking about the hookworm parasite, which he had recently found to be widely prevalent in several Southern States. The portion of his speech that had coincided with the drowsy auditor's sudden revitalization had dealt with the effect the hookworm has of causing in its victims an extreme disinclination to labor. The so-called "poor white trash" of the South, Doctor Stiles had said in substance, were probably not inherently lazy; their energy was being consumed by hookworms. What was there in that statement to galvanize a lethargic young man? That allusion, in Stiles's mind, was no more arresting than other parts of his address, his reference to the eosinophilia of the blood, as an aid to diagnosis, for example.

After the lecture, the sleepy young man — he was a newspaper reporter — took himself off into the night, leaving for history no explanation of his abrupt emergence from sleepiness — whether the startling thought had struck him that his own proneness to somnolence might be due to hookworms in his internal anatomy, or whether his interest had been awakened by the implications in the thought that so common a human trait as laziness might be caused by a microbe. In the anonymity that was the almost universal rule of newspaper writing in America during the early years of the century, the young man's name[2] disappeared into the limbo of that quite large number of persons whose contributions, in the course of the day's work, to the wit of the time or its enlightenment, or its wisdom or emotion, are unacknowledged by fame.

Stiles, the congratulations of his scientific colleagues tingling pleasantly in his ears, went home to a quiet night's rest, undisturbed by any dream that the day's occurrences had unleashed forces destined to make him, in turn, first, the target for newspaper and stage humorists the world over; next, the object of scorn and vituperation in all the region south of the Potomac River and east of the Mississippi; and, finally, years later, one of the heroes of medical science in his generation.

GERM OF LAZINESS FOUND?

DISEASE OF THE "CRACKER" AND OF SOME NATIONS IDENTIFIED.

Dr. Charles Wardell Stiles, Discoverer of the Hook Worm Disease, Describes Its Curious Effects to the Sanitary Conference of American Republics

WASHINGTON, Dec. 4.—The Sanitary Conference of American Republics closed its sessions to-day with a declaration almost sensational in its significance. Dr. Charles Wardell Stiles, Zoölogist of the Bureau of Animal Industry of the Agricultural Department and well known in the medical world as the discoverer of uncinariasis,

A headline that made history. Printed in the New York *Sun*, December 5, 1902, its whimsicality set the world a-laughing and, by focussing attention on an obscure scientist, helped make possible a great victory over disease.

II

The following evening, Stiles, after a routine day in his laboratory, went to the Cosmos Club for dinner. Afterward, while looking over the newspapers in the club library, his eye was caught by a head-line in the

2 Efforts made in 1928 to identify the reporter were unsuccessful.

New York *Sun:* "GERM OF LAZINESS FOUND?" Chuckling, he was about to turn the page when his own name seemed to leap out of the type at him. Aghast, Stiles read a description of his own speech at the preceding day's meeting of the Sanitary Conference, written by the young man whose drowsiness had so troubled him.

One of the pictorial jokes inspired by Doctor Stiles's lecture on Uncinaria Americana, renamed by the New York *Sun* "Germ of Laziness."

The despatch, in effect, declared that Doctor Stiles had found the germ responsible for that widespread human failing, chronic indolence.

Next day began the flood. On the authority of *The Sun's* despatch, accounts were telegraphed throughout America and to Europe. Some of the newspaper treatment was serious, taking the form, in part, of interviews with physicians. That, however, was minor compared to the explosion of facetiousness.

While the outburst was put in the familiar formulas of humor, it was more than that; it had a shading which made it an exceptionally accurate and characteristic expression of the American spirit. That spirit, in its deeps, had always had toward laziness an attitude that was not really condemnatory. Indeed, the attitude was one of tolerance, of approval that could not be direct but was the more genuine for being tacit. This trait of Americans was their adjustment to reality, the compromise by which they

THE UNCINARIASIS
OR GERM OF
LAZINESS

RESPONSIBLE
FOR THE FOLLOWING PHRASES!
"NOTHING DOING"   „
"THAT TIRED FEELING"
"WHATS THE USE"
"DEAD TO THE WORLD"

From the New York "Journal,"
December, 1902.

Cartoonist Powers's impressions of the "Germ of Laziness."

made a livable bridge between their austere ideals of theology and education and the realities of human nature. When Americans were, so to speak, intellectually and morally on parade, when they were at church or in school, they solemnly extolled the virtue of diligence; but when at their ease they gave smiling sympathy to the sinner against arduousness. In their pulpits, the preachers read the Bible passages about industry, repeated Solomon's counsel "Go to the ant, thou sluggard," while the congregations decorously nodded becoming approval. In their literature for the young, their Horatio Algers and their Samuel Smiles, they exalted assiduity and gave the successes of life, as represented in fiction, solely to the industrious and the sedulous. In their schools they required the children to read, memorize and recite the copy-book maxims of "Poor Richard" and others about

> Early to bed and early to rise
> Makes a man healthy, wealthy, and wise.

But the less self-conscious expression of the American spirit when in its spontaneous moods, and therefore the truer index, was smiling indulgence for those who ignored the cult of diligence, or flouted it. About the indolent, they made countless jokes — but always the sort that invited the victim to join in the smile. The cracker-barrel philosopher, the lazy office-boy, the "weary Willie," the fisherman truant from his task, were stock characters of American humor — but rarely did the joke really sting. Always it was touched with tolerance, even envy. The characters of song and story that America really loved were the ones who emulated the sloth, obeyed no routine, and left diligence to the ant and the bee — Rip Van Winkle, Old Dan Tucker, the old settler in "The Arkansas Traveler." The village vagabond, if he had wit and personality, was better loved and longer remembered than the local nabob who built the town hall and tried to perpetuate his name by fastening it to a suburban extension. In the true American estimation, the real frontier heroes were not the ones who tilled the land, built the factories, founded the banks, and acquired great possessions — the names of those were not preserved. The real American heroes were those who in life went their own way and at death left nothing in the bank — Kit Carson, Davy Crockett, Daniel Boone. It may reasonably be contended that it was as an incident of a later organization of American life that the "go-getter" came to the front, fruit of the period of the speeding-up of industry, when man was stimulated to conform to the machine. The more characteristic American hero in the earlier day, and the more beloved type at all times, was not the hustler but the whittler.

And now, here was a discovery that exonerated and exculpated all indolence; laziness was only a disease. The idea bore out what the American spirit had always wanted to believe — always the springtime impulse to loaf and wander and fish had been euphemized as an ailment, "spring fever."

In glad celebration of science's acquittal of sloth, editorial writers, professional jokesmiths, cartoonists, pressed the starter of imagination; newspaper rhymesters took up the challenge to their ingenuity inherent in the technical name of the new disease:

THE MICROBE OF SLOTH

I for long had believed that, concerning my case,
    There existed much popular haziness;
I for years had felt sure it was grossly unfair
    To regard as a failing my laziness;
Now, the truth has come out, thanks to good Doctor Stiles,
    And 'tis proved how unjust a strong bias is,
For I, if you please, for my idleness scorned,
    Have been suffering from uncinariasis!

Of course, I've been lazy — who wouldn't be so
    Who has known what the "hookworm's" fell trail meant?
Who wouldn't, I ask, who's endured all his life
    A confounded six-syllable ailment?[3]

Such "hookworm verse" became a recognized category of contemporary doggerel; in the offices of *Puck*, *Judge*,

[3] Originally published in *Truth*, London.

and *Life*, and in the fraternity of newspaper humorists, "hookworm jokes" became a staple commodity:

A dog belonging to a Virginia mountaineer howled so loudly it attracted the attention of a passerby who inquired, "What ails that houn' — sick?" "Naw — hookworm." "Hookworm! I didn't know that hurt." "Doesn't — dawg sitting on a burr — too lazy to get up, so he howls."

Among the thousands of jokes, cartoons, comic strips, and the countless parasangs of hookworm hectameters and dactyls, it was an editorial in the Salt Lake City *Herald*[4] that most accurately expressed the precise American shade of humor — mild jeering, softened by tolerance, touched indeed almost with envy:

Are you troubled with "that tired feeling"? Have you a settled aversion for getting up in the morning to start a fire in the kitchen range? If you have, folks say you are lazy, don't they? Well, they are wrong. The trouble with you, although you may not have known it until now, is that you have uncinariasis.

Uncinariasis? Yes; it's a disease. Dr. Charles Wardell Stiles is the discoverer. He has just returned from a sojourn among the laziest people in the world, the "crackers" of the South. Lazy? We beg their pardon. Those fellows are suffering so terribly from uncinariasis that they wait for the apples to fall off their trees, and then ask somebody to pass the fruit along. . . . Almost any fair day you can see on the corner of Main and Second South Streets whole droves of men who are in the very last stages of uncinariasis. Day after day the poor fellows stand around, stand around, looking at other people work. At intervals they go home and eat, provided the neighbors have sent in anything, but the rest of their time they put in just standing around.

The imagination of the humorists adventured into whimsical speculation about the possibilities of an "anti-laziness" serum that would convert office-boys into paragons of diligence, energize "weary Willies" into cap-

4 December 9, 1902.

tains of industry. The New York *World* announced, with a wink, the discovery of a hookworm antidote, "Staphylococcus anti-uncinariæ," discovered by "the eminent Prof. Weissnichtwarum," and described by him "in an article on Faulheitskur in the Vienna *Wochenschrift für Physiologie und Psychologie*," which was "produced by cultivating to a state of absolute perfection the germ of insomnia in a gelatine of agar-agar, a colorless oriental plant, stimulated with exhibitions of tincture capsicum and nitroglycerine." "English physicians," said *The World*, "acting, it is understood, upon representations made by the Home Secretary and the Premier, have cabled to their professional brethren in New York and Washington praying that under no circumstances shall any of the anti-laziness serum be given to J. Pierpont Morgan. 'He has our ships now,' they pleaded, 'and if he takes any of the Staphylococcus anti-uncinariæ his activity will be so increased that he will seize our railroads, our mills, our banks — aye, even the crown itself and the lion on the flag.'"

All of which, while it added to the gaiety of nations and portrayed an agreeable aspect of the American spirit, had a manner of forgetting about Stiles, though Stiles's name ran, of course, through the newspaper comment. Jokes lampooned him, and some of the serious comment chided him for a "sensationalism" for which the newspapers themselves, not the modest scientist, were responsible.

III

Charles Wardell Stiles, born the son of a Methodist minister at Spring Valley, N. Y., May 15, 1867, attended the Hartford, Conn., High School, where in one study, languages, he led his class, an achievement, however, which he attributed less to merit than to adventitious circumstance. His grandfather, like his father a Methodist of the old school, whom Stiles often visited in his boyhood, had the conviction that there were three ways, and only three, in which a boy might properly spend Sunday: he could read the Bible, or sing hymns, or walk in the churchyard. For young Stiles, walking in the churchyard had no allure; not for him the doleful contemplation, under the monitory eye of his Methodist grandfather, of the last resting-places of the local departed, the while his ears were tantalized by the joyous cries of those of his friends whose freedom was not so inflexibly encompassed. As for the hymnal, the first year of that yielded the satisfaction of exploration, but after he had come to know the book by heart the mere thought of hymn-singing caused him acute distress. Thus Stiles, bending his spirit to the least of three distastes, spent long hours, Sunday after Sunday, summer and winter, in what was, for a good many average American youths of the 1870's, the characteristic Sabbath-day recreation. After many months of it, Stiles, with a resourcefulness that was destined to enrich his future career, turned the chore into an intellectual adventure. Having begun the study of French only a few years later than he began English, he secured a French Bible and thereafter conducted his Sunday reading in French. Eventually he came to know the French Bible as thoroughly as the English one and increased his reading mastery of that language. In succession he took up the Bible in Latin, Greek, German, and Italian.

The cherished hope of young Stiles's family that he should become, like his father, a Methodist clergyman, was frustrated by his youthful satiety with churchyards, hymnals, and Bibles, and by a powerful urge within himself that already expressed itself in a boyish hobby. He was never so happy as when collecting insects or mounting butterflies or dissecting frogs; to this lad the common earthworm was not merely something to catch fish with, it was an animate marvel as enthralling as a tale in Grimm's. In his room he maintained as reasonably complete a collection of the smaller fauna of Connecticut, alive and dead, as could be concealed in odd corners from the suspicious eye of his mother's servant. He was proud of his collection and constantly on the alert to enrich it with new specimens. One thing he lacked to make it perfect in his mind; he wanted a skeleton, preferably the skeleton of a human being, but if that was impossible — and the attitude of his family left little doubt that it was — then the skeleton of an animal lower in the scale. One day, on his way home from school, a boyish divagation into a rubbish-strewn vacant lot revealed to him the cadaver, stiff in rigor mortis, of an alley cat which the hazards of a vagabond existence had stripped of the last of its nine lives. The lad, with his treasure-trove under his coat, rushed homeward, his blue eyes sparkling in an ecstasy of enthusiasm which, as he neared his front gate, partially disciplined itself to the restraints of caution, born of recollections which made him feel that his family might fail to share his rapture. By such artifice of smuggling as inspiration can always invent when zeal encounters obtuseness, he got the cat into his room, where, with the extemporized dissecting-tools that are available to a small boy, he stripped off the hide and removed the viscera. Since the separating of the hard stringy muscles from the bones was beyond the capacity of such tools of surgery as can be surreptitiously borrowed from a family sideboard, he decided to soften the flesh by boil-

ing. During a favoring absence of the family, he put
one of his mother's best kettles on the kitchen stove,
filled it with water, and placed the cat in it. There followed a catastrophe impossible to foresee, impossible to
guard against, heartrending in its consequences. A play-
mate happening along, young Stiles's interest in anatomy
was temporarily distracted to the perfecting of some
feats of acrobatic dexterity in the front yard. His experiment in taxidermy was recalled to him when he saw
smoke issuing from the kitchen windows and his nose
was assailed by a smell which he remembered throughout his mature life as the most offensive he had ever had
experience with — a convincing superlative considered in
the light of Stiles's subsequent acquaintance as a scientist
with extraordinary odors, in laboratories and elsewhere.
The hot fire had boiled away the water in the kettle,
and the hoped-for addition to his amateur museum was
a charred crisp.

In 1886, Stiles, then eighteen years old, went to Europe and studied at the Collège de France, the Universities of Berlin and Leipzig, the Trieste Zoological
Station, and the Pasteur Institute. In following his specialty, medical zoology, Stiles learned, as one detail of
the broad and thorough training he received, about a
parasite of animals, the hookworm, known to European
scientists for more than a hundred years as a pin-like
worm infesting the intestines of wild and domesticated
animals. In 1782, Goeze, a German clergyman and zoologist, found in the intestine of a badger he was dissecting a small, hair-like parasite which he called "der
Haarrundwurm" — the hair-round worm. Seven years
later, Froelich, another German zoologist, found a similar parasite in the intestine of a fox. Froelich, observing curious structures resembling hooks in the tail of the

worm, adopted the vernacular word Haakenwurm (hookworm), and gave the generic name Uncinaria to the genus he established. Stiles learned also that more recently another species of hookworm had been found in the intestines of human beings living in Europe and in the tropics; Angelo Dubini, in 1838, found hookworms in the body of a young woman who had died in a hospital at Milan. A book containing references to hookworm was published in France in 1888 while Stiles was a student there;[5] it cited, among the regions where hookworm disease had been found, in addition to the tropics, France, Italy, and southern Germany. As an inference from descriptions of afflicted persons, and from similarity of climatic conditions, it stated that hookworm probably existed in the American States bordering on the Gulf of Mexico, although few if any cases of the disease had been actually recognized and no definitely identified hookworm parasite had ever been found there.

IV

Stiles, returning to the United States in 1891, received an appointment as a consulting zoologist in the Bureau of Animal Industry of the Department of Agriculture at Washington. His duties as custodian of the helminthological collections of the National Museum, coinciding with his intellectual curiosity about everything in the field of zoology, led him to make a careful examination of the parasite collections under his charge. The mass of what he found was, after his extensive European experience, familiar; he was surprised, however, at not finding any specimen of hookworm of the species that infects man. No American scientific collection contained any hookworm specimen of this type;

5 "L'ankylostome duodénal et l'anémie des mineurs," by Raphael Blanchard.

no American scientific body presumed the existence of hookworm in this country. A study by Stiles of American medical literature for many years back revealed no definite assertion of the existence of hookworm disease in the United States. As late as the year 1901, hook-

From the report of the Rockefeller Sanitary Commission.
Dispensary group, Jacksonville, N. C. They came 20 and 30 miles by boat, train, and private conveyances.

worm disease, recognized as such or by that name, was unknown in the United States.

But if there was no hookworm disease, by that name, there were countless thousands of cases of a disease variously referred to as "chronic anæmia" and "continuous malaria," of a type associated with dirt-eating, medically "malacia." In whole regions of the South it was endemic. Dirt-eating — it was literally that — because it was so horrifying a contrast to normal human behavior, had a fascination for the kind of popular curiosity catered to by the "shocker" sections of Sunday newspapers.

Frequent articles about "dirt-eaters," "clay-eaters," "brick-eaters," "resin-chewers" dwelt upon the revolting symptoms and effects of the morbid diet-habit, usually with the implication that a moral stigma went with it. Occasional newspaper articles told of cultivated persons, formerly fastidious, who after affliction with this disease pathetically adopted furtive devices to conceal their revolting habit. As a rule, however, the disease was thought of in connection with an unhappy class in the South called "poor white trash," "crackers." Much of the writing about "dirt-eating," medical as well as popular, assumed that the unnatural diet was, in some cases, deliberately adopted as a means of bringing about a physical condition which would justify avoidance of labor.

To Stiles, the references to dirt-eating in the South had the illuminating effect of a searchlight. Dirt-eating, he recalled from his education abroad, was regarded in European medical circles as a concomitant of hookworm disease; in European medical experience, dirt-eating and hookworm were inseparable. To Stiles it was clear that American medical opinion about malacia had mistaken effect for cause; he was confident that the dirt-eating found in the Southern States was not a disease, but a symptom. The disease, Stiles felt sure, was hookworm, the existence of which in the United States was not even suspected by American medical science.

Stiles, when he recited his theory in American medical circles, encountered, sometimes polite scepticism, sometimes raucous disbelief. He was, in the eyes of physicians, merely a zoologist, a student of animals and small bugs, and therefore not as qualified to know about human disease as men who devote their lives to clinical medicine. The outstanding medical man in the United

States, Doctor William Osler of Johns Hopkins, hearing Stiles in 1896 assert his belief that hookworm disease existed in the Southern States, rebuked him for having reflected on American physicians. Stiles's reply, the only one he could make as yet, was, "Wait and see."[6]

Stiles used every opportunity to transmit to others his interest in hookworm and his conviction that it was widely endemic in the South. In addition to his work in the Bureau of Animal Industry he taught medical zoology at Johns Hopkins University, at Georgetown University, and at the Army Medical School, to students of whom many would ultimately have experience in the tropics. Always, at one time or another during his lectures, Stiles would explain what he had learned in Europe about hookworm, how to diagnose it, and what was then known of its geographical distribution. "Gentlemen," he would say, "if you are ever in the tropics and you find a case of anæmia you cannot explain, see if it is not due to hookworms."

v

Among the hundreds of medical students who during the early and mid-nineties listened to Stiles's talks about hookworms, was a young man named Bailey K. Ashford. Ashford, born in 1873, had attended grammar and high schools at Washington, had studied a year in the medical school of George Washington University and three years at Georgetown University, had absorbed much knowledge of medicine from his father, a practising physician, and had worked in several Washington hospitals. In November, 1897, Ashford entered the army as an assistant surgeon.

[6] Doctor Harvey Cushing, Professor of Surgery, Harvard University, former president of the American Surgeons Association, having read the proofs of this chapter in one of its stages, pencilled on the margin: "I was at Johns Hopkins when Stiles was lecturing on parasites and I well remember the skepticism with which his ideas about hookworm disease were met."

When war was declared against Spain, Ashford accompanied the first troops sent to Porto Rico. Had any one attempted a judgment, during those anxious summer days of 1898 when rehabilitated cattle-boats and tramp steamers were pouring out of Tampa Bay loaded with troops bound for Caribbean battle-fields — had any one sought to guess which of all the 20,000 duty-bound Americans landed in Porto Rico during the war would contribute most to history in the highest sense, the guesser would probably not have looked beyond the high-ranking officers; in all likelihood his choice would have fallen upon the expedition's leader, General Nelson A. Miles — head of the United States Army in a symbolic as well as an official sense, handsome, impressive, with a

Colonel Bailey K. Ashford,
U. S. A. retired.

picturesque experience of Indian wars behind him, just the type for a military hero—who during his thirty-five years of army service had, as "Mr. Dooley" said, "faced death an' promotion in ivry form."[7] Not conceivably could the prophet's choice have been that inconspicuous twenty-five-year-old assistant surgeon, Bailey K. Ashford, whose knowledge of warfare included

[7] An unforgettable passage from "Mr. Dooley" was his picture of General Miles preparing to make an appearance in public, in the days before serviceable khaki had displaced gorgeous colors in army uniforms, and when official rank was in the ratio of gold braid: "He took his bonnet out, had a goold beater in to fix up th' epylets, got th' ilicthric lights goin' in th' buttons, found th' right pair iv blue an' pink pants, pulled on th' shoes with th' silver bells, harnessed to his manly hips th' soord with the forget-me-nots on th' handle . . ."

nothing of destruction but only the amelioration of sufferings wrought by war. The most of fame that Ashford could reasonably expect would be, perhaps, a citation for bravery under fire, or, in another alternative, that his name should appear in one of the black-bordered newspaper lists of "Killed in Action." As for being the one American of the 20,000 whose name should outlive the oblivion that followed quickly upon the short-lived and bloodless Porto Rican campaign; who should come to be grouped by discriminating history with the great figures of medical science — Ross, Gorgas, Finlay, Walter Reed, and the rest — certainly Ashford's chance of that was very small. It could happen at all — and it did — only because Ashford possessed a scientific mind of high order, and because of several happenings and coincidences fortunately concatenated.

From the day of his landing in Porto Rico, Ashford's professional interest was stirred by the unhealthy appearance of many of the natives, particularly those living away from the cities and towns. They were wan, emaciated, listless, utterly lacking in energy; a blight seemed to weigh upon them. If Ashford would have liked to probe into the causes for their condition, duty denied him the time and the opportunity; night and day he was busy caring for sick American soldiers. Then, in 1899, a year after the war ended, occurred an event of a sort normally described as a cataclysm, but which, because of certain of its consequences, was of the nature of a beneficent dispensation. A hurricane of terrific force, sweeping northward from the equator, passed over Porto Rico, leaving in its wake a heavy toll of death. Relief hospitals were opened speedily to care for the injured, to one of which Ashford was assigned. Now, in his improvised clinic crowded with emaciated, sickly natives he could at last satisfy his zeal for investigation. Fully three-fourths of his patients, he found, were anæmic, a condition "which was then believed to be due to faulty diet."[8] He tried iron, arsenic, and full diet, all without effect. Other explanations of the natives' condition were "malaria, climate, lack of hygiene." None of these, Ashford decided, adequately explained the symptoms. He pondered the phenomena of a high eosinophilia in the blood samples he had taken and reviewed in his mind the disease of which this was characteristic. Eosinophilia of the blood was one of the characteristics mentioned by Stiles in his lectures on hookworm disease. The test for hookworms was simple — eggs of the parasite in the victim's fæces. Ashford went looking for eggs. He found them, in profusion, myriads of them. Ashford now knew, beyond possibility of mistake, what the blight was that lay upon the natives of rural Porto Rico; it was hookworm.[9]

What followed Ashford's discovery was sensational; to the disease-burdened peasants of Porto Rico it must have seemed miraculous. With thymol and epsom salts Ashford worked cures on thousands of sufferers, giving

[8] This was another instance of confusion of cause and effect.

[9] It was not quite so simple as that. Ashford's feat was not the mere putting of two and two together and adding up their sum. The symptoms Ashford found could have been accounted for by any one of a large number of diseases, or by such other factors as climate, bad living conditions, and the like. Other physicians, including the many excellent Porto Rican doctors who had been trained in the United States and Europe, had had the same symptoms to judge and none of them had suggested hookworm. Further, at the time of Ashford's discovery so little attention had been paid in America to hookworm, so little had been written about it, so completely lacking in knowledge of it was America, that Ashford's hitting upon it as the causative agent of the anæmia in Porto Rico was the equivalent of finding the needle in the haystack. Indeed, Ashford's achievement was greater than that. Up to the time of his observation of the patients in his hospital, physicians saw no mystery in the prevailing anæmia. It was regarded as being caused, in the majority of cases, by ordinary ailments. That people should suffer from it chronically, that they should die of it in alarming numbers, was believed to be the natural result of their poverty, of their supposedly innate laziness, and of the enervating climate in which they lived. Ashford displayed scientific imagination of the sort bordering on genius in rejecting this settled conviction of doctors older and more experienced than himself, and formulating an independent diagnosis of his own.

new life, free of misery, to young and old. When he went to Porto Rico in 1898, 12,000 people were dying annually from anæmia; within half a dozen years he had reduced this yearly toll to less than a thousand.[10]

VI

Stiles, in Washington, on receiving the news of Ashford's discovery in Porto Rico, wrote him a letter of congratulation. In 1901, when Ashford made a trip to Washington bringing a collection of hookworms for the Army Medical Museum, the two met for several long talks.

Stiles now knew: that hookworm was wide-spread in Porto Rico; that conditions of soil and climate in Porto Rico were similar to those in parts of the Southern States; that the symptoms of hookworm sufferers in Porto Rico were similar to the symptoms of some of the persons in the South whose affliction was supposed to be chronic anæmia, or continuous malaria, or dirt-eating.

To Stiles's conviction that hookworm was wide-spread in the Southern States, the discovery of the disease in Porto Rico by Ashford gave supporting evidence, but nothing more. Neither Ashford's discovery nor all the allusions to dirt-eating Stiles had found were enough to remove Stiles's conviction from the field of theory and place it in the category of tested, scientific fact; in 1901, it was, as it had been ten years before, a hypothesis, nothing more. In support of it Stiles had theoretical deductions but no proof; he had never seen in the United States a person who could be said with certainty to have the disease; he had never found eggs of the parasite — the one certain test — in the fæces of an American

[10] Ashford adopted the scene of his great beneficence as his home for life; he married in Porto Rico, and, in the year this chapter was written, 1930, still lived there. He held the rank of colonel in the Medical Corps of the United States Army, and was accounted an outstanding world authority on tropical diseases.

suspect; he had never seen a hookworm identified as coming from an American host.

Stiles's conviction had been fortified by Ashford's discovery in Porto Rico; in addition, news of Ashford's discovery had put American physicians on warning[11] that soldiers returning from Porto Rico might bring the disease with them, with the result that there was watchfulness for it on the part of some American physicians.

In October, 1901, Stiles read in a medical journal that a Texas physician, Doctor Allen J. Smith of Galveston, had found eight cases of hookworm among some eighty-odd medical students of the University of Texas. This, to Stiles, was illumination; in effect, definite proof. The cases could not compose a local infection brought from abroad; since university students come from scattered localities, the infection must be endemic and more or less wide-spread throughout Texas. Stiles wrote the Galveston physician requesting specimens of the worms. When these arrived, Stiles put them under his microscope. They were hookworms — not identical, he discovered, with the Old World hookworm. He compared them with the Porto Rican specimens sent to the Army Medical Museum by Ashford; these two were identical. Stiles named the new species *Uncinaria americana*, *Necator americanus* — "American Murderer."

VII

Up to this time, Stiles's opportunities had been limited by his routine duties as a subordinate in the Bureau

11 Stiles wrote, in a report of his bureau, in 1903:

"To one of my former pupils, Dr. Bailey K. Ashford, of the U. S. Army, is unquestionably due the credit for having first seriously directed the attention of American physicians and zoologists to this disease. Ashford in fact found this malady very common in Porto Rico, and his clinical observations placed the American medical profession on its guard for cases which might occur in returning American troops."

of Animal Industry at Washington; his study of hook-worm had been carried on as an avocation outside the scope of his official tasks. Since he was without private wealth he could not give up his post to devote himself to the travel that was necessary for the investigation upon which his heart and mind were intent. What might have happened under these conditions to a man of Stiles's zeal and concentration, what explosion of his temperament, or stunting of his talent, is hard to guess. It is not necessary to guess. Fate interposed a beneficent hand by transferring him to the United States Public Health and Marine Hospital Service, in which hookworm was as proper a subject for investigation as any other disease. The head of the Public Health Service, Surgeon-General Walter Wyman, happened to be one of those men whose contributions to scientific discovery are sometimes only less great than those of the discoverers themselves. General Wyman's temperament inclined him to regard men of one idea not as cranks but as possible harborers of the divine spark of genius; he believed in his subordinate, and he gave Stiles permission to do what he had long wanted to do, make a trip through the Southern States to determine by personal observation if his long-held theory was correct.

In September, 1902, Stiles set out. Now began one of the strangest odysseys ever recorded in the annals of any people. Indeed, such odysseys as Stiles's are rarely recorded in history, for that art, so far as it deals with travel, confines itself usually to the marches of warriors, the treasure-hunts of argonauts, or the crusades of religion. Stiles had much of the temperament and some of the ways of a religious pilgrim; in an earlier age, legends might have grown up about him that could have made him a Prester John. To the matter-of-fact persons with whom he came in contact in the Southern States of America, however, in the early years of the twentieth century, he could have been explained only as a person demented. Here was a man carrying little baggage besides a microscope — to most of the communities he visited the microscope was novel; a man who, judged by accepted interpretations of human motives, was obviously seeking something valuable, perhaps signs of gold or jewels, but jewels with an extraordinary setting, for his quest, his inquiry at each place to which he came, was for human ordure. Little wonder that at the Cumnock mines in Chatham County, Va., Stiles was subjected by the miners to the process described as being "run out of town" — leaving behind him, one feels sure, among those simple folk, extraordinary surmises that one would enjoy hearing told in the hillside cabins, tales that must have composed an extraordinary legend.

At Richmond, Va., Stiles's examination of some of the 1,200 convicts in the State penitentiary revealed no hookworms or hookworm eggs. In the brick-yards at Camden, S. C., Stiles found hookworm eggs in night soil, but no person he could be sure had the disease. In five hundred miles of travel, chiefly in cities and in the clay lands, south from Washington, Stiles, though he examined many people from among those classes who, according to his theory, should be infected, had found no convincing evidence to support his hypothesis.

In a mood of brooding doubt, Stiles's mind, winding backward over his past researches and reading, recalled that in several of the cases of hookworms in animals which he had studied, there had been repeated allusions to a soil condition which had not, until now, seemed significant. Alaskan seal pups infected with hookworms had been found on sand rookeries, sheep and goats infected with the parasites had been found in sandy pastures, an outbreak of the disease among dogs had occurred in a sandy yard.

Stiles, his mind now on soil as a possible factor, "learned that the land near the Haile gold mines in South Carolina was chiefly a granite sand." He went there, and:

I found a family of 11 members, one of whom was an alleged "dirt-eater." The instant I saw these eleven persons I recalled Little's (1845) description of the dirt-eaters of Florida. A physical examination made it probable that we had before us eleven cases of uncinariasis, and a specimen of feces from one of the children gave the positive diagnosis of infection with *Uncinaria americana.* There were hundreds of eggs present.

Inquiring for the largest plantation of this sand district, I was directed to a place in Kershaw County, South Carolina. There were about sixty white "hands" on this farm. Going to a field I found about twenty at work. . . . A physical examination showed that they corresponded to cases of uncinariasis. A family of ten members was selected and examined carefully. Specimens of feces from four were examined microscopically and found to contain hundreds of eggs of *Uncinaria americana.* The owner of the plantation informed me that it would be a waste of my time to examine the remaining forty "hands," as they were in exactly the same condition as the twenty already examined.

Driving to a neighboring farmhouse, I found a family of five, three of whom presented such severe and typical symptoms that I had no hesitation in diagnosing them as due to uncinariasis.

While driving back to Kershaw, I passed a country school house. The children, about twenty-five or thirty in number, were at play during recess, and a mere glance at them was sufficient to show that thirty to forty percent presented the same general appearance as the children on the neighboring plantation.[12]

Continuing his journey, Stiles found cases of hookworm disease in Charleston, S. C., in the neighborhood of Macon, Fort Valley, and Albany, Ga., Jacksonville, Ocala, and other places in Florida. In one rude cabin he

[12] Ch. Wardell Stiles, *Hygienic Laboratory Bulletin,* No. 10, February, 1903.

found an emaciated farmer and his wife and five stunted children. Uncared-for graves in the yard marked the resting-places of ten other children whose hookworm-debilitated bodies had been unable to survive the handicap of disease and poverty they had borne from birth.

VIII

Jubilant, Stiles returned to Washington. He had established the identity of one of the most common diseases in the South, a disease hitherto undiagnosed, hitherto regarded as incurable and unpreventable, hitherto accepted as an inevitable and unarrestable deterioration of hundreds of thousands of persons belonging to the best stock in the country. Stiles had proved it to be hookworm, and hookworm was curable by a brief and simple treatment costing less than fifty cents. Stiles was justified in feeling that measured in terms of curing those already afflicted and preventing future infection, his achievement would rank as one of the great medical triumphs of all time.[13] When realization definitely came to him, he had been sleepless for three nights. Before his mind's eye passed much of the fundamental history of the South: negro slaves had brought hookworms from tropical Africa, one of many unhappy accompaniments of an institution that had been supposed, with tragic error, to be the indispensable economic basis for civilization in the Southern States. From negroes the disease had passed to whites, with the result that men of English, Irish, and Scotch stock — who elsewhere in America had conquered the wilderness, established schools, built churches, founded successful self-government, created

[13] Doctor Stiles, reading the proofs of this chapter, crossed out the author's words — "his achievement would rank as one of the great medical triumphs of all time" — and substituted: "his work would have lasting results." Probably the correct estimate lies somewhere between the historian's enthusiasm and the scientist's modesty.

a glowing civilization — men of this same stock had in the South become "poor white trash," had sunk to the level of their recently savage neighbors, had indeed sunk lower, for the white sufferers from hookworm were downward bound toward degeneracy and extinction.

Back in Washington, Stiles rushed forward a preliminary report of his journey for publication as a bulletin of the Public Health Service. What he needed now was public attention for the disease. He could envisage the fruits of his report — the country would be stirred, an aroused country would galvanize Congress, Congress would provide the sinews for the kind of war Stiles contemplated — not cannon nor battle-ships nor regiments of troops, but tons of thymol and epsom salts, and flying squads of sanitarians.

Stiles's report, printed as an official document of the United States Government, created scarcely a ripple; there was hardly a sign even that any one had read it, let alone comprehended its significance. Sadly, Stiles concluded that his report, which he felt was the most important thing printed in the United States in 1902, which he had counted upon to awaken the country to the condition of wholesale sickness in the South, was not going to help him. If there was any concrete result, it was an invitation to address the Pan-American Sanitary Conference on December 4.

At that Conference a sleepy newspaperman, whose precarious foothold on a gypsy occupation depended upon a facility with words, wrote a report of Stiles's discovery, upon which a head-line writer struck off, as a spark of his day's work, a phrase "germ of laziness." Overnight came, not exactly the publicity Stiles had hoped for, but publicity. He was a robust fellow, and he took the goods that the gods provided. If the public attention he sought, for the opportunity to exterminate hookworm, had to come with the accompaniment of ridicule for himself, that partial misadventure was better than complete public indifference.

The jeering with which Stiles's discovery was now surrounded made it impossible to hope for organized action to relieve the South; nobody would take the idea seriously. Stiles began single-handed. In him were combined two types of public benefactor. Many a scientist would have regarded his discovery as a sufficient climax, would have left the public to make such use of it as public intelligence might devise, and for himself would have turned to further research in his laboratory for some new scientific triumph. In Stiles, however, was a trait having no relation to the scientific part of him, a characteristic American quality, a missionary streak, the better part of Puritanism, a zeal to carry healing to the afflicted, combined with an urge to exhort, to preach, to recruit converts and apostles to a good cause. In a series of journeys out of Washington over a period of eight years, journeys made possible by the sympathetic support of his chief in the Public Health Service, Surgeon-General Wyman, the idea-driven scientist made himself a lone exhorter, bringing together audiences in schools, clubs, and colleges, to whom he lectured.

In other trips out of Washington, southward, Stiles carried his own kit of salts and thymol. Rural folk in remote districts found occasion to wonder at the purpose of a traveller who showed an extraordinary interest in their insides. Suspicious of "furriners," especially of "city" people, they eyed him coldly. Occasionally, on approaching the cabin of a "hillbilly," he found himself waved on his way with a shotgun. So often did this happen that as the years went by cumulative experience provided Stiles with a technic to prevent guns going off in his face. He would stand stock still, smile, and say: "Now, my friend, let's talk this over." Fortunately, the illiterate, their eyes and minds not spoiled by reading too much print, sometimes have a more accurate observation and a shrewder divination of human qualities than the "educated," and Stiles's formula of directness and sincerity never failed him. More often than not, when he explained that he wanted to cure sickness if sickness was in the house, he was allowed to do as he pleased, watched by puzzled but friendly audiences.

After five years of almost solitary crusading, Stiles — intense individualist though he was — realized there must be organization. With the accustomed thinking of a government employee, his first hope had been that Congress would help. He knew from his own experience in the Bureau of Animal Industry that Congress made generous appropriations to stamp out crop-destroying insects and cholera in hogs. But he was compelled to realize that Congress would not give him even enough money to set up a single anti-hookworm unit in one of the regions where infestation was greatest. He must turn to private wealth.

To find a man able and willing to give away $2,-000,000 (Stiles's estimate of his need) — and to persuade him to give it — is a job calling for specialized skill, and that sort of skill was not in Stiles's equipment. He lacked not only knowledge of the psychology of organized money-raising, "drives"; he did not even know personally any men of great wealth. Perhaps his sheer naïveté helped him; he found a wealthy philanthropist who promised the money, who began making plans for carrying out the project — and then died, leaving his money to heirs who had uses for money quite distant from philanthropy.

IX

In 1908, Stiles's familiarity with conditions in the rural South caused him to be assigned as an attaché to a Commission on Country Life, appointed by President Roosevelt to make a nation-wide survey of rural living conditions. Members of the Commission included Walter Hines Page, editor of *World's Work Magazine*, and Henry Wallace, editor of an Iowa periodical, *Wallace's Farmer*. One morning, when the Commission's train was travelling through the South, Stiles, Page and Wallace happened to be together in the smoking-car when a stop was made at a small country station. On the platform they noticed a miserable figure, a type hardly to be recognized as

Walter H. Page. One of the most useful Americans of his generation.

human, misshapen, his dwarfish body small in proportion to his apparently elongated limbs and fingers and unnaturally swollen joints; shoulders hunched and pointed, neck attenuated like that of a very old man, his dropsically protuberant stomach forming a hideous contrast with his pathetically emaciated, unnourished frame; skin the greenish-yellow tint of tallow, shrivelled and parchmentlike, eyes like a fragment of faded rag, nose almost transparent, mouth sagging; his attitude, if he could be said to have an attitude, that of a three-fourths empty sack supported by contact with the station wall. To Page, as a Southerner-born, the sight was all too familiar, all too common, and all too tragic; but to Wallace, coming from Iowa, it was arresting. There ensued a conversation, which Stiles recalled years later to have run as follows:

Wallace: What on earth is that?
Page (sadly): That is a so-called "poor white."
Wallace: If he represents Southern farm labor the South is in poor luck.
Stiles: That man is a "dirt-eater." His condition is due to hookworm infection; he can be cured at a cost of about fifty cents for drugs, and in a few weeks' time he can be turned into a useful man.
Page (astonished): Is that really a hookworm case? Can he really be cured? You can make a healthy man out of that wreck? Good God! Stiles, are you in earnest?

Now occurred the very essence of history: the juxtaposition in a smoking-car of two travellers, of whom one, Stiles, had a scientist's information about hookworm, while the other, Page, had a passion about bettering the South; the detonation of the mind of the first by the spectacle of a chance figure dawdling on a station platform, coupled with the eagerness of the mind of the second, set great events upon their way.

Walter Page can be rated as one of the ten or fifteen most useful men who provided leadership to America during the early years of the present century. While his enthusiasm was responsive to every sort of good cause, his particular zeal was for the regeneration of the South. Born and educated in North Carolina, he realized poignantly how near the fire of civilization in that section had come to extinction through the Civil War and the aftermath that was worse than war. Hardly to this day has any unbiassed summation been made of the destruction that the North visited upon the South. Rarely has any conqueror in history been so ruthless — by comparison, the treatment of Germany by the Allies was the rebuke of a complaisant parent to a naughty child. The North, by abolishing slavery, wiped out five billion dollars' worth of the South's property. That was but the beginning. Abolition of slavery was the complete destruction of the South's economic system, land in the South was made valueless. Then the North, by conferring suffrage on the negro, set the former slave in power over his recent master, and for ten years maintained him there by arms. The very aorta of civilization in the South was more near to being completely severed than historians have commonly realized. In the University of South Carolina, a State institution authority over which rested in the legislature, a corn-field negro, barefooted, illiterate, sat in the chair and drew the salary of the Professor of Greek. Over a period of forty years, including war, reconstruction (ironic word!) and the aftermath of both, the lamp of education in the South was saved from complete extinction only by the devotion and patience of half a dozen men. With the other consequences went a discouragement which accepted the physical deterioration, through disease, of large portions of the rural South, as merely one detail of a fate it was useless to resist. To rescue the South from this fate was Walter Page's consuming passion. For generations many of his North Carolina country people had been disdained, wiped off the books, as hopeless dross, as people with a moral, mental and physical taint, well on the path to irresistible degeneracy — and now Doctor Stiles told Page that the great mass of them were merely ill, ill in the same sense as the tuberculosis patients in the Adirondacks, and much more readily curable. Free these masses from the parasite that consumed their energies — Doctor Stiles said it could be done — and a revitalized generation would result.

The hookworm, Stiles told Page, is about as thick as a pin and about half as long. By means of hard structures in its mouth — curiously and, when seen under the microscope, hideously adapted to the purpose — it fastens itself, in clusters of several hundred, on the mucous wall of the small intestine of its victim. There it spends its adult life, sucking the blood of its human host and ungratefully discharging into his system enervating poisons. Its eggs, passing out with the bodily wastes, hatch in any warm, damp soil. The new generation, so tiny as scarcely to be perceptible to the naked eye, lie in wait, sometimes as long as six months; to the sole of the next barefooted passer-by they attach themselves and bore through (causing an irritation known as "ground-itch," "dew-itch," "toe-itch," and by a multitude of other names in different communities). Entering the blood-stream the worms pass through the heart and lungs and eventually settle in the small intestine, where a new cycle begins.[14]

The victim of hookworm, Stiles told Page — and Page recognized each symptom and effect as ones he had observed a thousand times — becomes inert, mentally incapable of ambition, physically incapable of application. He does not always die from hookworm disease directly, but he becomes useless to himself or to society, and he is an easy and early victim to tuberculosis, pneumonia, typhoid, or any other disease. If the hookworm victim is young, and the infection severe or long-standing, physical and mental growth is inhibited; boys and girls twelve years old, look six; adults have the mental and physical development of a child of twelve, the appearance of either a young child or a very old person, often that of an elderly dwarf.

[14] As a rule, the hookworm cannot exist where the simplest hygienic measures are in force; where people do not go barefoot, and where the soil is not indiscriminately polluted with human offal. In addition to the manner described above, infection can take place through the use of human offal as fertilizer for green vegetables eaten uncooked, or through house-flies, or drinking-water.

Diagnosis, Stiles told Page, though easy when the process is understood, had in the past always been mistaken; usually the hypothesis had been chronic anæmia or continuous malaria, always something chronic, about which nothing could be done. But diagnosis of hookworm, once the "know how" was grasped, was one of the simplest possible operations of the laboratory; only a microscope was necessary, and identification of the disease consisted merely of finding eggs in the victim's excrement.

Cure, Stiles told Page, was equally simple, utterly inexpensive, and infallibly certain: a few repeated doses of thymol, which would cause the worms to relax their grasp on the intestines of their unwilling host, followed by doses of epsom salts to eject them. If the work of cure and prevention were organized, if it were carried far enough and long enough, the hookworm could be completely exterminated — a new generation growing up would be free of the menace of it.

To all Stiles said, Page listened with the fascination of one in whom a speaker's words inspire visions — how much of the South's past did Stiles's theory explain! how much for the South's future did it promise! Page's ardent spirit took fire. His interest in all sorts of good causes had given him the acquaintance and confidence of everybody in the North interested in philanthropy or given to benevolence. Once Page was convinced of the soundness of Stiles's theory and the dependability of Stiles as a man, messages flew North that set wires of altruism in motion.

x

Stiles and the rest of the Commission on Country Life, returning from their tour, stopped at Cornell University. At a reception in their honor Stiles heard a voice booming behind him, "Where is Stiles?" He turned and was introduced to a plump, jolly-looking man, Wallace Buttrick, at that time secretary of the General Education Board, an organization through which John D. Rockefeller carried on some of his philanthropic activities. Buttrick told Stiles: "Walter Page says you know something which I must know immediately; let us go to my room." Stiles and Buttrick talked hookworm almost all night.

John D. Rockefeller.

Back in Washington Stiles was settling into the routine of his office when a telegram came to him from Doctor Simon Flexner; Flexner was director of the laboratories of the Rockefeller Hospital for Medical Research, and his telegram invited Stiles to New York for a conference. Stiles went, armed with specimen case, microscope, drawings, photographs and statistics. At Rockefeller's office Flexner introduced Stiles to Frederick T. Gates, Rockefeller's chief adviser in his philanthropies. Stiles told his story, Flexner and Gates listening quietly. After about forty minutes Gates interrupted, rang for a messenger, and sent for Starr J. Murphy, whose place in the Rockefeller hierarchy of benevolence was described as "personal counsel and benevolent representative." When Murphy appeared, Gates said: "This is the biggest proposition ever put up to the Rockefeller office. Listen to what Dr. Stiles has to say. Now, Doctor, start from the beginning again and tell Mr. Murphy what you have told me."

After several more conferences, Gates called Stiles to his home one night and told him: "The Rockefeller office will support this work."[15]

XI

The announcement, early in November, 1908, that Rockefeller would give $1,000,000 to combat hookworm, started the newspaper humorists on a second instalment of the gibing with which they had greeted Stiles's "germ-of-laziness" address six years before — with the South substituted for Stiles as the chief victim of the jeering. Walt Mason, one of America's most fecund newspaper versifiers,[16] devoted one day's outpouring of his muse to his vision of what was about to happen in the South:

He was a mournful looking wreck, with yellow face and scrawny neck, and weary eyes that looked as though they had monopoly of woe. Too tired to get his labors done, all day he loitered in the sun, and filled the air with yawns and moans, while people called him Lazybones. One day the doctor came, and said: "Brace up, my friend! Hold up your head! The hookworm, deadly as an asp, has got you in its loathsome grasp! But I will break the hookworm loose, and cook its everlasting goose! Swing wide your mouth, and do not cringe —" and then he took his big syringe, and shot about a quart of dope, that tasted like a bar of soap, adown the patient's yawning throat — "I guess I got that hookworm's goat!" One gasping breath the patient drew, and bit a lightning rod in two, and vaulted o'er his cottage roof: and then, on nimble, joyous hoof he sped across the wind-swept plain, and burned a school and robbed a train. The doctor watched his patient streak across the landscape sere and bleak, and said: "It makes my bosom warm! What wonders Science can perform!"

[15] The quotations of conversations between Stiles and Rockefeller's men, and the accompanying statements of fact, are taken from an unpublished manuscript of Stiles.

[16] Walt Mason's daily verse, syndicated in newspapers throughout the country, was a conspicuous detail of the passing-show of the time. While its length and its form — rhyme printed solid like prose — were standardized, its content was daily a fresh delight of novelty, whimsicality, wisdom, and common sense.

The spectacle of hard-headed old John D. Rockefeller co-operating with a scientist-discoverer to make war on laziness was pictured as very, very funny. Humorist Irvin Cobb wrote a satire in terms of a prize-fight: "Kid Rockefeller versus Battling Hookworm . . . winner to take all . . . Rockefeller's going after him blood raw." Cobb, himself a Kentuckian with sympathetic understanding of the South, fell thoughtlessly into what the South justly regarded as a habitual attitude of the North, a jeering which the sensitive South resented as an addition of insult to the North's long-practised cruelties of "Reconstruction":

Photograph by courtesy of Dr. C. W. Stiles.

One of the thousands of Southern children examined by the Rockefeller Sanitary Commission.

But it's a question in my mind whether [the people] down South want the hookworm dispossessed from their midst by a rank outsider from the North. From what I can learn, intimate association with Brer Hookworm and his interesting household is productive of a most soothing languor. The owner of one of these pleasant little domestic pets doesn't care whether school keeps or not. All he craves is the shady side of the house, a couple of hound pups for company and a little bait of hoe cake a la pellagra three times a day. Sometimes he won't even drink coffee for breakfast, because it's liable to keep him awake all morning. Just give his wife all the washing she can do and let his kids have steady places on the night shift of a cotton mill, and he's too happy for words. His greatest physical exertion is voting the Democratic ticket once a year. But just picture what'll happen to his peace of mind when some Yankee comes around and deprives him of his private zoo. "My poor man," says the interfering stranger, "you have been freed of your affliction. You are no longer a slave. Go forth and seek employment." But the hookwormer won't agree with him. He'll resent being filled with a sudden and uncomfortable restlessness that'll start him out hustling for a job. With him slavery and work are synonymous, and if anything work is the more synonymous of the two.

Similar examples of Northern newspaper humor, not untouched in some cases with malice, caused some of the South to react in resentment: "Sir, [wrote a former president of the Georgia Bar Association[17] to the Columbus, Ga., *Enquirer-Sun*] up to 1865 nobody ever thought of charging the South with being lazy. . . . Then came the Civil War, the outgrowth of jealousy. For four years the lazy (?) indolent (?) South fought and successfully fought the whole world" [*sic*]. The Macon, Ga., *Telegraph* pointedly asked, "Where was this hookworm or lazy disease, when it took five Yankee soldiers to whip one Southerner?" Bishop Candler of Atlanta, a long-time critic of Rockefeller, sermonized against and urged the South not to permit the Rockefeller work to be carried on.

XII

To much of the South, Stiles, with his Rockefeller backing, "appeared in the light, not of a deliverer but of another damYankee bent upon holding the South up to ridicule. And they abused him with the proud fluency of which only a self-righteous Southern rhetorician seems to be master."[18]

Of all the abuse heaped by the South upon Stiles, as well as Rockefeller, the most violent came from Florida.

[17] Honorable Henry R. Goetchius, October 31, 1909.
[18] The quotation above is from an article by Gerald W. Johnson, in the Baltimore *Sun,* 1927.
The habitual juxtaposition of "damn" and "Yankee" was the subject of one of the most familiar stories of the post-bellum South, about a child born during the passions of the Civil War who lived to the age of fifty without ever learning that "damn Yankee" was not one word.

There was a special reason. Stiles, in accounts of the symptoms of hookworm, had enumerated what had been called by other observers before him "Florida complexion."[19] To a community just beginning to think of itself as a winter health resort that was infuriating. The editor of a Tampa, Fla., newspaper attacked Stiles in an editorial and threatened him with lynching if he ever set foot in that State. Somebody sent a copy of the paper to Stiles, who read it, packed a valise, and left at once for Tampa, went to a hotel and registered under his own name. For a week he loitered about the streets, and visited near-by rural schools, accosting people who to his practised eye appeared to be suffering from hookworm disease, and getting them to allow him to make microscopic examinations. When he had incontrovertible evidence of the existence of the disease in and around Tampa, he sent word to the editor who had attacked him, relating what he had been doing and what the results of his investigation had been, and added: "The lynching may begin when you are ready."

The editor called on Stiles, dined with him, spent half the night talking hookworms, and became a convert. Next day his paper published a generous retraction.

XIII

The first formal work done through Rockefeller's beneficence was a careful survey under Stiles's technical direction, during the early part of 1909, to determine the geographical extent of the hookworm infestation and the approximate number of sufferers. Before this was completed Rockefeller called a joint meeting of scientists and Southern leaders of thought, to whom he turned over $1,-000,000 to be used in a five-years' war on the hookworm.

---

[19] Ch. Wardell Stiles, *Hygienic Laboratory Bulletin,* No. 10, February, 1903.

The giver felt obliged to say, as almost apologetic placation to the aroused sensitiveness of the beneficiary, in a public letter read[20] to the trustees, that while he regarded it as "a privilege to act in any movement which offers assurance of relieving human suffering, it is a peculiar pleasure to me to feel that the principal activities of your Board will be among the people of our Southern States." It had been, Rockefeller said, "my pleasure of late to spend a portion of each year in the South, and I have come to know and to respect greatly that part of our country and to enjoy the society and friendship of many of its warm-hearted people; it will therefore be an added gratification to me if in this way I may in some measure express my appreciation of their many kindnesses and hospitalities."

The Rockefeller Sanitary Commission for the Eradication of Hookworm Disease began, largely, with activities designed to have the effect of ingratiation and education — lectures, demonstrations, talks with individuals and with local groups, items prepared for Southern newspapers, tactful enlistment of co-operation by local physicians, careful selection of local State directors to carry the work to every infected county. During the first year about 102,000 persons were examined in nine Southern States, of whom 42,945 were found to have hookworms. More convincing than the statistics were example after example of whole local communities cleaned up. A community known to their neighbors as "Forkemites" (because of their location in the fork of a creek) had seemed for generations to live under a curse; they were poverty-stricken, they were sickly — and they were called lazy; few of them could read and most of them were believed to be of a low order of mentality. During the first April of the Rockefeller commission's

20 October 24, 1909.

work (1910), a local physician, aided by the commission, began treating them for hookworm. In one school he found thirty-eight of the forty pupils infected, while forty-five of their brothers and sisters were too sick of the disease to go to school. A year later the teacher of the school said to a visitor: "Children who before the treatment were listless and dull are now active and alert; children who could not study a year ago are not only studying now but are finding a joy in learning. They have a new outlook on life. There is a new spirit in the school. Most of the forty-five who were sick at home are now well and coming to school."

In a Southern orphan asylum, many of the children, "when watched too closely to [get dirt to eat] otherwise, would gouge out the mortar between the bricks of their dormitory and swallow it." After treatment, "the children blossomed luxuriantly. From horrible, heart-rending caricatures of children, they were changed — it seemed almost over-night — into chubby, rosy, exuberantly healthy boys."[21]

Such striking examples, occurring in community after community, carried conviction to whole neighborhoods. The commission's work became easy. By 1914, half a million school-children and 392,765 grown persons had been examined, 382,046 of whom had been found infected and had been treated — composing, in the words of Doctor Eliot of Harvard, "the most effective campaign against a wide-spreading disease which medical science and philanthropy have ever combined to conduct."

Nevertheless, when the Great War combed the South for young men, from 12 to 33 per cent of the draftees were found to have the disease; it was estimated that there were still approximately 2,000,000 hookworm pa-

21 Gerald W. Johnson, Baltimore *Evening Sun,* 1927.

tients and carriers in the South. By 1927, however, after about 7,000,000 persons had been treated, the annual report of the International Health Board (into which the Commission had been merged) was able to declare:

At the present time it is fair to say that hookworm disease has almost disappeared from the United States and is rapidly coming under control in many parts of the world.[22]

XIV

During the thirty-nine years, from 1891 when Charles Wardell Stiles returned to the United States with the best scientific education obtainable in Europe, to the year in which this history was written, 1930, eight Presidents rode in swaying barouche or shining motor from Capitol steps to White House door; seventeen Congresses ground out thousands of statutes and millions of words of what is called history; two victorious armies returning from foreign wars paraded up Pennsylvania Avenue; some scores of generals and admirals and captains were borne on flag-draped caissons across the Potomac River to graves in the Arlington Memorial Cemetery. Upon it all, Stiles looked out from the dusty windows of a division of a bureau of a government department — if indeed he ever took time to look at all, if ever there was an occasion when even for a quarter-hour the spectacle of pomp or pageant was as alluring to him as the quaint creatures that wiggled beneath his microscope. After 1914, when he could see the work of hookworm extermination so organized as to be certain to succeed, he retired to his laboratory, allowing his great discovery to slip to the rank of a mere episode in his concentrated life. As he withdrew more and more

[22] Doctor Stiles, out of the caution engendered by almost half a century's study of parasites, characterizes this declaration as slightly rose-colored "due to the enthusiasm of young men."

continuously into his laboratory, devoted himself more and more to the work of his mature years, one thought of him as a man who had taken youth's fling in the form of an immense adventure in altruism. He had been but twenty-three when he first began his investigations of hookworm, thirty-four when he identified Necator americanus, and barely over forty when his rich and persistent vitality set the work of extermination upon its way. By the time he was fifty, he had receded from public consciousness in both North and South; the immense outburst of publicity and ridicule about the "germ of laziness" had become, to a new generation, merely an unimportant detail of the long-gone past — to them, one with Nineveh and Tyre — pre-war America.[23]

[23] For ten years Doctor Stiles has been engaged on his *opus magnum* (his tombstone as he calls it), a key to the parasitic diseases of the world.

10

PRE-WAR POPULAR SONGS

Together with Some Remarks about the Relation Between
Changes in the Vogues of Popular Songs, and Corresponding
Changes in Manners. Songs that Make Topical Allusions,
or Otherwise Serve as Footnotes to History. Songs of Sentiment, and of Childhood, and of Satire. Songs that Reflected Successive Waves of Immigration to America. Others that Reflected the Altered Status of the Negro.

To the historian, some songs constitute an index to
manners, vogues, even morals, the events and subjects
that engaged national interest, the times of economic,
philologic, and other changes. Others are comparatively
slight in their relation to contemporary events:

> Meet me in St. Louis, Louis,[1]
> Meet me at the Fair.

obviously referred to the World's Exposition at St.
Louis, 1904. The Harry Thaw murder trial gave rise
to "Why Don't They Set Him Free?" — "Just because
he's a millionaire, everybody's willing to treat him unfair"[2] (1913). "He'd Have to Get Under" (1913) referred to an incident of motoring, practically unknown to
drivers of the foolproof cars of 1930, but very familiar
in the days before the wayside garage became common,
and when part of the equipment for a ride consisted of a
"duster" or a pair of overalls with which one could trans-
form oneself into a mechanic when caught by trouble
with gear or transmission. "Come Take a Trip in My

---

[1] Meet Me in St. Louis, Louis" (1904). Reproduced with permission of the
copyright owner, Paull-Pioneer Music Co., New York.

[2] In this chapter, in every case, the figures in parenthesis after song titles are the
year of copyright. In some cases the period of the song's greatest vogue was
one, two or more years subsequent to its copyright.

Airship" (1904) was an attempt by a song artisan to take advantage of the current talk about aviation. The time of

> I must say good-by to you, Dolly Gray,[3]

is forever fixed by the allusion to the color of army uniforms in

> Don't you hear the tramp of feet, Dolly Gray,
> Sounding through the village street, Dolly Gray?
> 'Tis the tramp of soldiers true, in their uniforms of blue —[4]

"Good-Bye, Dolly Gray" was written in 1900, just after the war with Spain, when relays of American troops were starting off to put down rebellion in the Philippines. That was two years before the military authorities, largely as a lesson learned from experience in the Spanish War, discarded the blue, which had had historic and sentimental associations ever since America had an army, and replaced it with the more protective coloration of olive drab. In several respects "Good-Bye, Dolly Gray" reflected the spirit of the time. The

> murmur in the air, you can hear it everywhere

was martial. For the first time in history, American soldiers were going overseas to wage war. "Good-Bye,

Good - bye,   Dol - ly I must   leave   you,

Dolly Gray" carries a faint suggestion of "The Girl I Left Behind Me"; but the American soldier took his

---

[3] "Good-Bye, Dolly Gray" (1900) and "In the Good Old Summer Time" (1902) were indisputably the two most popular songs of the early years of the twentieth century in America. Their primacy lasted until about 1906.

[4] Reproduced with permission of the copyright owner, Paull-Pioneer Music Co., New York.

home-leaving, his departure to fight in foreign lands, more seriously and more sentimentally.

Another song associated with America's martial adventure overseas was "Blue Bell" (1904):[5]

And, of course, "There'll Be a Hot Time in the Old Town To-night," which, put out in 1896, became, in a sense, the official song of the Spanish War.

Popular songs identify vogues, conditions, eras. The future historian will know that "Her Golden Hair Was Hanging Down Her Back" (1894) must have been written in the pre-bobbing era. He will know, too, that the change from long hair to short accompanied a change in the attitude of women toward the world, and of the world toward women. Barbers clipped off more than hair, some romance, too, when women began coming to their shops.

In the early years of this century, a premier in drollness was a comedian named Raymond Hitchcock, who chose, as the background of his performances, farcical shows that told "joyous and impossible tales of carefree life in incredible kingdoms." In one farce-comedy, Hitchcock, as "Abijah Booze, the Yankee Consul"

[5] Reproduced with permission of the copyright owner, F. B. Haviland Pub Co., Inc.

(1904), sang some verses about one of the world's perennial topics for song and sermon, the regrettable desuetude of whatever happens at the time to be the recent and passing style in women's dress. Hitchcock's song, deploring several innovations, ran:

> It was not like that in the olden days.
> That have passed beyond recall.
> Then the new "straight-front" and the habit-back . . .[6]
> Had not even been foretold.
> Imagination had some play,
> In the days of old.[7]

The implication in the last line, about women's clothes of 1903, seems far-fetched twenty-five years later. In the intervening years women's dress made progress; at least its lower hem progressively inched itself upward.

Sir John Suckling wrote, in the early part of the seventeenth century:

> Her feet beneath her petticoat
> Like little mice stole in and out,
> As if they feared the light.

That description of women's feet as a fugitive and therefore alluring sight remained correct for nearly three hundred years, up to about 1910. But had Sir John been living in 1915, and disposed to bring his verse up to date, he would have been obliged to write

> Her *calves* beneath her petticoat,
> Like little mice ——

assuming that, as to the lady whose charms he was immortalizing, or indeed as to any lady, he would have felt

---

[6] "Straight-front" was a style of corset — the name is a sufficient description. "Habit-back" was a tight-fitting coat with a back similar to that of a riding-habit.

[7] Reproduced with permission of the copyright owner, M. Witmark & Sons.

1901   1908   1910

1920   1925   1927

Changes in women's skirts, as revealed by the pages of the style magazines. The skirt of 1901 was described by the *Ladies' Home Journal* as "the indispensable short skirt essential in a college girl's outfit."

he could say so truthfully and poetically. Had Sir John made a further revision a few years later, say in 1923, fidelity to the changing scene would have compelled some such form as

Her *knees* . . . like little mice

and he would have been obliged to omit the petticoat, for it had disappeared. By 1929 — but Sir John's delicate verses would creak under the burden of accommodating themselves to the increasingly visible expanse of female anatomy. Another poet, Whittier, about 1850, described Maud Muller's embarrassed response to the judge's request for a drink from the spring:

> She stooped where the cool spring bubbled up,
> And blushed as she gave it, looking down
> On her feet so bare ——

By 1930, Maud, if playing tennis, or even sometimes on city streets, would have had, not bare feet, but legs bare from ankle to thigh. If either party to the episode had blushed, it would have been the judge.

It was about 1912 that a Chicago dramatic critic, Percy Hammond, reproved what then seemed to him a daring brevity of skirts in a musical comedy, by remarking that "the human knee is a joint and not an entertainment." The high visibility of the adult female human knee, together with accompanying scantiness of all female clothing, became, during the 1920's — to the elder generation to whom the sight was novel — a subject for serious sermonizing, or for philosophic resignation. To the younger generation, younger in years or in carelessness of spirit, just beginning to take paucity of female raiment for granted, it was occasion for a wit that was like the wearer of the short skirt, uncertain just how daring it was safe to be. A newspaper humorist, "Abe

Martin," said in 1928: "I used to think women wuz all alike, but now I can see ther's quite a difference in 'em." By 1929, the condition having become more extreme, he remarked, "What to leave bare and what to cover[8] seems to be the question of the hour." A periodical in 1928 jested, under the caption "Try a Doily":

Flapper : "I would like to try on that vieux rose frock in the window."
Saleslady : "I'm sorry, that's a lamp-shade."

To identify the causes of any change, in any field, small or great, is a task which historians undertake with a confidence out of proportion to their success. Sometimes they make long-armed deductions, in which they may confuse mere sequence of events, or coincidence, with cause and effect. To the shortening of women's skirts, many agencies contributed — it was a symbol of, and a part of, a movement broader and more diverse than feminism, a movement that expressed itself, one way or another, in practically every field of human affairs, and in every quarter of the globe, including China and finally, in 1927, Turkey. The process, considered in the light of all its causes, effects and associations, was important, and can hardly be fully dealt with as one facet of a comment on popular songs.

With these very broad qualifications, it is worth while to call attention to what is at the least a coincidence, and may be more. The striking elevation of the lower hem of women's skirts began about 1910, in which year it advanced from about the knob of the ankle-bone upward as far as the shoe-top. In the same year, the automobile self-starter was perfected and put on the market. So

8 In 1929, *The Pathfinder Magazine* conducted a nation-wide contest in the invention of a type of aphorism which the slang of the day called "wise-cracks." The judges, Senators Moses of New Hampshire and Ashurst of Arizona, awarded second prize to "I never expected to see the day when girls would get sunburned on the places they do now."

long as automobiles had to be cranked by hand, it was taken for granted that women generally could not be drivers or owners. With electric self-starters came realization by automobile manufacturers that their market might be increased by persuading women they could now drive. When woman began to move her feet about among the pedals of a car, long skirts became an inconvenience.

In proportion as legs in the flesh became visible, so did the word become permissible in conversation, and also in song and in books. And in proportion as the word became permissible, so did it cease to provide occasion or material for jokes and stories of the sort whose point and interest depended upon suggestiveness of wickedness. The situations in song and story that constituted *double entendre* moved upward with the skirts, or, to put it in political terms, far over toward the radical left. In the Victorian 1880's a typical *double entendre* song, "Aching Heart" (1880), depended for its point upon the unmentionability and unprintability of a detail of woman's dress which, by the 1920's, was utterly familiar to every eye, completely casual in common talk. The song alluded to the nursery tale of Hickory Dickory Dock, about a mouse that ran up a clock, and added:

But the case that I refer to is particularly shocking.
The clock that this old mouse ran up was on a lady's st—

In proportion as the area expanded over which a lady might become sunburned, so did a host of songs, jokes and stories come into the light, whose circulation previously had been confined to furtive word of mouth, and to adolescents of all ages. Professional authors, of novels as well as songs, were quick to take advantage of the opportunity. James Branch Cabell turned some of the stag and stallion stories into exceptionally elevated literary form, and received applause as a pioneer of letters. In the field of song, every popular favorite had always had its obscene variation, for rendition in barrooms and at parties of "men only"; and songs of the "Frankie and Johnny" sort had flourished for generations in the musical underworld. By the 1920's, "Frankie and Johnny" was freely sung at mixed gatherings of young folks. In 1929, a volume entitled "Songs My Mother Never Taught Me" stood in the windows of sedate book-shops alongside the "Life of Abraham Lincoln" and "The Meditations of Marcus Aurelius."

Until the 1900's "double-meaning" songs — or songs that had only the ribald meaning — had been rigidly excluded from public performance in ordinary theatre and vaudeville houses. Unsanctified relations between men and women could be mentioned only if attended by a wholesome moral, as in "She Loved Not Wisely But Too Well" (1894) — "now she's fled to hide her shame." By 1907, "Be Good" took the tone of advising, not goodness for goodness' sake, nor goodness as a quid pro quo for a harp in heaven, but rather the appearance of goodness for artfulness' sake, and carefulness for safety's sake:

> Be good, very, very good . . .
> If you can't be good, be careful.[9]

Other songs lending themselves to the requisites of double meaning or suggestiveness included "Mary Took the Calves to the Dairy Show" (1908), "This Is No Place for a Minister's Son" (1909), "If You Talk in Your Sleep, Don't Mention My Name" (1910).

The movement was not wholly meretricious in motive, nor necessarily unwholesome in effect. This, like

[9] Reproduced with permission of the copyright owner, M. Witmark & Sons.

the change in women's dress, like feminism, like a new attitude about religion, was interlocked with other developments, in a mesh far too intricate to permit any historian safely to assert any sure relation of cause and effect — too intricate, also, to permit any moralist dogmatically to say how much of the new is evil, how much good. The area of the discussable was enlarged not only in songs and novels, but everywhere.[10]

The coming of the day when women and children were employed in great numbers in factories, oftentimes supplanting men, made it inevitable that fathers of families should have more leisure, enforced or otherwise, than when they were the sole breadwinners. This shifting of burdens from strong shoulders to weak was signalized by a song in which the son or the daughter of the family complained:

> Everybody works but father, and he sits around all day,
> Feet in front of the fire,[11] smoking his pipe of clay;
> Mother takes in washing, so does Sister Ann,
> Everybody works at our house but my old man.[12]

Most of those who sang "Everybody Works But Father" thought of it merely as a good song. It had

---

[10] The world had become alarmed at the ravages of two familiar diseases mainly associated with sex, whose spread had been partly facilitated by the refusal of common print and speech to acknowledge their existence; it was about 1910 that the world was permitted to read warnings against them, with the names of them used. Similarly, the world had been shocked by the existence of commercialized sex relations on an organized scale in large cities, involving odious semibondage for some women; exposure and cure of the conditions involved familiarity with the word "prostitution" in newspapers and common speech.

[11] This 1906 conception of fathers as inert sit-by-the-fires changed, twenty years later, to the picture suggested in a joke printed in 1928:

"I wish to goodness I could go home, but dad wants to stop for three more dances."

"I know, my dear; they're a trial. But, after all, one can only be old once."

[12] "Everybody Works But Father" (1905). Reproduced with permission of the copyright owner, Edw. B. Marks Music Co.

economic and social pointedness, however, in circles where the relationship of the daughter-worker's pay-check to the family budget was the occasion of some tartness about the whole obligation of bread-winning being on the father. Whether it was the duty of a good daughter to "bring the pay-envelope home unopened" on Saturday night was a question occasionally mooted in not a few families. Apart from economic asperities, "Everybody Works But Father" coincided with the beginning of an attitude toward parental dignity which, in the year of this song, 1905, was merely good-humored irreverence, but by 1929 had become outright flouting tempered by affectionate condescension.

II

Songs That Are Footnotes to History

One wonders why Theodore Roosevelt, with the warmth of appeal he had, his spectacular quality, the universal interest in him and his actions, gave rise to no political ballads or campaign songs, such as had been used in the campaigns of Harrison and Cleveland. There were allusions to Roosevelt in many topical songs, and some having "Teddy" or "Theodore" as their title, but no song having Roosevelt as its hero became popular. The Roosevelt followers in the Progressive party movement of 1912 put the ardor and reverence of a crusade into two old and familiar songs, one religious, "Onward, Christian Soldiers"; the other semireligious, a revival of the Civil War, "The Battle Hymn of the Republic."

A song political in its inspiration and allusions, which pictured certain aspects of the spirit of New York, including its self-complacency and occasional cynicism toward some ideas held elsewhere in America, was

Tammany, Tammany (Drawn out) Ta-a-a-man-e-e-e . . .
Swamp 'em, swamp 'em, get the " wampum,"
Tammany.[13]

In the verses of "Tammany," New York politicians and
other public figures were given characteristic Indian
designations — allusions acutely diverting to a day in
which every newspaper reader recognized them — but
to a later generation as cryptic as Greek.

"Paleface preacher" . . .
[who] said he would run Manhattan like a Sunday School,

was the Reverend Charles H. Parkhurst, a trenchant
reformer. "Young Chief Breaks-in-where-they-gam-
ble," referred to a crusading young District Attorney,
William T. Jerome, who on one occasion broke down
the door of New York's most conspicuous gambling-
house. "Man Behind" was a variation, dictated by the
exactions of metre, for "The Man Higher Up," at that
time a mystic phrase for a mysterious and potent character — quite frequently to the front in discussions of how
New York was governed, but as to all other respects,
conspicuously in the background.

Though the quick passing of the characters made most
of the stanzas of "Tammany" ephemeral, the music and
the words of the chorus remained familiar. It was the
custom of Tammany, on trips to Democratic National
Conventions at Denver, San Francisco, or St. Louis, to
take a special train, which carried more than merely the
Tammany delegation; it was a microcosm of New York,
keeping New York hours, practising New York manners, and using New York devices for elevation of the
spirits, including a band which blared out "Tammany"
across the sleeping prairies.

[13] "Tammany" (1900). Reproduced with permission of the copyright owner,
M. Witmark & Sons.

One ditty was sung with direct reference to a Presidential candidate, Champ Clark, a Missouri Congressman, Speaker of the House from 1911 until 1919:

> Ev'ry time I come to town
> The boys keep kickin' my dawg aroun';
> Makes no diff'rence if he is a houn',
> They gotta quit kickin' my dawg aroun'.[14]

The refrain, passing into current slang, was sung as "They Gotta Quit Kickin' My Dawg Aroun'," under circumstances where the intention was merely to make an impersonal observation; but became "You Gotta Quit" when direct personal resentment was meant. The song was very old; for generations it had expressed occasional emotions entertained by mountaineers in Virginia, Kentucky and Tennessee. After Daniel Boone and the other early settlers carried it across the Mississippi, it came to be thought of as essentially a Missouri song; and "They gotta quit kickin' my dawg aroun' " was supposed to express a characteristic Missouri state of mind.

The song had aptness to Clark's fortunes. In 1912 circumstances seemed to mark him for the Democratic Presidential nomination and seemed to destine the Democratic nominee for success, because of the split in the Republican party. In the Democratic nominating convention at Baltimore, William Jennings Bryan was one of the delegates; he was Clark's personal friend, under the additional obligation of direct instructions from his State, Nebraska, to vote for Clark. At a stage of the balloting when Clark had more than a majority, and by every precedent, as well as by common consent, seemed certain to get the necessary two-thirds, Bryan, in a sensational speech, repudiated Clark and helped turn the

---

[14] "They Gotta Quit Kickin' My Dawg Aroun'" (1912). Reproduced with permission of the copyright owner, M. Witmark & Sons.

tide to Woodrow Wilson. Clark never forgave Bryan, called him "William Judas Bryan," and spent his remaining years in the sullen resentment of a man whose deserts had been unnecessarily kicked around.

III

The popular songs[15] that had their brief blooming between the turn of the century and the Great War, were for the most part almost as ephemeral as the emotions they evoked. Few had the robustness to endure; none concerned itself with anything so hardy as a will to survive. A few of them dainty, many merely antic, all fragile — they sang the youths of their day into love, and themselves succumbed to the vicissitudes that at all times beset them. Each was jostled by the next newcomer; whole groups were elbowed aside by new vogues

---

[15] The musical experience of the average American was limited almost exclusively to popular songs together with hymns, which, in the period this chapter deals with, were as familiar as secular airs.

As late as the 1890's, hymns were frequently sung under circumstances having no especial religious connotation, and with no religious intention — merely as the vocal expression that came first to the mind of a person or a group when in one of several moods. An ordinary social gathering, or a picnic, or young folks on a moonlight straw-ride, would sing familiar hymns as readily as "Oh, Don't You Remember Sweet Alice, Ben Bolt," or "Annie Laurie." Such gatherings would as often wind up with "God Be With You Till We Meet Again" as with "Auld Lang Syne." A farmer in the fields, or a woman in the kitchen or at the sewing-machine, would express a mood of contentment or of busyness having no religious connection, with "Rock of Ages" or "Nearer My God to Thee," or "Bringing in the Sheaves" or "Work, for the Night Is Coming." Other hymns that were, in a strictly accurate sense, popular songs, and were rather more familiar in the eighteen-nineties than many of the songs classified as "popular," included: "Beulah Land," "From Greenland's Icy Mountains," "Whosoever Will May Come," "I Love to Tell the Story," "Shall We Meet Beyond the River?" "Ninety and Nine," "Jerusalem the Golden," "Rocked in the Cradle of the Deep," "Sweet Hour of Prayer," "What a Friend We Have in Jesus," "Onward, Christian Soldiers," "Blest Be the Tie That Binds," "Hark, the Herald Angels Sing," "Lead, Kindly Light," "Jesus, Lover of My Soul," "Rescue the Perishing," "How Firm a Foundation."

After about 1900, the singing of hymns, while still an important and beloved part of the musical life of the people, came more and more to be confined to churches and gatherings definitely religious in nature.

in song and in manners. By the year in which this chapter was written (1930), they had retreated to remote corners of the memories of those whose heyday had been one with theirs.

Several friendly collaborators who searched the attics of their memories to ascertain which of the songs of 1900–1914 lingered most lovingly in the affections of those who as youths had sung them, agreed that the rusts of a quarter-century had been best resisted by a melody whose theme and name was "In the Good Old Summer Time" (1902), beginning

> There's a time in each year
> That we always hold dear . . .

"In the Good Old Summer Time" achieved glamour by a metrical listing of the more agreeable phenomena of the season[16] it extolled. In the cataloguing, difficulty was encountered, through the disinclination of some familiar words to accommodate themselves to rhyme, resulting in such disconcerting assonances as "breezes" and "trees-es". That duplication of a sibilant syllable may seem awkward to generations who will know the song only in cold print; on persons sensitive to locution it may have the effect of a deliberate false start, as if the verses were meant to be burlesque; or it may seem an interruption, as if the singer had stuttered and momentarily changed his vocal step, and his mood. Actually, to the zestful generation that sang the air in its pristine freshness, the "trees-es" was an added lusciousness. One accented it, feelingly, with volume; it became a vocal spring-board from which one swung with accelerated

---

[16]Other songs of this period that depended for part of their appeal on seasonal allusions were "When the Harvest Days Are Over, Jessie Dear" (1900), "Wait Till the Sun Shines, Nellie" (1905), "Where the Morning Glories Twine Around the Door" (1905), "When the Frost Is on the Pumpkin" (1904), "When It's Apple Blossom Time in Normandy" (1912).

momentum into the lilting sweep of sentiment about young love, young love at a time when

> Strolling thro' the shady lanes with your baby mine;
> You hold her hand and she holds yours . . .

was as daring as a popular song was likely to be — some fifteen to twenty years before expressions like "petting" and "necking"[17] ogled their way into permitted speech.

The appeal of "In the Good Old Summer Time" lay partly in its sentimental motif, and partly in a quality that made this ditty a humble little sister of Whittier's "Maud Muller." It evoked rural scenes and summer scents, half remembered or wholly dreamed, expressed the mood of "spring fever," suggested vacation, voiced the longing of dwellers in drear city canyons for the wide bright fields of country-bred childhood. The adult city people of the early nineteen-hundreds had for the most part been born and reared on farms or in villages, either in America or abroad, and had been drawn into urban life by the fast-growing industrialization of that day. Their rural background made them poignantly susceptible to "In the Good Old Summer Time's" suggestion of the unshadowed sunniness of country meadows, the scents of ripening orchards, and the other allurements, real or dreamed, of country life.

A similar tug on the same heart-strings was made by "In the Shade of the Old Apple Tree" (1905). A chorus, that asked no aid from summer, buzzing bees or apple trees, that sang of love only and put concentrated sentiment into the drawn-out, almost wailing, tenor echoes on which it chiefly depended for its effect, was "Sweet Adeline" (1903).[18] For the vogue it enjoyed, it received

---

[17] The 1900's equivalent for these words was "spooning."

[18] In 1927, the author of "Sweet Adeline" was described in a newspaper interview as still living, "a friendly, stocky man with a shiny bald head, bending over

help from a most unusual source. The Mayor of Boston in 1906–7 and 1910–14, John Francis Fitzgerald, earlier a member of Congress, used to sing this song on occasions when the more usual expectation from a politician would have been a speech — a laudable consideration for audiences which contributed to his being called "Honey Fitz," and facilitated a locally successful political career:

> In all my dreams (in all my dreams),
> Your fair face beams (your fair face beams);
> You're the flower of my heart, sweet Ad-e-line (sweet Ad-e-line).[19]

The height of "Sweet Adeline's" vogue was about 1906. Many a youth, in college during the 1920's, taught by modern teachers curious new theories about eugenics and the laws of mating, about "fixations" and "complexes," could have learned from his parents that a considerable element in the determination of his immediate ancestry had been the fortuitous conjunction of a spring night, a full moon, and "Sweet Adeline" — followed in due course by "Oh, Promise Me" and the "Wedding March."

IV

They were artlessly direct in sentiment, those early years of the century, and likewise robust in humor. The period had relish, gusto. The people liked songs in which the quality could be savored, lustily. When a tune had an easily grasped chorus, the audience liked to join in. One high-spirited song that thus invited the audience's

---

a desk, figuring accounts in the New York Post Office" — but carrying a memento of his earlier glory on his card, which read:

RICHARD H. GERARD.

Author of the World Famous Song, "Sweet Adeline."

[19] Reproduced with permission of the copyright owner, M. Witmark & Sons.

participation was the narrative of an immigrant Irishman, Michael Kelly, who, arriving with his sweetheart from County Cork, became separated from her in the crowds of New York City. The sweetheart, searching for him, climbed to a perch along a St. Patrick's Day parade, and addressed the marchers:

Has anybody here seen Kelly? K-E double L-Y.
Sure his hair is red, his eyes are blue, and he's Irish thro' and thro'.

Whereupon "five hundred Kellys" left the ranks of the paraders to answer the lady's summons.

Similar to the Kelly epic, in its use of orthography set to music, was George M. Cohan's[20]

H-A double R-I-G-A-N spells Harrigan,
Proud of all the Irish blood that's in me;
Divil a man can say a word agin me;
H-A double R-I-G-A-N you see,
Is a name that a shame never has been connected with.
Harrigan — that's me![21]

A hilarious expression of the robustious gusto of the early 1900's, and the decade preceding, was "Throw

[20] George M. Cohan, actor, singer and composer of popular songs, prominent, as child and man, for more than a generation, beginning in 1888, when he was ten. His versatile talent produced, among others, "Mary's a Grand Old Name" (1905), "So Long, Mary" (1905), "I Was Born in Virginia" (1906).

Cohan's occasional use of patriotism as a theme for popular songs, as "I'm a Yankee Doodle Dandy" (1906) and "You're a Grand Old Flag" (1906) — originally "You're a Grand Old Rag" — was criticised as, in the words of the Providence *Journal*, "playing on the patriotic sensibilities of the public." Cohan was sometimes banal but when the Great War came, he wrote one of the two or three songs that most satisfied the emotions of the soldiers; for his "Over There" he received public thanks from President Wilson.

Cohan as a writer of songs that went all over the country shared and fostered a characteristic New York City attitude toward that part of America lying west and south of the Hudson River. His songs of the early 1900's contain frequent allusions to "hicks," "rubes," "jays," "one-night-stands." His affection was for New York City, and he expressed it in "Give My Regards to Broadway" (1905).

[21] "Harrigan" (1907). Reproduced with permission of the copyright owner, Paull-Pioneer Music Co., New York.

Him Down, McCloskey" (1890), indissolubly associated with the name of Maggie Cline.[22] Rarely has
there been such propitious union of song and singer.
The verses celebrated the Irish trait of bellicosity, as exhibited in a prize-fight which be-
gan regularly enough under the
rules of Queensberry but ended in
the tradition of Kilkenny. Miss
Cline, "daughter of Hercules and
descendant of Stentor," sang it
first at Tony Pastor's, next door to
Tammany Hall, New York City,
and thereafter from coast to coast,
with a frequency and verve that
made this union of personality and
song as familiar and as beloved
as DeWolf Hopper and "Casey
at the Bat." As Maggie Cline
fog-horned the chorus, the whole
house roared it with her, "hand-
clapping and stamping the while;
the orchestra was as drowned as if
it did not exist; the stage devices
behind the scenes that tried their
hardest to bang out the illusion of
smashing furniture and falling

From the Albert Davis Collection.
Maggie Cline.

walls — became merely a gentle obbligato to the crowd's
delighted bellowing of the rapturous line: 'T'row him
down, McCloskey.' With all due reverence," William
O. Inglis wrote me in 1926, "I say that if I had my
choice of hearing again Patti or Maggie, it would be
Maggie. With Maggie Cline in my corner, I'd take a
crack at time and age."

[22] Miss Cline's vogue rested also on her recitation of "Slide, Kelly, Slide."

V

Songs of Sentiment

The period covered by this chapter, 1900 to 1914, spanned, in music, two extremes, from the tranquil "Rosary"[23] to blatant ragtime,[24] the former a vogue in 1900, the latter a rage by 1914. Between those two, about the only characteristic in common was that both were written in musical notes — a more complete revolution could hardly be. Beneath the revolution, however, and serenely undisturbed by it, continued sentiment, and the expression of sentiment in song. The love-songs of the early 1900's were neither greater nor less in proportionate quantity, neither better nor worse in quality, than those of the decades that preceded or succeeded. There was possibly a greater emphasis on permanence, in contrast with a later tendency to emphasize exclusiveness of possession, or intensity of passion. A song of 1911 that could hardly have been sung by any one coldly contemplating nothing more than companionate marriage was:

> Till the sands of the desert grow cold
> And their infinite numbers are told . . .
> Till the mysteries of Heaven unfold,
> And the story of judgment is told,
> I'll turn, love, to thee,
> My shrine thou shalt be.[25]

Love in wedlock, fireside love, romantic love as a continuing accompaniment of marriage, love associated with home, was quite within the imagination, and, in spite of mounting divorce statistics, commonly within the practice, of the early 1900's. "Little Grey Home in the

---

[23] See page 419. [24] See page 413.
[25] "Till the Sands of the Desert Grow Cold" (1911). Reproduced with permission of the copyright owner, M. Witmark & Sons.

West" (1911) was the song of the home-faring husband; "Just a Wearyin' for you"[26] was of the waiting wife:

.3. Eve - nin' comes, I   miss you more   When the dark gloom's round the door,
Seems just like you   or - ter be   There to o - pen   it for me. Latch goes tink-lin,'
thrills me through, Sets me wear-y - in' for you.

The generation that lived through this period was sometimes described by its descendants as having been oversentimental. It took sentiment as it took its other moods, as it took the seasons and the weather — in their natural place and proportion. One of the richest men in America, an ironmaster named Henry C. Frick, who bought fine old paintings and endowed an art gallery, had in his mansion a pipe-organ proportioned to his wealth, from which, in his hours of ease, it was his custom to have "Dearie" (1905)[27] summoned:

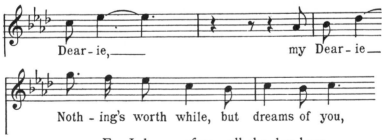

Dear-ie,_____   my Dear-ie__
Noth - ing's worth while, but   dreams of you,

. . . For I dream of you all the day long,
You run thro' the hours like a song . . .

Dearie, my dearie, nothing's worth while but dreams of you,
And you can make ev'ry dream come true; dearie, my dearie!

[26] (1901.) Reproduced with permission of the copyright owner, Carrie Jacobs-Bond.

[27] Reproduced with permission of the copyright owner, Edw. B. Marks Music Co.

Artlessness and sincerity characterized "Love Me and the World Is Mine" (1906):[28]

> I care not for the stars that shine,
> I dare not hope to e'er be thine,
> I only know I love you!
> Love me, and the world is mine!

Another expression of romantic love much sung by the early 1900's was the "Gypsy Love Song" (1898):[29]

> Slumber on, my little gypsy sweetheart,
> Dream of the field and the grove;
> Can you hear me, hear me in that dreamland
> Where your fancies rove?

A mere ephemeral coon song was "Can't Yo' Heah Me Callin', Caroline?" (1914). It had no particular elevation of quality, nor was it more familiarly known than many others. Its value as an illustration lies in its very averageness. If it is psychologically true that the emotion of love is associated with all the other exaltations the lover has experienced from beauty in nature or elsewhere; if it is psychologically true that thought of the sweetheart has potency to evoke memories and visions — in short, if romance is the true reality, then "Can't Yo' Heah Me Callin', Caroline?" is, as a love-song, faithful to nature; certainly it is faithful to romantic love, as the early 1900's felt it and sang it:

> Can't yo' heah me callin', Caroline?
> Lordy, how I miss yo', gal o' mine . . .
> I miss yo' in de mornin', when ole bob-white gives his call,
>   Caroline, Caroline;
> I miss yo' at de sunset, when de evenin' shadows fall,
>   Caroline, Caroline;[30]

A charming musical expression of the period covered

---

[28] Reproduced with permission of the copyright owner, M. Witmark & Sons
[29] *Idem.*
[30] *Idem.*

by this chapter was a vogue of songs about childhood.[31] The number of these, the proportion that were good, and the popularity they had, were a sign of that day, its simple heartiness, its unaffectedness. It was characteristic of such a generation that it produced a lullaby with a lighter and more joyous lilt than is usual with bedtime songs, "All Aboard for Blanket Bay" (1910) — and even more characteristic that it adopted this lullaby for additional service as a dance-tune.

There's a ship sails away at the close of each day
  Sails away to the land of dreams;
Mama's little Boy Blue is the captain and crew,
  Of this wonderful ship called the White Pillow Slip . . .[32]

Familiar in songs of childhood was the theme of the mother gone to Heaven; combined with it, in "Always in the Way" (1903)[33] was the plaint of the unappreciated stepchild:

[31] Called, in the terminology of the song-writing profession, "kid songs."

[32] Reproduced with permission of the copyright owner, Harry Von Tilzer Music Pub. Co.

[33] Reproduced with permission of the copyright owner, Chas. K. Harris.

Please, Mister, take me in your car; I want to see mamma.
They say she lives in Heaven; is it very, very far? . . .
Always in the way, so they always say,
I wonder why they don't kiss me, just the same as Sister
    May. . . .

An ancient theme, lament of a child for its mother in heaven, was brought up to the date of a modern invention in a song which told its story in the opening line, "Hello, Central, Give Me Heaven, for My Mamma's There" (1901). Rather too often, and more generally than happens in nature, self-pity was put into the mouths of children; there was almost a cult of songs about children who were misunderstood, or so considered themselves. Probably greater fidelity to child nature was achieved in "They Always Pick on Me" (1911),[34] about a child who asked no sympathy, but proposed practical revenge for his woes:

They always pick on me
They never, never let me be. . . .
But I know what I'll do by and by,
I'll eat some worms and then I'll die.

Childish indignation was also expressed in "Smarty, Smarty, Smarty" (1908):

You're nothing but a smart-y cat,
So there, there, there.[35]

An echo of school-days was in

"B.l.n.d." and "P.g.,"
That spells blind pig, don't you see?
Teacher says with some surprise,
"Oh, my! You've left out both 'i's.'". . .
"Blind pig has no 'eyes' you see?"
"You're right!" the teacher said to me.[36]

Several "kid songs" dealt with childhood as a distant and affectionately remembered experience. One of the most familiar was the easily sung and easily remembered "School Days" (1907):

Readin' and ritin' and 'rithmetic, taught to the tune of a hick'ry stick.

In the same spirit were the charming "Sunbonnet Sue" (1908) and "To My First Love" (1900)—"That was many years ago; don't let anybody know!"

No list of the "kid songs" widely sung between 1900 and 1914 would be complete without three whose popularity held over from the nineties of the preceding century: "Kiss and Let's Make Up" (1891), "Daddy Wouldn't Buy Me a Bow-wow" (1892), and "Two Little Girls in Blue" (1892).

Not classifiable in any ordinary grouping, not romantic because it had nothing to do with love, hardly even sentimental in the ordinary sense, but powerful to move many hearts, was "The End of a Perfect Day"[37] (1910), described by one who liked it as "the story of an aching heart in music." "The End of a Perfect Day" was written as the spontaneous expression of a sincere emotion evoked by beauty and an experience of fine pleasure. The author, Mrs. Carrie Jacobs-Bond,[38] had been motoring with friends: "Arriving at Riverside, California, late in the afternoon, we traveled to the top of Mt. Rubidoux, sat down and watched the sunset. . . . That night, while dressing for dinner, I sat down and wrote a few verses on little cards used as place-cards for the dinner. It didn't take me more than ten minutes; at dinner I read them, and my friends were all pleased":

[37] Reproduced with permission of the copyright owner, Carrie Jacobs-Bond
[38] Mrs. Bond also wrote "I Love You Truly" (1905).

More than five million copies were sold, more, perhaps, than of any other American song except "Home, Sweet Home"; it drew royalties from twenty-nine manufacturers of phonograph records, player-rolls, and other forms of mechanical music; and enriched the woman who, by an unusual combination of talent, wrote both words and music — a widow, who, before this success, had kept lodgers, painted china, made dresses, and sung at church entertainments to eke out the income of the hall-bedroom shop in which she carried on a small business in sheet-music. "The End of a Perfect Day" evoked moods of peace and repose for literally millions of average Americans. The wife of President Warren Harding[39] (she had much need of peace) cherished it as her favorite song, often asked official musicians to play it as the closing number on White House programmes. One of them, remembering, played it at her funeral.

There were songs in which the dividing-line between sentiment, and satire on sentiment, was made deliberately narrow; songs that could be sung soulfully and received in the same spirit — or sung and received as conscious

[39] 1921–23.

burlesque. (Awkwardness occurred only when the singer and the audience had conflicting moods.) For example, concentrated dolefulness, yet with the wink of a pun, was in

> Annie Moore, sweet Annie Moore,
> We will never see sweet Annie any more;
> She went away, one summer's day,
> And we'll never see sweet Annie any more.[40]

Similarly,

> Ev'ry morn I send thee violets[41]

could be taken with extreme seriousness, or it could give rise to harsh remarks about bleating tenors. It was much the same with a group of ballads about lost love, or unrequited love, or love frustrated by circumstances. One could indulge in a mood of melodrama, or one could smile at melodrama, as in:

> She was happy till she met you,
> And the fault is all your own.
> If she chooses to forget you,
> You will please leave her alone!
> She is with her dear old mother;
> In this world she has no other,
> There is no-o place like home, sweet home![42]

Another ballad of affection misplaced, in which love became involved in unhappy complications through trying to bridge an economic chasm, was told in words and music designed to make hearers feel very sad:

[40] "Sweet Annie Moore" (1901). Reproduced with permission of the copyright owner, Paull-Pioneer Music Co., New York.

[41] "Violets" (1905). Other songs of this period that depended for their appeal on one of the most potent stimuli to sentimental memories, the remembered aroma of flowers, were "You're as Welcome as the Flowers in May" (1902); "Love Sends a Little Gift of Roses"; "That's What the Rose Said to Me" (1906); "When You Wore a Tulip, a Bright Yellow Tulip" (1914); "Garden of Roses" (1908); "The Wedding of the Lily and the Rose" (1892); "Where the Morning Glories Twine Around the Door" (1905).

[42] "She Was Happy Till She Met You" (1899). Reproduced with permission of the copyright owner, Paull-Pioneer Music Co., New York.

> She's only a bird in a gilded cage,
>   A beautiful sight to see;
> You may think she's happy and free from care;
>   She's not, though she seems to be.
> 'Tis sad when you think of her wasted life,
>   For youth cannot mate with age.
> And her beauty was sold for an old man's gold,
>   She's a bird in a gilded cage.[43]

The author[44] of "A Bird in a Gilded Cage" (1900) made another effort, also unsuccessful, to unite economic strata by the cement of emotion in "When Wealth and Poverty Met" (1901). Neither that nor "A Bird in a Gilded Cage" would be written or become popular in the America of a quarter-century later, about 1927. The picture would be so different from the new conditions as to seem too far-fetched even for burlesque. Economic and social changes had given a girl too many careers alternative to selling her beauty "for an old man's gold," and there was literally no such thing as "a

---

[43] Reproduced with permission of the copyright owner, Harry Von Tilzer Music Pub. Co.

[44] Harry Von Tilzer. He was easily head of the fraternity of professional song-writers who sought for what would make a "hit" with the indefatigable zest with which prospectors seek gold. Von Tilzer's quest was successful, again and again and again. By the number of his compositions that made a "hit," he stands, in this period, alone; by the adaptability of his talent, the number of different themes and topics he dealt with, his distinction is equally unique, and more elevated. Among the more than three thousand songs Von Tilzer wrote, some of the popular successes were: "Wait Till the Sun Shines, Nellie" (1905); "In the Mansion of Aching Hearts" (1902); "Where the Morning Glories Twine Around the Door" (1905); "Last Night Was the End of the World" (1912); "All Aboard for Blanket Bay" (1910); "A Little Bunch of Shamrocks" (1913); "Under the Yum Yum Tree" (1910); "Down Where the Wurzburger Flows" (1902); "On a Sunday Afternoon" (1902); "Row, Row, Row" (1912); "What You Goin' to Do When the Rent Comes 'Round?" (1905); "Don't Take Me Home" (1908); "Please Go Way and Let Me Sleep" (1902), "Goodbye, Liza Jane" (1903); "Are You Coming Out Tonight, Mary Ann?" (1906); "The Beautiful Sea" (1902); "Down Where the Cotton Blossoms Grow" (1901).

girl in a ragged dress," and no corroding consciousness of "wealth and poverty side by side." A girl of 1930 who married for money and found the bargain unsatisfactory did not seek sad sympathy in a song — she stepped out briskly to the divorce court, and exchanged the clanking chains of matrimony for the gayer jingle of gold in the form of alimony.

VI

Songs of Satire and Cynicism

Excess of melodrama[45] or of sugariness invited amiable satire. There had been since 1901 a universally familiar "Florodora" song, by no means excessively sentimental; rather it was sentiment with a twinkle, a song with which a youth could give a comedy touch to a proposal, "Tell Me, Pretty Maiden" (1901):

> For I must love some one, really,
> And it might as well be you.[46]

One of the Florodora lines, becoming a current quip, was incorporated into a satirical song called "Mamie."[47] "Mamie" made use of other slang idioms of the day —

[45] Periodically, song vogues about lost loves and broken hearts run into other vogues that jeer at them with burlesque, or supplant them with new themes. But sentiment comes back. In the 1920's, the newest of inventions, the radio and the phonograph, gave affectionate welcome and a considerable proportion of their programmes to songs written in the style and mood of more than fifty years before, such as "Lay My Head Beneath the Rose," "Prisoner's Song," and "When I'm Gone You'll Soon Forget Me."

[46] "Do you know," wrote William O. Inglis in 1926, "anything in the wide world of music more sumptuous, sensuous, intoxicating than the orchestration that went with 'Tell Me, Pretty Maiden'? That, and the dancing and the come-hither winks under the flapping hats, rather than the words, made this Florodora sextette song the most popular musical comedy feature that ever swept America."

[47] "Mamie" (1913). Reproduced with permission of the copyright owner, Paull-Pioneer Music Co., New York.

will a reader in the distant future recognize the pun in
"notion" and in "Mamie got the sack"?[48]

> Mamie was a girlie, Mamie was her name.
> Ev'rywhere that Mamie went, something went the same;
> She took well at parties, very well, in fact;
> Mamie was a klepto-mamie, kleptomamiac.
> Once she took a notion in a dry goods store,
> She would be a lady, that and nothing more;
> But a bold floorwalker made her put it back.
> Mamie took a sealskin, Mamie got the sack.
> M-M-M-M-Mamie, don't you feel ashamie,
> Tell me, are there any more at home like you?

Cynicism about melodic declarations of true love was
introduced into a satiric popular song, by the device of
giving a voice, and a worldly mind, to one of those products of the taxidermist's art which at that time were
frequent adornments of feminine headgear,[49] "The Bird
on Nellie's Hat"[50] (1906):

> Ev'ry Saturday Willie got his pay, then he'd call for Nell . . .
> On Nellie's little hat there was a little bird . . .
> "I'll be your little honey, I will promise that!"
> Said Nellie as she rolled her dreamy eyes.
> "It's a shame to take the money!" said the bird on Nellie's hat,
> "Last night she said the same to Johnny Wise!"
> Then to Nellie Willie whispered as they fondly kissed,
> "I'll bet that you were never kissed like that!"
> "Well, he don't know Nellie like I do,"
> Said the saucy little bird on Nellie's hat.

"The Bird on Nellie's Hat" was impersonal cynicism
from a detached observer. "I Wonder Who's Kissing

---

[48] The 1928 equivalent for "got the sack" was "canned."
[49] In 1907 *Puck* lamented:

> We have the horseless carriage,
> The wireless and all that,
> Also the loveless marriage,
> But not the birdless hat.

[50] Reproduced with permission of the copyright owner, Paul-Pioneer Music Co.

Her Now?"[51] (1909) was direct reproach by an injured party:

I wonder who's kissing her now, wonder who's teaching her how;
I wonder who's looking into her eyes, breathing sighs, telling lies.

VII

Songs of Inebriation, and of Moods Ensuing Therefrom

The period which in bibulous history is designated

From a photograph by Sarony.
Nora Bayes in "The Follies of 1907."

"Pre-Volstead" was marked by several songs of conviviality. "Down Where the Wurzburger Flows"[52] (1902) antedated by nearly a score of years the taking effect of the Eighteenth Amendment; for singing it to the de-

[51] Reproduced with permission of the copyright owner, Chas. K. Harris.
[52] Reproduced with permission of the copyright owner, Harry Von Tilzer Music Pub. Co.

light of hundreds of audiences, Miss Nora Bayes[53] became known as "The Wurzburger Girl":

it   Just or-der two seid-els of la-ger, or three If 1

don'twantto drink it,please force it on me, The Rhine may be fine but a   cold stein for

mine,   Down where the Wurz-burg-er flows.

Twin to that, though less successful, was:

Come, come, come and make eyes with me under the Anheuser
    Bush.
Come, come, drink some Budwise with me under the Anheuser
    Bush.[54]

The other side, the "morning after" of alcoholic conviviality, was celebrated by George Ade in a song about

[53] Miss Bayes's versatility enabled her to sing, with equal charm, the German
"Down Where the Wurzburger Flows" and the Irish "Has Anybody Here Seen
Kelly?" A competent judge (Mr. Odell Long Whipple, manager of the sheet-
music department of the house of Droop's, at Washington, D. C.), speaking
from an experience of thirty-nine years, regarded Miss Bayes as "the best popular stage singer I ever heard." In 1927, some twenty years after her early successes, and a little while before her death, Miss Bayes made one of those familiar tours in which a stage favorite of a former generation renews old acquaintance. "When she appeared in Washington," said Mr. Whipple, "I sat with my
heart in my mouth, fearing to see our idol of past days go down under the disapproval of the modern-day jazz demands. She began in her accustomed manner; clear-voiced, dramatic when necessary; always enunciating clearly every
word (the secret of the success of most of our popular singers). At first, the
audience was mild, but before she finished, the same old-time roar of applause
greeted her and she carried off easily the evening's honors."
    Another of Miss Bayes's songs about liquid refreshment was "What Good Is
Water When You're Dry?" in which she concluded that water "For a ship to sail
on, it is fine; but to drink — well, not me."
[54] "Under the Anheuser Bush" (1903). Reproduced with permission of the
copyright owner, Harry Von Tilzer Music Pub. Co.

the Sultan of Sulu.[55] This Filipino potentate was introduced by American soldiers to the Occidental institution
known as a cocktail, and after the experience, sang:

> The cocktail is a pleasant drink;
> It's mild and harmless, I don't think.
> When you've had one you call for two,
> And then you don't care what you do!
>
> Last night I hoisted twenty-three
> Of these arrangements into me.
> My wealth increased, I swelled with pride,
> I was pickled, primed and ossified
> But [spell out] R-E-M-O-R-S-E.
>
> These dry martinis did the work for me;
> A dark brown taste, a burning thirst,
> A head that's ready to split and burst.
> Last night at ten, I felt immense;
> To-day I feel like thirty cents.
>
> Now I'm feeling mighty blue —
> Three cheers for the W. C. T. U.
> It is no time for mirth and laughter
> The cold, gray dawn of the morning after.[56] . . .

The Sultan's renunciation being acute, was temporary.
A pledge of total abstinence, carrying more convincing
assurance of permanence, was expressed in a song made
familiar by the Primrose and Dockstader minstrels,
called by them "A Coon Temperance Ditty," but better
known as "Good-bye, Booze"[57] (1901):

> So good-bye booze, forever more!
> My drinking days are surely o'er.
> We've had a good time I will agree,
> But just look what it's done to me.
> So good-bye booze, forever more!

Whether the farewell was to be voluntary by indi-

[55] In Ade's play of the same name.
[56] Reproduced with permission of the copyright owner, M. Witmark & Sons.
[57] Reproduced with permission of the copyright owner, Edw. B. Marks Music
Co.

viduals, or universally enforced by law; and whether it was to be permanent or merely "until we meet again" — those and associated questions became a leading political issue in the United States during and after the passage of the Prohibition Amendment to the Constitution in 1920.

VIII

Two stage figures who richly satisfied the popular zest were Marie Dressler and May Irwin — custodians

From the Albert Davis Collection.
Marie Dressler.

in their generation of the heritage of the comic muse — twins in jocosity, obesity and racy verbosity. While both in their long careers sang many songs, each had one with which she was tagged in the public's affections. As Joseph Jefferson played many parts but was always summoned back to "Rip Van Winkle," so was Marie Dressler put under affectionate compulsion to sing "Heaven Will Protect the Working Girl"[58] (1909). This ditty burlesqued, or, as the slang of that day would have put it, "joshed," the melodrama in some of the popular songs and plays of that period, which, as that generation itself recognized, were rather over-theatrical. Miss Dressler's satire began:

A village maid was leaving home, with tears her eyes were wet
Her mother . . . says to her: "Neuralgie dear, I hope you won't forget
The city is a wicked place,
And cruel dangers 'round your path may hurl."

[58] Reproduced with permission of the copyright owner, Chas. K. Harris.

Refrain.

You are go-ing, far a-way, But re-mem-ber what I say, When you are in the ci-ty's gid-dy whirl, From temp-ta-tions crimes and fol-lies, Vil-lains tax-i-cabs and trol-leys Oh! Heav-en will pro-tect a work-ing girl.

The mother's foreboding was borne out — in the person of a city villain. The country girl "supposed he was a perfect gent," but was disillusioned when, at dinner one night in a "table d'hote so blithe and gay," "he says to her: 'After this we'll have a demi-tasse.'"

Whereupon Neuralgie, recalling her mother's warning and instantly alert to peril, exclaimed:

"Stand back, villain; go your way! Here I will no longer stay,
Although you were a marquis or an earl;
You may tempt the upper classes with your villainous demi-
tasses,
But Heaven will protect the working girl."[59]

Of the many choruses which May Irwin[60] stirred thousands of audiences to sing with her, one of the most

[59] "Heaven Will Protect the Working Girl" had an English antecedent, published in 1901, called "I'm a Respectable Working Girl," in which the heroine pu.s her rebuke in terms of British social stratification:

I'm a respectable workin' girl while you're of the upper classes.
But you can't come none of your games on me with wine and demi-tasses;
I could 'ave sworn that you was a gent as would never treat me so,
For I'm a respectable workin' girl I'd 'ave you know.

[60] Miss Irwin's versatility, in voice and personality, enabled her to give pleasure with a range of song that included "Mamie, Come Kiss Your Honey Boy" (1893), "When Yo' Ain't Got No Money, Well, Yo' Needn't Come 'Round" (1898), "May Irwin's Frog Song" (1896), "May Irwin's Moonlight Serenade," and Robert Louis Stevenson's "My Bed Is a Little Boat" (1899), sung to music composed by Cissie Loftus, the actress.

enduringly popular was the "Bully Song"[61] (1896). To see Miss Irwin's broad features take on the semblance of a negro in a darkly angry mood, to watch her massive chin move slowly forward into the symbolism of bellig-

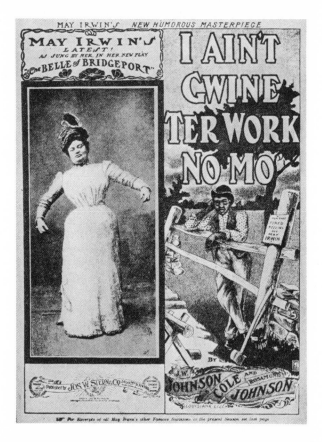

erency, to see her stride back and forth across the stage with the hunched shoulders and menacing swing of a confident negro whose only request of fate was that he be allowed just one sight of his enemy — to witness that was to recognize a really gifted impersonation. "You had no doubt," wrote Henry O. Osgood, editor of *The*

[61] Reproduced with permission of the copyright owner, White-Smith Music Pub. Co.

Musical Courier, "that that nigger *must* be found — and felt sorry for him when he should be."

When I_____ walk dat lev - ee round, round, round, round,

When I_____ walk dat lev - ee round, round, round, round,

When I_____ walk dat lev - ee round,_____ I'm a

lookin' for dat bully an' he must be found._____

IX

A Transition in Songs About Negroes, from Old-Time "Darky Songs" to Modern "Coon Songs," Together with Some Allusions to Changes in the Status of Negroes, Which Were Associated with the Altered Mood and Tempo of Negro Music

About the time when negroes had ceased to be called "Sambo" and were coming to be addressed, generically, as "George"; after Aunt Dinah, illiterate and happy in the kitchen, had yielded, as a symbol of the race, to her granddaughter Clara, destined for the high school and self-consciousness; when amiable darkies gave up saying "Marse Tom" with easy native grace, and stiff-necked colored gentlemen began to say "Mister Page"[62] with embarrassed lack of ease; about the time when the negro had been fully deprived of the homely privileges of dependence, in exchange for the dubious gift of civil

[62] The allusion is to Thomas Nelson Page (1853–1922), Ambassador to Italy in the Presidency of Woodrow Wilson, distinguished Virginia author of "Befo' de War," "The Old South," and other books about Southern characters and Southern history. As an author, and as gentleman in private life, no American knew the negro better, nor treated him more sympathetically.

rights — unshackled in Virginia "so's he could be lynched in Ohio," as "Mr. Dooley" put it; when a colored workman ceased to be grateful for a hand-me-down suit of broadcloth and took pride in a gaudy new one of shoddy; when the younger colored woman became a little ashamed of her mother's turban and bought for herself a concoction of feathers, plumes and plush; when writers and song-composers left off thinking of a cabin in the cotton-fields as the negro's exclusive background, and began to write of him in a Harlem apartment; when young negro "intellectuals" were starting periodicals whose editorial pages truculently demanded equality and independence — but whose advertisements of "anti-kink" suggested that they really aspired toward imitation; when a negro comedian, Bert Williams, wrote and sang,[63] in 1901, about a lady of his own race, "She's Gettin' Mo' like the White Folks Ev'ry Day," and cited, as signs of the change, that she used to wear "calico patterns" but now wants "silks and satins," that she had taken to kalsomine "to help to make her fair," and that she used to "sing Swanee River" but now she "warbles Il Trovatore" — about the time, in short, when the colored man became less a type faithful to its own characteristics, and more an imitation of a white man — about that period, and in somewhat that spirit, there came a change in negro songs: the old-time "darky songs" began to be jostled, quite roughly, by the quite different "coon songs" of the early 1900's; the mellowly sentimental "Old Folks at Home," began to be subjected to rude elbowing by songs like "Mister Johnson, Turn Me Loose."

Neither as to the upgrowth of a new type of negro song nor as to other changes in negro life, was the evolution brought about by the negro himself. So far as he

[63] With his partner, George Walker.

contributed to it, he did what subject races commonly do, what the negro had always done since he was first brought to America in slavery — he adapted himself to what the white man wanted him to be, or what the white man's conditions made him. The difference between

PERFORMED BY

HARRIGAN & HART.

WORDS BY ED. HARRIGAN. ⑤ MUSIC BY DAVE BRAHAM.

Typical cover of sheet music of the old-time "darky song" during the 1870's and preceding.

the darky song and the coon song — between "Old Black Joe" of 1877 and "Pullman Porters' Ball" of 1901 — was chiefly a difference between contrasting conditions of negro life, both conditions being products or reflections, in different times and places, of the white man's social organization. The darky song reflected negro life of slavery days and immediately after, the bondsman's acceptance of dependency as the natural order, his self-protective deference to the ways of the superior race, his pleasure in what good his condition provided, his contentment with a simple existence, his freedom from concern about money or any other aspect of an economic lot for which he had no responsibility.

Similarly, the difference between the darky song and the coon song was in part a difference between the ways in which two generations of white folks looked upon the black. Of the two, it was the earlier generation that had the more sympathetic attitude. The authors of such early darky songs as Stephen Foster's "Old Folks at Home" (1851) and "My Old Kentucky Home" (1853), had had familiar and affectionate contact with the old-time negro, called him "Uncle Ned" and his wife "Aunt Dinah." Often they built their songs upon melodies spontaneously evolved by the negroes themselves. Because the negro was at that time in bondage, or the hardly less pathetic condition immediately succeeding slavery, the best of the early darky songs were wistful, mournful.[64]

[64] While most of the early darky songs, especially those that survived and became classics, were mournful, there were darky songs that were lively and comic, many of them. Upon darky songs of the comic type was built the whole of negro minstrelsy, which, like everything else associated with the old-time darky, came to an end during the period covered by this history. By 1910, the black-face minstrel show fulfilled literally Shakespeare's phrase for one of the saddest of experiences, lingered superfluous on the stage. It had begun something more than a lifetime before, about the 1830's, when an actor (whom theatre lore names variously "Adelphi" Rice, "Daddy" Rice, and "Thomas" Rice) borrowed the clothes of a negro porter in a Pittsburgh hotel, blacked his face, and sang a ditty he had heard from a negro stage-driver, accompanying the singing with "most remarkable jumps and gyrations":

> "I came from ole Kentucky,
> Long time ago,
> Where I first larn to wheel about
> An jump Jim Crow.
> Wheel about and turn about,
> And do jis so,
> Ebry time I wheel about
> I jump Jim Crow."

"Jim Crow" became the progenitor of literally thousands of comic darky songs, many of them made familiar to the public during the seventy years or so of the vogue of negro minstrelsy. But no darky song of the lively type, and no "nigger minstrel" song achieved permanence, as did the mournful "Swanee River," and also "Old Black Joe" and "Old Uncle Ned" and "Massa's in de

X

"Darky Songs" in Partial Eclipse

While the old-time darky songs had to endure rough shoving from the coon songs of the 1900's, their popularity was not seriously disturbed. The darky songs were superseded only in the sense that none appeared as new during this period; it was the coon song that was the current vogue. But the old ones were sung. At all times there were millions of Americans who could hum, from memory,

All up and down de whole cre-a-tion Sad-ly I roam, Still long-ing for de old plan-ta-tion, And for de old folks at home.

"Old Folks at Home," "Old Black Joe," and their companions of a preceding era had achieved a secure pedestal in American song-lore, an enduring place in American affections. This favor they retained after the social order that produced them had passed away. They retained it despite the disapproval, expressed through ignoring them, of cabaret and dance-hall orchestras. One heard them chiefly in homes, though they were also

Cold, Cold Ground." The case tends to prove Herbert Spencer's analysis of the genesis of melody, in which he argues that the best folk-music, because the most natural and genuinely personal, is that which arises out of suffering.

"Jim Crow," among several contributions to the American scene, provided the white man with a generic name for institutions associated with discrimination between the races, such as "Jim Crow" cars, to which the negroes on railroad trains in the South were required to confine themselves, "Jim Crow" laws, and many social usages which segregated the negro.

used by concert singers who, in a spirit of amiably condescending largesse, occasionally sang them as encores
following more pretentious arias. To one was given, during the 1900's, a special prominence, in the nature of a
happy resurrection, by a concert singer, Alma Gluck,
who recalled and gave to a second generation the pleasure
of "Carry Me Back to Old Virginny"[65] (1878):

> Carry me back to old Virginny,
> There's where the cotton and the corn and 'tatoes grow.
> There's where the birds warble sweet in the springtime,
> There's where this old darky's heart has long'd to go.

Those darky songs — the negro songs of the cabin
and the cotton-field, of the turban and the bandanna, of
the curtsey and the memories of slave days, figured in
this period as part of the permanent stock of American
songs, or as a hold-over or a revival. No new ones were
written. The last "darky songs" — and some of the best
that appeared at any time or from any source — were
written about 1880, by James Bland, himself a negro.
Bland's songs pictured his own people, the old-time
darky, as he was seen, and sung about, in the 1870's and
1880's, a character whose life was associated with the
cabin and the cotton-field, whose lack of earthly riches
was compensated by confident expectation of Heavenly
ones, and whose visions of the future life included emphasis on golden aspects of Heavenly architecture. The
more familiar of Bland's songs, many of them plaintive
or semireligious, included: "De Golden Wedding"
(1880), "Oh Dem Golden Slippers" (1879), "Carry
Me Back to Old Virginny" (1878), "In the Morning
by the Bright Light" (1880), "In the Evening by the
Moonlight"[66] (1880):

[65] Reproduced with permission of the copyright owner, Oliver Ditson Co.
[66] Reproduced with permission of the copyright owner, Hitchcock Pub. Co.

In de ebe - ning ?by de moon-light, you could hear us dar - kies . sing - ing, In de

ebe - ning by de moon-light you could hear de ban - jo ringing, How de old foll·s would en - joy it, Th· would

sit all night and lis - ten, As we song In de ebe - ning by de moon - light.

XI

The Transition to "Coon Songs"

The difference between those darky songs and the "coon songs" that displaced them is illustrated by comparing two airs, both about the same theme, but written a generation apart. "Gib Me dat Watermillion"[67] was true darky — composed some time before 1882, in Tennessee:

> Oh, de dew it am a fallin', dat 'million's gwineter cool,
> An' soon it will be very, very fine.
> But bless yo' soul, my honey, dis darkey ain' no fool
> To leave it dar a hangin' on de vine.
>
> Oh, de ham bone am good, de bacon am sweet,
> 'Possum meat am very, very fine;
> But gib me, oh, gib me, oh how I wish you would,
> Dat watermillion hangin' on de vine.

That had the mellow mood, the gentle tempo, the rich melody, the characteristic point of view of the old-time darky song. Contrasting[68] with it is a coon song

---

[67] Among many evidences of enduring appeal, "Gib Me dat Watermillion" was sung for more than thirty years, beginning in 1894, at the Gridiron dinners at Washington by Major Alfred J. Stofer, correspondent, in 1930, of the Birmingham, Ala., *News*. In the course of this one perennial exhibition of the "Watermelon Song's" appeal, it was heard with unvarying delight by eight Presidents of the United States. William H. Taft used to seek opportunities to hear Major Stofer sing it.

[68] A penetrating critic who has read these proofs contends that the distinction between darky songs and coon songs as here made, has implications that go too far. He insists that no question of better or worse is involved, that it is merely a matter of different types, and that the modern coon song is as faithful to one type of negro as the older darky song was to the negro of earlier days. In each generation, song-writers wrote about, and stage characters imitated, the

dealing with the same theme — the more strident, slightly nasal, "Lam', Lam', Lam' "[69] (1900), written in a later period and a good many miles from Tennessee:

Cow meat am good and sweet, roast veal it am fine,
Kidney stew I love, too; pork chops am divine;
But of all de meats dat's good to eat, from turkey down to ham,
De one dat tickles ma palate de most is lam', lam', lam'.

XII

"Coon Songs" Become the Vogue

In a subtle way, recognizable by those who knew both the old-time darky and the modern coon, "Lam', Lam', Lam'," reflected a change in the negro and especially in the characteristics of negro songs. Many of the newer type, the coon songs, were written by persons not familiar with negro life, or only familiar with it as it was in the profoundly changed conditions of a New York City background. Their attitude toward the negro was coldly objective, wholly without sentimental glamour. Many merely tried to imitate negro psychology and speech. Some coon songs were written with the frank intention of caricature — and were better than those that achieved caricature without intending to. Those that attempted accurate characterization at all, dealt with the new negro, reflected his altered economic and social status, his beginning sophistication, his engaging "triflingness," his strutting show-offiness, the discomforts he experienced in trying to adjust himself to an economic system evolved by the white man. They depicted the negro as he was

---

type of negro that would be familiar to their audiences. To discuss whether the 1910 type of negro is "better" or "worse" than the 1880 type would be more than any cautious historian would care to undertake, since it would involve definition of standards of civilization, and standards of individual human happiness. "Better" for himself? "Better" in the eyes of his white neighbors?

[69] Reproduced with permission of the copyright owner, Paull-Pioneer Music Co., New York.

after a generation of freedom, and therefore of responsibility.

Anticipation of the new lot, as imagined by a negro

Cover of the sheet music of an old-time darky song, "De Golden Wedding"
(1880).

who himself bridged the transition between slavery in
the South and wages in the North, was expressed in "Ole
Shady"[70]:

> Good by, hard work widout no pay.
> I'se gwine up North, whar good folks say
> Dat white wheat-bread an' a dollar a day
> Is a comin', comin'.

[70] Reproduced with permission of the copyright owner, Oliver Ditson Co.

Dawning disappointment was in "The Best I Get Is 'Much Obliged to You'" (1907); and harsh reality, in the unaccustomed form of a certain landlord, came in:

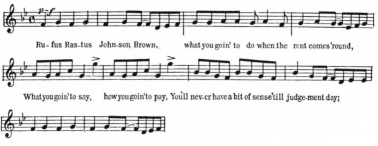

Ru-fus Ras-tus John-son Brown,　what you goin' to do when the rent comes 'round,

What you goin' to say,　how you goin' to pay, You'll nev-er have a bit of sense 'till judge-ment day;

You know, I know, rent means dough, 71

Cold insistence upon eternal economic verity became a dolorous refrain in many of the songs about the new negro, about the coon as distinguished from the old darky — the negro who had left slavery behind him and had now to share the white man's concern about balance between income and expenditure, who had left the happy-go-lucky ease of a cotton-field cabin and was now required to meet the rent in a city apartment, and to adjust himself to the other problems and attributes of what may have been a more elevated stage of civilization, but could hardly have seemed, to the negro's temperament, a more easy one. There was sheer Ethiopian sordidness — acquired, one feels sure, from the Caucasians — in

When you ain't got no money, well, you needn't come 'round;
Ef you is broke, Mister Nigger, I'll throw you down.72

The desirability of money, the imperious necessity of having money — and keeping it, was the doleful theme of several ditties sung, with deliberately didactic effect,

71 "What You Goin' to Do When the Rent Comes 'Round?" (1905). Reproduced with permission of copyright owner, Harry Von Tilzer Music Pub. Co.
72 "When You Ain't Got No Money You Needn't Come 'Round" (1898). Reproduced with permission of the copyright owner, M. Witmark & Sons.

by two negro comedians, Bert Williams and George
Walker. Williams was the most talented negro that ever
appeared upon the American stage. His personality, superbly adapted to acting the simplicity, indolence and
credulity of the negro, filled many rôles
in which, through hard luck, or too
much trustfulness, or a game of craps
conducted by smarter negroes, or other
misadventure, he has been forced to a
firmness about money not native to his
naturally generous soul. In "In Da-
homey" (the first piece written and
performed by negroes ever on the
boards of a Broadway theatre), Williams was a simple, good-natured
darky; Walker a smart, sophisticated
one. The latter, having already made
free with a good deal of Williams's
money, asked for a final loan, and was
answered in a dialogue ending:

Bert Williams, singer
of modern "coon
songs."

Williams: And I say No.
Walker: Do you mean to say that you
refuse?
Williams: No, I don't refuse. "No"
and "refuse" is two diffunt words. They
don't sound alike. You don't even spell 'em alike. I say No!
N-O-E, Noe!!

In the same play, the same theme, preoccupation with
money, was expressed musically in a song written and
sung by Williams and Walker jointly:

You know how it is wid money, how it makes you feel at ease;
De world puts on a big broad smile, and yo' friends am thick
          as bees.
But oh, when you' money is runnin' low . . .
Dat am de time, oh dat am de time —

When it's all goin' out and nothin' comin' in,
Dat am de time when de troubles begin.[73]

Even when a negro reached his maximum imaginable economic elevation, his achievement was attended by unforeseen qualifications. The rise of the American

New type of cover for sheet music of the modern "coon song," 1910.

negro in the economic scale is described in a hundred books, proved by masses of statistics. But do all combined suggest it as compactly or vividly for the historian of a hundred years from now, or fix the date when the negro had risen and knew he had risen, as adequately as the fact that in nineteen hundred and nearby years, a song was popular which had for its title: "I've Got a White Man Workin' for Me"[74] (1901), in which

Jim Jackson got a dollar and a half to shovel in a load of coal,
But said unto a white man passing by, "if you will put this down the hole,
I'll give you just two dollars for the job.". . .

The white man, having accepted, saw the colored man "swell" and "sneer" as he said to a gathering crowd of his own race:

I've got a white man workin' for me.
Don't care what it costs, I'll stand all the loss;
It's worth twice the money for to be a boss . . .

[73] When It's All Goin' Out and Nothin' Comin' In" (1902). Reproduced with permission of the copyright owner, Edw. B. Marks Music Co.

[74] Reproduced by permission of the copyright owner, Paull-Pioneer Music Co., New York.

Whereupon

That white man felt so very much insulted that he left off
shov'ling coal,
And grabbed that black man by the kinky, woolly head and
dropped him down the hole . . .

"You hired me for to do this job, and I'm a-goin to clean
up right;
"So down the hole goes everything that's black that I can
see round here in sight."

XIII

In many of the coon songs, fiscal troubles were combined — in dreadful complexity — with matrimonial
difficulties.

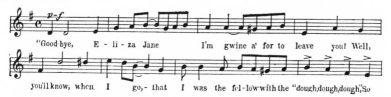

"Good-bye, Eliza Jane"[75] (1903), was answered,
about a year later, by the repentant despair of the lady
in "Alexander!"[76] (1904):

[75] Reproduced with permission of the copyright owner, Harry Von Tilzer
Music Pub. Co.
[76] Reproduced with permission of the copyright owner, Harry Von Tilzer
Music Pub. Co.

Similar to that epic of "Alexander's" marital discord was a song popular in 1901, reciting a domestic tragedy in the life of William Bailey, who, having left his home in anger, came back in repentance, calling:

> Ain't dat a shame, a measly shame,
> To keep yo' honey out in de[77] rain?
> Won't you open dat door and let me in?
> I stand yere freezin', wet to de skin.[78]

The following year appeared what apparently was meant to be a sequel, with a happy ending of remorse and forgiveness:

> Won't you come home, Bill Bailey, won't you come home? . . .
> I'll do the cooking, darling, I'll pay de rent,
> I knows I've done you wrong.
> 'Member dat rainy eve dat I drove you out,
> Wid nothing but a fine tooth comb?
> I know I'se to blame, well, ain't dat a shame?
> Bill Bailey, won't you please come home?[79]

Most of the coon songs reflecting the harsh dawn of economic understanding dealt with the negro who had gone North and to the city. The negro who remained in the South retained much of his native quality, and songs about him treated him as a carefree person. There was never a better portrayal of the negro when in high spirits than the lively "Whistling Rufus"[80] (1899), which, together with "Smoky Mokes" (1899), often provided the music for the dance called "cake-walk," in vogue about 1900:

[77] Many of the popular songs quoted in this chapter had, as respects words, variations of spelling. Negroes were sometimes represented as saying "dat," sometimes orthodoxly "that." In printing quotations here, the author has occasionally made immaterial changes in the interest of consistency and clarity.

[78] "Ain't Dat a Shame" (1901). Reproduced with permission of the copyright owner, Paull-Pioneer Music Co., New York.

[79] "Bill Bailey, Won't You Please Come Home?" (1902). Reproduced with permission of the copyright owner, Paull-Pioneer Music Pub. Co., New York.

[80] Reproduced with permission of the copyright owner, Paull-Pioneer Music Co., New York.

A great musician of high position
Was whistling Rufus, the one man band . . .
Nothin' could touch him in Alabama when he played on his
    old guitar.

Bert Williams (with his partner, Walker, also colored) wrote both words and music of "Ready Money" (1899), "The Voodoo Man" (1900), "I Don't Like No Cheap Man" (1897), "Not a Coon Came Out the Way He Went In" (1899), "The Blackville Strutters' Ball" (1900), "The Colored Band" (1900), "The Game of Goo Goo Eyes" (1900), "He's Up Against the Real Thing Now" (1898). Williams composed the music, and by singing, or by a superb art he had for semi-recitation, made familiar many songs of which the words were by various authors, including: "Chink, Chink Chinaman" (1909), "The Darktown Poker Club" (1914), "My Landlady" (1912), "My Ole Man" (1909), "Nobody" (1905), "You're On the Right Road, But You're Going the Wrong Way" (1912).

Contemporary with Williams and Walker, and of the same race, were Cole and Johnson, the Johnsons being two. The Williams and Walker partnership and the Cole and Johnson trio were frequently associated with each other both on the stage and in the composition of songs, singing each other's songs and otherwise making joint contributions to such a degree that it is now difficult to say, as to some songs, whether they were Williams and Walker's, or Cole and Johnson's. The productions commonly assigned to Cole and Johnson suggest that they attempted, and succeeded, in creating music some degrees above the standard of coon songs written by white artisans of coon songs. Their productions included "The Maiden with the Dreamy Eyes" (1901), "Congo Love Song" (1903), "My Castle on the Nile"

(1901), "Good Morning, Carrie" (1901), "Mandy" (1906), and "Under the Bamboo Tree"[81] (1902), written in a dialect that seemed Italian, but presumably was South Sea:

> I love-a-you and love-a-you true, and if you-a love-a me,
> One live as two, two live as one, under the bamboo tree.

Perhaps it was a wish they had to preserve a greater dignity for themselves and for their race that caused Cole and Johnson to adopt a pseudonym, "Will Handy,"[82] to designate the authorship of the most familiar, if not the most elevated of all the songs they wrote, "Oh, Didn't He Ramble?"[83] (1902), of which the chorus was

> Oh! didn't he ramble, ramble?
> He rambled all around, in and out of the town;
> Oh! didn't he ramble, ramble?
> He rambled till the butchers cut him down.

Tradition said that the song, in its earliest version, had an authentic hero, an old billy-goat wise in the ways of the world as observed while prospecting in garbage cans along the alleys back of Armour Avenue, Chicago, who "got mixed up with a band of goats being driven to the stock-yards for slaughter and was killed by mistake." Probably no American popular song of the twentieth century suffered so many parodies, some of which were more singable (by males) than printable. Of the standard version, the first stanza ran:

Old Beebe had three full-grown sons, Buster, Bill and Bee,
And Buster was the black sheep of the Beebe family;
They tried their best to break him of his rough and rowdy
    ways,
At last they had to get a Judge to give him ninety days.

[81] Reproduced with permission of copyright owner, Edw. B. Marks Music Co.

[82] Not to be confused with W. C. Handy, composer and introducer of negro "blues."

[83] Reproduced with permission of the copyright owner, Edw. B. Marks Music Co.

XIV

The coon songs that were familiar at one time or another between 1900 and 1914, some as new "hits," others enduring from the decade preceding, included: "Coon, Coon, Coon, I Wish My Color Would Fade" (1900); the darkly menacing "You'll Get All That's Coming to You" (1898); "All Coons Look Alike to Me" (1896) — that title was a chilling negation of what had been the old-time darky's sacred tie and cherished wish, to have an individual relation of informal but warm and very special friendship with some one white man or white family who would be his particular "folks," who would stand sponsor for him in the community, indorse him to strangers, especially to minions of the law; respond to his childlike dependence, help him when in need, protect him in time of trouble.

A song which gave to current slang a derisive phrase, "Go Way Back and Sit Down, Coons in Your Class Are Easy Found" (1901) . . . The plaint of a colored woman who left her unhappy home, "I Don't Know Where I'm Goin' But I'm On My Way" (1905) . . . Advice of a disillusioned colored woman who had been married for her money, "The Bee That Gets the Honey Doesn't Hang Around the Hive" (1906) . . . A song the early phonographs used to blare forth:

> Any rags, rags? any bones, any bottles today?
> There's a big black ragpicker comin' this way.[84]

Not all the "coon songs" dealt with the troubles attending the negro's new estate; some turned appealingly to universal sources of happiness: "Come Along, My Mandy, Sweet as Sugar Candy" (1907) . . . "I'd Leave Ma Happy Home for You,' oo, oo" (1899) . . .

[84] "Any Rags?" (1902).

"My Gal Is a High-Born Lady — She's Black, But Not Too Shady" (1896) . . . "Just Because She Made Them Goo-Goo Eyes" (1900) . . . "Little Alabama Coon" (1893) . . . "At a Georgia Camp-Meeting" (1897) . . . "Rastus on Parade" (1896) . . . the early telephone song,

Hello my baby, hello my honey, hello my ragtime girl,[85]

the plaintive

Way down in my heart I've got a feelin' for you,
And if we should part I'd be a-kneelin' to you.[86]

I have said that all the negro songs appearing between 1900 and 1913 were coon songs, that no important song of the older darky type appeared after 1900. There was one that did not quite belong in either class — at least it was far from the coon type, though it had something in common with the older darky songs. "Mighty Lak' a Rose" (1901) had distinguished authorship, the music by Ethelbert Nevin,[87] the words by Frank L. Stanton. Stanton was a gentle, lovable, unworldly Georgian, who spent nearly forty of the seventy years of his life at the very centre of the clattering distractions of the Atlanta *Constitution* office, writing a poem a day, always about homely or humorous themes and characters — striving to keep alive the old in a world fast turning away from him toward cynicism and jazz. His "Mighty Lak' a Rose" was a lullaby, about a little boy, his own:

Sweetes' li'l feller —
Everybody knows;
Dunno what ter call 'im,
But he mighty lak' a rose!

[85] "Hello My Baby" (1899).
[86] "Way Down in My Heart" (1904).
[87] See page 423.

Lookin' at his mammy
Wid eyes so shiny-blue,
Mek' you think dat Heaven
Is comin' clost ter you!

XV

Melting-Pot Songs. By Which Is Meant, Not Songs Brought to America from Other Lands; Nor Songs Written by Immigrants After Arriving Here; but Rather Those Written by Americans About Immigrants, Reflecting the American's Conception, Not Invariably Correct, of His Newer Fellow Citizen

The successive waves of immigration to the United States gave rise to corresponding vogues of song; to some extent they contributed toward changed trends in American popular music. It was not so much that the newcomers brought their native songs with them. What is commonly meant by an Irish, or a German, or an Italian song, is one about an immigrant, about a "greenhorn" — written usually by an American, or by an immigrant already here long enough to acquire, toward his newer fellow American, a sophisticated air of humorous condescension.

In this spirit of amiable burlesque, three songs associated with the early influx of German immigrants became American popular classics. One, composed by Gus Williams (called a German comedian though born on the Bowery), was about those strolling German bands — trombone, horn, and piccolo[88] — that every American town and village learned to expect with the same confidence, and about the same time, as the burgeoning of buds in the spring. "Dot Leedle German Band,"[89] as

---

[88] One player had also a pair of cymbals attached to his shoulders, with a rod running down to his heels, by means of which he "kicked" the music.
[89] The title was "Gus Williams's German Band" (1873).

song and as institution, continued to be familiar in the affections of America until the early 1900's.[90]

Dot leedle German band, dot leedle German band;
De beoble cry und say, "Oh my!" as ve march drough de
    land.

Ve go around de sdreeds almosd every day,
Und set de beoble vild mit de music dot ve blay;
"Good-by, Sourheart,"[91] und "Hime Sweed Hime," ve blay
    so fine,
But ve always do our best ven ve blay "Die Wacht am Rhein."

The strolling German band of the villages and towns was contemporary with another itinerant transplanted from the Fatherland, the German peddler of the country roads, who trudged from farm to farm carrying strapped upon his bent shoulders a pack wrapped in black oilcloth, as big as an ordinary trunk and hardly less heavy. On the tables in farmhouse kitchens, he spread his little outpost of Cathay and the bazaars — gaily colored cloths, ribbons, sparkling jewels of a sort, braidings, beads, glass ornaments. If it was late afternoon, he requested permission to spend the night on the kitchen floor, or in the haymow of the barn. Food he never needed to ask for; the best in the cupboard was pressed upon him by the generous farmer folk as partial return for the pleasure that his coming gave them.[92] At least two of New York's largest department stores, having

[90] The last "little German band" of the authentic type seen by the writer of this history played for half an hour on the steps of the Harvard Law School, Cambridge, Mass., in the spring of 1903.

[91] Such perversions of English words as "sourheart" for "sweetheart" were supposed to be amusing results of the effort of the German immigrant to master the American idiom.

[92] The last peddler seen by the writer of this history plodded the road between West Grove and New Garden, in southeastern Pennsylvania, in the fall of 1886, and gave a stick of striped candy to a little boy. But in New York City, as late as 1910, I knew a great merchant whose bent shoulders and sturdy, short legs, no less than his shrewd understanding of human nature, were the permanent marks of his earlier career.

The greatest metallurgical business in America was founded by a German

branches in other cities, had their beginning in that sort of merchandising celebrated by a very old native German song, formally entitled "Buy a Broom,"[93] but equally well known by a phrase from the chorus: "Ach du Lieber Augustin":

> From Deutschland I come,
>   With my light wares all laden . . .
> Oh listen, fair lady
>   And young pretty maiden,
> Oh, buy of the wandering Bavarian a broom.
>
> O mein lieber Augustin, Augustin, Augustin,
> O mein lieber Augustin, Alles ist weg.

Equally familiar was a ditty of which the music was German, but the words, sung wherever beer was drunk, were by an American:[94]

> Oh where, oh where iss mein little dog gone,
> Oh where, oh where can he be?
> 'Mit his ears cut shord und his tail cut long —
> Oh where, oh where can he be?[95]

All three of these songs, and many others, owed their vogue to the wave of German immigration that began with the German revolution of 1848 and lasted until the 1880's, the period when newly arrived Germans were a daily sight to the average American, who did not distinguish between them and Hollanders, and often called them "Dutchmen." All three became part of the permanent stock of American songs, familiar to each suc-

---

Jew who had begun his business career as a peddler. Two brothers who helped to found one of New York's first-rank banking houses, and whose sons continued to be partners in 1930, had begun as peddlers. Many of the peddlers, while German by birth and nationality, were Hebrew by race.

[93] "Buy a Broom" in its original version was associated with the beginning of the waltz during the eighteenth century.

[94] Septimus Winner, who wrote under the curious pseudonym "Alice Hawthorne," was author, also, of "Ten Little Injuns" and "Listen to the Mocking-Bird."

[95] "Oh Where Iss Mein Little Dog Gone?" (1864).

ceeding generation. To think of "Dot Leedle German Band" or "Oh Where Iss Mein Little Dog Gone?" as German is to fail to distinguish the song's theme from its place of origin and its spirit. They were American songs, they became American institutions, and they expressed the American feeling about the Germans among us. That feeling was one of true affection in no wise modified by the humor, also American, which sang burlesque songs about them. Later, about 1903, appeared a German song in which the burlesque was a little touched by jeering, a mocking note, inspired less by any tangible friction between the Americans and German-Americans than by the grandiosity with which the Kaiser was at that time striving to impress the world — and for which the German nation paid so dearly in the good opinion of most of its neighbors:

> Who were the greatest race of men, in this or any age?
> Who always led the world? It was the Dutch.[96]

To which, in the same year, and in a similar mood, answer was made — on behalf of another race,[97] also, in some of its ways, grandiose, or, at the least, instantly ready to respond to the challenge of grandiosity in others:

The Germans are a mighty race, improving ev'ry year;
They lead the world in science, sauerkraut and lager beer.
But there's a race surpassing them in this world and the next,
And on the tomb of Germany some day you'll read this text:
It takes the Irish to beat the Dutch.[98]

[96] "It Was the Dutch" (1903).

[97] From the earliest presence of the Irish side by side with the Germans in America, the former regarded themselves — with some justification — as more nimble-witted than the Teutons, and therefore as licensed to "kid" their more serious-minded neighbors. It was the custom of John W. Kelly (the "Rolling Mill Man"), a monologue entertainer of the 1870's, to acknowledge his first burst of applause from an audience by saying, "Thank God the house is full of good Irish people — you never got a roar like that from a German except when he's losing money."

[98] "It Takes the Irish to Beat the Dutch" (1903). Reproduced with permission of the copyright owner, F. B. Haviland & Co.

XVI

Irish songs did not bulk so large in the period this chapter covers as in previous decades. New influences were making themselves felt among song-writers, on the stage and in every quarter of American life. Comedians reflecting a later tide of immigration, such as Weber and Fields and the "Rogers Brothers," were taking the place formerly occupied by Irishmen like Harrigan and Hart, and by Americans in black-face.

The change in its fundamental aspect, from the great immigrations preceding 1880 to those coming after that year — from the Germans, Irish, Scotch and Scandinavians to the Italians, Poles and Russians, as well as Jews from eastern Europe — was one of the most important of the developments that influenced modern America. A comparatively trivial facet of it was the theme of a popular song about, "The Argentines, the Portuguese and the Greeks."[99] The writer of the song was not accurate in the races he chose as symbols, since neither the Argentines nor the Portuguese ever came to the United States in large numbers — it was not they who gave the American of about 1910, in parts of some large cities, an occasional sense of being among strangers in his own land. The song began with an epitome of the country's beginnings:

> Columbus discovered America
> In fourteen ninety-two;
> Then came the English,
> And the Dutch, the Frenchman
> And the Jew.
> Then came the Swede
> And the Irishman.

[99] (1920.) Reproduced with permission of the copyright owner, Edw. B. Marks Music Co.

But now, said the song:

> There's the Argentines,
> And the Portuguese,
> The Armenians, and the Greeks.
> One sells you papers,
> One shines your shoes,
> Another shaves the whiskers off your cheeks.

Time, however, changes all. After twenty years, according to the song:

> There's the Oldsmobile,
> And the Hupmobile,
> And the Cadillac,
> And the Ford.
> They are the motors
> You and I can own,
> The kind most anybody can afford —
> But the Cunninghams —
> And the Mercedes and the
> Rolls-Royce racing freaks —
> Ah! they all belong to the
> Argentines, and the
> Portuguese, and the Greeks.

In spite of the shrinking of the Irish strain in the melting-pot, "The River Shannon" flowed melodiously about 1911. "My Irish Molly O" was frequently reminded in 1906 that "springtime is ring-time." "It's a Long, Long Way to Tipperary," composed in England, appeared in America first in 1912, was neglected, and then, two years later, was cabled here in news despatches as the marching-song of the first British contingent in the Great War, the "Contemptibles,"[100] as they embarked at Dover for the battle of Mons — whereupon "Tipperary" became one of the three or four outstanding songs of the war, in America as well as England.

---

[100] So called because the Germans thus estimated them.

In 1909 there came to America an Irish-born singer, destined to popularize a lovely song:

Sure I love the dear silver that shines in your hair,
And the brow that's all furrowed and wrinkled with care;
I kiss the dear fingers so toil-worn for me,
Oh, God bless you and keep you, Mother Machree!

"Mother Machree"[101] (1910) was deeply and truly Irish,[102] including the right Irish shade of attitude and expression toward a revered mother. To hear John McCormack's tenor lead up to the devotion of the last line was to get a thrill that was little short of solemn. "Mother Machree" called for complete surrender to emotion, and permitted the surrender without damage to taste.[103] Irish songs, true Irish ones, enabled a singer to be sentimental without causing shivers to the discriminating listener.

From a photograph by Hartsook.
John McCormack.

[101] Reproduced with permission of the copyright owner, M. Witmark & Sons. "Mother Machree" was written by Ernest R. Ball. Writing songs designed to strike the popular taste was his career, and he was exceptionally successful, achieving more than twenty "hits." Ball's songs were more than a shade higher in quality than most of those composed by persons who made song-writing a profession; they included "Love Me and the World Is Mine" (1910), "Till the Sands of the Desert Grow Cold" (1911), "I Never Knew What Love Could Do" (1906), "In the Garden of My Heart" (1908), "When Irish Eyes Are Smiling" (1912).

[102] While "Mother Machree" was the best Irish song of this period in the sense of faithfully reflecting Irish sentimentality, the best in the sense of fulfilling the common notion of the Irishman in comedy and on the stage, the swashbuckler, Rory O'More, "divil-a-bit-do-I-care" type, was either "Harrigan" or "Has Anybody Here Seen Kelly?" See page 350.

[103] A change in popular manners and point of view is epitomized in the contrast between the "Mother Machree" of John McCormack in 1910 and the

An actor with a charming brogue and a tenor voice, who made a specialty of plays built around Irish heroes, Chauncey Olcott, gave momentum to:

From a copyrighted photograph by F. C. Bangs.

Chauncey Olcott.

When Irish eyes are smiling,
    sure, it's like a morn in
    spring,
In the lilt of Irish laughter you
    can hear the angels sing;
When Irish hearts are happy
    all the world seems bright
    and gay,
And when Irish eyes are smil-
    ing, sure, they steal your
    heart away.[104]

In 1899, Olcott, then just reaching his prime, gave the country the best of his songs, one that continued to be sung after a quarter-century, "My Wild Irish Rose"[105] (1899):

The sweetest flow'r that grows,
You may search ev'rywhere, but none can compare
With my wild Irish Rose.

XVII

To confine this discourse about Irish songs to the rather late harvest of them that bloomed between 1900

"Mammy" and "Red-Hot Mama" songs of fifteen years later. The earlier ones were designed to go to the heart and cause emotion; the later ones to go to the feet and cause liveliness. In 1929, a parody of "Mother Machree," written in New York patois, by Frank Sullivan in the New York *World*, ran:

"Mother Machree" (Park Avenue)

Sure I love the dear henna that shines in your hair,
And the face they've unwrinkled and lifted with care;
But as for those fingers so toilworn for me —
Excuse me, I'm leffing, Mater Machree.

104 "When Irish Eyes Are Smiling" ((1912). Reproduced with permission of the copyright owner, M. Witmark & Sons.

105 Reproduced with permission of the copyright owner, M. Witmark & Sons.

and 1914 would be to let mere chronology work injustice to the richest, most varied, and most lively type of popular song that America has known. The real heyday of Irish songs was earlier, from the 1860's to the 1890's, synchronizing with the presence among us of native Irishmen in large numbers and fresh from the "old country" — a period when practically every American had familiar, and almost always affectionate, acquaintance with them; when the Irish "greenhorn" was as frequent in daily contact and conversation as "greenbacks" in politics and pocketbooks; when most of the jokes and stories that amused the average American began, "Once there were two Irishmen" — their names were always Pat and Mike, invariably they said "be Jabers," and usually the stories dealt with a presumably universal Irish trait of lighting a match by means of friction on the seat of the trousers, or with an equally widely assumed characteristic of spitting on the hands before taking hold of a pick. At that time, when the bulk of the names on construction crew pay-rolls began with "O" or "Mc," when Irish immigrants were laying the ties and breaking the rocks, and blasting the mountain passes of America's railroads, the song that was the bench-mark of his status was "Drill, Ye Tarriers, Drill"[106] (1888):

> Oh, ev'ry morn at seven o'clock,
> There are twenty tarriers on the rock;
> The boss comes along and says "be still,
> And put all your powder in the cast-steel drill."

Spoken: Stand out there with the flag, Sullivan,
Stand back there! Blast! Fire! All over.

Chorus

Then drill, ye tarriers, drill;
Drill, ye tarriers, drill;

[106] Reproduced with permission of the copyright owner, Leo Feist, Inc.

Oh it's work all day with no sugar in your tay,
When ye work beyant on the railway,
And drill, ye tarriers, drill.

> *Spoken: Stand out there forninst the fence
> with the flag, McCarthy. Where's the fuse,
> McGinty? What? He lit his pipe with it?
> Stop the Belt car coming down. Stand
> back! Blast! Fire! All over.*

Last week a premature blast went off,
And a mile in the air went big Jim Goff,
When pay-day next it came around,
Poor Jim's pay a dollar short he found.
"What for," says he; then came this reply,
"You were docked for the time you were up in the sky."

Presently the Irishman stepped up in the world, and, in a phrase of modern slang, stepped out; exchanged his laborer's clay dhudeen for a briar or meerschaum, or even a fifty-cent cigar; gave up his blackthorn stick brought from Ireland for a gold-headed cane bought on the Avenue; rose, often symbolically and sometimes literally, from the hand-car of a laborer on the right-of-way to the private car of the president of the road — and found his affluence sometimes dogged by the mood expressed in the soliloquy of Cassidy in "Shanahan's Ould Shebeen":

In me bran' new brownstone manshin' — Fift' Av'noo over
th' way,
Th' Cathedral round th' corner, an' the Lord Archbishop to
tay,
Sure I ought to be sthiff with grandeur, but me tastes are
mighty mean,
An' I'd rather a mornin's mornin' at Shanahan's ould shebeen . . .
That's why, as I squat on th' cushins, wid divil a hap'orth to
do,
In a mornin' coat lined wid velvit, an' a champagne lunch at
two,
Th' mem'ry comes like a banshee, meself an' me wealth between;

An' I long for a mornin's mornin' in Shanahan's ould shebeen.
I've got to meet th' Archbishop — I'm a laborer now no more,
— But, ohone! those were fine times, then, lad, an' to talk o'
    them makes me sore.
An' whisper — there's times, I tell you, when I'd swap this
    easy chair,
An' the velvit coat, an' th' footman wid his Sassenach nose
    in th' air,
— An' th' Lord Archbishop himself, too — for a drink o' th' days
    that ha' been,
For th' taste o' a mornin's mornin' in Shanahan's ould she-
    been.[107]

The earlier period, when Cassidy had been a laborer,
the period of the Irish immigrant who fought in the
Civil War and built the railroads, was entertained by
"Lanigan's Ball" (1863). The opening verses recited
that Lanigan, while young, had wasted his substance in
the pleasures of his day and place, but was restored to
solvency and the respect that goes with it when

His father he died, and made him a man again,
Left him a farm of ten acres of ground.

Whereupon young Lanigan

. . . gave a large party to all his relations.
That stood beside him when he went to the wall.
So if you will listen, I'll make your eyes glisten,
With the rows and the ructions at Lanigan's ball.

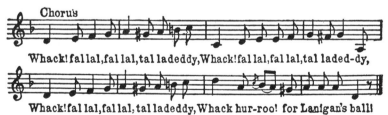

Whack! fal lal, fal lal, tal ladeddy, Whack! fal lal, fal lal, tal laded-dy,

Whack! fal lal, fal lal, tal ladeddy, Whack hur-roo! for Lanigan's ball!

[107] "Shanahan's Ould Shebeen" is attributed to an Irishman, Gerald Brennan,
who lived in New York in the 1890's. It was not, so far as I know, a song;
as a recitation, however, to introduce a note of mellowness to parties where good
fellows were gathered together, it was a favorite for many a year and in every
part of America.

Kitty O'Hara, a nate little milliner,
Tipped me the wink, and asked me to call . . .
Whin we got there they were dancing the polka,
All round the room in a quare whirligig;
But Kitty and I put a stop to this nonsense,
We tipped them a taste of a nate Irish jig;
Oh, Mavrone, wasn't she proud of me?
We bathered the flure till the ceiling did fall.

"Lanigan's Ball" remained familiar until the 1890's. Current during the same period were "Finnigan's Wake" (1863); "The Mulligan Guard" (1873), which supplied a march tune for practically every military band during half a century; "Saint Patrick's Day Parade" (1874); "The Gallant 69th" (1875); "Are You There, Moriarty?" (1876); "Branigan's Band" (1876); "No Irish Wanted Here" (1876); "Barney McCoy" (1881); "I'll Take You Home Again, Kathleen" (1876); "Pat Molloy" (1878); "The Little Widow Dunn" (1879); "The Mulligan Braves" (1879); "Paddy Duffy's Cart" (1881); "The Irish Christening" (1884); "The Irish Jubilee" (1890); "Arrah, Go On! You're Simply Tazin'!" (1895); "Sweet Rosie O'Grady" (1896).

By 1900 and after, the Irish-born in America, failing renewal because of dwindling immigration, had become a less pungent ingredient in the melting-pot. Those who had arrived in the first great immigrations slept beneath the crosses of a thousand Catholic graveyards; with them slept many of the characteristics and customs that had given distinctive flavor to the race. The Irish strain in the American scene now depended upon the somewhat attenuated blood of second and third generations who had, in the expressive Irish phrase, "lost the brogue," had exchanged the soft Irish "R" for the harsh American one, had ceased to exclaim "be Gorra" and, with other American youths and flappers, said "by Golly," or even "by heck"; had forgotten the pious custom of their parents who never mentioned a dead person without adding "God rest his soul," and never failed to say, when any one sneezed, "God bless us." The new generation

---

ORDER OF DANCE.

—o—

1.—Grand March.

2.—Lancers.

3.—Polka.

4.—Quadrille.

5.—Double Lancers.

6.—Military.

7.—Waltz.

8.—Lancers

9.—York.

10.—Portland Fancy.

11.—Quadrille.

12.—Polka.

13.—Saratoga Lancers.

14.—Military.

15.—Caldonia.

16.—Waltz.

17.—York.

—SUPPER.—

18.—Virginia Reel.

19.—Polka.

20.—Newport.

21.—Lancers.

22.—Waltz Quadrille.

23.—Military.

24.—Waltz.

25.—New York Lancers.

26.—Waltz.

27.—"Home, Sweet Home "

Dance programme for May party given by the Pastime Club, Thursday evening, May 1, 1890, Marion, N. Y.

---

had dropped the "Bridget" and called themselves "Belle" or "Barbara," had exchanged "Mary" and "Mollie" for "Marie" or "Mae," had exchanged "Kathleen" for "Kathryn" — to find a "Bridget" one would have been obliged, by 1900, to rub the moss from a tombstone somewhere. They had forgotten "Shule, Shule, Shule Agradh," and joined with American voices in singing "Daisy Bell"; had exchanged Irish jigs for American jazz; had sent their mothers' sturdy shawls and "hoods" to the attic and wore shirt-waists and picture hats. They had made, within one generation, the leap between thousands of years of ancestors who had spent ten hours a day in the sun and in contact with the soil, to a status in which many of them spent the whole day indoors at a desk, and bought chemicals to give themselves the artificial tan that was a poor substitute for the wholesome rich color their parents had brought from Ireland. In the processes of sophistication and elevation, if it was elevation, the second and third generation Irish lost much that had made their parents simple and happy, much that made America colorful and agreeable. The effect wrought upon the American scene by the ascent — if it was an ascent — of the Irish to white-collar occupations, and especially by the eclipse of the Irish relative to later immigrations, was illustrated by a whimsical editorial in the New York *Herald Tribune:*[108]

It is still the fashion to assume that if it were not for Ireland this city would be lacking a police force, that if you scratch one of "the finest" you find a "harp," that the New York police force marches with a livelier tread when the band plays "The Wearing of the Green." Yet a perusal of the list of recent graduates from our Police Academy will soon convince one that this notion, once grounded in fact, is now merely traditional. There are some Irish names proudly bunched among the Ms and the Os and a thin scattering elsewhere, but all are submerged in a Saragossa Sea of monickers — Italian, Jewish, Polish, Bohemian, Russian, Swedish and plain Yankee — that are as strange to the Emerald Isle as they are common to the metropolis. Take, for example, the "Ss" among the members of the class of July, 1929, who have received warrants of appointments to the force — Saggese, Savino, Schaefer, Scheller, Schillbersky, Schleimer, Schloemer, Schrimpf, Schuchman, Schuck, Sellger, Seymour, Shaffer, Silvey, Smith, Smith, Smith, Solomon, Sparacino, Staib, Stainkamp, Stanton, Sullivan, Sullivan, Svendsen.

What company for a couple of Sullivans!

[108] In 1929. The editorial is here paraphrased in part.

As the Celt rose from Officer Mike of the police force to become His Honor the Mayor in City Hall, as he was promoted from swinging a pick with the tarriers to issuing orders as superintendent of the division, the place he vacated was taken by the newer immigrant, the Italian. The change impressed America. In the Hartford, Conn., *Courant* a scholar familiar with ancient Roman history, observing a gang of Italians digging a trench under the supervision of an Irish boss, put his reflections into hexameters:

One of "The Finest" in 1907–1908.

Yonder one pushing the shovel might be Julius Cæsar —
Lean, deep-eyed, broad-browed and bald, a man of a thousand.
Farther along stands the jolly Horatius Flaccus.
Grim and grave, with rings in his ears, see Cato the censor.

On the side of the street in proud and gloomy seclusion,
Bossing the job, stood a Celt — the race enslaved by the
    legions,
Sold in the markets of Rome to meet the expenses of Cæsar;
And, as I loitered, the Celt cried out: "Worruk, ye Dagos!"
Meekly the dignified Roman kept on patiently digging.

Such are the changes and chances the centuries bring to the
    nations . . .
Now the Celt is on top, but Time may bring his revenges
Turning the Fenian down, once more to be bossed by a Dago.

The height of the presence of Italian immigrants in America came between 1900 and 1914, about the time the little German band gave way to the Italian with a hurdy-gurdy. In this period bloomed such songs as the Italians gave rise to. An early one recited some of the first designations of them — extended by persons with imperfect ethnological information, to all recent immigrants who were dark-complexioned:

> First dey call-a me a Dago, den Guinie, Guinie, Guinie!
> Now it's Wop! Wop! Wop![109]

"My Mariutch"[110] (1907) described one of those exercises which are called dances, though accomplished without use of the feet:

Mariutch she make-a de hootch-a-ma-kootch[111] down at Coney Isle.
She make me smile, she go like-a dis, like-a dat, like-a dis.
She make-a such a dance and never move-a de feet, that's a funny style.

America sang "My Mariutch" as a comic song. Actually it was the pathetic plaint of an Italian lad whose sweetheart had become Americanized and, in his view, "gon-a ta hell":

> That dance, it make-a me seek
> Mariutch, you break-a my heart.

America complacently assumed that Americanization was always benevolent and good for the alien's soul; the subjects of the process sometimes had occasion for doubt.

---

[109] "Wop, Wop, Wop" (1908). Reproduced with permission of the copyright owner, M. Witmark & Sons.

[110] Reproduced with permission of the copyright owner, Harry Von Tilzer Music Pub. Co.

[111] The "hootchy-kootch," described in this song, originated with so-called "Egyptian Dancers" on the Midway at the Chicago World's Fair in 1893. A later name for a similar dance was "the shimmy."

Jews wrote much music, both classic and popular, and became important as purveyors of popular music; but songs written about Jews were comparatively few. Some were sung in burlesque theatres by slapstick Jewish comedians; but outside the theatre, in the country at large, they failed to win the favor of the public as had the earlier Irish and German songs. For the most part they lampooned the Jews' supposed preoccupation with money, as in "Maxie, Don't Take a Taxie" (1910). Other Jewish songs were "Becky, Do the Bombashay" (1910), and Irving Berlin's "Yiddisha Eyes" (1910).

Surprisingly the vast Scandinavian immigration to the United States evoked but one popular song, "Ay Vant to Go Back to Sweden" (1904). The immigrations from eastern and southeastern Europe, Poles, Russians, Hungarians, Slavs of all nations, gave rise to no popular songs whatever.

XVIII

An innovation of this period was a vogue of Indian songs.[112] The popular "Hiawatha" appeared in 1901. "Red Wing"[113] (1907) was a simple little song with a lovely melody, about an Indian maid whose lover died in battle:

Now, the moon shines to - night on pret - ty

Red Wing,_____ the breeze is sigh - ing,_____ the night bird's

[112] They had one worthy and authentic progenitor, the classic "Indian Suite," taken from the Sioux, in which Edward McDowell created the first contribution of symphonic rank ever made to indigenous American music and, appropriately, made himself the first American to be internationally acknowledged as a composer of classical music. McDowell, said a witty critic, Philip Hale, is "not a Boston genius but a real one."

[113] Reproduced with permission of the copyright owner, Paull-Pioneer Music Co., New York.

cry - ing,_____ For a - far 'neath his star her brave is

sleep - ing,_____ While Red Wing's weep - ing_____

her heart a - way._____

In the spirit that animated the field of popular music in 1906 and near-by years, the song publishers kept alertly on the watch for the waning of any one vogue, intent on guessing what would be next. Either as a reflection of that state of mind, or more probably as a satire on the swift passing of vogues, some composer, taking the attitude of one uncertain whether the next fad would be Irish or Indian, achieved a fantastic miscegenation, unique in the variegated results of America as a melting-pot:

Arrah-Wanna, on my honor, I'll take care of you;
I'll be good and true,
We can love and bill and coo. in a wigwam made of sham-
    rocks green.
When you're Mrs. Barney, heap much Carney,
From Killarney's Isle.[114]

XIX

One can imagine the learned societies of Mars having commissioned one of their number to make, in the most scientific spirit, a meticulously literal record of the musical sounds with which the inhabitants of earth gave expression to their various emotions; one can picture the expert, as he approached the surface of the United States, on January 1, 1900, for his fourteen-year vigil, holding his note-book ready with scholarly care to take down in order each vocal sound as it reached him in the upper air, his aural tentacles alert, his recording-apparatus

[114] "Arrah-Wanna" (1906). Reproduced with permission of the copyright owner, F. B. Haviland & Co.

poised — a little pedantic, perhaps, but finely faithful to the spirit of scholastic inquiry; one can imagine him painstakingly recording every shred and fragment of sound as it floated upward — and one can visualize, later on, the Martian learned societies patiently endeavoring to untangle the melodic jumble, and from it make erudite deductions about the emotional nature of the average American, about the aspects of life that moved him to song, the kind of event that he considered of sufficient importance to write a song about. Such application of scientific methods to the interpretation of melodic vocal sounds would have presented exceptional difficulty in a period, 1900–1914, when song-titles and lines from songs with which America expressed its moods at one time or another, composed a peculiarly chaotic babel. The medley would yield rather more to the average American who lived through the period, to whom not only meanings but memories, happy emotions, old associations would be evoked by "I Hear You Calling Me" (1908) . . . "On a Sunday Afternoon" (1902) . . . "By the Light of the Silvery Moon" (1900) . . . "Could You Be True to Eyes of Blue if You Looked Into Eyes of Brown?" (1902) . . . "Will You Love Me in December as You Do in May?" (1905), written by James Walker, later Mayor of New York City . . . "Next to Your Mother Who Do You Love?" (1909) . . . "Rip Van Winkle Was a Lucky Man But Adam Had Him Beat a Mile" (1909) . . . "Why Did I Pick a Lemon in the Garden of Love?" (1906), sung by Richard Carle in "The Spring Chicken" . . . "Every Little Movement Has a Meaning All Its Own" (1909), sung in "Madame Sherry":

> Ev'ry little movement has a meaning all its own,
> Ev'ry tho't and feeling by some posture can be shown.[115]

115 Reproduced with permission of the copyright owner, M. Witmark & Sons.

"Please Go 'Way and Let Me Sleep" (1902) . . .
"Little Alabama Coon" (1903) . . . The wooing of
an Indian maid by a "copper-colored aborigine" celebrated in "My Sweet Iola, Iola List to Me" (1906)
. . . "The Whole Dam Family" (1905):

There was Mr. Dam and Mrs. Dam, the Dam kids, two or three,
With U. B. Dam and I. B. Dam and the whole Dam family.[116]

(What would the Martian scholars make of that?)
"Waiting for the Robert E. Lee" (1912) . . . "The
Warmest Baby in the Bunch" (1897) . . . "I'm Goin'
to Live Anyhow Until I Die" (1901) . . . "If a Girl
Like You Loved a Boy Like Me" (1903) . . . Unfor-
tunate episode at a social event, described in a song of
1898: "Who Threw the Overalls in Mrs. Murphy's
Chowder?" . . . "Way Down Yonder in the Corn Field"
(1901) . . . "Is Everybody Happy?" (1905) . . . "On
the Old Front Porch, Oh! Charley! On the Old Front
Porch" (1913) . . . The girl who was a "baseball fan"
celebrated in "Take Me Out to the Ball Game" (1908):

Katie Casey was baseball mad
Had the fever and had it bad.[117]

"I'd Like to See a Little More of You" (1906), very
suggestive for the early 1900's . . . Good-natured willingness expressed by the lad who was not too "choosy,"
"Any Little Girl That's a Nice Little Girl Is the Right
Little Girl for Me" (1910) . . . Similar undiscrimi-
nating longing of a lonesome girl, "I Want Someone to
Call Me Dearie, Someone I Can Love" (1908) . . . One
hopes they found each other "On the Old Fall River
Line" (1913) . . . George M. Cohan's liking for the

---

[116] Reproduced with permission of the copyright owner, Broadway Music
Corp.

[117] Reproduced with permission of the copyright owner, Broadway Music
Corp.

name Mary, voiced in two songs: "So Long, Mary"
(1905) and "Mary's a Grand Old Name" (1905) . . .
"Alice, Where Art Thou Going?" (1906) . . . "Honey-
suckle and the Bee" (1901) . . . "My Little Georgia

From "The Herald Tribune," New York, September 26, 1928

Rose" (1899) . . . "The Yama-Yama Girl" (1908)
sung by Bessie McCoy, who married Richard Harding
Davis . . . "He's Me Pal" (1905) . . . "Little One,
Good-bye; Little One, Don't Cry" (1906) . . . "Moon-
light Bay" (1912) . . . "The Belle of the Ball" — "the
queen of them all" (1905) . . . "Asleep in the Deep"
(1904) . . . "What You Want and What You Get"
(1904), sung by Fay Templeton . . . Marie Cahill's
"Arab Love Song" (1908) . . . "I Remember You"
(1908):

> I remember you; yes, indeed, I do;
> Weren't you the fellow with the open umbrella

That I met one rainy day upon the avenoo? . . .
Gee! I'm awful glad I metcha, betcha life I don't forgetcha[118]. . .

"Oceana Roll" (1911) . . . "Absence Makes the
Heart Grow Fonder" (1900) . . . "Ain't You My
Lulu?" (1900) . . . "Heart of My Heart" (1907)
. . . "Oh, You Candy Kid" (1909) . . . "Teasing"
(1904):

> Teas-ing, teas-ing, just to see what you would do,
> Teas-ing, teas-ing, to find out if your love was true.[119]

"San Antonio" (1907) . . . "I Just Can't Make My
Eyes Behave" (1906), sung, rather naughtily for that
time, by Anna Held . . . "Ev'ry Little Bit Added to
What You've Got Makes Just a Little Bit More"
(1907) . . . "I'll Do Anything in the World for
You" (1906) . . . An apotheosis of bathos which pro-
vided unintended amusement, "The Curse of an Aching
Heart" (1913):

You made me what I am today, I hope you're satisfied,
You dragged, and dragged, and dragged me down till my soul
> within me died.[120]

"Cheyenne" — "shy Ann, shy Ann, hop on my pony"
(1906) . . . How a whispering campaign starts: "A
Friend of Mine Told a Friend of Mine in a Confidential Way" (1906) . . . "When It's Apple Blossom Time
in Normandy" (1912) . . . "Mr. Dooley" (1901) . . .
"That's the Fellow I Want to Get" (1910) . . . "September Morn" (1913) . . . "What's the Matter With
Father?" (1910) . . . "Little Grey Home in the West"
(1911) . . . "Won't You Come Over to My House?"

[118] Reproduced with permission of the copyright owner, Harry Von Tilzer
Corp.
[119] Reproduced with permission of the copyright owner, Broadway Music
Corp.
[120] Reproduced with permission of the copyright owner, Leo Feist, Inc.

(1905) . . . "The House of Too Much Trouble" (1900) . . . "Trail of the Lonesome Pine" (1913) . . . "Raus Mit Im" (1899) . . . "He's All Right" (1899) . . . "The Best I Get is Much Obliged to You" (1907) . . . "Bedelia" (1903) . . . "I've Got Rings on My Fingers" (1909) . . . "Casey Jones" (1909), a ballad of derring-do on the Illinois Central Railroad, one of the best songs of an occupation ever written . . . "He's a Cousin of Mine" (1906), in which Julie Brown's "feller" found Julie "spooning" with her "long-lost Cousin Jeremiah," whereupon Julie tried to exculpate herself with " 'Tain't no harm for to hug and kiss your cousin" . . . Several songs aspersing the old refrain, "There's no place like home": "I'm Afraid to Come Home in the Dark" (1907), in which a husband elaborately — but except to a particularly trusting wife, not very convincingly — states his reasons for remaining away all night . . . Similar lack of domesticity in "Home Was Never Like This" (1899) and "Any Old Place I Hang My Hat Is Home, Sweet Home to Me" (1901) . . . "It Looks to Me Like a Big Night Tonight" (1908), in which a henpecked husband rejoices over his wife's absence:

For when the old cat's away, why the mice want to play.

And "Don't Take Me Home" (1908), plea of an inebriated husband — "I'm with you in anything you do, but don't take me home" . . . "Coax Me, Go On and Coax Me" — "I'll be your tootsie wootsie if you'll coax me" (1904) . . . "I'm Trying So Hard to Forget You" (1904) . . . "There's a Dark Man Coming With a Bundle" (1904) . . . Curious example of musical miscegenation, "Navajo" (1903):

If you'll have a coon for a beau, I'll have a Navajo.

George M. Cohan's philosophic "Life's a Funny Proposition After All" — "imagination, jealousy, hypocrisy and gall" (1904) . . . "Would You Care" — "if I should leave you?" (1905) . . . "A Little Class of One" — "to learn to love your teacher is your A B C" (1905)

A Pre-War Song Cover.

. . . "Down on the Farm" (1902) . . . "On a Sunday Afternoon" (1902) . . . Tuneful greeting popular with young people, "Good Evening, Caroline" — "never saw you looking finer, how's your ma? how's your pa?" . . . The very doleful "Last Night Was the End of the World" (1912) . . . "You Made Me Love You" — "I didn't want to do it" (1913) . . . "All Alone" (1911) . . . "The Mansion of Aching Hearts" (1902) . . . "I Want a Girl" — "just like the

girl that married dear old dad" (1911) . . . "Put On
Your Old Grey Bonnet" (1909) . . . "Bessie and Her
Little Brown Bear" (1906), which celebrated the Teddy
Bear, and provided many a highly colored souvenir postal card with the sentiment, "And the big round moon
saw them kiss and spoon, Bessie and her little brown
bear" . . . Irving Berlin's "Stop, Stop, Stop" — "don't
you dare to stop; come over and love me some more"
(1910) . . . The Italian dialect song that Jesse Lasky
wrote, "My Brudda Sylvest" (1908) . . . "Down By
the Old Mill Stream" (1910) — "where I first met
you" . . . "When the Midnight Choo-Choo Leaves for
Alabam'" (1912) . . . "In the Valley of the Moon"
(1913) . . . "Good-night, Nurse" (1912) . . . "Little
One, Good-by" — "little one, don't cry" (1906) . . .
"When It's Nighttime Down in Burgundy" — "I want
to be with you" (1914) . . . "I'm the Guy" — "that
put the salt in the ocean" (1912) . . . "If You Don't
Want Me, Why Do You Hang Around?" (1913) . . .
The language of flowers in "That's What the Rose Said
to Me" (1906) . . . "Won't You Fondle Me?"
(1904) . . . "That Railroad Rag" (1911) . . . Final
summing up of an unprofitable matrimonial venture,
"Nothin' from Nothin' Leaves You" (1905):

> You can't learn nothin', 'cause you don't know nothin',
> I've forgot more than you ever knew;
> And the only way I can figure you out
> Is nothin' from nothin' leaves you.[121]

Two importations from London, "Poor John" (1906)
and "Waiting at the Church" (1906) . . . Harry
Lauder's Scotch songs: "Stop Your Ticklin', Jock"
(1904), "She Is Ma Daisy" (1905), "I Love a
Lassie" (1906), "Roamin' in the Gloamin'" (1911),

---

[121] Reproduced with permission of the copyright owner, Paull-Pioneer Music
Co., New York.

"A Wee Deoch-an'-Doris" (1911), "It's Nice to Get Up in the Mornin' " (1913).

"Do You Take This Woman for Your Lawful Wife" — "I do! I do!" (1913) . . . "Somewhere" (1906) . . . "Oh You Spearmint Kiddo With the Wrigley Eyes" (1910) . . . "Here Comes My Daddy Now" — "Oh pop, oh pop, oh pop!" (1912) . . . Ernest Ball's "Love Me and the World Is Mine" (1906), of which the Rochester *Times-Union* said, after Ball's death in 1927, "So long as good fellows get together, that famous chorus will ring out" . . . "Wait Till the Sun Shines, Nellie" (1905) . . . "Down Where the Cotton Blossoms Grow" (1901):

> Hear the darkies singing soft and low.

"You Can't Give Your Heart to Somebody Else and Still Hold Hands With Me" (1905) . . . "Mother, Mother, Mother, Pin a Rose on Me" (1905) . . . "Are You Coming Out Tonight, Mary Ann?" — "don't say you can't, when you can!" (1906) . . . "Back, Back, Back to Baltimore" (1904) . . . "In Dear Old Georgia" (1905) . . . "Someone Thinks of Someone" (1905) . . . George M. Cohan's "Yankee Doodle Boy" (1904):

> I'm a Yankee Doodle Dandy,
> A Yankee Doodle do or die;
> A real live nephew of my Uncle Sam's,
> Born on the Fourth of July.[122]

"Somewhere" — "the sun is shining, somewhere a little rain" (1906) . . . "Because I'm Married Now" (1907), the explanation given by a man who declined invitations to "have a drink," to "bet a ten-spot on Shogun," or to be "introduced to Mame" — "I would if I

[122] Reproduced with permission of the copyright owner, Paull-Pioneer Music Co., New York.

could, but I can't; Why? Because I'm married now"
. . . "Tessie" — "you make me feel so badly, why don't
you turn around?" (1902) . . . "Honey-Boy" — "I
hate to see you leaving, you know my heart is grieving"
(1907) . . . Ungracious attitude of a prospective
bridegroom: "I Don't Like Your Family" — "they
don't make a hit with me" (1906) . . . "Waltz Me
Around Again, Willie" — "around, around, around;
the music is dreamy, it's peaches-and-creamy; oh, don't
let my feet touch the ground!" (1906) . . . "Yip-I-
Addy-I-Ay" — "I don't care what becomes of me
when you play me that sweet melody" (1908) . . .
"Alexander's Rag-time Band" (1911), with which

Come on and hear,......... Come on and hear............. Al - ex - an - der's rag-time band,......... Come on and hear.......Come on and hear,............ It's the best band in the land,...........

(Reproduced with permission of copyright owner, Irving Berlin, Inc.)

Irving Berlin "set the shoulders of America swinging
with [a new] syncopated jubilance"[123] and raised rag-
time dancing to the apotheosis of a popular vogue, a
vogue described the same year in "Everybody's Doin' It
Now" (1911) . . . "The Spaniard Who Blighted My
Life" (1909) . . . "Sympathy" — "ain't it funny, when
you look for money, all you get is sympathy" (1912)
. . . "I Wish I Had a Girl" (1907) . . . The boy who
lectured his sweetheart for using slang and was told, "If
you think I'm too tough, and you don't like my stuff,

[123] The quotation is from Alexander Woollcott's biography of Irving Berlin,
Inc.

Ev - 'ry - bo - dy's do - in' it,   (Spoken) Do - in' it, do - in' it,

Ev - 'ry - bo - dy's do - in' it,   (Spoken) Do - in' it, do - in' it, See that rag - time

cou - ple o - ver there,

(Reproduced with permission of copyright owner, Irving Berlin, Inc.)

why" — "Make a Noise Like a Hoop and Roll Away" (1908) . . . Irving Berlin's "That Mesmerizing Mendelssohn Spring Song Tune" (1909) . . . George M. Cohan's "I'll Be There With Bells On" — "count on me rain or shine" (1906) . . . "Virginia Song" (1906), composed by George M. Cohan and often sung by Ethel Levey (of Paris and elsewhere in Europe):

> I was born in Virginia, that's the State that will win yer;
> If you've got a soul in yer . . .

Arboreal melodies following the vogue of "Under the Bamboo Tree"[124] (1902), the successors including "Under the Yum Yum Tree" (1910), "Up in the Cocoanut Tree" (1903), and, finally, a burlesque, "Any Old Tree at All" (1905) . . . "My Wife's Gone to the Country" (1909), of which Irving Berlin was one of the authors:

> My wife's gone to the country, hurrah! hurrah!
> She took the children with her, hurrah! hurrah!
> I don't care what becomes of me, my wife's gone away.[125]

"And a Little Bit More" (1907) — "I'd like to be a friend to you, and a little bit more" . . . "Show Me the Way to Go Home" . . . "My Jersey Lily" (1909) . . . "Steamboat Bill" (1910) . . . "Oh, You Beautiful Doll" — "you great, big, beautiful doll, let me put my arms about you, I could never live without you" (1911)

[124] See page 384.
[125] Reproduced with permission of the copyright owner, Irving Berlin, Inc.

... "Broke" (1908), much of the merit of which lay in the way Lew Dockstader sang it:

> Sounds real funny, but it ain't no joke.

"Ev'ry Little Bit Helps" — "give me just one loving smile, ev'ry little bit helps" (1904) . . . "I'd Rather Be Outside a-Lookin' In, Than Inside a-Lookin' Out" (1906) . . . "Cubanola Glide" (1909) . . . "Just a Little Rocking Chair and You" (1905) . . . "Keep a Little Cosy Corner in Your Heart for Me" (1906) . . . "Oh, Mr. Dream Man, Please Let Me Dream Some More" (1911) . . . "I'm Crying Just for You" (1913) . . . The sentiment-charged song of 1904:

CHORUS.

Good bye, my la-dy love, Fare-well, my tur-tle-dove,

(Reproduced with permission of copyright owner, Charles K. Harris.)

and "Sing Me to Sleep" (1902):

> Love, I am lonely, years are so long;
> I want you only, you and your song.

The very popular Hawaiian song, written by Queen Liliuokalani, "Aloha Oe":

Fare - well to thee, fare well to thee, Thou charm-ing one who dwells a-mong the bow-ers One fond em-brace, be-fore I now de-part, Un-til we meet a- gain.

"Dreaming" — "years have not changed, the old love still remains" (1906) . . . "In the Good Old-Fashioned Way" (1901) . . . "Ain't You Coming Back to Old New Hampshire, Mollie?" (1906) . . . "For Old Time's Sake" (1900) . . . and a song of 1916 that summed up much of the spirit of all these songs, "Turn Back the Universe and Give Me Yesterday":

Unclasp the hands of time that hold life's golden ray . . .
It seems so long ago, although it was only yesterday.[126]

XX

Most of these songs were mere tiny bubbles of iridescence on the surface of the time. To regard them as landmarks, musical or social, would be the last thing those humble little ditties would ask of history. To future generations they will be no more than quaint or amusing or otherwise entertaining reflections of the sentiments and manners of the America of the early 1900's. They will mean more to those who as youths sang them — now in early middle age — than they ever will mean again. So soon as the generation of which they were a part passes away, the bulk of the tunes will be as "forgotten[127] as the forms of last year's clouds."

They made no pretentious claims for themselves; so far as they had merit it was more in the melody[128] than in the words, hence some injustice is done by a recital of them that can appeal only to the eye. The mass of them were composed in a febrile region of New York called, by one obliged to hear the sounds from it, Tin Pan Alley. The denizens of that district, in the period this chapter covers, reversed the art of the old-time balladwriter, whose first concern was to tell a story. The aim of the later race of song artisans was to hit upon some

---

[126] Reproduced with permission of the copyright owner, M. Witmark & Sons.

[127] The residuum of the songs of any comparatively modern period that achieve any degree of permanence is small indeed. In the 30's, 40's and 50's of the last century there were many popular songs, but only an occasional "Old Oaken Bucket" or "Sweet Alice Ben Bolt" survived. The more modern the period the smaller, relatively, will the residuum be, for the reason that the total output of the song-writing and song-purveying trade increases prodigiously.

[128] "It is the air which is the charm of music, and it is that which is most difficult to produce." — Haydn.

James William Fitzpatrick, discussing the song-writing practice of the period this chapter covers, said: "The song writer hits on a good melody and proceeds to write — or gets a lyric writer to do it for him — words to fit the tune. It is the tunes which endure; you can take any of the songs that have lasted, fit totally different words to it, and the song is just as appealing."

new combination of sounds, or some rearrangement of a
old combination, that would fall agreeably upon the human ear. With the melody accomplished, the finding of
words was a secondary consideration, facilitated by the
amiable disposition of some words associated with sentiment to unite euphoniously with each other in rhyme —
love and dove, coo and woo, heart and part, tune and
croon, you and true, moon and June,[129] as in:

> Honey moon, keep a shining in June,
> To my honey I'll croon love's tune . . .[130]

— the final union of the words to the melody being
achieved in a spirit which said, in the words of one popular song of the day:

> So the tune has a right good ring
> It doesn't much matter what words you sing.

The Martian observer might have made a not too
wide-of-the-mark guess had he said, as to the mass of
the fragments of harmonious sounds floating upward,
that they were the love sounds, the equivalent of dove-
calls, availed of by the unfeathered and songless bipeds
of earth during the period of susceptibility to mating.

The youths of any generation, when the adolescent
imagination is burgeoning, do not commit the cold-
blooded atrocity of passing critical judgment on the popular songs of their time; to them any song heard under
any fortuitous conjunction of romantic circumstances
has an aura that endures so long as they live. From the
critical or historical point of view, the successive cycles
of songs that happen to be popular during successive
generations of adolescents are as ephemeral as the moods
with which they were associated. To have a longer life

---

[129] A classic satire on Tin Pan Alley, its denizens and its products, was composed, in 1929, in the form of a successful comedy, "June Moon," by Ring Lard-
ner and George S. Kaufman.
[130] "By the Light of the Silvery Moon" (1908).

than the love-time of one particular age-group, a song must have, in some degree or other, the quality that makes the "Iliad" immortal. Either there must have been in its authorship some elevation of enduring genius; or the song itself must have some musical "IT,"[131] some of the essence of universality, which gives it protection " 'gainst the tooth of time, the 'rasure of oblivion."[132]

[131] A term that came into popular use about 1924, meaning, among other things, charm of personality, or exceptional magnetism.

[132] The making of this compilation of the popular songs of the period has encountered difficulties, difficulties great at this time and likely to be, for several reasons, greater in future. In the overcoming of extraordinary handicaps, the author of this history came under obligation to — and the value of this compilation (whatever it may be) is indebted to — among others: The Honorable Sol Bloom, Congressman from New York City, himself once a composer as well as publisher of popular songs, and possessor of valuable information about copyrights; Mr. Caspar G. Dickson of the Congressional Library at Washington, who, in addition to technical information about dates and copyrights, has a well-informed and thoughtful interest in the relation between popular songs and phases of culture; Carolyn Wells (Mrs. Hadwin Houghton), who, in the course of a versatile literary activity, wrote some songs, sang most of them, and remembers many; Franklin P. Adams, whose "fly-speck-memory" caught errors in the proofs; Mr. George Ade, author of "R-E-M-O-R-S-E"; Mr. George O'Connor, of Washington, D. C., amateur but skilled performer in melody and savant in its lore, who knows the distinction between old-time "darky songs" and modern "coon songs"; Judge Louis B. Hart, of Buffalo, N. Y., probably the best-informed student of the lore of American popular songs and generous friend to all other explorers in that field; Mr. Thomas F. Woodlock, formerly a financial writer on the *Wall Street Journal,* later Interstate Commerce Commissioner, who knows, and loves, the old-time type of Irish song; Mr. Odell Long Whipple, manager of the sheet-music department of Droop's, Washington, D. C., whose warm liking for the songs of an earlier day makes him willing to take generous pains to have the record of them accurate; Mr. William G. McAdoo and Mr. Norman Chandler, of Los Angeles, who gave generous help to an effort to explore the history of "Casey Jones" (an effort of which the results must remain for the present unpublished); Mr. James William Fitzpatrick, of New York; Mr. Herndon Morsell and Mr. George East, of Washington, D. C.; Mr. J. C. Rosenthal and Misses Lillian K. Braun and Gertrude Winter of the American Society of Composers, Authors, and Publishers, New York City; Mrs. Ethelbert Nevin, Mr. William O. Inglis, Mr. R. Cameron Rogers, and many, many others.

In the research that was a partial preparation for this chapter, many books were consulted, so many that I cannot be sure the following list is even approximately complete:

"Bert Williams, Son of Laughter," edited by Mabel Rowland; "The American Songbag," by Carl Sandburg; "The Life of Ethelbert Nevin," by Vance Thompson; "The Story of Our National Ballads," by C. A. Browne; "Frontier Ballads," by Charles J. Finger; "On the Trail of Negro Folk-Songs," by Dorothy Scarborough; "Read 'Em and Weep," by Sigmund Spaeth; "Pious Friends and Drunken Companions," by Frank Shay; "After the Ball," by Charles K.

XXI

"The Rosary"

One song popular during the period this chapter covers, "The Rosary," touched hands with the most exalted in poetry and in music; it stands out in this record of popular songs like a solitary tall lily in a garden rather given to marigolds and zinnias. As to its words, it was one of the few songs of sentiment that would parse; as to its music, it was one of the rare American popular songs of which the composer had a background of sound training in classical music. The author of the words, Robert Cameron Rogers, could have had a high place among American poets. That he fell short was due to a cynicism about his function, a disdain toward his own best, which, whether real or a pose, is usually a corrosive of talent; and to an intellectual curiosity about fields other

---

Harris; "Twenty Years on Broadway," by George M. Cohan, and "The Story Behind the Song," a series of articles by J. J. Geller in the New York *Herald Tribune*.

But the book of books — indeed, it is literally more than a book, it is an encyclopædia — is the sequence of pamphlets numbered from 1 to 89, each called "Delaney's Song Book." Each of the numbers contains roughly from 175 to 200 songs, and the aggregate of them contain — literally without exception, I imagine, every song, important or trivial, that was published in the United States between 1891 and 1921, together with many songs of older date. These books are utterly priceless and utterly unpretentious, each about 30 pages, printed on inexpensive paper, with blue, pink, yellow or purple covers. They contain, as respects each song, all the words (not the music), together with the names of the authors, composers, and date of copyright. In few fields of American culture or lore has any individual taken the pains to assemble so complete a collection of the data as William W. Delaney assembled in his humble song books.

A collection not attempting to be so comprehensive, but more scholarly and discriminating, and in all respects worthy and valuable, is that which Judge Louis B. Hart contributed to the Grosvenor Memorial Library in Buffalo, N. Y.

Mr. M. A. Richmond of the Paull-Pioneer Music Company, New York, generously gave permission to print extracts from many songs; the name of the firm is printed in a foot-note in connection with each song. Similar permission, similarly acknowledged, was given by Mr. Edward B. Marks of the Edward B. Marks Company; also the White-Smith Music Publishing Co., Broadway Music Corporation, Oliver Ditson Co., Boston and New York, Leo Feist, Inc., Charles K. Harris, Harry Von Tilzer Music Pub. Co., Boston Music Co., Boston, Mass., M. Witmark & Sons, F. B. Haviland & Co., Irving Berlin, Inc., The Hitchcock Pub. Co., Remick Music Corp., all of New York City, and Carrie Jacobs-Bond of Hollywood, Cal.

than his own, an interest in other pursuits, which made perseverance and concentration unlikely. Another handicap this poet had, which was not within himself: "Inherited wealth, cancelling the obligation of hard work, made of his life an easy schedule of to-morrows that proved ever pleasant but ever barren of yield, a masterpiece of genial laziness."[133] "He loved living and sitting in the sun better than working, so he never developed his mine but at that he has written some of the best poetry in the language."[134] The most compact explanation of Rogers's frustration is to be found in the humorous cynicism, the too great self-tolerance, which he compressed into an epitaph he wrote for himself, while still in his twenties:

> He was patient in the pursuit of pleasure,
> and ambitious for his father.

Rogers, born in Buffalo in 1862, graduated at Yale in 1883, studied at the Harvard Law School, practised in his father's Buffalo office, grew weary of an inherited career and went to live in California. There he followed pursuits listed by Stewart Edward White, who, in his novel "Rose Dawn," pictured Rogers as "Gordon Carlson":

He . . . was a poet, and one with a very genuine voice. He was also a hard rider, a tremendous climber of mountains, a redoubtable poker player, an enthusiastic hunter and fisherman, and a conscientious punisher of booze. His poems were exquisite, but he concealed the side of him that produced them as though it were a vice. [He] would have resented being called a poet as he would have resented an epithet. He was sick and tired of poets, and he did everything he could think of in the way of rude, rough, coarse things to prove he did not belong to that breed.

---

[133] For most of the information about the author of "The Rosary" I am indebted to his son, Cameron Rogers. The quotations are from an article by Mr. Rogers about his father in *The Saturday Review of Literature*.

[134] David Gray, author of "The Boomerang," "Mr. Carteret and Others."

In 1894 Rogers wrote "The Rosary," saw it when set to music acquire the greatest current vogue of any American poem, saw it become the inspiration of a sentimental

Part of the original score of "The Rosary."

British novel whose sales went over a million — and lived until 1912 enduring the irony of seeing the world adore his popular song while ignoring what he regarded as by far his better poetry.[135]

"The Rosary," published in a magazine, caught the

[135] Which included "Lochaber No More" (considered by his widow and some others to be his best), "A Health at the Ford," "A Ballad of Dead Camp Fires,"

eye of a chance woman reader, who happened to be writing to a friend, an American composer named Ethelbert Nevin; with her letter she enclosed the verses. By that incident, the poem came to another artist whose career, more typically American, had had the stimulus of poverty and stern discipline, as Rogers's had had the opiate of inherited wealth.

The father of Ethelbert Nevin, mirroring the common thought of a generation which regarded money-making as the most worthy and satisfying of careers, got the boy a clerkship in a Pittsburgh railroad office. Young Nevin, however, pleaded successfully for release and went through a long period of study in both the writing and playing of music under the best teachers, with professional experience in Boston, and in Germany, France, and Italy — a thoroughness of training which helped make it possible for him to compose music satisfying at once to the general public and to exacting critics,[136] to have the simplicity and directness that make for popu-

"To Great Britain," "Charon," "The Blind Polyphemus," "Odysseus at the Mast," and "I Will Lift Up Mine Eyes Unto the Hills." The range of poetic moods of which Rogers was capable is suggested by the contrast between "The Rosary" and his poem about a Greek statue, "The Dancing Faun":

> Thou dancer of two thousand years,
>   Thou dancer of today,
> What silent music fills thine ears,
>   What Bacchic lay,
> That thou shouldst dance the centuries
>   Down their forgotten way? . . .
>
> Ah! where is now the wanton throng
>   That round thee used to meet?
> On dead lips died the drinking song
>   But wild and sweet,
> What silent music urged thee on . . .

[136] A discerning analysis of Nevin's work was written by Willa Sibert Cather, novelist: "His work is unique among the world's beautiful creations. His harmony and melody are his own, like no one else's. He has no affectations. He is not afraid of simplicity, of directness. As someone has said, his melodies 'gain a certain distinction from their very unconsciousness of the danger of vulgarity.' To everything he writes, however slight, that rare grace and distinction cling; an aroma of poetry, a breath from some world brighter and better than ours; an exhalation of roses and nightingale notes and Southern nights."

larity and at the same time the grace and finish that make for distinction.[137]

The words of "The Rosary" reached Nevin one evening while at home with his family. He read them, came under their spell, and walked up and down the room repeating them until he had them by heart:

> The hours I spent with thee, dear heart,
>   Are as a string of pearls to me;
> I count them over, every one apart,
>   My Rosary, my Rosary.
>
> Each hour a pearl, each pearl a prayer,
>   To still a heart in absence wrung;
> I tell each bead unto the end,
>   And there a cross is hung.
>
> O memories that bless and burn!
>   O barren gain and bitter loss!
> I kiss each bead, and strive at last to learn
>   To kiss the cross;
>   Sweetheart! to kiss the cross.[138]

Next day, Nevin, arriving home from his studio, handed his wife the pencilled music for the song — he had written it, says Mrs. Nevin, "in less than an hour, and never changed a note." Notwithstanding his speed, he had practised expert craftsmanship, subtly combining the emotions of love and religion in a melodic outline in which the eighth-notes of the music suggest the manner in which the smaller beads of the Rosary slip through the fingers of a pious devotee, while at the end of each phrase of the music comes a long note and a pause, corresponding to the larger beads that divide the Rosary into tens. Upon audiences, singers observed, the song had always the same effect. As the listeners caught the

---

[137] Nevin wrote the music for over seventy songs. The best known, aside from "The Rosary," were: "Oh, That We Two Were Maying" (1888); "Mighty Lak' a Rose," published after the composer's death in 1901 (see page 386); and "Narcissus" (1891), of which Nevin's biographer, Vance Thompson, said: "No composition by an American composer has had to stand such wear and tear."

[138] Reproduced with permission of the copyright owner, The Boston Music Co.

first familiar phrase there was a spontaneous burst of applause. Then came silence that grew tenser and tenser. "I can see and feel on every face before me," said Mme. Schumann-Heink, "that what is in my heart is in theirs."[139]

"The Rosary" was first sung publicly in Steinert Hall, Boston, in 1898. Almost a generation later, in 1925, Alexander Woollcott could write: "Every publisher's ear is strained to catch the first notes of another 'Rosary,' for they all doff their hats to a song that is still in great demand at the beginning of its second quarter century."[140]

[139] Some of the sophisticated said "The Rosary" was "sugary." Others argued that Nevin's putting it to music was a case where an accomplished composer, sure of his powers, including his versatility, set himself to devise a song that would please the most sentimental yet not depart from sound standards of taste and technic; a song, let us say, that would satisfy sentimentality, yet avoid banality. To all demeaners, Alexander Woollcott retorted (in 1925) that he had "grown a little weary of those cultural parvenus who consider it a showy sign of sophistication to achieve an attitude of disdainful superiority towards that world favorite." What Rogers and Nevin produced was a song which was to music what Watts's "Hope" is to pictorial art, something so definite and concrete as instantly to thrill the simplest understanding of beauty, while conveying no necessary offense to those most conscious of being æsthetes. "The Rosary" was an important contribution to the emotional enrichment of the average man; a contribution also to the elevation of the people's taste — a service best understood when "The Rosary" is compared with the music and words, especially the words, of some of the other sentimental songs common during this period.

[140] The yearly sales of all arrangements of "The Rosary" in the United States States from its first year were:

Year	Sales	Year	Sales
1898	1,990	1914	228,324
1899	18,410	1915	184,946
1900	32,500	1916	103,847
1901	37,500	1917	98,020
1902	36,655	1918	59,201
1903	35,945	1919	67,011
1904	23,332	1920	71,296
1905	33,094	1921	69,738
1906	39,808	1922	80,170
1907	48,665	1923	90,690
1908	46,459	1924	93,157
1909	72,743	1925	87,015
1910	71,288	1926	73,207
1911	199,780	1927	68,096
1912	264,561	1928	48,735
1913	287,267		

Grand total...2,670,750

11

1906

Forebodings of Fiscal Troubles. Marshall Field Dies. "Mr. Dooley" Discusses the Current Vogue of Parlor Socialism. Woodrow Wilson Arraigns the Automobile. America's Cry for Hair. Maxim Gorky Comes and Goes. The Last of the Heretics—Algernon Crapsey. The Thaw Murder Trials. Secretary Root Expounds at Rio Janeiro an Important Point of Doctrine. Rioting by Negro Troops at Brownsville—and Precipitate Punishment by Roosevelt. Taft Succors Cuba. Bryan is Welcomed Home. The California-Japan Imbroglio.

January 4. Jacob Schiff, far-sighted New York banker, member of Kuhn, Loeb and Company, predicted that if the American monetary system were not reformed the country would "get a panic . . . compared with which the three which have preceded would be only child's play." For several months call-money on the New York Stock Exchange had been fluctuating between 10 and 125 per cent, a condition which, Schiff said, was "a disgrace to a civilized community." Ex-Secretary of the Treasury Lyman G. Gage agreed "that a stunning panic will come unless

Jacob Schiff.

something is done." The panic came, October 21, 1907 (see page 502). It, with warnings such as Mr. Schiff's, led to a movement which in 1913 resulted in the creation by Congress of the Federal Reserve System.

(The characteristic, at that time, of our banking system, so far as it could be called a system, was that, speaking roughly, each bank stood alone. Each had to maintain within its own vaults enough reserves to meet at any time any possible call upon it by depositors. The result

Marshall Field.

was that in proportion as need for money by borrowers and business was greatest, in that proportion was the bank obliged to withhold money; the coming of panics was, in a sense, automatic. The change wrought by the Federal Reserve System was that, again speaking roughly, the resources of all the member banks are pooled and are available to meet the needs of each.)

January 17. Marshall Field, multimillionaire dry-goods merchant of Chicago, died. He was, intoned the wealth-defending New York *Sun*, "the first as well as the richest citizen" of Chicago. "The red-mouthed yapping at the rich spared him." *The Sun*, however, did not accurately reflect the times. In Field's life and also after his death the hundred and forty millions he left his children was one of the subjects of querying reflection by critics over the arising of financial dynasties in America. An occasionally expressed belief of that day, often put in words by William Jennings Bryan, was that "no man could earn a million dollars honestly" — Henry Ford was not yet upon the scene, and Bryan had not amassed from his lecturing and writing the million and a quarter of dollars that he was destined to bequeath in his will in

1925. Marshall Field's death and Marshall Field's fortune were taken as a text by a gilded young Socialist, Joseph Medill Patterson, scion of one of Chicago's wealthiest families and an heir to the Chicago *Tribune*. Young Patterson wrote for *Collier's Weekly* a biting analysis of the sources of the Field fortune. Of the more than 10,000 persons employed by Field, he wrote, 95 per cent received $12 a week or less. "The female sewing-machine operators, who make the clothes which are sold in the Field establishment, get $6.75 per week. . . . The makers of socks and stockings are paid: finishers, $4.75 per week of fifty-nine working hours . . . knitters,

Marshall Field's Store, Chicago.

$4.75 per week of fifty-nine and one-half working hours."

The New York *Sun*, seeing in young Patterson's article damage to the conservative interests for which *The Sun* was spokesman, and being much too astute to reply directly, sardonically and most shrewdly sent a reporter to interview the young crusader's father, Robert W. Patterson, who was known to have the orthodox views that should go with his position as editor of the

Chicago *Tribune* and son-in-law of its late owner, Joseph Medill. The elder Patterson talked, willingly; what he said *The Sun* published under the head-line:

PATTERSON SR. SCOFFS

SAYS HIS SON IS SOWING HIS POLITICAL WILD OATS

— which paternal serenity was abundantly justified when the younger Patterson came into his patrimony;

From a photograph by Bachrach.   *From a photograph by Clinedinst.*

Feminine Fashions of the Early 1900's.

Left: Evening dress.   *Right:* The high collar.

became one of the owners of the Chicago *Tribune* as well as of the New York *Daily News* and the weekly *Liberty*, in which positions the young Socialist of 1906 was, in 1930, decidedly not a menace to the established order.

January. Wealthy young gentlemen and ladies taking up Socialism, Socialism as an incident of pink teas, current prevalence of a type later denominated by Roosevelt "parlor Socialists," inspired "Mr. Dooley" to discourse, his foil being, for this one occasion, not the familiar Mr. Hennessy (who as a Celt might have lacked the patience to listen) but Mr. Dooley's fellow saloon-keeper on the German side of the town, Mr. Schwartz-meister:

'Twas diff'rent in the goolden days. A gr-rand chance a So-cialist had thin. If annybody undherstood him he was kilt be infuryated wurrukin-men. It was a good thing f'r him that he on'y spoke German, which is a language not gin'rally known among cultivated people, Schwartzmeister. They used to hold their meetin's in a cellar in Wintworth Avnoo, an' th' meetin' was most always followed be an outing in th' pathrol wagon. 'Twas wan iv th' spoorts to go down to see th' Brotherhood iv Man rushed off in th' on'y Municipal Ownership convey-ance we had in thim days, an' havin' their spectacles busted be th' hardy an' loyal polis. 'Tis far different now. No cellars f'r th' Brotherhood iv Man, but Mrs. Vanderhankerbilk give a musical soree f'r th' ladies iv th' Female Billyonaires Arbeiter Verein at her iligant Fifth Avnoo mansion yisterdah afther-noon. Th' futmen were dhressed in th' costume iv th' Fr-rinch Rivolution, an' tea was served in imitation bombs. Th' meet-in' was addhressed be th' well-known Socialist leader, J. Clar-ence Lumley, heir to th' Lumley millyons. This well-known prolytariat said he had become a Socialist through studyin' his father. He cud not believe that a system was right which allowed such a man to accumylate three hundherd millyon dollars. He had frequently thried to inthrest this vin'rable mossback in industhreel questions, an' all he replied was: "Get th' money." Th' ladies prisint cud appreciate how fool-ish th' captains iv industhree are, because they were marrid to them an' knew what they looked like in th' mornin'. Th' time had come whin a fierce blow must be sthruck f'r human freedom. In conclusion, he wud sing th' "Marsellaisy" an' accompany himself on a guitar. Th' hostess followed with a few remarks. She said Socialists were not dhreamers but practical men. Socialism was not a question iv th' hour, but had come to stay as an afthernoon intertainment. It was less expinsive thin bridge, an' no wan cud call ye down f'r ladin' out iv th' wrong hand. She had made up her mind that ivry-body must do something f'r th' cause. It was wrong f'r her to have other people wurrukin' f'r her, an' she intinded to free or bounce her servants an' go to live at a hotel. She wud do her share in th' wurruld's wurruk, too, an' with this in view she was takin' lessons in minichure paintin'. A lady prisint asked Mr. Lumley wud large hats be worn undher Socialism.

He answered no, but th' more becomin' toque; but he wud look th' matther up in a book be Karl Marx that he undherstood was an authority on these subjects. Th' meetin' thin adjourned afther passin' a resolution callin' on th' husband iv th' hostess to go an' jump in th' river.

The Rural Free Delivery as it was in the first decade, before being motorized. The horse in the illustration travelled 55,000 miles, carrying the mails, before being retired in 1928.

January 25. General Joseph Wheeler died. He had fought on the side of the Confederacy during the Civil War, rising to the rank of lieutenant-general and becoming at the age of twenty-eight senior cavalry officer. Thirty-four years after surrendering to the Union forces, Wheeler volunteered upon the opening of the war with Spain for service in the United States Army, was commissioned Major-General and led American cavalry in Cuba. His action attracted sentimental attention as a landmark in the passing of emotions associated with the Civil War and the restoration of national unity. A few Southerners of the type called "unreconstructed" criticised him. At his funeral in 1906 veterans of the North stood side by side with veterans of the South in tribute; over his coffin both the Stars and Stripes and the Stars and Bars were draped.

February. A characteristic whimsicality of the American press of this time was illustrated by the cumulative accretions to a bit of verse, marine in flavor:

> Flo was fond of Ebenezer —
>   "Eb," for short, she called her beau.
> Talk of "tide of love" — great Cæsar!
>   You should see 'em, Eb and Flo.
> > *— Cornell Widow.*

> Eb and Flo they stood as sponsors
>   When Flo's sister was a bride,
> And when bride and groom receded
>   They, too, went out with the tied.
> > *— Yonkers Statesman.*

> When their first child came, a daughter,
>   The nurse, for a larger fee,
> Went to someone else who sought her,
>   Leaving Eb and Flo at sea.
> > *— Chicago Record-Herald.*

> Next came triplets, heaven bless 'em!
>   Ebenezer looked quite grave,
> Then quoth he to his Floretta,
>   "This looks like a tidal wave!"
> > *— Boston Post.*

> The triplets now are cutting teeth,
>   And, alas, it hence befalls
> That in Eb and Flo's life voyage
>   There are many grievous squalls.
> > *— Rex H. Lamoman.*

March 1. Woodrow Wilson, president of Princeton University, addressing the North Carolina Society, asserted that "nothing has spread socialistic feeling in this country more than the use of the automobile." The reason, he elucidated, was that "to the countryman they are a picture of arrogance of wealth, with all its independence and carelessness."

Whatever of truth there may have been in Doctor

Wilson's picture of the countryman's feeling about the automobile, he erred in assuming that to the owner of an automobile in 1906 life was all joy and irresponsibility.

The truth was synthesized in a joke first published in the New York *Sun* and thereafter told countless times until its point was killed, about 1913, by mechanical progress:

A physician, starting a model insane asylum, set apart one ward especially for crazy motorists. Taking a friend thru the building, he pointed out with particular pride the automobile ward and called attention to its elegant furnishings.

"But," said the friend, "the place is empty; I don't see any patients."

"Oh, they are all under the cots fixing the slats," explained the physician.

President Wilson, of Princeton, and Andrew Carnegie.

More seriously, Woodrow Wilson was probably correct in saying that in 1906 the farmer-owner of one or two literal horses felt resentment against and envy of the possessor of twenty horse-power in the form of an automobile. In the development that came about after 1910, however, the owner of a twenty horse-power Ford felt no conscious inferiority to, or bitter envy of, the owner of an eighty horse-power Lincoln. The spread of the automobile was a clearly recognizable emollient of caste-consciousness, a part of that immense diffusion of wealth, and that enrichment of the average man, which came during the first quarter of the twentieth century, with effects as beneficial to society as to the individual.

March 1. The president of the Dressmakers' Association, Miss Elizabeth White, as quoted in New York City newspapers, delivered a dictum of 1906 style:

From "The Ladies' Home Journal," March, 1906.   *From "The Ladies' Home Journal," 1907.*   *From "Vogue" May, 1930.*

1. Eton jacket suits worn in the Spring of 1906. 2. Tailored suit of dark-blue serge for the girl of 12 to 18 for the Autumn of 1907. 3. A one-piece dress of flat crepe with box-pleated flounce.

"What's the use of having pretty shoes and then having your dress so long nobody can see them? It is quite proper to have the skirt of a white summer dress as high as six inches from the ground. The short skirts must be full, of course, and they must have underneath them a plain petticoat with a hair cloth flounce."

March 25. A business that flourished in the era preceding bobbed hair was described in a New York *Sun* article appearing under the caption:

AMERICA'S CRY FOR HAIR

PRICES TREBLED IN THE LAST FOUR YEARS.
EUROPE MEETS PART OF THE DEMAND FOR NEW YORK WOMEN, CHINA A PART, AND THE GOATS OF TURKESTAN SUPPLY SOME MORE.

BUSY TIMES IN A BLOND HAIR FACTORY

Crescent Hair Roll.

No. 18T2590 Crescent Hair Roll, thick in the center, tapering to a point at the ends. To be used where the parted front and large back hairdressing is desired. Made of clean genuine hair combings covered with marcelled mohair and a very fine invisible net. Colors, blonde, light brown, medium brown, dark brown or black. State color desired. Length 24 inches. 50-cent value. Our price......33c If mail shipment, postage extra, 3 cents.

Sears-Roebuck's catalogue for 1910, taking account of the vogue in women's hair-dressing then current, devoted several pages to advertising the various ingenious devices necessary to get the effects decreed by fashion, among them turbans, braids, cluster puffs, pompadours, hair-rolls, switches.

From "Scribner's Magazine," June, 1927

From "The Theatre Magazine," September, 1906.

Walk-Over shoe, Style No. 956. In 1908 women wore high buttoned and laced shoes. Here is a Walk-Over model for that year.

April 14. Maxim Gorky, Russian author and revolutionist, arriving in New York for the purpose of interesting America in freedom for the Russian people, was received with distinguished attention from American authors under the leadership of Mark Twain, from sympathizers with liberty, and from newspapers and public. He expressed him-self as overwhelmed by the warmth of his welcome and deeply impressed by the prevalence of peace and or-der in America unaccom-panied by display of military authority.

Seven months later, in November, Gorky departed from the United States, in a state of national feeling which may best be pictured by quoting one among hun-dreds of similar newspaper comments: "Maxim Gorky has left us, unwept, unhon-ored, and, fortunately for him, unhung."[1]

Maxim Gorky.

Gorky's fall in esteem occurred soon after his arrival, when, in the midst of the homage to him, newspapers discovered, published, and republished, with an effect of hounding,[2] that the lady accompanying him was not his wife. Though Gorky's friends explained that the nov-elist's marital status was understood in Russia and not disapproved there, the disclosure arrayed public opinion against him. He cancelled his remaining lecture engage-ments and contracts for newspaper articles and slipped unobtrusively away to a little cottage in the Adiron-

[1] The Savannah *News*.

[2] Oswald Garrison Villard, editor of *The Nation*, having read the proofs of this paragraph in 1930, commented: "The brutality and hypocritical ferocity of the attack on Gorky can hardly be over-stated."

dacks. A New York *Times* man who had witnessed the tumultuous welcome to Gorky on his arrival as well as his very different departure wrote, sympathetically: "He was not well when he came here; he has grown

much thinner, and he has a racking cough. His leave-taking was sad. He had been received at first with such enthusiasm, and he went away so quietly. He stood on the deck of the steamer, a big, quiet, sad, patient figure."

Gorky later, in a book "In America," pictured, with Slavic violence, horrors he saw awaiting the United States, among them a revolution of the unemployed who would "spring one day upon that city [New

From a photograph by Underwood & Underwood.
Mark Twain.

York] with hands unfettered and unrestrained, and like rapacious marauders, reduce all to dust and ashes — bricks and pearls, gold and serf-flesh, the unwashed and the idiots, the churches, the dirt-poisoned hotels, and the subtle 20-floor [*sic*] skyscrapers . . . yes, reduce the whole city to a muckheap, a pool of stench and human blood, into the original chaos whereout it came."

April 18. At 5.13 A. M., in San Francisco, an earthquake unparalleled for its violence in American history, killed hundreds of people in their sleep and injured thousands. Immediately afterward, gas from broken mains, exposed electric-light wires, and overturned stoves started scores of fires; by noon whole sections of the city were ablaze. The temblor having damaged the water system, soldiers[3] attempted to stop the spread of the conflagration by razing, with dynamite, gunpowder,

From a photograph by Underwood & Underwood.

The San Francisco earthquake of 1906. Northeast from Powell and Post Streets toward the Jewish Synagogue.

and artillery, the buildings in its path, among them half a mile of mansions on the city's finest residence street.

[3] Wallace Irwin, having read in the proofs this reference to the San Francisco earthquake, wrote me: "General Fred Funston was in command at the Presidio. When the earthquake came and the first smoke began to rise, he marched all available troops into the city at once, established martial law, and got busy. He did this on his own responsibility, without waiting for instructions from Washington. So the disaster was efficiently policed; and further he furnished men who could handle explosives. No one can estimate how much the city owes to his prompt and super-efficient action. Survivors have often told me of Funston's dramatic entry. The disaster; the fires rising; a series of lighter shocks; the police inadequate in numbers; the Fire Chief dead in his own fire house; the people just standing round in groups as though paralyzed. Then, at about 8 o'clock in the morning, comes a regiment of U. S. infantry four abreast, picking its way through the debris of Market Street — and everyone woke to life."

From a photograph by Arnold Genthe, New York.

The San Francisco Earthquake.   All buildings shown in the photograph were the same day destroyed by the conflagration following the earthquake.

For three days the holocaust continued, wiping out fully half the city and rendering two hundred thousand people homeless. The country's sympathy responded with money, food, medicines, doctors, and nurses. Congress, at the request of President Roosevelt, appropriated $2,-500,000. From abroad came many offers of help; these the President declined. The people of San Francisco faced their situation with characteristic spirit; a despatch from the city to a New York paper saying: "She's crippled, thirsty, hungry, and broke; she has a few whole churches, only half her schoolhouses; not one French restaurant; not a theatre; she is full of people without homes, jobs or clothes; she is the worst bunged-up town that ever was.[4] But the spirit of her is something to bring tears to an American's eyes."

Last of the Heretics

April 18. At Batavia, N. Y., began the trial for heresy of the Reverend Algernon Sidney Crapsey, an event which engaged the attention of the modern world as intently and, because of modern mechanisms of news dissemination, much more generally, than any of the long series of similar trials that went back through the Middle Ages to the early centuries of the Christian Church. The historic background of the event, its arguments over points of ancient canonical law, its citations of Arius and Athanasius, the eminence of the counsel, lay and ecclesiastic, who accused and defended — the whole atmosphere of a mediæval religious inquisition which the trial had, interested people of all creeds and, most of all perhaps, people of no creed. Equally wide-spread was another kind of interest, which saw the attempt to unfrock a clergyman as the oppression of an

---

[4] As a local poet put it, in a characteristic American spirit:
"Where the buildings that are standing sort of blink and blindly stare
At the damnedest finest ruins ever gazed on anywhere."

individual human being by authority and organization.

Doctor Crapsey, rector in 1906 of St. Andrew's Protestant Episcopal Church, Rochester, N. Y., had during his early years in the ministry regarded himself as

From a photograph by Dudley Howe, Rochester, N. Y.

The Rev. Algernon S. Crapsey.

Left: At the time of his trial (1906) for heresy. *Right:* In 1924. Both photographs are by courtesy of the New York *World.*

a "ritualist," as "High-Church," normal fruit of his education (at the General Theological Seminary, New York City), which had included instruction in Dogmatic Theology, Old Testament Exegesis, the Hebrew language, the Greek version of the New Testament, Church History, Ecclesiastical Law, and Liturgiology. In the leisure of his early pastorates, however, he had explored secular literature; his temperament, naturally susceptible, had, he said later, "been influenced by the master minds of Darwin and Karl Marx," as well as by Renan, and he had become what was described, in a then new terminology of religious controversy, as a "rationalist."

During 1905, Doctor Crapsey, whose habit was to write out his addresses a day in advance of delivery "for the most part without lifting pen from paper except to dip it in the ink,"[5] gave a series of talks on Sunday evenings in his church setting forth the "advanced" beliefs he held on religious doctrine. One of the talks, or lectures, bore the title, suggestive of the temper of all of them, "The Commercialized Church in the Commercialized State." In the last one of the series, called "The Present State of the Church," delivered February 18, 1905,[6] he boldly took issue with a tenet of most Christian churches except the Unitarian:

In the light of scientific research the founder of Christianity, Jesus the son of Joseph, no longer stands apart from the common destiny of man, in life and death, but he is in all things physical like as we are, born as we are born. . . . Scientific history proves to us that the fact of his miraculous birth was unknown to himself, unknown to his mother, and unknown to the whole Christian community of the first generation.

That was an application to the New Testament of a form of interpretation currently known as "Higher Criticism." Higher criticism, the reading of the Scriptures in the light of and by the tests of modern historical knowledge and scientific hypothesis, had been applied to the chapters of Genesis and to other parts of the Old Testament, without great offense to, or at least with tolerance upon the part of, many church authorities.

[5] Doctor Crapsey, in his autobiography, twice uses this phrase to describe the expedition with which he prepared his sermons, a method he characterized in afterthought as "hazardous in the extreme" — meaning, apparently, that if he had thought twice about it he would not have said the words that changed him from an obscure clergyman to a figure that, for a time, held the attention of the world.

[6] Doctor Crapsey's lectures, published as a book under the title "Religion and Politics," became a part of his offense.

Crapsey's application of the new criticism to the Biblical
account of the birth of Christ created a furor; the
lecture, "reproduced in whole or in part by nearly every
paper in the United States . . . [and] telegraphed almost in full to England,"[7] led to an outburst of excited
sermons and indignant editorial comment in every part
of the Christian world. Doctor Crapsey's bishop "made
an immediate demand upon me that I either repudiate
what had been published as my utterance, or I should
make formal retraction." Crapsey refused. After indictment by the Standing Committee of the Diocese of Western New York, Crapsey's trial before an ecclesiastical
court of five clergymen, opening in the parish-home of a
church in the quiet country town of Batavia, was transferred, for the better accommodation of newspapermen
and the crowds of curious, to the county court-house.
Crapsey's lay counsel included two men distinguished
throughout the country as lawyers, scholars and public
figures — Edward M. Shepard, once a reform Democratic candidate for mayor of Greater New York, often
suggested as Democratic candidate for the Presidency,
author of a biography of Martin Van Buren; and James
Breck Perkins, member of Congress and author of several French histories, among them, "France Under
Richelieu and Mazarin." Crapsey's ecclesiastical counsel included Doctor Elwood Worcester of Boston and
Doctor Samuel McComb.[8] For the accusers, the ecclesiastical counsel was Doctor Francis J. Hall, Professor
of Dogmatic Theology in the Western Theological Seminary. Lay counsel for the prosecution included John
Lord O'Brien, a distinguished lawyer and public official

[7] "The Last of the Heretics," Doctor A. S. Crapsey.
[8] Doctor McComb, Irish by birth, provided the one touch of comedy that occurred during the trial, by saying, in a gathering prone to detect violations of
nicety in language, "If it please the court, we are in the presence of three alternatives."

of Buffalo, N. Y. One of the lawyers for the Church, in making the opening address for the prosecution, said: "All we hear of this defendant is most lovely and Christlike, but that makes his crime all the greater; he, an officer of his church, in his official capacity, denies the fundamental doctrines of his church, in his pulpit he denies the creed; for this offense we demand from this court a verdict of guilty, with the consequences that follow."[9] The judgment of the court was, in effect, that it could not "permit a clergyman of the church to use the pulpit of the church to defame the creed of the church." The decision, sustained by the Court of Review, was followed by the formal ceremonial of deposal on December 5, 1906.[10]

April 27. Ground was broken for Gary, a fiat city decreed by the United States Steel Corporation (and named after its head), on the shores of Lake Michigan east of Chicago. The conditions which normally determine the planless birth and growth of cities were entirely lacking on the desolate sand plain where Gary rose; there was no harbor, no labor supply, no raw materials,

[9] The public, following the case, did not distinguish between two questions, whether Christ was or was not divinely conceived, and whether an official of an organization has a right to deny fundamental principles of the organization and at the same time insist upon continuing an official. One indignant clergyman, addressing Doctor Crapsey at a meeting, charged: "You are not basing your dogma on the infallible authority of the church, you are basing it on your own fallible reason."

[10] Doctor Crapsey and his wife, paying a quiet visit of farewell to the church where he had ministered for twenty-seven years, walked up and down the empty aisle, crying; most poignant of their experiences was their moving from the rectory, their home, in which their six children had been born and two had died, to a house provided for the unfrocked clergyman without cost by a generous stranger who was not a member of his church and had never seen him. More than twenty years later, Crapsey, completing his autobiography under the title "The Last of the Heretics," wrote, with perhaps more self-pity than the circumstances need have called for: "There is no more pitiable object than an unfrocked priest . . . if he be a married man his wife and children are the greatest sufferers; he has the glory of his martyrdom, they suffer in silence and obscurity the consequence of that martyrdom." In the same autobiography he set down, apparently in pride, that "I was the first man in this country to publicly apply the principle of the higher criticism to the New Testament stories."

no ore, no coal. Some of these lacks were overcome, and
the rest cancelled out, by careful engineering; a harbor
slip almost a mile long was dug inland from the lake
edge, wide and deep enough to permit manœuvring by
fleets of great cigar-shaped ore-carriers from the Lake
Superior region; great foundries and steel-mills erected;

Gary, Indiana, when under construction.

thousands of workmen's homes built; sewage, electric
light, water, and gas systems installed; millions of cubic
yards of fertile soil brought from distant places to cover
the sterile sand wastes and permit the planting of grass
and trees; a system of public-school education inaugurated which attracted wide attention and was taken as a
model by other cities. By 1930, twenty-five years after
its founding, Gary had a population of almost 100,000.

Harry Thaw

June 25. At 11 o'clock in the evening, on the roof of
Madison Square Garden, New York City, the comedy
"Mamzelle Champagne" was concluding its first performance. A soloist had finished singing "I Could Love
a Million Girls," when a young man in evening clothes

left his seat near the stage and walked toward the rear of the audience. He was recognized by many as Harry Kendall Thaw, a familiar figure at first-night theatrical performances. Sitting alone at a table was Stanford White, fifty-three years old, America's most famous architect. Thaw drew a revolver from under his coat, held the muzzle close to White's head, and shot him, three times. White fell to the floor, instantly dead. Thaw walked back, holding his hands above his head and letting his revolver hang down, as if to signify to the audience that he intended to shoot no more; a fireman disarmed him. Somebody sent for a policeman, who arrested Thaw and took him, without resistance, to a near-by police station.

Harry Thaw was the scion of a Pittsburgh, Penn., coal, steel and railroad fortune, the son of William Thaw, in his lifetime a director of the Pennsylvania and other railroads, a generous endower of art and education, his money the source of fellowships in science at Harvard and Princeton Universities. The son had long been known on Broadway as a profligate spender; in a career of some dozen years after coming of age he had left, in what was known as the "White Light"[11] part of New York City, and in Paris as well, a wake of lurid stories and newspaper publicity about wrecked cafés, a cab-horse ridden at breakneck speed down Broadway, another horse ridden up the steps of the Union League club-house, cigars lighted with five-dollar bills, lavish entertainments of chorus girls, a dinner in Paris that had cost eight thousand dollars exclusive of costly gifts of jewelry to women guests.

The murdered man, Stanford White, in association with his firm, McKim, Mead and White, had designed

---

[11] So called from the electric signs then beginning to be lavish along midtown Broadway and in the theatrical district about Herald Square.

the Washington Arch, New York City, and the Columbia University Library; he had designed the buildings of the University of New York, the new buildings of the University of Virginia, the Madison Square Presbyterian Church in New York, the Detroit Savings

Bank, the battle monument at West Point, the Metropolitan and Century clubhouses in New York, and the Madison Square Garden, in the tower of which he lived and upon the roof-garden of which he was murdered.

Thaw said he shot, among several reasons, to save his young wife from the elderly White's attentions.[12] The circumstances leading up to the murder, the life-stories of the wastrel murderer, the voluptuary victim, and the "lady in the case," who had formerly been a chorus girl and artists' model, as recited in literally thousands of newspaper columns with a welter of detail in which fact was interwoven with theatricality, composed for the America of the day a drama such as stage nor fiction ever provided, a Clarissa Harlowe romance with all the physiological details of eighteenth-century frankness. For months and years it exceeded, in

Courtesy of the New York "World."
Stanford White.

[12] The necessary limitation upon space in this history forbids amplification of Thaw's charges against White; it forbids also mention of the partial defense of White by Richard Harding Davis — it forbids, indeed, any but the briefest epitome of the more essential details of a murder which, in the circumstances that attended it, may reasonably be described as the most sensational in the history of a country in which murders are numerous and murder trials dramatic.

the sensational quality of its climaxes, as well as in the number of persons who eagerly followed it through the press, any melodrama that went by the name of melodrama.

The hardly less spectacular and rather more important aspect of the Thaw case lay in the demonstration it provided, before the eyes of the public during a period covering nearly twenty years, of how long and how successfully atonement may be averted by a murderer who has much money, supplemented in this case by the practically endless financial resources of a doting mother.

Thaw was indicted for murder in the first degree, and the opening one of literally more than a score of trials and legal proceedings began January 22, 1907. The prosecutor was the District Attorney of New York County, William Travers Jerome, able as a lawyer, high in the esteem of the public, attractive and powerful in personality, resourceful and effective in his methods with juries and judges — in the Thaw case, the forces on the side of the law were much better equipped to achieve conviction than in any average murder trial. On the side of Thaw, the six major counsel included one imported from San Francisco because of a Pacific Coast reputation he had built up for an emotional way he had with juries, Delphin Delmas, whose oratorical arts in the Thaw case struck the East as overdone. Delmas told the jury that Thaw "struck for the purity of the wives and homes of America." Coining a new phrase (which instantly passed into universal use) he said Thaw had had a "brain-storm." Amplifying his plea for the benefit of the "unwritten law," Delmas invented a new category of mental aberration — not to be called a disease because it was creditable to those who had it. Delmas said that Thaw had shot White during a fit of "dementia Americana," a form of mental *furor* presumed to be confined to persons of the male sex living between the twenty-fifth and forty-ninth parallels of latitude and between the Atlantic and Pacific Oceans, indigenous to the United States, where it is at all times endemic, and not to be found in less admirable nations.

The trial, after being under way for several weeks,

Courtesy of the New York "World." William Travers Jerome at the time he was District Attorney.

was halted upon application by District Attorney Jerome, who asked that a commission be appointed to inquire into Thaw's sanity. The commission pronounced Thaw sane, the trial proceeded, and the case went to the jury on April 10, 1907. The jurors were out forty-seven hours; seven of them voted for a verdict of murder in the first degree, but they were at last compelled to report disagreement. In the second trial, beginning January 6, 1908, Thaw's defense relied upon a formal plea of insanity. To prove Thaw's chronic and constitutional paranoia, his mother took the stand. The jury, after being out twenty-five hours, reported a verdict: "Not guilty because insane." The judge committed Thaw to the State hospital for the criminal insane.

In the status Thaw now had before the law, he had been tried in a trial that had gone the full length to verdict by the jury; therefore he could never be put in jeopardy of his life again (for that crime). He had been found insane, and as a criminal lunatic was confined in an institution for that class; but if in the future he could establish that he was not insane, or that he had recovered from his insanity, he would go free. In this state of facts, began an extraordinary series of actions — legal, non-legal and illegal, to get Thaw out of the insane asylum. During year after year hardly a month passed without the spectacle of newspapers reeking with the beginning or the course or the end of one or another attempt in Thaw's behalf, initiated by himself, or by his mother, or by the lawyers whose ingenuity the mother's money was able to hire. In only one instance — and that did not touch the courts — was there a charge of bribery or money improperly used. The frequence and persistence of Thaw's presence in the courts was brought about by his lawyers' taking advantage of accepted legal procedures. What Thaw had that other murderers had not was money to keep up an endless testing of the law to find a weak link, a complaisant court, an amiable jury, or a technicality.

May 6, 1908,[13] Thaw secured a writ of *habeas corpus;* the court dismissed it, saying Thaw's release would be "dangerous to the public." June 13, 1908, he applied for transfer from the hospital for the criminal insane to the homœopathic hospital for the insane; the court refused it. June 29, 1908, he demanded a jury trial to determine his sanity; the court refused it. January 4, 1909, he appealed this decision; the appellate court denied the appeal. August 26, 1909, he carried the appeal to the highest court of New York State; this court likewise denied the appeal. December 30, 1909, he carried his appeal to the United States Supreme Court; this court likewise, the fourth in order, denied his appeal. Meantime, July 14, 1909, Thaw made a second use of *habeas corpus;* the courts dismissed it. April 15, 1912, he made a third attempt to get free through *habeas cor-*

[13] The dates in this paragraph are, in some cases, the date of the beginning of an action, in others the date of conclusion, or of a step in the course of the action.

pus, and a third time the court refused. November 22, 1912, Thaw gave $25,000 to a lawyer to influence public officials to obtain his release — the lawyer was tried, convicted and sentenced to prison. March 1, 1913, Thaw a fourth time availed himself of *habeas corpus*, and again the court dismissed the writ. May 15, 1913, Thaw appeared in court as a witness against the lawyer whom he had employed to bribe in his behalf, saying that he hoped by his bearing and testimony to prove to the court and to the public that he was sane. August 17, 1913, Thaw walked through the gates of the hospital while they were open to admit a milkman, stepped into a waiting automobile, and vanished. Two days later, being found in Canada, he began a series of proceedings under the laws of that country to resist extradition to the United States. (District Attorney Jerome, who had gone to Canada to conduct the fight to get Thaw back, was arrested — as a gambler; he had playfully thrown dice for small coins with some newspapermen.) September 10, 1913, Thaw was deported from Canada and upon arrival in New Hampshire was arrested; in the New Hampshire courts he resisted return to the jurisdiction of New York State. November 19, 1913, in New Hampshire, he was freed of a charge under which he was being temporarily detained, and immediately re-arrested. December 22, 1914, he was delivered to the jurisdiction of the New York courts. Meantime, October 24, 1913, he had been indicted in New York for conspiracy, in connection with his escape from the hospital for the criminal insane. January 25, 1915, he was back in the jurisdiction of New York, and in prison. July 16, 1915, at the close of a jury trial on his sanity, he was declared sane and released. April 20, 1916, he secured a divorce from his wife. Early in 1917 he was indicted for a new crime, abducting and whipping a boy. January 11, 1917, he was adjudged insane; for safety's sake, as a fugitive from New York, he accepted commitment to an insane asylum in Pennsylvania. In August, 1923, he was given a vacation from the asylum and

Russell Sage.

allowed to visit his mother. In 1924 the case against Thaw arising out of his assault on a boy was settled by his mother, out of court. In April, 1924, he had, in Pennsylvania, another trial for his sanity. On May 20, 1924, he was finally released as sane.

Let us pass on, hastily.

July 21. Russell Sage died, aged eighty-nine. "Every country village," said the New York *Evening Post*, "has its keen money-lender, ready to screw the last cent from his neighbors, on mortgage or note. Russell Sage was this village skinflint writ large. He operated in the mar-

Courtesy of the New York "World."

Russell Sage's "brown stone front" house at 506 (left) Fifth Ave., New York.

ket of the continent, but the magnitude of the enterprises in which he shared did not expand his mind or quicken his sense of responsibility. From the individual in his grip he relentlessly exacted the pound of flesh; and he never made even a pretense of reparation in the form of public benefactions. He wanted money; he got it; he kept it."

What *The Evening Post* could not know, in writing its harsh obituary, was that Sage's entire fortune, amounting to between $60,000,000 and $80,000,000 was destined to be given by his widow to humanitarian causes.

July 27. Secretary of State Root, addressing the Pan-American Conference of American Republics at Rio de Janeiro, made a statement of the policy of the United States toward other American countries that was destined to rank as one of the great pronouncements of American statesmen:

We wish no victories but those of peace, no territory except our own, and no sovereignty except sovereignty over ourselves, which we deem independence.

The smallest and weakest member of the family of nations is entitled to the respect of the greatest empire, and we deem the observance of that respect the chief guaranty of the weak against the oppression of the strong. We neither claim nor desire rights, privileges, or powers we do not freely concede to every American republic. We wish to increase our prosperity, expand our trade, and grow in wealth and wisdom, but our conception of the true way to accomplish this is not to pull down others and profit by their ruin, but to help all our friends to common prosperity and to growth, that we may all become greater and stronger together. Within a few months for the first time the recognized possessors of every foot of soil on the American Continent can be, and I hope will be, represented with acknowledged rights as equal sovereign states at the great World's Congress at The Hague. This will be the formal and final acceptance of the declaration that no part of the American Continent is to be deemed subject to colonization.

From a photograph © by Clinedinst, Washington, D. C.

Elihu Root about 1903.

August 14. At Brownsville, Texas, negro soldiers of the United States Army rioted, killing and wounding several citizens. Inspector-General of the Army E. A. Garlington, a South Carolinian, investigated but failed to discover the offenders who, he said, "appeared to stand together to resist the detection of the guilty." Garlington recommended to President Roosevelt the discharge, without honor, of every member of the three colored companies stationed at Brownsville and their debarment from re-enlistment and from employment in any capacity by the government. Roosevelt approved Garlington's drastic recommendations and on November 26 they were put in effect.

Immediately arose discussion, argument, vituperation. Senator Foraker of Ohio, making himself the champion of the dismissed soldiers, began a prolonged fight for their reinstatement. Many Northern papers, some for one reason and some for another, treated the various developments in the episode with head-lines raucously critical of the President. The negro press, in a frenzy of indignation, metaphorically turned black in the face. Said the negro New York *Age:*

> It is carrying into the Federal Government the demand of the Southern white devils that innocent and law-abiding black men shall help the legal authorities spy out and deliver practically to the mob black men alleged to have committed one sort of crime. . . . It is an outrage upon the rights of citizens who are entitled in civil life to trial by jury and in military life to trial by court-martial. . . .

Roosevelt, sure he was right, or almost right, stuck by his guns. The criticism of him by Foraker and other public men in and out of the Senate he termed "academic"; that by newspapers he ignored. To visitors calling to intercede for soldiers with good records among those discharged, Roosevelt said, "Show me evidence of non-participation," and promised to make exceptions to his order against reinstatement.

Congress, nearly three years later, created a court of inquiry composed of Army officers to investigate and report the names of soldiers eligible for re-enlistment. The court reported the names of fourteen innocent, all of whom re-enlisted.

August 23. Estrada Palma, President of Cuba during the four years that country had been an independent Republic, asked the United States for aid to quell a seriously threatening revolt that had grown out of a dispute over elections. Roosevelt, a sincere friend of the Cuban people and an ardent well-wisher for the success of their experiment in self-government, held off, hoping that the quarrelling factions might settle their differences amicably. At the end of three weeks, however, the increasingly numerous reports of burnings and lootings in various parts of the Island convinced Roosevelt that further delay was unwise, and he summoned Secretary of War Taft, Secretary of the Navy Bonaparte, and Assistant Secretary of State Bacon to Oyster Bay for a consultation. Immediately thereafter Taft and Bacon left for Havana where, unfortunately, Taft's tact and skill as a conciliator failed to bring the government and the revolutionists into peaceable agreement; on September 29, one day after President Palma had resigned his office, leaving the government without an executive head, Taft reluctantly proclaimed intervention by the United States. The revolutionists now returned to their homes and the people, once again feeling secure in their persons and property, returned to their normal ways of life. On October 12, thirteen days after he had taken over the government, Taft relinquished it to Charles E. Magoon, and himself returned to Washington.

August 29. William Jennings Bryan, arriving in New York after an eight months' tour of the world, was met in the harbor by a delegation of his "home-folks," one of whom, James Dahlman, Mayor of Omaha, Neb., lassoed him from the deck of a tug. Crowds lining both sides of Broadway cheered him as he rode from the dock to his hotel. As an incident of his home-coming, Democratic leaders arranged an immense meeting in Madison

Square Garden, at which Bryan delivered one of his best-known but least fortunate speeches. (See page 275.)

October 15. The San Francisco Board of Education excluded Japanese from the public schools of that city on

Delegation of "home-folks" meeting Bryan. Mayor Dahlman of Omaha, Neb., carrying a lasso.

the ground that many of the Japanese pupils were adults and as such should not be taught in schools designed for and patronized by white children. The Board maintained a separate school for the free education of Orientals, largely attended by Koreans and Chinese, and the Japanese were invited to avail themselves of its facilities. The Board's action stirred angry feeling in Japan. President Roosevelt was seriously embarrassed. Because of the peculiar construction of the American governmental system, by which the individual states retain jurisdiction over affairs within their borders, the President was powerless to do more than exert pressure upon California. He sent a member of his cabinet, Secretary of the Navy

Metcalf, a Californian, to San Francisco; later Mayor Schmitz and members of the San Francisco School Board went to see Roosevelt at Washington. After much criti-

Mr. and Mrs. Nicholas Longworth shortly after their wedding.

cism of Roosevelt by California newspapers, and much criticism of California by newspapers elsewhere in the country, a compromise was arranged providing for the admission of Japanese children to San Francisco schools, while Japan undertook by its own regulations to limit emigration of its subjects to the United States to the merchant and student classes only, preventing the coming of coolies.

November 15. Mayor Eugene Schmitz of San Francisco and "Abe" Ruef, political boss of the city, were indicted on five bills charging extortion, following exposure of sensational corruption. The trial brought three men to national fame, Francis J. Heney, who conducted the prosecution until incapacitated by an attempt to murder him, Hiram W. Johnson, who succeeded Heney as prosecutor, and William J. Burns, the detective who unearthed the evidence.

Other events of 1906, important, colorful, or otherwise interesting, included: *January* 21. President G. Stanley Hall of Clark University, deploring a trend of the day, said that the Bible was "less read in the home than it was a few years ago; the number of children who have a fair knowledge of it is growing smaller." * * * *January.* A great new hotel in Atlantic City, the Traymore, advertised: "Completely appointed with every modern equipment; twenty-five private baths; capacity 450." * * * *February* 3. Colonel George B. M. Harvey, editor of *Harper's Weekly*, at a Lotos Club dinner in honor of President Woodrow Wilson of Princeton, proposed Dr. Wilson as the next Democratic candidate for President of the United States. * * * *February* 17. Literally world-wide attention was focussed upon the wedding of Miss Alice Lee Roosevelt, eldest daughter of President Roosevelt, to Nicholas Longworth, a young Congressman from Cincinnati, Ohio, in the East Room of the White House. A color vogue associated with Miss Roosevelt, "Alice blue," was conspicuous in the aigrettes, cloak-linings, and gowns of women guests. * * * *February* 27. Professor Samuel P. Langley, distinguished scientist and pioneer in aviation experiments, died. (See "Our Times," Vol. II.) * * * *March* 8. Six hundred Moros were killed in battle with American troops and constabulary near Jolo. * * * *April.* The United States won the Olympic Games at Athens with a score of 75 points. England was second with 41; Sweden third with 28. * * * *May* 1. The Night and Day Bank, open at all hours (except between midnight Saturday and midnight Sunday), was inaugurated. * * * *May* 21. The action of Mrs. J. B. Henderson, widow of ex-Senator Henderson of Missouri, a woman a social prominence in Washington, in emptying the contents of her wine cellar into the street, was extolled at a meeting of the Frances E. Willard Union as "a tremendous step in advance." * * * *May* 23. Edward Payson Weston, professional pedestrian 68 years old, walked from Philadelphia to New York, ninety-six miles, in twenty-three hours and thirty-one minutes, beating his own record of twenty-three hours and

Courtesy of the New York "World."

At Reno (Nev.), Joe Gans won from Battling Nelson in forty-two rounds on a foul, Sept. 3, 1906.

forty-nine minutes made in 1863. * * * *May* 25. Contracts involving $35,000,000 were awarded by the Pennsylvania Railroad for the construction of a terminal station in New York City. * * * *June* 10. Thousands of followers of the Christian Science faith attended the dedication of the First Church of Christ Scientist in Boston, one of the largest religious structures in the United States. * * * *June* 15. Roy Knabenshue's sailing around the dome of the Capitol at Washington in his dirigible balloon caused so many Representatives and Senators to leave their desks to watch the strange sight that for an hour both Houses lacked a quorum. * * * *June* 16. President Roosevelt signed the bill granting statehood to Oklahoma and Indian Territory; "Roosevelt" he wrote with an eagle's quill from Oklahoma. * * * *August* 13. The Pennsylvania Railroad announced that all passenger cars going into service in the future on its lines would be of steel. The company's wooden coaches receded to backwater branches from which they finally disappeared in 1928. * * * *September* 22. In one of the worst race riots in the history of the South a frenzied mob of white people, incensed by several recent attacks by negroes on white women, ran riot for five hours in Atlanta, killing a score of negroes and wounding hundreds more. * * * *September* 30. President Joseph F. Smith of the Mormon Church was arrested charged with living unlawfully with wives to the number of five. Not long before, said newspaper despatches, his forty-third child had been born. * * * *October* 10. Southern negroes filed with the Interstate Commerce Commission a complaint against the forcing of negroes holding interstate tickets to ride in "Jim Crow" cars. * * * *November* 15. President Roosevelt visited the city of Panama, the first occasion of an American President setting foot on foreign soil. * * * *December* 5. Jews in New York demanded that the school board prohibit Christmas compositions or instructions concerning Yuletide in public schools. * * * *December* 10. President Roosevelt was officially informed that the Norwegian Parliament had awarded him the Nobel Peace Prize for bringing the war between Russia and Japan to an end. The President announced he would donate the prize, amounting to $37,000, to the advancement of industrial peace.

Books of 1906

Books popular during 1906 included: "The Future of America," in which H. G. Wells entertainingly recorded observations on contemporary phases of the United States as he found it during a visit. . . . "The Jungle,"[14] by Upton Sinclair. . . . "The Conquest of Canaan," by Booth Tarkington. . . . "White Fang,"[15] by Jack London. . . . "Lady Baltimore," by Owen Wister. . . . "The Spoilers," by Rex Beach. . . . "Coniston," in which Winston Churchill, departing from romance of colonial America, wrote about a New England political boss named "Jethro Bass."

[14] See "Our Times," Volume II.
[15] See page 150.

The Theatre in 1906

William Vaughn Moody had beautifully written, and Henry Miller and Margaret Anglin in 1906 superbly acted, "The Great Divide," a drama of the Southwest, portraying "the rough right of might in conflict with self-righteous Puritanism," which, said John Corbin, "sets a new mark in the American drama"; another cultivated critic, James S. Metcalfe, said that "Miss Anglin has scored what seems to be a fixed position among the stars."

From the Albert Davis Collection.
Henry Miller.

That judgment, as of the day, about what constituted the most important dramatic event of 1906, might be queried by an estimate made with the benefit of a quarter-century of perspective. In influence upon the evolution of the stage and upon American thought, possibly more important was the fact that 1906 was a high tide of George Bernard Shaw. His sardonic reversal of accepted ways of thinking, his mocking impiety toward cherished traditions and reverences, his violent attacks upon familiar conventionalities, were part of a broad wave of iconoclastic influence, which included the plays of Henrik Ibsen, the influence of Darwin trickling down among the masses, and the wide-spread reading, by Americans brought up in an austere Christian religion, of an Oriental philosophy of life and death alluringly expressed in Omar Khayyam. These and other causes accounted largely for the beginning of new ways of thought in America which, when they became common twenty years later, were incorrectly attributed to the Great War, and to subsequent and contemporary authors, such as Eugene O'Neill.

During 1906, or the dramatic season 1905–6, six plays by Shaw were on the New York stage: "Cæsar and Cleopatra," played by Mr. Forbes-Robertson and Miss Gertrude Elliott; "Arms and the Man," produced and played by Arnold Daly; "Man and Superman," played by Robert Loraine; "John Bull's Other Island" was a failure; "Mrs. Warren's Profession" was denounced by newspapers and clergymen and banned by the police. Bizarrely, "Cashel Byron's Profession" was produced with an ex-prize-fighter, James J. Corbett, in the star part, causing a facetious critic to say that the "ex-champion had a mill with Bernard Shaw and knocked him out in three rounds."

From the Albert Davis Collection.
Margaret Anglin.

Other important or interesting aspects of the stage in 1906 included the continued popularity of "The Lion and the Mouse," in which playwright Charles Klein "daringly and brilliantly dramatized, in thinly veiled form," the current popular conception — which was the melodramatic conception — of John D. Rockefeller, Sr., "unscrupulous, self-satisfied, cold-blooded man of money, who allows nothing, not even his own honor, not even a man's life, to stand between him and his financial" purposes. "The Lion and the Mouse," by running for two years in New York City, while four other companies played it throughout the country, made a record that, up to 1906, had not been equalled in the history of the American stage. . . . At continued high tide also was Maude Adams in James Barrie's "Peter Pan"; women and children went to see it over and over — a New York seamstress was said to have sought in 47 attendances the escape from reality to illusion that "Peter Pan" provided. . . . Equally popular, for different reasons and to another type of audience, was "The Chorus Lady," written by James Forbes and made engaging by Rose Stahl who, as "an ill-favored but waywise and humorously right minded veteran of the musical stage

From the Albert Davis Collection.

James O'Neill.

standing guard over a pretty but light headed younger sister who is in the toils of a gay deceiver,"[16] gave out worldly wisdom in pungent slang:

If a girl's good she's good anywhere. But, say, if you're scrimping along on twenty per, and the next girl to you in your dressin'-room comes down to the show shop every night in a benzine wagon in ermine capes and diamonds big as oysters, it ain't religion so much as a firm grip on home and mother that makes you sit tight an' keep on handin' out the frozen mit an' the icy eye to the man behind the bank-roll.

Mme. Sarah Bernhardt, by this time a venerable actress, appearing in a repertoire of French plays (including of course "Camille"), was described gallantly

[16] John Corbin, New York *Sun.*

by Mark Twain, then seventy, as the youngest person of his acquaintance — except himself; while Madame Bernhardt, in gracious Gallic riposte, said that of all Americans, next to George Washington, Mark Twain was the greatest. . . . James O'Neill,[17] having played Edmund Dantes in "Monte Cristo" 4,802 times, declared he would not appear again in that rôle after the close of the current season. . . . George Ade's "The College Widow" ended, on April 19, 1906, a run of 372 performances in New York City. . . .

From the Albert Davis Collection.
Alla Nazimova.

Mme. Alla Nazimova, who had come to America with a much-praised band of Russian actors, played, in English, Ibsen's "Hedda Gabler"; Mme. Nazimova "can draw herself up like a serpent, with a quick, boneless heave that begins nobody can say exactly where, until, though she is but of medium height, she seems to tower over everybody on the stage."[18] . . . Mrs. Minnie Maddern Fiske acted in Langdon Mitchell's "The New York Idea" — the "idea" being to follow your whim and let the divorce court do the rest, and the play following the fortunes of an off-again-on-again couple to whom New York was a city bounded on the north, east, south and west by the State of Divorce.

[17] Father of Eugene O'Neill, famous, twenty years later, as author of a type of play that seemed consciously to scorn the sort of old-fashioned drama in which his father had made his fame.

[18] Quoted from a critic of exceptional elevation of taste, Arthur Ruhl.

Miss Ruth St. Denis, a dancer, one of the most charming ever on the American stage, by her skill as well as by her "personality of chaste and exquisite grace,"[19] conveyed to audiences a height and delicacy of exaltation not exceeded by music, poetry or any other

From the Albert Davis Collection.
Ruth St. Denis.

of the arts, an ecstasy that persons who had sat enraptured before her tried to express by saying it was like Mendelssohn's songs without words. Tall, sinuate, supple as a willow, lithe as a tuning-fork, she "suggested the vestal quite as much as the artist in flesh and fibre"; her face, poised upon her slender form, had "the delicacy of a flower, and its beauty, as of a tryst of earth and heaven." Miss St. Denis's programme in the season of 1906 was "Hindoo dances," including "The Spirit of the Incense" and "The Snake Charmer."

[19] The quotations are from John Corbin.

Mme. Yvette Guilbert sang, in costumes of the various periods, "Chansons Pompadour and DuBarry," "Chansons Crinoline," "Chansons Modernes" and

"English Songs," the latter including: "Mary Was a Housemaid," "The Keys of Heaven," "The Dumb Wife Cured."

In grand opera, Geraldine Farrar made her American début, having first, said *The Theatre Magazine*, "made slaves of half the population of Berlin." . . . Oscar Hammerstein opened in New York City, on December 3, 1906, a second opera-house, the Manhattan, rival to the Metropolitan, producing a preponderance of French and Italian operas in contrast with the Metropolitan's emphasis upon German; the venture lasted until the close of the theatrical season 1909–10, when Hammerstein sold out to the Metropolitan Company, agreeing not to produce opera again in New York City.

From the Albert Davis Collection.

Geraldine Farrar as Carmen.

There had been for many years two — not two, a team, of Jewish comedians, their names as inseparably coupled as Damon and Pythias, as "Haig & Haig," as "Amos 'n' Andy," as, indeed, "ham and eggs"; in the current talk of the day they were not "Weber and Fields" but "Weber-'n'-fields." Their jokes, the humorous stage conversations they built up, depended upon the complementary contributions of their separate personalities. Weber, small, fat, naïve, susceptible to alarums, would sadly draw out the insides of his empty pockets, saying: "I got notdings." Such bankruptcy, tragic to Weber, was to the shrewd, slender, resourceful Fields, merely opportunity: "You got notdings, I got notdings, ve both got notdings — den ve vill form a trust." After many years the two had a disagreement, some seriousness or other of private personality behind the façade of the public one — what it was about was the subject of far more speculation and concern in New York than the contemporary falling out of Russia and Japan. To a distinguished scholar who was then the dramatic critic of the New York *Sun*, John Corbin, the separation of Weber and Fields portended tragedy, the doom of low comedy, "one of the richest gifts of the muses." Sadly Corbin reviewed the succession of racial dynasties: "The day of the negro minstrel is long over; then came the Irish invasion and in its train Harrigan and Hart; this is the era of the Jew." And since Weber and Fields, as a team the greatest of Jewish comedians, had now gone separate ways, Mr. Corbin anxiously asked, "Is low comedy doomed?" "The fact is," he said, "these two artists were born brothers; neither, without the other, is more than a poor fraction of himself." In 1906 Fields, minus Weber, but supported by a company justly described as all-star, since it included Peter F. Dailey, Blanche Ring, Edna Wallace Hopper and Vernon Castle, played "About Town" and "The Great Decide" (burlesque of "The Great Divide"). Weber, minus Fields, but with a cast which included Charles A. Bigelow, Marie Dressler, Trixie Friganza and Bonnie Magin, played, in the spring of 1906, "Twiddle-Twaddle," described as "a merry-go-round of mirth, melody and madness, in two goes." In the fall Weber played "Dream City" — dialogue and lyrics by Edgar Smith, music by Victor Herbert — with a cast which included Cecilia Loftus, as well as Will T. Hodge in the rôle of "Seth Hubbs, village hackman and the oracle of Malaria Center."

Otis Skinner, in "The Honor of the Family."

In 1906 Richard Mansfield acted Reverend Arthur Dimmesdale in "The Scarlet Letter" . . . John Drew and Margaret Illington in Arthur W. Pinero's "His House in Order" . . . William Gillette in a comedy-drama by himself entitled "Clarice" . . . Mrs. Sarah Cowell Le Moyne in Browning's "Pippa Passes," produced under the direction of Henry Miller . . . Annie Russell as "Puck" in "A Midsummer Night's Dream" . . . Virginia Harned in Victorien Sardou's "The Love Letter" . . . James K. Hackett and Mary Mannering in "The House of Silence" . . . Henry Miller in "Grierson's Way" by H. V. Esmond . . . Henrietta Crosman in "Mary, Mary, Quite Contrary" and in "Madeline," with a cast which included Guy Standing . . . John Barrymore and Lionel Barrymore in "Pantaloon," a one-act play by James M. Barrie . . . Eleanor Robson in four new plays, including "The Girl Who Has Everything" and "Nurse Marjorie" and "Susan in Search of a Husband" . . . Viola Allen, soon to be lost to the stage, in "Cymbeline" . . . William H. Crane in "The American Lord" . . . Otis Skinner in "The Duel" . . . Blanche Walsh in "The Kreutzer Sonata," which, in the original Yiddish, had already run for almost a year on the Bowery . . . Henry Woodruff in "Brown of Harvard" . . . Benjamin Chapin in "Lincoln," described on the programme as "a drama of life in the White House in war times" — "war times" meaning, in that period, Civil War times . . . Nat Goodwin in "The Genius," written by William C. and Cecil de Mille . . . Raymond Hitchcock in "The Galloper" by Richard Harding Davis

From the Albert Davis Collection.
William H. Crane.

. . . Fritzi Scheff in "Mlle. Modiste" . . . Francis Wilson in a farce called "The Mountain Climber" . . . Montgomery and Stone in "The Red Mill" . . . Fay Templeton in George M. Cohan's "Forty-five Minutes from Broadway" . . . Louis Mann and Clara Lipman in "Julie Bonbon" . . . May Irwin, coming toward the close of her stage career, in "Mrs. Wilson, That's All"; and Lillian Russell, likewise approaching her final exit to private life, in "Barbara's Millions" by Paul M. Potter.

"The Man of the Hour" by George Broadhurst . . . "Brewster's Millions" produced by Frederick Thompson and Winchell Smith . . . "The Hypocrites" by Henry Arthur Jones, which, so said a headline of the day, "flays conventional moralities" . . .

"The Fascinating Mr. Vanderveldt" by Alfred Sutro
. . . Winston Churchill's "The Crossing," dramatized
by Louis Evans Shipman . . . "The Man on the Box"
by Harold MacGrath . . .

From the Albert Davis Collection.
Fritzi Scheff.

"The Embassy Ball," written by Augustus Thomas to fit Lawrence d'Orsay . . . "The Rose of the Rancho" by David Belasco and Richard Walton Tully, the leading rôle played by Charles Richman . . . Mrs. Edith Wharton's "House of Mirth," dramatized by herself and Clyde Fitch . . . "Mr. Hopkinson" by R. C. Carton, a farcical satire on greed for money in the British aristocracy . . . A first adventure by a distinguished novelist, Winston Churchill, into playwriting, entitled "The Title Mart."

On the last day of the year, at the Herald Square Theatre, New York City, began a comedy of fantasy by B. M. Dix[20] and E. H. Sutherland, "The Road to Yesterday."

[20] The "B. M." stood for Beulah Marie. At that time it was thought that feminine authorship of a play was a handicap in getting the attention of the public. Mary Roberts Rinehart has told me that when she wrote her early plays she deemed it prudent to describe herself as "Roberts Reinhart." On the other hand, Mr. Clayton Hamilton doubts if there was any wide-spread feeling that a woman could not write a successful play. Mr. Hamilton cites, as examples of women playwrights of this time or before who were in one degree or another successful, Madeline Lucette Riley, author of "An American Citizen," in which Nat Goodwin starred during the 1890's; and Marguerite Merrington and Rachel Crothers. Mr. Hamilton adds, "women playwrights in America were unusual before 1900 merely because any American playwrights were unusual."

12

1907

Tom Johnson, and the Commotion that Revolved about Him. John Alexander Dowie, and Zion. The Orchard Confession and the Haywood Murder Trial. Augustus Saint-Gaudens Dies. Judge Landis Imposes the Largest Fine in History. Vogue of the Peek-a-boo Shirtwaist. Maiden Voyage of the *Lusitania*. Wireless Progress. Business Depression and the Panic of 1907, Together with Some Speculation about the Causes of Panics. Charles Glidden Tours the World in his Automobile. First of the "Gary Dinners." Round-the-World Cruise of the Battle Fleet. The First Steel Sleeping-car. Books and Plays of 1907.

January 11. The New York *Tribune* published a choleric letter from "An Old Housekeeper": "Sir: Twelve years ago, in 1894, I employed, as I do now, three women servants, the work being the same and in the same house. At that time two received $16 each, and the third, the cook, $18 — a total of $50 a month. Now for the same duties the total a month is $67 — an increase of $17!"

Tom Johnson

January 12. In Cleveland, Ohio, three-cent street-carfare went into effect, with Mayor Tom L. Johnson acting as motorman of the first car, an incident in a long fight waged by Johnson against private ownership of public utilities. Johnson, beginning business life at the age of eleven as a newsboy on the railroad, became successively bookkeeper, cashier, and superintendent of the mule-power street-railway system of Louisville, Ky. With some twenty thousand dollars acquired by inventing a fare-box, and help from friends, he bought, when twenty-two, a majority interest in the franchise and property of a street-railway in Indianapolis, Ind., and subsequently a franchise and line in Cleveland. While on train trips between the two cities of his business interests he read Henry George's "Progress and Poverty"[1] — and became the most energetic "single-taxer," the

From a photograph by Marceau.
Tom L. Johnson.

most forceful and resourceful foe of franchises, monopolies and private ownership that flourished in America during his generation. The aggregate enemy, Johnson called "Privilege," with a capital "P"; and Privilege he defined,[2] awkwardly, as "the advantage conferred on one by law of denying the competition of others." A rich man himself — made rich by municipal franchises, patents and other forms of monopoly or privilege — Johnson became an earnest, if good-humored, crusader against the system of which he had been a beneficiary. Continuing to make money as a steel manufacturer, and therefore as a beneficiary of the tariff, he got himself elected to Congress and with the leverage of that office conducted nation-wide propaganda for free trade; he and five other Congressmen arranged that each should use his "leave-to-print" privilege to insert in *The Congressional Record*, in connection with their speeches on a tariff bill,

[1] The first of George's books that Johnson read was "Social Problems"; when the train-boy offered it to Johnson, he supposed it was about the "social evil" and said he was not interested. The train-conductor, hearing the conversation, urged Johnson to buy, saying he would refund the half-dollar if Johnson did not find the book interesting.

[2] In his autobiography "My Story."

one-sixth of Henry George's "Protection or Free Trade"; then Johnson combined the parts and distributed more than a million copies at a cent a copy, as campaign material in the Presidential election of 1892 between Cleveland and Harrison. Johnson, continuing to make money by expanding his street-railway interests into St. Louis, Brooklyn, Detroit, and other cities (as incidents of the substitution of electricity for horse power), preached everywhere the doctrine of municipal ownership — preached it even to the city councils from whom he was soliciting franchises — to the puzzlement of many who could not understand such a paradoxical relation between financial interest and intellectual conviction.

Johnson's great fight to bring about city ownership occurred in Cleveland. In his conduct of his side of the fight, he was humorous, high-spirited, poised — sincere without feeling called upon to say so and without being gloomy about it — gaily frank in confessing that so long as he had been a monopolist he had "played the game as he found it," resourceful in attack because of his familiarity with the ways of the business world in which he had formerly functioned, vivid as a journalist or a showman in devising ways to make the public understand the inner workings of the alliance between big business and politics. When Johnson's opponent for the mayoralty, the scholarly Theodore E. Burton, opened his campaign with a quotation, *jacta est alea*, Johnson genially volunteered to translate for the benefit of voters un-erudite in Latin, saying it meant, "Let 'er go, Gallagher." His opponents, the public utility interests of Cleveland and most of the banking and other large business interests, convinced that both Johnson's theories and his practices were unsound, regarding him as a traitor to his former business associates, an ingrate toward the system that had

made him rich; and, shocked and angered by some of his
political and financial[3] methods, conducted their side of
the fight sometimes with the bitterness of personal
malevolence. The warfare was described by one of
Johnson's disciples,[4] from a standpoint of strong sym-

About 1907. "Quick lunch," an American institution that got its start in the
eating-rooms of railroad stations and from there spread out
to the country's cities and towns.

pathy for Johnson, a sympathy that Johnson would have
been the last to ask, for his rotund, eupeptic, cheery personality took pleasure in giving as good as he got, or a
little better:

I doubt if any of the border cities like Washington and Cov-
ington during the Civil War were more completely rent asunder
than was Cleveland during those years. There was but one line
of division. It was between those who would crucify Mr. Johnson and all of his friends, and those who believed in him. . . .
If any kind of cruelty, any kind of coercion, any kind of

[3] A "Depositors' Savings and Trust Company" which Johnson promoted "in
the interests of the low-fare people," and of which he was president, failed, with
loss to stockholders, though not to depositors.
[4] Frederic C. Howe.

social, political or financial power was left untried in those years to break the heart of Mr. Johnson, I do not know what or when it was.

While the Cleveland fight stood alone, the agitation for a three-cent fare, partly for itself but chiefly as a step toward public ownership, went on in many cities. The high tide of it coincided with the period of Johnson's mayoralty in Cleveland, from 1901 to 1910 (when Johnson was defeated for re-election).[5] During about the same period a new theory about public utilities spread over the country, a theory of retained private ownership accompanied by regulation of rates and other practices through "public utility commissions" which were set up by most of the States. Three cents as an arbitrary fare had already been made obsolete by rising costs of goods and rising wages for labor, due to increased gold supply from South Africa and elsewhere. With the coming of bus competition and the inflation that accompanied the Great War, even five cents became too small a fare in practically every city. The movement toward municipal ownership receded through adoption of the public utility commission as a device for regulating private ownership, through the eclipse of public interest in every sort of domestic reform when the Great War came to preoccupy the thought of everybody, and through other causes, including, as is often the case, invention. Street-railways were usually in the same ownership as the plants for generating electricity for light and other purposes. With improvement in the means of transmitting electricity

[5] Newton D. Baker, City Solicitor of Cleveland during Tom Johnson's administration, later Secretary of War, thinks this account should include "another phase of Mr. Johnson's work which seems to me epochal." When Johnson became Mayor of Cleveland, municipal government in America was generally corrupt and inefficient: "Johnson became at once the outstanding municipal executive — was guide, counsellor and friend to all other American cities; was visited almost daily by men from everywhere who were interested in rescuing city government. When Johnson ceased to be Mayor of Cleveland, he had set new standards of city government throughout the nation."

over long distances, local electric plants tended to become parts of wide-spread systems, in which condition municipal ownership of individual plants was less expedient.

Dowie

March 9. John Alexander Dowie died, revered by a few people — chiefly at Zion City, Ills. — as a second Elijah; regarded by thousands all over the world as one of the great religious charlatans of history. Dowie, born in 1847 in Scotland, studied at the University of Edinburgh, followed his parents to Australia and was ordained a clergyman of the Congregational Church. After a few years, proclaiming it is wrong for a clergyman to accept a salary, he established an independent church in a tabernacle he built at Melbourne, in which he crusaded against drink and tobacco as causes of sin and disease, advocated free education and social reform, and after a time announced that he believed in divine healing as a direct answer to prayer. Coming to San Francisco in 1888 on what he intended as a journey to Europe and back to Australia, he found California exceptionally susceptible, and remained for two years travelling up and down the Pacific Coast, establishing branches of what he called the Divine Healing Association, without offense to the churches, many of which gave shelter to his gatherings. In 1890 he came to Chicago, where he set up first a Zion's Tabernacle and subsequently "Divine Healing Home No. 1." In 1895 he spent parts of 120 days in court defending himself against more than a hundred warrants incited by physicians and clergymen. The same year, having acquired a following from the fringes of various denominations, he ordered them to separate themselves from other church affiliations; with this nucleus he set up "The Christian Catholic Church," with himself as "General

Overseer." Dowie as he appeared at this time was a short-framed man with a tendency to fatness, bow-legged and bald, but nevertheless attractive; he really wore the aspect of benevolence and looked the patriarch; his shoulders were straight and ample, his eyes bright and piercing, his beard white and flowing.[6] In 1901, he took his motley following away from Chicago to a site of about ten square miles on the western shore of Lake Michigan,[7] where he established a combination of religious Mecca and industrial city, with a central "Shiloh Tabernacle," a bank, business houses, a printing plant which published "Leaves of Healing," and several industries of which the most successful was a lace factory, the whole valued at some ten million dollars — formidable start toward realizing his confident prediction that in ten

Courtesy of the New York "World."

John Alexander Dowie.

years he would have the strongest and wealthiest church the world had ever seen. His followers, whom he now called "Zion's Restoration Host," numbered about a hundred thousand throughout the world, about ten thousand of them resident at Zion City. Them Dowie required to sign a vow reading in part:

... and I declare that I recognize John Alexander Dowie, General Overseer of the Christian Catholic Church in Zion ... in his threefold office, as the Messenger of the Covenant, the Prophet foretold by Moses, and Elijah the Restorer. ... I

[6] This description of Dowie's physical appearance is paraphrased from an article by I. K. Friedman in *Everybody's Magazine.*

[7] The site, about midway between Chicago and Milwaukee, was described by Dowie as "half way between Beer and Babel."

promise to obey all rightful orders issued by him . . . and that all family ties and obligations, and all relations to all human governments shall be held subordinate to this vow, this declaration and this promise. This I make in the presence of God and of the visible and invisible witnesses.

In 1903, at high tide of success, Dowie determined to make a spectacular evangelistic invasion of New York, and that brought upon him national attention of a sort that in his gradual growth at Chicago he had not encountered. His announcements, shrewdly designed by him to get the kind of attention he wanted for his proposed exhorting and healing, were treated by the New York press in a manner giving Dowie precisely the kind of publicity he could not want. Preliminary news stories spoke of the coming host as "Satan-stormers." "A considerable element in New York," said *The World*, with subtly provocative encouragement, "will 'have fun' with Dowie."

Dowie and his followers came in eight special trains, a host three thousand strong, three hundred of them uniformed as a special bodyguard of "soldiers of Zion" carrying Bibles in leather holsters. From the Jersey City ferry, Dowie was driven to the Plaza Hotel in a carriage brought on from Chicago, drawn by four horses draped with the colors of Zion, while his followers marched to Madison Square Garden. The discrimination between leader and followers was one of scores of details that the New York newspapers picked up for purposes of jibing:

> "Hark! Hark! The dogs do bark!
> The Dowies have come to town.
> Some in rags, some in jags,
> But ONE in a velvet gown."[8]

Against the atmosphere of sceptic jeering that was partly the habitual attitude of the metropolis and partly

[8] New York *Press,* October 18, 1903.

had been built up by the newspapers, Dowie could make
no headway. Jeering from the press was reinforced by
denunciation from the pulpit. The crowds, in the mood
in which they went to hear Dowie in Madison Square,

From a photo by International Newsreel.

A change of the quarter-century. The young woman on the left is dressed in
the style of 1907 and working at the primitive typewriter of that
era. The one at the right typifies the year 1928.

turned the meetings into a farce. A competitor in rab-
ble-rousing, Carry Nation, happening to be in New
York, went to a meeting and from the floor challenged
Dowie to debate; Dowie ordered his guards to eject the
disturber. The scenes in the Garden were described by
the newspapers in terms of rowdyism and burlesque.
The Prophet — angry at abuse and ridicule of a form
and intensity that were new to him, humiliated in the
presence of his own loyal followers — turned to savage
invective against the metropolis. One New York paper

counted thirty-five epithets that he habitually used, "eleven of them, or 30 per cent, being" canine in form or implication, variations or approximations of America's most resented term of reproach, "dog," "cur," "hound," "dirty yellow dogs," "dirty hungry dogs," "stupid dogs," "hungry filthy curs." A further draft made by the enraged Prophet on the animal kingdom supplied him with "rats," "pigs," "swine," "lice," "maggots," together with "stink-pot," "whiskey-pot," "drug-pot."

Probably it might be said, in leniency to a former student of moral philosophy at the University of Edinburgh and ordained pastor in the Congregational Church, that the deterioration had already begun which soon after 1903 became plain. The New York hegira destroyed[9] Dowie, undermined his prestige with his followers, broke him physically. September 24, 1905, he suffered a stroke. December 3, in a pitiable effort to assert his power over his people in an address in the Tabernacle at Zion, he was overcome by weakness, abandoned the service, and went off to the West Indies, leaving at Zion City first a triumvirate which in a month he deposed by telegraph, and setting up next a regent-dictator, Wilbur Glenn Voliva, whom likewise he quickly tried to depose. Voliva, in a telegram of outright treason, refused to be deposed. Dowie tottered back to Zion City and on April 29, 1906, at a meeting of his aforetime followers, tried to crush the rebellion. In the outcome he was himself formally deposed, with the assent of his wife and son. On March 9, 1907, at

[9] "It is creditable to the intelligence and moral sense of New York that failure complete, humiliating and, let it be hoped, smashing, has come to this preacher whose own prominence and profit are his only gospel. Dowie in seeking a metropolitan triumph has but pilloried himself. It is seen that he has no message to humanity; that he is a posturing and bellowing pretender, that he is without intellect, or eloquence, or wit, or zeal for anything save his own glorification as the leader of a band of human misfits that would follow any leader who cared to shout orders to them." — New York *Examiner*, October 22, 1903.

Zion City, he died, palpably insane — the fates' answer to the questions of one New York newspaper that
had tried to take a serious view of him: "Who is he, what
is he, is he a prophet or a megalomaniac, is he a fakir or
the bearer of a message, is he crafty or crazy?"[9]

June. Quantity of hair as a desirable attribute of

From the *"Theatre Magazine,"* 1908.
1908: The Psyche knot.

From the *"Theatre Magazine,* 1926.
1926: The mannish haircut.

feminine charm was the subject of a *Puck* quip:

"And her hair," cried Claude, "is something to dream
over!"
"It would make a good mattress, for a fact," assented Mel-
travers, ever anxious to display fine sensibilities.[10]

The Murder of Steunenberg; the Confession of Orchard; and the Trial of Haywood

July 28. William D. Haywood was acquitted of the
charge of being an accessory to the murder of ex-Governor Frank Steunenberg of Idaho.

Steunenberg, a big-framed, silent, self-educated man,
simple in manner and attire, had been elected Governor
of Idaho ten years before, as a Populist and sympathizer

[9] New York *Press,* October 18, 1903.
[10] Pickings from *Puck,* June, 1907.

with labor — he was a member of the typographical union. During his second term, in April, 1899, he had taken an important part in a dramatic event: In the Cœur d'Alene lead-mining region the Bunker Hill and Sullivan mine had been dynamited during a quarrel over wages, the owners had appealed to the Governor, and Steunenberg had called on President McKinley for Federal troops; the soldiers — the first were negro companies — had arrested hundreds of union miners without warrants and detained them for months in a "bull pen," and had arrested and confiscated the plant of a local editor, Stewart, for criticising them. Steunenberg had known that his action would arouse strong feeling, had recognized that it meant his political death, but had said that his duty was to his State, not to his own political career; he had declared that "for years the county officers had been either in sympathy with, or intimidated by, criminals; that there could be no compromise with crime, and that in applying the remedy, 'nothing less drastic than the disease itself will cure.'" On the expiration of his second term, he had refused to try for reelection and had returned to private life. For more than six years he had lived in quiet retirement, devoting himself to his sheep-ranch and other business interests.

Steunenberg, at about 6.30 on the evening of Saturday, December 30, 1905, closed his office in the small town of Caldwell and started the short walk to his home for supper. Behind him, with a companion, was his eldest boy, twenty years of age. The early winter night was dark. Steunenberg opened the gate before his house, passed through, and turned around to close it. There was an explosion which literally tore the flesh from the bones on his right side. When Mrs. Steunenberg reached her husband's side she found him still conscious. He said to her: "What's the matter, mother? What does this mean?" In twenty minutes he was dead. When the neighbors sought gently to place Mrs. Steunenberg on a couch in the parlor, they found it covered with broken glass from the windows, which were a considerable distance from where the explosion took place.

The sheriff, notified of the murder, quickly swore in deputies whom he stationed in a cordon about the town. It was believed the murderer was still in Caldwell and a systematic search for him was begun. A light snowfall during the evening gave hope that any one attempting to escape would be tracked and overtaken.

Governor Steunenberg of Idaho.

Three weeks before the murder of Steunenberg there had come to Caldwell a man a little above medium height, of stocky build, and of dark complexion — not a bad or vicious looking man when well-dressed, and upon his visit to Caldwell he was garbed in a neat suit, a derby hat, and well-polished shoes. He took a room at the Hotel Saratoga,[11] registering under the name of T. S. Hogan, and told people he was in Caldwell for the purpose of buying land for some friends.

Ten minutes after the bomb explosion that killed Steunenberg, "Hogan" slipped into a chair in the dining-room of his hotel and was calmly eating his supper

[11] "Hotel Saratoga" — in the early nineteen hundreds there was one in nearly every city and large town in the country, a memento of the time, twenty years before, when Saratoga, N. Y., enjoyed unique and glamourous and slightly naughty fame as America's first pleasure resort.

when the hunt for the murderer began. The following day, when the entire town was excitedly discussing the murder, "Hogan" called a local official from a group and asked if he knew where a "band of wethers[12] could be bought cheap." The very calmness of the question, a little too deliberately matter-of-fact in a time of intense excitement, aroused suspicion; a man was set to watching the stranger and his room was searched. A small amount of plaster of Paris and a pinch of explosive powder, found in his valise, led to his being called before an informal inquisition. "Hogan's" apparently frank answers to the questions asked him, and his unruffled ease of manner, convinced the authorities he was innocent and he was released. In the crowd that witnessed the questioning, however, was Sheriff Harvey K. Brown[13] of Baker County, Ore., who identified "Hogan," the supposed land buyer, as a miner named Harry Orchard whom Brown had known in the Cracker Creek District of Oregon, where Orchard had been an officer of the Bourne Miners' Union. This information led to the man's re-arrest and eventually, as the result of the finding of other evidence, to his being charged with the murder.

To Caldwell, and later to Boisé (whither Orchard was transferred), attracted by the large rewards offered for the arrest and conviction of the murderer of Steunenberg, came scores of detectives, among them one whose name, when later it was spread abroad in the newspapers, seemed to older Americans like an echo

12 Sheep.

13 Sheriff Brown was later assassinated in exactly the same way as Steunenberg. Brown, fearing assassination, had the gate to his house taken off its hinges. But the assassins got him by hiding in a ditch alongside the house and pulling a string as he passed in. It was generally supposed that the assassination of Brown was in retaliation for his identification of Orchard and to prevent his being a witness in the subsequent trial of one of the inner circle of the Western Federation of Miners.

from the past. James McParland was the most remarkable detective who ever followed that vocation in America, one who worked alone, whose success was based upon his own skill, patience, and perseverance; in short, a detective who devoted himself to detecting, a type different from those organizers of great detective businesses whose names became headline words. Thirty-two years before, in Pennsylvania, McParland had entered the employ[14] of the Philadelphia and Reading Coal and Iron Company to unearth the inner workings of a terrorist secret society in the anthracite coal regions, the "Molly Maguires." McParland had taken a job about the mines, had frequented the saloons in which the "Mollies" foregathered, had gained their

James McParland.

confidence, had become indeed "the biggest 'Molly' of us all," had become secretary of the inner organization that planned the murders — and after two years had gone upon the stand, where as a quiet, grave, intelligent, spectacled witness dressed in plain black and looking like a college professor, he had given testimony which resulted in the hanging of ten "Mollies," the complete disruption of the organization, and the flight of most of its members.

Now, thirty years later, McParland, an aging man of sixty-seven, came to Boisé[15] and for a week spent long

[14] As an operative of the Pinkerton Detective Agency.

[15] From Denver, where he was managing a branch of the Pinkerton Detective Agency.

hours daily visiting Orchard in his cell. Then he made an astounding announcement. He said he had secured from Orchard a full and detailed confession: that he was the murderer of Steunenberg; that he had murdered eighteen other people during ten years preceding; and that all his crimes had been at the behest and in the pay of the "inner circle" of the Western Federation of Miners — William D. Haywood, Charles H. Moyer, and George A. Pettibone.

Harry Orchard at the time of his arrest.

Orchard in his confession said that the "inner circle" had ordered Steunenberg's murder in revenge for Steunenberg's action as Governor more than six years before, when he had called in Federal troops following the dynamiting of the Bunker Hill and Sullivan mine. That crime had been one of a long series of acts of violence committed by, or charged against, the leaders of the Western Federation of Miners. The Federation composed one side of a long feud, of which the other side was the corporations owning the mines, their managers, and often the State and local officials who, for the most part, sided[16] with the mine owners. The weapon of the Western Federation of Miners had been violence, the weapon of the other side had been as a rule control of, and help from, organized govern-

[16] Not always. In many cases local county or town officials sided with the Western Federation of Miners. See Governor Steunenberg's comment on conditions in the Cœur d'Alene, page 482.

ment. "For every murder," said a thoughtful editor, "there was an unjust decision in the courts; for every bomb a misuse of the State's power."[17]

The Western Federation of Miners had been organized following a strike in the Cœur d'Alene lead-mining region in Idaho in 1892. The Federation in the beginning took in all the miners' unions of the Cœur d'Alene, Butte, Mont., the Black Hills of South Dakota, and of several Colorado mining communities. From the outset, control had been in the hands of men of violence — direct-action terrorists.[18] An early president had advised the unions to form rifle-clubs "so that in two years we can hear the inspiring music of the martial tread of twenty-five thousand armed men in the ranks of labor." A member of the "inner circle," George A. Pettibone, during a battle between union men and deputies defending the Helena-Frisco mine, the year before the Federation was formed, broke open a powder-house, took two hundred pounds of dynamite to the hillside in the rear of the mill, and slid it down the penstock. There was a terrific explosion and the mill was wrecked. For this crime Pettibone served eight months' imprisonment.[19]

When Orchard made his confession, the men he accused of having employed him, Haywood, Moyer, and Pettibone, were living in Denver, Colo., and were there-

[17] *Collier's,* May 11, 1907.

[18] The mass of the miners were decent, law-abiding men, fair-minded and uncovetous, but they feared to resist the lawless leaders, feared reprisals from the leaders, feared to be regarded as traitors to their class.

[19] "It is impossible to believe that the rank and file at large of the Cœur d'Alene miners were responsible for these crimes and persecutions, or even at heart countenanced them. I have found these men in the jury box as keen to uphold the law as any class, and in their natural instincts fairer than most men, but, in common with entire communities, they were in dread of the tyranny of the lawless ones, and dared not openly repudiate them." — C. P. Connolly, *Collier's,* May 11, 1907.

fore beyond the jurisdiction of Idaho authorities. To be
tried they must be extradited. It was obvious they would
resist. How to extradite them presented a nice problem
in law and resourcefulness. "The foundation of extradition between the states is that the accused should be a
fugitive from justice from the demanding state, and he
may challenge the fact by habeas corpus immediately
upon his arrest."[20] To have the status of a "fugitive
from justice," an accused person must have been in the
State where the crime was committed and have subsequently absconded. None of the three men accused of
employing Orchard was known to have been in Idaho;
their alleged relation to the crime was that of "acces-
sories." Under the current interpretation of the law, it
would be impossible, often, to extradite an accessory,
for an accessory may never have been in the State where
the crime was committed. In this anomalous state of the
law, authorities had often resorted to stratagem or force
to get accused persons into the jurisdiction of the States
where the crimes were committed; and the Supreme
Court of the United States had frequently held that the
right of the State in which a crime was committed to
try an abducted person could not be questioned, whatever the means used to secure his presence.

In this state of the law, sheriffs from Idaho bearing
Orchard's confession as evidence of the complicity of
Haywood and his companions in the murder of Steu-
nenberg, and armed with a request from Governor
Gooding of Idaho for their extradition, went to Denver
and requested extradition of the three men. Governor
McDonald of Colorado granted the request. That was
in the middle of the week. On Saturday, February 17,

[20] Justice McKenna of the United States Supreme Court, in an opinion dissenting from the approval by the remainder of the Supreme Court of a decision
of an Idaho court upholding the legality of the arrest of the three labor leaders.

1906, after the courts had closed for the week, and when it was difficult or impossible for the accused to get a writ of habeas corpus, the Idaho sheriffs arrested the three labor officials, kept them in jail all night, and early next morning took them aboard a special train and hastened back to Idaho.[21]

William D. Haywood.

Long before it began, and for months after it ended, the trial of Haywood, "a big sturdy fellow with a square head and solid jaw, who has lost one eye and overworks the other in much reading of socialistic and idealistic literature," held the attention, at times alarmed, at times angry, of the entire country. Newspapers and magazines, taking account of the public interest in the case, sent scores of writers to report it. Throughout the spring and early summer the streets of the quondam sleepy little town of Boisé were alive with throngs of labor men, reporters, sheepmen from near-by ranches, country lawyers in wide-brimmed Stetson hats, witnesses from as far away as California and Minnesota, delegations of travelling men holding an intermountain convention, an excursion of Omaha business men. Outside Boisé, throughout the country excitement

---

[21] The legality of these proceedings was upheld, when challenged, in the United States Circuit Court of Idaho. The Supreme Court of the United States, December 3, 1906, sustained the lower court, on the ground that what had taken place did not constitute a violation of the Federal laws or of the Federal Constitution. Justice McKenna dissented, terming the action of the officers "kidnapping."

was continuous. Behind Haywood had rallied labor, organized and unorganized, and all the sympathizers with radicalism from Socialists up and down. In cities two thousand miles from Boisé men paraded, waved red flags, sang the "Marseillaise," carried banners with provocative inscriptions. At times so vociferous was the ranting din that excitable persons believed orderly government was at stake, that bloody civil war impended. There appeared to be no limit to the violence of the attack on authority. President Roosevelt edged into the mêlée with a public letter in which, as an aside, he mildly referred to Haywood as being, like the railroad magnate Harriman, an "undesirable citizen," a phrase sufficiently tepid, whether considered as a description of Haywood, or as a sample of Roosevelt's vocabulary of disapproval. Immediately a stream of sulphurous invective was turned upon the President. Socialist leader Eugene Debs said Roosevelt had the "cruel malevolence of a barbarian." With a forcefulness of language which Roosevelt himself could not excel, Debs charged the President with having "uttered a lie as black and damnable, a calumny as foul and atrocious, as ever issued from a human throat." Even the Supreme Court was abused and insulted; when it upheld an action of an Idaho court in the case the radicals called it the "tool of capitalist masters" and its members "thieves" and "murderers."

The counsel for Haywood's defense was headed by Clarence Darrow, already famous as a criminal lawyer; a fund of $250,000 raised by popular subscription insured him every assistance that money could buy. The prosecution, equally able, included a young man, William E. Borah, then almost unheard of outside of Idaho, who in the January preceding had been elected to the

United States Senate,[22] but had not yet taken his seat.

In the trial, the star witness was, of course, Orchard. On the witness-stand, with every appearance of exactness and truthfulness, and in the most cold-blooded and callous way, he told of having destroyed nineteen human lives at the direction of Haywood, Moyer, and Pettibone. He had blown up the railway-station at Independence, Colorado, killing fourteen men. He had placed a bomb in the shaft of the Vindicator mine, killing two. He had shot down a detective in Denver after following him for two miles. A bomb he had set for a Colorado judge (Luther M. Goddard) had missed its intended victim and killed a chance passer-by.[23]

Courtesy of the New York "World."

William E. Borah, counsel for the prosecution in the Moyer-Haywood trial.

Counsel for the defense, recognizing that Orchard's testimony was terribly damaging to them, sought by every means to discredit it. By cross-examination they showed that Orchard was a bigamist; that he had been a hard drinker and an inveterate gambler all the time he lived in the West; that he had

[22] During the trial Borah displayed the independence of judgment which was one of the most outstanding of his qualities during his years in the Senate. His associates wished to call Orchard as a witness in the trial of Haywood. Borah opposed this, urging that both men be tried independently. He was overruled.

[23] To the great majority of Americans, Orchard's descriptions of his crimes, as given on the witness-stand and published by newspapers everywhere, had the unreality of a chapter from De Quincey. Orchard, as an assassin for hire, was a new phenomenon, which America could not understand. We had had experience with "bad men" of course — Jesse James and the Dalton brothers were still

been in the pay of railroad detectives in Colorado when he first met Haywood; that he had tried to sell information to the State authorities or the mine owners or both while he was, as he claimed, the paid assassin of the unions. Orchard, the defense claimed, was the tool of a conspiracy between the Pinkerton detectives and the

From a photograph © by Underwood & Underwood.

Clarence Darrow, counsel for Haywood.

Mine Owners' Association to discredit and exterminate the Western Federation of Miners.

Clarence Darrow, devoting more time and eloquence to giving the trial the appearance of a struggle between capital and labor than to proving his client's innocence, said it was "the spiders and vultures of Wall Street" — queer figure! — and those "who hate Haywood because he works for the poor," who wanted Haywood convicted. He pictured honest working men, before the coming of the union, stripped to their waists, working twelve hours a day in the mills and smelters to increase the dividends of the wealthy mine owners. As the

fresh in men's minds — but Orchard was not of the "bad-man" breed; the murders he had committed lacked the palliative of the "bad man's" bravado; a soap salesman could not have gone about his work with less emotion. America was further puzzled that Orchard, having committed his crimes, should talk so unreservedly about them, so unctuously even. Orchard's frankness, he himself explained on the ground that he had "got religion":

"I believed it was my duty to tell the truth, regardless of the consequences to myself or to anybody else. I did not see any other way. I felt I owed it to society. I owed it to God and to myself. . . . I'd been thinking over my past life and I did not believe the grave ended it all, and I was afraid to die, I had been such an unnatural monster. Finally I came to believe that if I sincerely repented of my sins I would be forgiven, and I have never been in doubt since."

sickening and dreadful fumes of arsenic arose from the melting ore, they paralyzed the arms and legs of the workers. The teeth in their jaws loosened and fell out. Five years, Darrow said, was the average length of life of workers under such conditions. When the Western Federation of Miners was formed, it had, Darrow said, spread out its protecting wings to the helpless and almost hopeless workers. It had built and maintained stores, libraries, hospitals, and union halls for the comfort and education of its members. It had supported the sick, buried the dead, and cared for the widows and orphans. He charged that secret spies in the employ of the mine owners, to render less effective the work of the union, had gained admission and planned and plotted to betray their associates. One of his statements, widely quoted and criticised, was: "Labor-unions are often brutal, they are often cruel, they are often unjust. . . . I don't care how many wrongs they commit. I don't care how many brutalities they are guilty of. I know that their cause is just."[24]

To all of which, Borah, for the prosecution, replied that "this is merely a murder trial; we are not fighting organized labor." The trial, Borah said, had no other purpose or implication than conviction and punishment of the assassins of ex-Governor Steunenberg. Borah's marshalling of the evidence into logical and dramatic sequence was admired by those who appreciated his skill. His presentation of the State's case "might have been likened more than anything else to the setting of a series of mines for the defense. This was the strength of the

[24] In comment on this much criticised remark, Mr. Darrow, in a letter to the author in 1930, wrote: "I meant that however unjust and cruel they sometimes are, their cause is just. The statement 'I don't care how many wrongs they commit; I don't care how many brutalities they are guilty of,' was used in the sense that regardless of how many wrongs they commit, or how many brutalities they are guilty of, their cause is just. I don't believe anybody can fairly interpret it in any other way."

State's case, greater than the force of its direct proof. The manner in which the disconnected but significant threads of evidence have been interwoven has shown the hand of a master."[25]

Of the jury eleven members were over fifty years of age, all were or had been farmers. Nine were American-born, two Scotch, one Canadian. They knew little about labor-unions or class struggles. After deliberating a day and a night they brought in a verdict of not guilty.

By common consent, it was not the eloquence of Darrow that freed Haywood, but the charge made to the jury by Judge Wood, whom the Socialists all along had been denouncing as a "tool" and a "puppet of plutocracy." The Judge had said: "Under the statutes of this State, a person cannot be convicted of a crime upon the testimony of an accomplice, unless such accomplice is corroborated by other evidence." The jurors, though, as one of them afterward said, "all thought Haywood guilty," considered the evidence presented by the prosecution as not sufficiently corroborative of itself to justify a conviction, and made their decision accordingly.

"The verdict at best," said the Richmond, Va., *Times*, expressing the general feeling of the country, "was the old Scotch verdict of not proven. It cannot be called a vindication by the most enthusiastic friends of Haywood."

Important, and also amusing, was the effect of the outcome of the trial on the noisy element among the Socialists and radicals who for months had been charging that the scales of American justice were loaded against Haywood. The trial had been conducted with dignity and decorum by serious men. The Judge had instructed

[25] C. P. Connolly, *Collier's*, July 27, 1907. Clarence Darrow comments, in a letter to the author in 1930: "What you say of Mr. Borah's argument I think is fully justified. I have often said that I have defended a great many criminal cases and I never heard a fairer argument on the part of the prosecution."

the jury in the law. The jury had considered the facts and the law bearing on the case and had reached the decision indicated by these factors. As a result those who had decried American justice, who had alleged the im-

Eugene V. Debs, American Socialist leader.

possibility of a fair trial for Haywood, found themselves discredited with all persons of common sense. Up to that time there had been a country-wide trend toward Socialism as a cure for various of the ills of democratic government; the hysteria and excesses of Debs and the other extremists among the Socialists, during and before the Haywood trial, had the effect of a brake applied to this trend, indeed brought it almost to a halt, at a time when in France, Germany, and England it was going forward strongly.[26]

August 3. Augustus Saint-Gaudens died, greatest American sculptor and dominating American influence upon the forms of art in which he excelled, leaving to Amer-

From the painting by Ellen Emmet.
Augustus Saint-Gaudens.

ica a rich heritage: the statue of "Grief" (known also as "Death" and "The Peace of God") in Rock Creek Cemetery, Washington, D. C.; the Shaw memorial near the State House, Boston, monument to the white Boston Colonel of a negro regiment in the Civil War; equestrian statue of General William T. Sherman at 59th

[26] Following a much less spectacular trial, Haywood's associate, George A. Pettibone, was acquitted, January 5, 1908.

Street and Fifth Avenue, New York; "Diana," colossal figure for the tower of Madison Square Garden, New York; statues of Abraham Lincoln and John A. Logan in Chicago; "The Puritan" (Deacon Chapin) in Springfield, Mass.; Admiral Farragut and Peter Cooper in New York; the familiar relief medallion portrait of Robert Louis Stevenson. Designer, upon invitation from President Roosevelt, of several American coins.

Saint-Gaudens' equestrian statue of General Sherman at the Plaza entrance to Central Park, New York

August 3. Kenesaw Mountain Landis, United States District Judge, fined the Standard Oil Company of Indiana $29,240,000, following indictment April 13 on 1,462 counts for accepting rebates in violation of the Elkins Act of 1903. The Indiana company not possessing assets equal to the fine, Judge Landis ruled that the holding company, the Standard Oil Company of New Jersey, must pay; whereupon John D. Rockefeller remarked, so newspaper despatches said, "Judge Landis will be dead a long while before this fine is paid." The fine was never collected. On appeal, Judge Landis's decision was reversed and the fine remitted, with costs thrown on the government. The publicity accruing to

Judge Landis was a principal reason for the selection of him, a few years later, as a kind of super-umpire on questions of morals and the like arising in organized baseball, at a salary described as more than ten times that of a Federal district judge.

Judge Kenesaw Mountain Landis.

Nineteen-seven was the year of the high tide of prosecutions and arraignments of the Standard Oil Companies. In Ohio, on January 14, the Standard of New Jersey was indicted on 539 counts for illegal acceptance of rebates. Two weeks later, the Interstate Commerce Commission published a report of its investigation of the Standard's methods of doing business, described by the press as a "most scathing arraignment." On May 19, the Commissioner of Corporations made public a report charging that the Standard Oil Company, largely through its control over transportation, had for thirty-five years maintained a practical monopoly of the petroleum industry. On June 1, a jury at Austin, Texas, rendered a verdict for the State of $1,623,900 against the Waters-Pierce Oil Company, an affiliate of the Standard, and advocated the ousting of the company from the State. In September, Government Prosecutor Frank B. Kellogg[27] brought the suit under the Sherman Anti-Trust Act which ultimately ended in the dissolution of the parent Standard Oil Company, the Standard of New Jersey.

[27] Later Senator from Minnesota, Ambassador to Great Britain, and Secretary of State.

August. A shirt-waist, supposed to be an extreme of daring, in which embroidered perforations permitted sight of female epidermis upon the arms and as much as two inches below the nape of the neck, was called the "peek-a-boo." Parsons denounced them; *Puck* made quips about them:

From "*The Modern Priscilla,*" *December, 1907.*

The "peek-a-boo" waist, perforated with clusters of daisies and heads of wheat.

The Thin Skeeter: Well, say, *you* look like ready money. You must be having a prosperous season. Where you stopping?

The Fat Skeeter: Me? Oh, I'm living in the back of a Peek-a-boo waist.[28]

From "*Pickings from Puck,*" *June, 1907.*

Left: Three Homeless Hooks. *Right:* From the *Pictorial Review Quarterly,* Autumn, 1930.

The many 1907 quips about women's dresses buttoned or hooked up the back disappeared with the slip-on styles of some twenty years later.

[28] Pickings from *Puck,* June, 1907.

And

Mose : What kin' of fool target yo' done call dat, —huh?
Sam : Dat ain't no target. Mah wife she's hankerin foh one
o' dem peek-a-boo waists an' Ah's renovatin' de material wif
bird-shot, dat's all.

September 12. A British steamship, the *Lusitania,*
arrived in New York Harbor on her maiden voyage,

The *Lusitania* leaving her dock in New York harbor.

notable because she was the largest ship in the world,[29]
and because she had broken all previous speed records
by travelling from Queenstown to New York in five days
and fifty-four minutes[30] — and destined to become more
notable, to have, indeed, a dramatic place in important
world history, through being sunk by a German subma-
rine off the coast of Ireland while carrying a large number of American passengers, on May 7, 1915.

The first arrival of the *Lusitania* in American waters
was occasion for lament over the long eclipse of Ameri-

[29] 709 feet long, beam 88 feet, moulded depth 60 feet, rated at 32,500 tons, her
turbines having 68,000 horse-power.
[30] Six weeks later the *Lusitania* steamed from Sandy Hook, N. Y., to Queenstown, Ireland, in four days, twenty-two hours, forty-six minutes.

can shipping. The spectacle should, said the New York *Evening Post*, "stamp this as a day of humility for all our citizens who wish to see the American flag restored to the place it occupied in the fifties, when our clipper ships were in every harbor on the globe. There are no

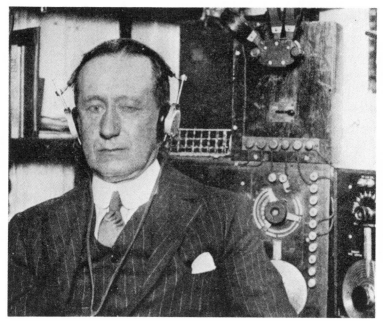

From a photograph © Kadel & Herbert News Service. Courtesy Radio Corporation of America.

Guglielmo Marconi, inventor of wireless communication.

reports of projected American ships to surpass the *Lusitania*, no rumors that American invention is busy with a plan to develop a vessel that will cross within four days. Our chief American line is precisely where it was in 1892."

October 18. A young man sitting at a desk in a lonely station at Glace Bay, Nova Scotia, talked by wireless telegraphy to Clifden, Ireland, an achievement which crowned six years of experimenting by Guglielmo

Marconi, following his initial success, on December 14, 1901, in transmitting the letter "S" by wireless from Cornwall, England, to St. John's, Newfoundland.

From a photograph by Louis H. Dreyer.

When the Knickerbocker Trust Company closed its doors, at the beginning of the panic of 1907, the New York *World* published this photograph.

The Panic of 1907

October 21. With the coming of daylight, people, congregating first by scores, then by hundreds, and later by thousands, were herded by policemen into lines stretching away from the marble entrance to the Knickerbocker Trust Company, New York. First in line, hold-

ing his place with difficulty against the surging and
jostling of the desperately anxious people behind him,
was a solidly built man, messenger of the Night and
Day Bank — serviceable agent of persons who had
shrewdly bethought themselves of the one bank that
kept open all night. In a satchel chained to the Night

A specimen of "Roosevelt Currency." Wall Street attempted to even the score
against Roosevelt by attributing paternity for its troubles to him. It gave
the name "Roosevelt Panic" to the financial collapse of 1907 and that of
"Roosevelt Currency" to the Clearing House Certificates which during the
panic the banks issued in lieu of money.

and Day Bank messenger's waist were thousands of
checks that had been signed by depositors of the Knickerbocker Trust Company and presented during the night
at the Night and Day Bank for collection. To him, at
intervals of an hour all night long, runners from his
bank had brought more checks.

When the Knickerbocker's doors opened at nine
A. M., October 22, the throng fought its way inside to
the windws of the paying tellers. All day the run continued; at three o'clock, when the bank closed, hundreds were still in line. Next day witnessed a similar
scene, which came to an end at noon, when the Knickerbocker's directors, their stock of cash almost exhausted,
decided to suspend payments.

The spectacle of the run on the Knickerbocker precipitated (with other causes, before and after) runs on

other banks in New York and elsewhere throughout the country. So many were they as to to suggest a humorous exaggeration to *Life:*[31]

"Hello, Dinny, you look prosperous — got a job now?"
"You bet, an' it's a good one!"
"What is it?"
"Gettin' in early on de bank runs, an' sellin' me place in de line."

These runs constituted a "currency panic," a condition in which depositors in banks had the experience of writing out checks, presenting them at the paying teller's window, and being told they could not have their money. This was a phenomenon different from (though in the past often associated with) a "business depression" or a "stock-exchange panic." The currency panic, as distinguished from the other phenomena, was due fundamentally to the lack of a national banking system, to the fact that, speaking roughly, each bank stood alone. The condition was later cured, largely under impetus from the rueful memory of the 1907 currency panic, by the adoption in 1913 of the Federal Reserve System, under which, again speaking roughly, the resources of all the banks in the system are pooled to meet the demands of any member bank threatened with a run by its depositors. Since the adoption of the Federal Reserve System, a currency panic can hardly again occur; though of course there have been and will continue to be business depressions and stock-exchange panics. No banking system or any other device can prevent these, since they appear to have their roots in the deep ground-swells of mass psychology which affect humanity at irregular intervals, causing waves of exaggerated optimism and pessimism, but it is probable that wise financial leadership, both economic and political, can reduce the oscillations and mitigate their effects.

31 November 14, 1907.

The spectacular series of financial phenomena of 1907 began with a business depression of the familiar sort that arises once in so often in the economic cycle.

Wall Street during the run on the Trust Company of America.

What caused the business depression, no one can say — though in fact many did say. It is doubtful if any person has ever been able to say, as to any business depression in history, just what was the order of the various causes that contributed, and what was the relative contribution of each. Economics, political science so called, is the science that overlaps two fields, on the one hand material goods and money, on the other hand human psychology in the mass. Within the area where those two meet, overlap and merge, are elements too volatile and eccen-

From photographs by Underwood & Underwood.

Wall Street about 1895.   Wall Street in 1930.

tric to submit to analysis or control, to prediction or exact post-mortem. At intervals more or less irregular in the business cycle, depressions come. Some specific signs[32] can be detected in advance, many specific causes identified afterward; but the aggregate of causes in their interrelation to each other baffles analysis, however expert the analyzer.

[32] The best book ever written in America on the limited phase of the business cycle to which it devotes itself is "Financial Crises and Periods of Industrial and Commercial Depression," by Theodore Burton, for an interval in his scholarly life president of the Merchants National Bank in New York, previously and later Representative and Senator from Ohio. Burton's book dealt with the period preceding the adoption of the Federal Reserve System, and was therefore to a degree, but only to a degree, rendered obsolete by the coming of that institution.

When the business depression of 1907 came, it resulted, quite according to both past precedent and subsequent rule, that the pot and the kettle exchanged the usual epithets. Business blamed politics, politics business. Probably had Edward H. Harriman been Presi-

Fifth Avenue at 33d Street, Waldorf Astoria in background. Horse-drawn Fifth Avenue stage; early electric taxi. Note style in women's dress early in the century.

dent of the United States, and had Theodore Roosevelt been president of the Union Pacific Railroad, the business depression of 1907 would have come in the course of nature, without material variation in degree or time. So many and violent were the charges made by business leaders against Roosevelt that there arose a public psychology in which the Augusta, Ga., *Chronicle* termed him "our chief panic-maker,"[33] and the New York *Sun* addressed to him the ironic salute, "Hail, Cæsar! We who are about to bust salute thee!" Roosevelt, reply-

[33] Railroad men derisively gave the name "Teddy-bears" to the country's 8500 idle locomotives.

ing,[34] was wise enough, or was so wisely advised, as not to misstate the true origin of the depression; in his preamble he said that "most of it I believe to be due to matters not particularly confined to the United States and to matters wholly unconnected with any government action." But Roosevelt felt he could not afford to fail to

J. P. Morgan.   Marshall Field.

strike back at those who falsely blamed the depression on him. The depression was caused, he said, in part by "ruthless and determined men" hiding "behind the breastworks of corporate organization. . . . It may well be that the determination of the government to punish certain malefactors of great wealth has been responsible for something of the troubles, at least to the extent of having caused these men to bring about as much financial stress as they can in order to discredit the policy of the government and thereby to secure a reversal of that policy so that they may enjoy the fruits of their evil-doing." "As far as I am concerned," Roosevelt con-

[34] In a speech at Provincetown, Mass., August 20, 1907.

cluded with unabated belligerence, "and for the eighteen months of my administration that remain, there will be no change in the policy we have steadily pursued, no let-up in the effort to secure the honest observance of the law, for I regard this contest as one to determine who shall rule this government."

As a corollary to the business depression, there was on March 14, 1907, a panicky fall on the New York Stock Exchange. Out of all the conditions came bankruptcies for important business firms; out of one of these arose scandal affecting a New York City bank; out of this and out of the conditions as a whole arose uneasiness by depositors in

From a photograph by Pach Bros.
Henry Clay Frick.

banks — an uneasiness, however, which need not have arisen but for the lack of a national banking system, and which, even if it should arise, could do no great harm if a national banking system had been in existence. The uneasiness of depositors expressed itself in runs upon the banks, of which the one on the Knickerbocker Trust Company was the most spectacular, and in its effect on public psychology the most disastrous. Bank after bank throughout the country was unable to give to depositors the money that belonged to them. In the common impotency of checks, and since the amount of government currency could not be sufficient to carry on the country's business on a cash basis, improvised currencies came into use, certificates made out by corporations for circulation among their employees, and in the local communities where the corporations had their plants; clearing-house certificates, many forms of informal currency, illegal but justified by the conditions.

When the panic was at its worst, J. Pierpont Morgan, by character and force of personality as much as by his resources, came clearly into his own as the dominant figure of American finance. To Morgan in his office at Broad and Wall Streets came the financial chieftains of America, some by invitation, some out of voluntary deference to Morgan's leadership, many drawn irresistibly by that subtle and powerful force through which, in time of crisis, the smaller gravitate to the greater. "In came a gentleman, who, without being announced, opened the gate of the railing which surrounds Mr. Morgan's desk. Mr. Morgan nodded and said, 'Good morning, Mr. Frick.' The two men sat chatting quietly for a few minutes. You would have thought they were engaged in an informal and unimportant conversation. But, in reality, Frick was offering millions of the highest grade of securities for a purpose that Mr. Morgan had in mind. When Frick went away a little man came in with a quick, nervous step. Mr. Morgan greeted him with a nod; the visitor was E. H. Harriman. In a similar manner, one after another, some ten or fifteen. . . . At

From a photograph © *by Harris & Ewing.*
George B. Cortelyou.

last, James Stillman, president of the National City Bank, came; receiving a most casual greeting, he went with Mr. Morgan into an inner room."[35]

Morgan and Stillman, with one or two others, brought about the importation of a hundred million dollars in gold from Europe. John D. Rockefeller, Sr., put up ten million dollars in government bonds, without charge. The Secretary of the Treasury, George B. Cortelyou, announced readiness to deposit with the national banks of the country a hundred and fifty million dollars of government money, and more up to the limit of the law. By these and other de-

Charles T. Glidden.

vices — but principally by those emanations from Mr. Morgan's personality that people call confidence — banks were put in a position to meet runs, or to disarm them. Within a comparatively few weeks the currency panic, as such, was over; the business depression, of course, went its slow way to normal recovery.

October. An automobile tour of the world, begun six years before by Mr. and Mrs. Charles T. Glidden, was described as "epoch-making" in an article in the London *Car*, containing flashes of unintended humor for the motorist of a quarter-century later:

The tour began in London in 1901, upon a twenty-four horse-power four-cylinder Napier car . . . and the same vehicle has carried Mr. and Mrs. Glidden ever since, only being sent to the

[35] The quotations describing the scene in Morgan's office are from "The Life-Story of J. P. Morgan," by Carl Hovey.

makers twice, and for minor repairs. Often the travelers have been hundreds, if not indeed thousands, of miles from any repair shop, so that they have had to thank the extraordinary reliability of the Napier car for bringing them through so successfully. Mr. Glidden begins his arrangements for the necessary stores of petrol and lubrication some two years ahead of time. He is very careful in starting, taking corners, and especially in avoiding the use of his brakes as far as possible by using the engine compression. He has obtained excellent results with his tires, often running 4,000 miles on a pair of rear tires and sometimes 10,000 miles on the front tires.

From "Ladies' Home Journal," August, 1907.
1907.

From "Pictorial Review," Fall, 1930.
1930.

Little boys' suits.

November 7. *Life* reprinted a story originally published in *Everybody's Magazine*, and apparently then new, which included a remark that became almost universal, as an epitome of situations at once impossible to conceive, but nevertheless actual:

An aged Jersey farmer, visiting a circus for the first time, stood before the dromedary's cage, eyes popping and mouth agape at the strange beast within. The circus proper began and the crowds left for the main show, but still the old man stood before the cage in stunned silence, appraising every detail of the misshapen legs, the cloven hoofs, the pendulous upper lip, and the curiously mounded back of the sleepy-eyed beast. Fifteen minutes passed. Then the farmer turned away disgustedly.
"Hell, there ain't no such animal!"

November 20. The first of a long series of what the public came to call familiarly "Gary dinners" was held at the New York home of the head of the United States Steel Corporation, Judge Elbert H. Gary, with competitors as guests. The dinners were denounced as a revival of the old "pools," perfumed to be not too odorous to

Elbert H. Gary.

the public attitude about restraint of trade and price-fixing. That the "Gary dinners" had the result of stabilizing the steel business, there is little doubt; about the desirability of the stabilization there was difference of opinion. Increasingly the public tended to approve it.

December. Current styles in women's hats were the subject of quips in comic journals:

"Been to the theatre this week?"
"Yep."
"What did you see?"
"A black velvet bow, some tortoise-shell combs, a couple of plumes, a chiffon knot and a stuffed bird the size of a hen."[36]

And

We have the horseless carriage,
The wireless and all that,

[36] *Life*, April 4, 1907, credited to the Louisville *Courier-Journal.*

Also the loveless marriage,
But not the birdless hat.[37]

December 16. Sixteen battle-ships, with officers and crews numbering about 12,000 men, under command of Admiral Robley D. Evans, sailed from Hampton Roads, Va., on the first round-the-world cruise ever undertaken by an American fleet — an incident of America's coming of age in the family of nations. The project was initiated by President Roosevelt; in formulating his plans he refrained from consulting his Cabinet and permitted his intention to be known to no one except a few high officials of the Navy. The fleet, after rounding South America, arrived in San Francisco in March, 1908; from the Golden Gate it proceeded around the world by way of Australia, Japan, and China, returning to Hampton Roads on February 22, 1909.[38]

From the "Millinery Herald," 1907.

A split straw hat.

Other Events of 1907

January 16. New York newspapers carried a full-page advertisement of Budweiser: "The king of bottled beers — in 1906 scored a sale of 137,722,150 bottles; the largest brewery in the world — covers 128 acres. * * * *February* 20. The Senate voted, 42 to 28, not to unseat Reed Smoot, Mormon Senator from Utah. The effort to oust Senator Smoot was based on the allegation that he, as an Apostle and member of the hierarchy of the Mormon Church, had taken an oath

[37] Pickings from *Puck*, December, 1907.

[38] Admiral Evans remained in command until the fleet reached San Francisco, when, at his request, the command was turned over to Admiral C. S. Sperry.

"which implied disloyalty to the United States." There was also objection to him on the ground that his church countenanced polygamy, though Smoot himself was not accused of that practice. * * * *February*. Much talk about Gelett Burgess's whimsical division of human beings into "bromides" and "sulfites" — the bromides being the majority of mankind who "all think and talk alike," and "may be depended upon to be

From the "Millinery Herald."
Bird-trimmed hats, Summer, 1908.

trite, banal, and arbitrary," while the sulfites were those who do their own thinking, who "eliminate the obvious from their conversation," and have surprises up their sleeves. A few months later, Mr. Burgess coined another word, destined to live longer, "blurb," defined by its creator as "a noise made by a publisher." * * * *March*. Information from Europe included inconsp cuous mention of "Sinn Fein" (meaning "ourselves alone"), a movement initiated by a university teacher for the revival of the Irish language, and destined, about ten years later, to take on proportions much wider. * * * *April* 26. President Roosevelt opened the Jamestown Exposition and reviewed the naval parade at Hampton Roads. Among the exhibits which never failed to attract crowds was a current

The U. S. fleet under Admiral Robley D. Evans, which made a world tour, starting in December, 1907.

Admiral Robley D. Evans, commanding the U. S. fleet, and Admiral Togo of the Japanese navy.

novelty, the first sleeping-car of steel, built by the Pullman
company. It was admired not only for its superior safety, but

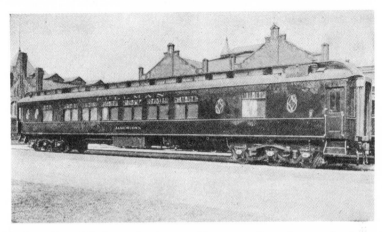

The first all-steel Pullman sleeping-car, "Jamestown," put in operation in 1907
after being exhibited at the Jamestown Exposition, was still
in service in 1930.

also "on account of the decorative features which have all
the beauty of graceful outline and pleasing color treatment

An early taxi.

which are characteristic of recent Pullman cars built of wood."
This first steel sleeper, the "Jamestown," was still in service
in 1930. * * * *May*. A flotilla of "taximeter cabs" imported
from Paris arrived in New York, forerunners of hordes of

"taxis" that a few years later congested the streets of American cities. * * * *June* 4. Fines aggregating $284,000 were imposed in the United States Court at Mobile, Alabama, upon thirty-one promoters of the Honduras Lottery, successor to the Louisiana Lottery, the defendants agreeing to surrender all their paraphernalia, close their printing-office, and go out of business. This ended lotteries in the United States, except furtive and unformidable ones; at one time they had been recog-

Union Station, Washington, D. C.

nized by law and approved by public opinion; one of the buildings of Harvard University was built from the proceeds of a lottery. * * * *June* 26. Lord Curzon, bestowing upon Mark Twain, on behalf of Oxford University, the degree of Doctor of Letters, said, in Latin: "Most jocund, pleasant, and humorous man who shakes the sides of all the circuit of the earth with your native joyousness, I, by my authority and that of the entire university, admit you to the honorary degree of Doctor of Letters." * * * *July* 5. Miss May Sutton, an American, won the women's lawn tennis championship of England. * * * *July* 30. The first Filipino general election was held without disorder. * * * *July.* An importation from Europe that acquired the proportions of a craze was a diversion called "diabolo" played with a piece of wood shaped like an hour-glass which was spun on a cord held by two sticks; the brief but intense popularity of diabolo in America was a repetition of a recurrent experience it had many times in Europe, and before that for centuries in China. * * * *August* 29. The almost-completed cantilever bridge spanning the St. Lawrence River near Quebec collapsed, killing eighty men. Following the accident the project was taken over by the Dominion government and completed September 21, 1917, at a cost of $22,662,-000. Its official opening, delayed until after the Great War, took place August 22, 1919, with the Prince of Wales in attendance. * * * *November* 17. The new union station at Washington, one of the loveliest buildings in America, costing more than $4,000,000, was opened for traffic.

Books of 1907

Books that were "best sellers," or otherwise popular, valuable or conspicuous during 1907, included "The Lady of the Decoration," by Frances Little, regarded by *The Bookman* as in some ways "the most successful book of 1907"[39] — by 1930 "The Lady of the Decoration" was

From a painting by Oliver Hazard Perry.
F. Hopkinson Smith.

utterly unknown. . . . "The Port of Missing Men," by Meredith Nicholson. . . . "Half a Rogue," by Harold MacGrath. . . . "New Chronicles of Rebecca," by Kate Douglas Wiggin. . . . "The Brass Bowl," which "marked the success of an absolutely new writer," whose name was Louis Joseph Vance. . . . "Jane Cable," by George Barr McCutcheon. . . . "The Doctor," by Ralph Connor. . . . "Satan Sanderson," by Hallie Erminie Rives. . . . "Alice-for-Short," by William de Morgan. . . . "The Second Generation,"

[39] Published April, 1906.

by David Graham Phillips. . . . "The Younger Set," by Robert W. Chambers. . . . "The Fighting Chance," by Robert W. Chambers. . . . "Pam Decides," by Baroness von Hutton. . . . "Silas Strong," by Irving Bacheller. . . . "The Awakening of Helena Richie,"

by Margaret Deland. . . . "If Youth But Knew," by Agnes and Egerton Castle. . . . "The Beloved Vagabond," by William J. Locke. . . . "A Lady of Rome," by F. Marion Crawford. . . . "The House of a Thousand Candles," by Meredith Nicholson. . . . "The Wheel of Life," by Ellen Glasgow. . . . "The Woman in the Alcove," by Anna Katherine Green (Mrs. Charles Rohlfs). . . . "Tides of Barnegat," by F. Hopkinson Smith. . . . "Friday the Thirteenth," a weird book in which a spectacular figure of the lower floors (perhaps the basement) of "high finance," Thomas W. Lawson, having turned, for a very brief interval, to the rôles of informer and reformer, made sensational disclosures of big business, accompanied by dire prophecies of its fate on a doomsday which Lawson predicted. . . . And "Three Weeks," by Elinor Glyn, which because of its commercial success led other authors to imitate its preoccupation with sex; which, in the vogue it gave rise to, caused William Marion Reedy to remark in 1915 that "it's sex o'clock"; and which, soon after its appearance, inspired an indignant rhymster to say:[40]

Elinor Glyn.

[40] In *Life,* December 19, 1907. The author was Ruth Moselle Mould.

"Have you read it?" "Have you read it?"
They hummed it in my ear,
And everybody said it
With a most suggestive leer.

Then I read it. Yes, I read it,
As my blushes have confessed,
And I'm proud of dear old England —
She had the book suppressed.

In 1907, on October 6, died a woman whose passing engaged only condescending attention from circles that thought of themselves as "the literati" but who had written a larger number of standard novels than any other American author,[41] and had had a larger following of readers over a greater length of time. The aggregate sales[42] of the novels of Mrs. Mary J. Holmes, upward of two million, considered with regard to the type of person with whom they were favorites — village and country women likely to be members of large families, likely also to be given to book lending and borrowing — must have accounted for fully half the adult population of America. It was about the middle of the last century, in 1854, the same year as Thackeray's "Newcomes" and a year after Dickens's "Bleak House," that Mrs. Holmes (born Hawes) wrote "Tempest and Sunshine." The story had the simplicity, the artless sincerity, the instinctive high ethics that she had breathed in her own experience as a teacher in a New England country school. From the standards of that background

41 Standard in the sense of selling originally at $1.50 and being published by a standard house, for many years D. Appleton & Company. (Mrs. Holmes's publisher at the time of her death was G. W. Dillingham Company.)

42 It is possible this aggregate may have been exceeded by the books of another writer who made somewhat the same kind of appeal to roughly the same stratum of American life, Reverend E. P. Roe (died 1904), author of "Opening of a Chestnut Burr," "Nature's Serial Story," etc. There were other authors, of a sort, writers of dime novels, as well as Laura Jean Libby, who may have had a larger aggregate circulation; but they did not write standard books, and were different from Roe and Mrs. Holmes in both the kind of book they wrote and the level of American life they appealed to.

she never departed; correspondingly she pleased the level of American life of which she was typical, the very heart and substance of what America then was. It loved her and sustained her for half a century and a little more, during which she produced nearly a novel a year. Her forty-second, and last, novel was published in 1905,

Photograph by Culver Service.

Dancing in statelier days. The cotillion given by W. C. Whitney, January 4, 1901, in his Fifth Avenue home. — Drawn by A. I. Keller for *Harper's Weekly.*

after Thackeray had been dead for twoscore years and more, in a year when the popular novel of the day, in a greatly changed America, was "The House of Mirth."

Commonly reckoned best among Mrs. Holmes's novels was her fourth, "Lena Rivers," published in 1856, and after fifty years still alive as a book, on the stage, and as a motion-picture. Other titles by Mrs. Holmes that lived long in the affections of loyal readers were "Homestead on a Hillside" (1855), "Dora Deane" (1858), "Cameron Pride" (1867), "Dr. Hathern's Daughters" (1895), "The Abandoned Farm" (1902),

"Lucy Harding" (1905). She married an official of a normal school, Daniel Holmes, in an old-fashioned American town, Brockport, N. Y.; made a large fortune from her writing, and devoted some of it, according to her code, to providing education for persons who otherwise might lack it; upon her death she had the largest funeral ever seen in her part of the State, with flags half-mast, schools and business places closed. Mrs. Holmes and her "Lena Rivers" belonged in an America that drove a horse and buggy through covered bridges, said grace before meals, went to church twice on Sunday, and on week-day evenings took part in the meetings of the Christian Endeavor Society and the Epworth League; that danced the "Virginia Reel" — so far as it danced at all, for as a rule churchgoing folks tabooed the dance; got thrills from "Uncle Tom's Cabin" and "Ten Nights in a Barroom" — so far again, as it went to the theatre at all; that rarely got into the newspapers and never into the divorce courts — an America that by 1907 was beginning to fade into the backwaters of national life, surviving on farms and in country villages.

The Theatre in 1907

As respects popularity achieved, and perhaps by some other standards as well, an outstanding dramatic event of 1907 was the first American production of the "Merry Widow,"[43] destined to charm America for years by its gay music, its rhythmical melodies, and especially by the sinuous, languorous grace of its waltz. The "Merry Widow" was comic opera, operetta. It aimed merely to charm and amuse; it concerned itself not at all with new theories about marriage and organized society, the strange yeast that was being introduced into Ameri-

---

43 At Syracuse, N. Y., on September 23, 1907. Originally produced in Vienna as "Die Lustige Witwe," on December 30, 1905.

can thought by the stage productions of Shaw, Ibsen and others. Yet the "Merry Widow Waltz" had a relation to American folk-ways.

Of all the dances that had been familiar to America

The Merry Widow waltz as danced on the stage.

for half a century or more — schottische, polka, galop, lanciers, quadrille, and from 1890 on the two-step — of them all the waltz was the most beloved. Its gentle sentimentality and stately dignity were a part and a symbol of the standards of manners that accompanied it, its tempo the tempo of the national pulse. By 1907 the waltz and the national rhythm that went with it were

beginning to give way to a new spirit and new manners,
a faster tempo of American life. The "Merry Widow"
by the glamourous, alluring tune it provided, gave to the
waltz a new lease of life, an Indian summer reprieve;
rescued it, for a while and
partially, from a vandal
invasion of hoydenish
dances just then coming
over the horizon — push-
ing newcomers called,
generically, "rag-time
dances" — the one-step,
the fox-trot, the turkey-
trot, the grizzly-bear, the
bunny-hug. The reprieve
of the waltz was short-
lived; its standards of gentle manners knew no way
of repulsing the rowdy
gate-crashers that elbowed
it to the side of the room.

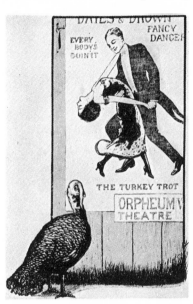

By half a dozen years after
1907 the waltz was defi-
nitely passé, wallflower
for a time to the popular

A drawing published in *Judge* November,
1912, shortly after the "Turkey Trot"
had become the current dance vogue.
The turkey is pictured as indignantly
repudiating authorship of the new
dance: "No, sir; nothing like that in our
family."

taste, almost companion in desuetude of the minuet.

In 1907 "Mrs. Warren's Profession," described on the
programme as "Bernard Shaw's greatest play," was given
without interference — the courts had reproved the police for stopping it a year before. "The play," said John
Corbin, "is neither as wicked nor as diverting as it appeared in that former fever of prurient imagination."
. . . 1907 was the first year in America of a form of
entertainment known as the "Follies," a conglomeration

of songs, dances, girls and vaudeville specialties — regarded, in 1907, as a little "sporty," something a father
would hardly take his family to see. (In the 1907 "Fol-
lies" Nora Bayes made her first American appearance.)

From a photograph by Frederick H. Evans,
London.

G. Bernard Shaw.   John Galsworthy.

. . . An Italian, Ermete Novelli, introduced to America as the "most versatile actor in the world," played
in the Italian tongue several Shakespearean and other
classic dramas, including "Hamlet," "The Merchant of
Venice," "Othello," and "The Taming of the Shrew."
. . . Richard Strauss's music drama "Salome" was produced by the Metropolitan Opera Company — once;
and was denounced as "revolting," "degrading." J. Pierpont Morgan (the elder), uniting with W. K. Vanderbilt,
August Belmont, and other directors, insisted upon the
performance being stopped; Morgan was said to have declared that he would be willing to refund from his own
pocket the entire cost of the production rather than have
another performance given. "Salome in her transports

of rage and gross sensuality," said *The Theatre Magazine*,[44] "is no less respectable a person than the Sapphos, the Zazas, the Mrs. Warrens and other red-light heroines of the contemporary stage; it was not the character of Sa-

From a photograph by Sarony.
John Drew.

Richard Mansfield.

lome nor her voluptuous dance of the Seven Veils which offended; it was the repulsive gruesomeness, the shuddering horror of the woman fondling a decapitated head."

In 1907, Richard Mansfield played in Ibsen's "Peer Gynt." . . . John Drew and Miss Billie Burke in "My Wife." . . . Alla Nazimova in Ibsen's "A Doll's House." . . . Ellen Terry in Bernard Shaw's "Captain Brassbound's Conversion." . . . Eleanor Robson in "Salomy Jane," composed by Paul Armstrong upon Bret Harte's California romance "Salomy Jane's Kiss." . . . Blanche Walsh in "The Straight Road," by Clyde Fitch. . . . E. H. Sothern and Julia Marlowe in "John the Baptist," by Herman Sudermann, and in "The Sunken

[44] March, 1907.

Bell" ("Die Versunkene Glocke"), by Gerhart Haupt-
mann, as well as "Twelfth Night." . . . Ethel Barrymore disguised her lovely face and form in the rôle of a
scrubwoman in the first play by John Galsworthy produced in America, "The Silver Box" — by 1925 seventeen Galsworthy plays had been produced here.

"The Movers" depicted what was, even then, regarded as the "seething restlessness" of New York life.
. . . "The Thief," by Henri Bernstein, adapted from
the French by C. Haddon Chambers, in which Kyrle
Bellew and Margaret Illington played. . . . "The Three
of Us," by Rachel Crothers. . . . "The Mills of the
Gods," by George Broadhurst. . . . "Widowers' Houses,"
by George Bernard Shaw. . . . "Paid in Full," by Eugene Walter.

Nine plays, all new during the 1906–7 season, had re-
markable runs; by June, 1907, the number of perform-
ances of each was: "The Chorus Lady," 299; "The Red
Mill," 274; "The Great Divide," 234; "The Three of
Us," 227; "The Hypocrites," 217; "The Man of the
Hour," 195; "The Rose of the Rancho," 192; "The Rich
Mr. Hoggenheimer," 187; "The Parisian Model," 179.

Seven other plays, a year or more old, had had, by
June, 1907, exceptionally long runs: "The Music Mas-
ter," 631; "The Lion and the Mouse," 586; "The Girl
of the Golden West," 397; "Peter Pan," 291; "Mlle.
Modiste," 202; "The Social Whirl," 195; "Brown of
Harvard," 178.

In 1907, on August 30, Richard Mansfield, greatest
American actor — possibly, with Henry Irving dead,
greatest in the English-speaking world — died.

13

1908

Prohibition Advances. Smoking by Women. Hard Times. New York Ends Race-track Gambling. Taft and Bryan Are Nominated. Fred Merkle Makes Baseball History, Unwillingly. Josephus Daniels Attacks the Republicans. Mrs. Astor Dies — and an Era Comes to Its End. The "Sheathgown" Causes Controversy. J. P. Morgan Speaks on America. The Motion Picture in Its "Nickelodeon" Stage. The First Sunday Evening Newspaper. Books and Plays of 1908.

January 1. A State-wide prohibition law went into effect in Georgia. One hundred and twenty-five of the hundred and forty-six counties had already been dry under a local-option law.

January 25. The Baltimore and Ohio Railroad Company announced that all employees engaged in running or directing trains must be total abstainers.

February 20. The New York *Herald* deemed it fitting to use large type for a head-line reading:

WOMEN SMOKE ON WAY TO OPERA

―――

Are Discovered Puffing Cigarettes When Electric Light Beams Into Their Carriage

By the 1920's, when smoking by women in America became common, it was generally assumed that the practice was a part of the shattering of standards that accompanied the Great War, or came as aftermath of it. Actually, the custom was started in the early 1900's, chiefly by American women who had passed some time in Europe, had become familiar with smoking in "smart" circles there, and introduced it in America. In the New York *Herald* for July 12, 1908, a despatch from San

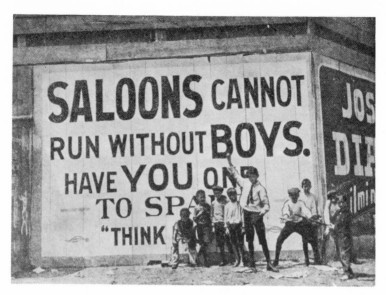

A memento of the days when the fight against the liquor traffic had the moral fervor of a crusade. The scene is of a billboard in Wilmington, Del. (about 1908), on which is painted the slogan of the reformers, "SALOONS cannot run without BOYS. Have YOU one to spare? 'Think it over.'" Wherever in Wilmington a billboard advertised liquor, beside it, the "cold waterites," as they were called, put one bearing their slogan.

Martin's, 26th Street and Fifth Avenue, formerly Delmonico's.

Francisco said that a woman of some social importance
in that city and New York, Mrs. Teresa Fair Oelrichs,
"has been brave
enough to give the
continental custom
the seal of American
approval and San
Francisco women
have now an unques-
tioned precedent for
smoking if they feel
so inclined. In Tait's
Café, Mrs. Oelrichs
and Mrs. McCreery
lighted their ciga-
rettes after dinner
and puffed their
smoke rings with the
men as if there had
not been anything to
disapprove in their
action."

From a drawing in the New York "Herald," April 26, 1908.

The itinerant umbrella-mender, who in the early 1900's was a familiar figure in American cities, had by 1930 become as great a rarity as the dancing bear and the organ-grinder's monkey.

The editor of one
New York paper
sent a reporter to
interview the mana-
gers of restaurants.
Mr. A. Miller, man-
ager at Rector's, on being asked: "Would you permit
a woman to smoke here now?" replied: "Decidedly not,
if we saw her. Of course there is no law against it, as
far as I know. For that matter there is no law to prevent a woman from smoking in the street. If she was
arrested at all, it might be for disorderly conduct." Mr.
John B. Martin, proprietor of the Café Martin, said:

"I am afraid the average American is still too Puritanical to allow the innovation." An assistant manager at the Waldorf said: "We have never given the question much

Marble soda fountain of the first decade.

thought, because it is seldom brought up. Probably once in six months an Englishwoman unfamiliar with conditions in this country will light a cigarette. We tell her it is against the rules, and the matter ends in her frank apology. We have never seen an American woman smoke here, and so never have been obliged to ask an American to stop, although everyone knows they smoke in their own homes."

Eventually the troublesome problem was treated in New York City by passing a law against it, the Sullivan Ordinance,[1] which made smoking by women illegal, made it an offense for the manager of a public place to allow women to smoke therein. "Will the ladies rebel," asked the New York *Times*, "as the ladies of New Amsterdam did when Peter Stuyvesant ordered them to wear broad flounces?"

February. Hard times, unhappy sequel to the panic of 1907, continued into 1908. Two thousand more needy persons than in normal years applied daily to the Bowery Mission, New York, for free coffee-and-roll breakfasts; so great were the demands for lodging that

[1] January 21, 1908.

the Mission was compelled to keep open until five in the
morning. Wide-spread unemployment, continuing over
a period of six months, had the usual effect of demoraliz-
ing wages for workers not belong-
ing to strong unions:

SITUATION WANTED — Book keeper,
23, thoroughly competent double entry,
German, French, Swedish and English
correspondent, typewriter; quick, accurate; good penman; highest references;
salary $12. Address S., 187 Herald.[2]

SITUATION WANTED — Butler (English), good worker; city or country;
salary $25 monthly; excellent references.
Harry Colpus, Mills Hotel, 7th Av. and
36th St.[3]

SITUATION WANTED — Barkeeper,
would accept $10 weekly; experienced,
respectable, careful, sober, steady, reli-
able man; good faithful worker, highly
recommended. Address B. B., 265.[4]

April 30. Worcester, Mass., having voted in favor of local prohibition, became the largest dry city
in the country. (Population, about
130,000.) Seventy-six saloons were

*Designed by the Ladies'
Home Journal for the
Winter of 1908.*

"For the girl who loves
fresh air and exercise."

closed, two thousand men thrown out of employment.
Seventeen other Massachusetts cities, including Haver-
hill and Lynn, and 249 smaller towns went dry the
same day.

May 9. The Senate debated, and rejected, a resolution providing for official observance of Mothers' Day,
to be honored by the wearing of a white carnation. Senator Kean of New Jersey moved to substitute the Fifth
Commandment. Senator Fulton of Oregon contentiously
argued that "if we are to have a Mother's Day, I for

[2] New York *Herald,* January 1, 1908.
[3] New York *Herald,* February 2, 1908.
[4] New York *Herald,* October 13, 1908.

one want to have a Father's Day, also," as well as a Grandfather's Day and a Mother-in-Law's Day. Senator Gallinger of New Hampshire felt it "almost a reproach and a burden upon me that I must wear a flower of a certain kind to remind me of my mother; I need no

The bread line at the Bowery Mission, 1908.

outward demonstration to keep my mother's memory green."

May 14. The Henry C. Frick Company, subsidiary of the United States Steel Corporation, posted an order that employees of the company must not use liquor either while on or off duty.

June 3. Henry Ford, in a brief departure from the production of cheap and serviceable, but not very ornate or speedy, four-cylinder automobiles, advertised:

Henry Ford is the pioneer manufacturer of six cylinder cars. Now they all make "sixes." Ford "sixes" are in use all over the world, and every one to the entire satisfaction of the owner. . . . Permit us to appeal to that sporting blood that's in every man with the Ford Six as a sport satisfying car.

The price was $2,800.

June 8. Members of the United States Brewers' Association, in convention at Milwaukee, announced a crusade to stem the tide of prohibition by themselves declar-

From the "Delineator," November, 1908.

Handling the long skirt going down stairs.

Going up stairs. Graceful possibilities of the long skirt.

ing open war against dives. They had a slogan: "Let us clean house; down with the immoral saloon." The convention greeted with roars of laughter the receipt of a facetious telegram reading:

The Prohibition State Convention of Minnesota, now in session, sends condolences to your association. Your business is doomed as your outposts are now carried and the prohibition army is about to move against your main body. The church and society have now declared and the State will soon say "The saloon must go."

June 11. Race-track gambling was prohibited in New York State by a law passed by the legislature, on the insistence of Governor Charles E. Hughes, who made a stirring issue of it. . . . *June* 23. The Louisiana Legislature prohibited race-track gambling in that State.

June 17. At the Republican National Convention at Chicago, when Chairman Henry Cabot Lodge said, in the course of his speech, that Theodore Roosevelt was "the best abused man in the United States, but also the most popular," the 12,000 men and women present started a demonstration that lasted forty-five minutes, exceeding the record set after Bryan's "Cross of Gold" speech of 1896, when the tumult lasted thirty minutes.

The following day, the Convention nominated Secretary of War William H. Taft for President on the first ballot, giving him 702 votes.

June 24. Grover Cleveland, President·of the United States 1885 to 1889 and 1893 to 1897, died in Princeton, N. J.

June 28. Senator Tillman of South Carolina read into *The Congressional Record* an official statement showing that in the District of Columbia there were 540 licenses to sell liquor and that 865 internal revenue tax receipts for the same purpose had been issued. The population of the District of Columbia at this time was about 310,000 (by the 1900 census, 278,718).

June. Nineteen-eight was the year of the phrase "Ain't it awful, Mabel?" — at first a byword among actors, later universal. The phrase was originally the refrain of some verse by John Edward Hazzard, purporting to be a dialogue, in twelve stanzas, between two chorus-girls:

> The way folks talk about us too;
> For the smallest thing we do —
> 'Nuff to make a girl feel blue.
> Ain't it awful, Mabel?

My Gawd! is that the overture?
I never will be on, I'm sure —
The things us actresses endure.
Ain't it awful, Mabel?

July 1. Count Zeppelin at Friedrichshafen remained aloft twelve hours in his dirigible and traversed the greater part of northern Switzerland at an average speed of thirty-four miles per hour. . . . *August* 2. Henry

The first Zeppelin.

Farman flew one-third of a mile in thirty seconds in his airplane at Brighton Beach, New York. . . . *September* 10. Orville Wright flew for 62 minutes 15 seconds at Fort Myer. . . . *September* 17. The Wright brothers' airplane, flying at Fort Myer, fell from a height of seventy-five feet, seriously injuring Orville Wright and killing Lieutenant Selfridge, his companion. . . . *October* 3. Wilbur Wright at Paris made a world's record for flight with a passenger by staying in the air with a French journalist 55 minutes 37 seconds.[5] . . . *December* 18. Wilbur Wright broke aviation records at

[5] In 1930, at Chicago, two Americans, the Hunter brothers, remained in the air 553 hours — more than 23 days, ending July 4. They were refuelled from another plane 273 times.

Le Mans, France; he rose to a height of 360 feet, travelled 120 kilometres, and remained in the air 113 minutes. . . . United States Postmaster-General George von L. Meyer was asked if he thought airships would

One style of hair dressing in vogue in 1908.

ever be used in the postal service, and was said to have replied, meditatively: "Yes, they might be, if you didn't care when your mail was delivered — or where." . . . Thomas A. Edison was quoted[6] as having said: "The dirigible has no future, speaking commercially. It has no great future any way you take it. It may be utilized in some measure in war, but the heavier-than-air machine that can go straight against the wind — ah, that is the thing that must come. . . . . I'll tell you what I think about this sky-sailing business. As I have said, it's sure to come. They haven't got it yet, but they will. But when the question is solved you will find that the machine that goes straight up in the air — screws itself vertically into the air — has answered the riddle." "The helicopter?" he was asked. "Right," he answered.

July 10. The National Democratic Convention at Denver, Colo., nominated William Jennings Bryan for President. Bryan's name was cheered for an hour and 28 minutes — eclipsing the endurance Marathon of cheering at the Republican Convention the preceding

[6] In the New York *Tribune*.

month, when Roosevelt's name had evoked an uproar
that lasted forty-five minutes.

Perils of the Theatre Lobby.

Once it was her hatpin.

From the New York "Herald Tribune," September 8, 1929.
Now it is her cigarette.

July 21. Melvin W. Sheppard, an American, won the
800-metre race at the Olympic Games in London. His
time, 1 minute 52 4-5 seconds, broke the previous record

of 1 minute 56 seconds. *July* 24. J. J. Hayes, an Amercan, won the Marathon race, in 2 hours 55 minutes 18 seconds. An Italian, Dorando, was first to cross the

line, but was disqualified on the ground that he had received assistance from onlookers. Dorando was delirious and several times during the last few yards collapsed and had to be helped to his feet. . . . The Washington *Post* remarked: "The British will have to console themselves with reflections on the running-record they made when George Washington was after them."

August 13. Ira D. Sankey, evangelist, associated with Dwight L. Moody, died. He was the composer of many hymns: "The Ninety and Nine" (of which millions were sold), "When the Mists Have Rolled Away," "A Shelter in the Time of Storm." He compiled "Gospel Hymns," of which more than fifty million copies were published.

Fred Merkle, whose failure to touch second base in a crucial game with the Chicago Cubs, September 23, 1908, will be remembered as long, at least, as Steve Brodie's leap from Brooklyn Bridge.

A Historic Event in Baseball

September 23. At the Polo Grounds, New York, a dispute historic in baseball, which enriched the language with two exceedingly forceful words, "bonehead" and "boner," arose over whether Frederick Charles Merkle did or did not touch second base. The game was between New York and Chicago and its outcome would determine which of the two teams should lead the National League. The setting of the play was the most dramatic that baseball provides — the last half of the ninth inning, the score 1 to 1. New York was at bat; there were two men out, one on third base and another, Merkle, on first. In this status, the New York player at bat, Bridwell, made a safe hit into centre field. The runner on third ran home, with what almost everybody took to be the winning run for New York. However, the play was not yet completed and it would not be completed unless and until Merkle reached second base ahead of the ball. What Merkle actually did do, following Bridwell's hit, is one of the unsolved enigmas of baseball history and is a point about which the chronicler of "Our Times" declines to be authoritative. The natural thing for Merkle to do was to get to second base with all the speed he could command; he insisted after the game that this was what he had done. It is equally plausible that when part way to second base he saw that Bridwell had made a safe hit and that the runner on third had got safely home with the winning run; he may have reasoned, prematurely, that the game was over, and may have turned and started for the club-house without touching second base. Whatever the fact may be, the resourceful "Johnny" Evers, second baseman for Chicago, took advantage of the situation for his team. Shouting to the umpire that Merkle had not touched second, Evers signalled to the outfielder to throw him the ball. This the outfielder attempted to do, but was interfered with by New York players and "fans" who had streamed onto the field. Somebody got the ball and threw it into the stands. Meanwhile there was a tussle over the person of the bewildered Merkle, his New York teammates seeking to drag him to second base, the Chicago players holding him back. In the stands a spectator friendly to Chicago scuffled for the ball, got it, and with a fine aim threw it to Evers, who, a short man, was now almost swallowed up by the milling mob of police, spectators, and players. Evers, with the ball in his hand, touched second base and frantically looked about for the umpire to get his decision on the play. The umpire had departed, however, precipitately, some minutes before, under the protection of an escort of police. New York newspapers next morning credited the game to New York, but President Pulliam of the National League decided that the evidence favored Chicago and called the game a tie, and as such it stood. In their wrath at Merkle, an excellent player, the New York fans fixed upon a previously anæmic and almost meaningless word, and gave to it a significance with which every reader is familiar. For more than twenty years, there has been rarely a game when from some part of the stands there did not arise from time to time, in shrill falsetto or hoarse bellow, the cry "bonehead" directed at any player disapproved, not always justly, by a "fan."[7]

October 14. Democratic editor Josephus Daniels, chairman of the press committee of the Democratic National Committee, advocating the election of Bryan, implied that the Roosevelt administration had not really been so very fierce against the trusts. Whereupon the Attorney-General in Roosevelt's Cabinet, Charles J. Bonaparte, produced statistics: Since Roosevelt became President in 1901, 46 antitrust suits under the Sherman law

---

[7] In a letter to the author, August 27, 1930, John A. Heydler, president of the National League, gave some additional details:

"The evidence clearly established that Merkle ran down part way toward second, then turned to right for the club house. . . . Some eight thousand people at that time signed a great protest in which they averred they actually saw Merkle touch second. The umpires ruled it a tie. President Pulliam sustained the umpires. The New York club appealed. The Board of Directors of the League ordered the game re-played in New York October 8th, one day after the season's close. The Chicago club was ordered from Chicago to New York, and in a pitcher's duel between Mathewson and Brown, Chicago won the game 4 to 2 and the championship. . . . Those were seething times in the old town!"

had been started. Nineteen ended in success, 6 in failure, and 21 were still pending. Under Presidents Harrison and McKinley 10 had been commenced, of which 5 were successful and 5 unsuccessful. Nine had been in-

From a photograph by Brown Bros.

Entrance hall and stairway, Astor residence.

stituted under President Cleveland, of which 5 were successful and 4 unsuccessful. The New York *Sun,* which disapproved "trust-busting," carried the Attorney-General's statement under an impish head-line: "Bonaparte Counts the Bag." Mr. Daniels asked why the Republican Attorney-General "did not take up the Steel trust, which received more benefits than any other from the government and contributed the most to the Republican campaign fund."

Passing of a Dynasty, and an Era

October 30. Mrs. William Astor died at her home, 842 Fifth Avenue, New York. With her passed not only a social dynasty but almost the whole idea of hereditary or otherwise arbitrary social supremacy in America; with her, indeed, passed "Society" in the old sense. For more than a generation, attendance at "Mrs. Astor's ball" had been the test of social position in New York. "If she invited you, you were in; if she did not, you were out." Mrs. Astor's rule over New York society coincided with a time when it was a compact, definite, limited body, largely composed of the older families of the city. In her prime, her box at the Metropolitan Opera House, No. 7, was a social throne — "it was always Mrs. Astor who gave the signal as to the proper time to leave; the time bore no relation to the stage to which the opera had advanced, but was selected because it happened to suit the matron; the time she chose was usually just after an intermission." Her later years were characterized by further and further retreat into retirement; she had given up her annual ball in 1904, and had discontinued her large dinners of which formerly she had given three or four yearly. Since 1906 she had not attended the

Mrs. William Waldorf Astor.

opera. To circumvent photographers, she carried, on the rare occasions when she left her house, a small parasol. During a year or more preceding her death, she was cautious about going even to the windows of her house, "so

© *Brown Bros.*

The sheath skirt at the Paris races, 1908.

great was her horror of being seen by the rubberneck wagons."[8] Born in 1830, a Schermerhorn, and therefore a descendant of the earliest Dutch families of New Amsterdam, she had married, in 1853, a grandson of the original John Jacob Astor. The disintegration of "Society" in the old sense that followed Mrs. Astor's death can hardly be comprehended by a generation who never knew the magic that once went with the name Astor. In the popular mind the name was often associated, not wholly accurately, with the name Vanderbilt, which came to prominence in New York life somewhat later than Astor, and was the symbol of a phase of New

[8] Sight seeing busses.

York society that did not quite attain the glory of
Society in the Astor sense. The two names became, in
a popular and even a literary sense, almost the Ameri-

Sheath bathing suits, 1908.

can and nineteenth century equivalent of Tudor and
Plantagenet, Capulet and Montague. "Astorbilt" was
the standard satirical or comedy term for a person or institution having, or pretending to have, social importance; a really clever invented word, current for a while,
was "Astorperious."

November. Nineteen-eight was the year of the "sheath" gown, called, on its arrival from Paris, the "Directoire," which "rang the knell of the rustling petticoat." When the first woman wearing one appeared

From "Theatre Magazine," September, 1909. *From the "Ladies' Home Journal," January, 1927.*

'This is to be a bandeauless season. Up and down Fifth Avenue, and in and out of the side streets, you may search and never a single bandeau will you find. Every hat sits way down on the head, and were it not that we are blessed with a goodly amount of hair, grown or purchased, would surely rest on the ears." — From *The Theatre Magazine,* September, 1909.

in the shopping district of Chicago "the police had to rescue her from a jeering insulting crowd."

> A skirt whose meagre gores necessitate
> The waddle of a Chinese lady's gait . . .
> A waist promcted half way up the back
> And not a shred that's comfortably slack.
> A figure like a seal reared up on end,
> And poking forward with a studied bend.[9]

The comic papers made quips about it: "The sheath gown uncovers a multitude of shins." A popular song celebrated it:

> Katie Keith, she wears a sheath
> With very little underneath.

[9] *Life.* Copied from London *Punch.*

Life[10] contrasted the slimness of its effect with the vogue of a few years before, when amplitude of hips had been thought desirable:

> We don't wish to insinuate
> That they were not real before;
> But where, oh, where, are the hips that we
> Don't notice any more?

In South Norwalk, Conn., the Haute Ton Whist and Literary Club, an ultrafashionable[11] social organization, concluded "that the sheath gown was but one big step backward toward the fig-leaf," and voted that "the sheath gown is both immodest and homely and this club will do everything in its power to put it down."

Nineteen-eight, summer and fall, was the period also of the "Merry Widow" hat, with wide brim, many of them roosts for dead birds, causing *Life*[12] to say: "Ten gorgeous little father birds were killed to trim the hat with; ten somber little mother birds were left sitting on their nests with nobody to feed them — and the hat was called the Merry Widow."

Nineteen-eight was the period also of dotted veils, good for the business of oculists; and of the boned collar, extreme ones reaching five inches with an added inch of lace ruching; and of what was supposed to be a rather bold stocking, about which *Puck*[13] quipped:

The Old Man. — No wonder m' sore throat ain't no better this mornin'. Asked Bessie for a stockin' to wrap around m' neck an' durned if she didn't give me one o' them fish-net open-works.

December 6. (*Sunday.*) Frank A. Munsey inaugurated in Washington a Sunday evening edition, the first

---

[10] November 19, 1908.
[11] So designated in a despatch to the New York *Herald.*
[12] November 19, 1908.　　　　　　[13] December, 1908.

The Merry Widow hat.

A Washington belle of 1908.

The chenille dotted veil.

A fashionable costume about 1907–1908; later the importation of aigrettes was banned by law.

Feminine fashions of the first decade.

in America, of a newspaper he owned, *The Times*. The innovation was not widely imitated and ultimately was abandoned.

December 11. J. Pierpont Morgan was quoted in newspapers as having recited to a group of friends and business associates at the Chicago Club, an axiom that had been handed down to him by his father:

Frank A. Munsey.

> Remember my son, that any man who is a bear on the future of this country will go broke. There may be times when things are dark and cloudy in America, when uncertainty will cause some to distrust, and others to think there is too much production, too much building of railroads, and too much other enterprise. In such times, and at all times, remember that the growth of this vast country will take care of all.

Publication of Morgan's statement was believed to have a helpful effect on the current business depression. The axiom continued to be quoted for more than twenty years.

December 21. Count Johann Heinrich von Bernstorff arrived in New York to become German Ambassador to the United States; his leaving, nine years later, was a dramatic incident of the entry of the United States into the Great War.

December 21. Andrew Carnegie, at tariff hearings before the Ways and Means Committee of the House of Representatives, urged abolition of the tariff on steel. "Take back your protection," said Mr. Carnegie, shaking his finger at the committee; "we are now men, and we can beat the world at the manufacture of steel."

An Early Phase of Motion Pictures

December 24. In 1908, the motion-picture was just midway between its grub stage, the nickelodeon, and the faint beginnings of what was, twenty years later, to

One of the early nickel movie houses.

be its gorgeous chrysalis — nearer the former than the latter. The day before Christmas, Mayor McClellan of New York revoked the licenses of 550 nickelodeons "because of the serious opposition by the rectors and pastors of practically all the Christian denominations in the city and because of the further objections of the Society for the Prevention of Crime." Future licenses would be granted, the Mayor said, only on written agreement that the licensees would not operate their places on Sundays and that they would not show pictures tending "to degrade the morals of the community."

Earlier in the year, the New York *Herald*, moved by a fire in a moving-picture theatre at Boyertown, Penn., which had destroyed more than a hundred lives, inves-

An announcement of one of the 1908 5-cent "movies."

tigated the moving-picture theatres of New York City and found that they were patronized daily by about two hundred thousand people, more than three-quarters of them women and children. "In almost every case a long, narrow room, formerly used for more legitimate business purposes, has been made over into what is popularly known as a 'nickelodeon.' At the rear a stage is raised. Across it is swung a white curtain. Before the

curtain is placed a piano, which does service for an
orchestra. Packed into the room as closely as they can be
placed are chairs for the spectators, who number from
one hundred to four hundred and fifty. Directly above
the entrance is placed the moving-picture machine,
which flashes its lights and shadows upon the white curtain dropped in front of the stage. Many of the machines are operated by means of a tank filled with gaso-
line or some similarly inflammable material."

While the motion-picture houses had not yet risen
above the low esteem that attended their early stage, a
few ambitious proprietors were beginning to picture
Shakespeare, and in other ways were initiating developments that constituted a milestone in an evolution destined
to bring about what in 1908 few would have predicted
or admitted, a status in which, by the 1920's, the motion-picture occupied more theatres and employed more
actors than the spoken drama. *The Theatre Magazine*
for October, 1908, in an article entitled "Where They
Perform Shakespeare for Five Cents," made what then
seemed daring predictions:

Whatever there may be crude about the kinetoscope of the
present, we cannot say that the kinetoscope of the future will
not be much nearer perfection. The scientific brains are at
work improving it, so that the slightest facial expression may
soon be caught, so that those looking for any length of time
upon the screen may not go away with wearied eyes, which
at present is not only a painful defect, but a danger to be
guarded against. . . . The actor has a formidable rival in the
kinetoscope. The time is not far distant when we will see
along Broadway theatrical agencies specially catering to the
manufacturers of moving-picture films. The Edison Company
of New York, the Vitagraph Company of America, the Pathé
Frères of Paris, each has its regular stock company. These men
and women, employed at good salaries, are richly costumed
for the dramas and the ballets and fairy tales and the dances
that are performed before the machine. It is remarkable to what
extent the moving-picture manufacturer will go in his anxiety
and determination to obtain realism in his kinetoscopic play.

Other Events of 1908

January 7. The Cunard Lines advertised "special low saloon rates to Europe" — *Mauretania*, $72.50. Twenty years later the minimum saloon rate on the *Mauretania* was $280.50. * * * *January* 15. The Senate passed a joint resolution remitting to China about $11,000,000 of the indemnity[14] paid by China on account of damage done during the Boxer rebellion eight years before. * * * *January* 24.

Edward MacDowell.

Edward MacDowell died; foremost American composer, first to give American music a standing in the world of art. * * * *January*. The boycotting of firms advertising their wares on bill-boards was proposed by Clinton Rogers Woodruff, lawyer and reforming æsthete of Pennsylvania, as a step toward the elimination of the ugly from America's landscapes and skylines. Mr. Woodruff deplored "the profanation of the skyline and the elimination of dignity through the unrestrained use of bill-boards. Cities spend hundreds of thousands for beautiful buildings, for parks and parkways and playgrounds, and then allow the bill-poster to use them as a background for his flaming advertisements." * * * *January*. Much discussion initiated by a suggestion from France about "trial marriages" for a specified period under legal safeguards protecting the interests of both parties. * * * *February* 3. Thomas Mellon (father of Andrew W. Mellon, Secretary of the Treasury under Presidents Harding, Coolidge, and Hoover), who accumulated a great fortune during his lifetime in oil, real estate, banking and traction promotions, died at Pittsburgh on his ninety-fifth birthday. Years before he had turned his great fortune over to his sons, preferring a quiet, peaceful old age to one distracted by cares. * * * *February* 3. John Mitchell made his last address as president of the United Mine Workers of America at a convention at Indianapolis. (See "Our Times," Vol. II.) * * * *February* 5. Passenger service was inaugurated on part of the railroad being

[14] See "Our Times," Vol. I, pp. 512–513.

built by Henry M. Flagler over the Florida keys south from Miami to Key West, called the "ocean-going railroad." For about half its length the road was on a concrete viaduct built over open water. * * * *February* 12. The six contestants in the 20,000-mile automobile race from New York to Paris arranged by *Le Matin* and the New York *Times* (3 French cars, 1 Italian, 1 German, 1 American) started from Times Square, New York, westward bound at 11.15 A. M. The American Thomas car won, reaching Paris on July 31, 1908. * * * *March* 9. No woman is physically fit to run an automobile, stated Mayor Markbreit of Cincinnati in a communication to the City Council recommending the appointment of a commission for the examination of all who seek to manage automobiles. * * * *April* 9. A bill was introduced in the Massachusetts Legislature authorizing the Selectmen of Nantucket to exclude automobiles from that island — incident in a long but losing struggle waged by a few communities, including Mount Desert Island, Maine,[15] to resist invasion by speed and noise. * * * *April* 12. Chelsea, Mass., was practically wiped out by fire; ten thousand people were left homeless, and ten millions in property destroyed. * * * *April* 13. The New England Methodist Episcopal Conference voted to remove the church ban from dancing, card-playing, and theatre-going. * * * *April* 24. First and second places in the Briarcliff Road Race near New York were won by two Italian cars, an Isotta and a Fiat. A Stearns and an Apperson, both American, were third and fourth; another Italian, a Bianchi, was fifth. The winning Isotta, driven by the American racer Strang, maintained an average speed of forty-nine miles for the two hundred sixty miles of the course. * * * *April.* Transatlantic steamship companies reduced the rate for steerage travellers from New York to Genoa to $12. * * * *May* 11. Thomas J. Heflin, representative in Congress from Alabama, was indicted by a Federal Grand Jury at Washington for shooting Lewis Lundy, negro, in a street-car fight several weeks before. Heflin claimed the shooting was in self-defense. * * * *May* 30. *The Call,* a one-cent, four-page daily newspaper dedicated to the interests of the "proletariat," was launched in New York; most of the contents was about labor and socialist activities. * * * *June.* President Roosevelt called a conference of governors of the States, which became an annual event of considerable importance. * * * *July* 21. Bishop Henry C. Potter, of the Episcopal Diocese of New York, died at Cooperstown, N. Y. He was the first person to be buried in the new Cathedral of St.

[15] A leader in this movement was President Charles W. Eliot of Harvard University, a summer resident of Mount Desert.

John the Divine at New York. * * * *July*. An inventor, Carl M. Wheaton, of Newtonville, Mass., convinced after nine years of experimenting that lethal gas could be made an effective instrument of war, urged the government to make gas-projecting equipment part of the nation's military organization. Mr. Wheaton claimed he had invented a gas having the property of putting to sleep whoever breathed it, the formula

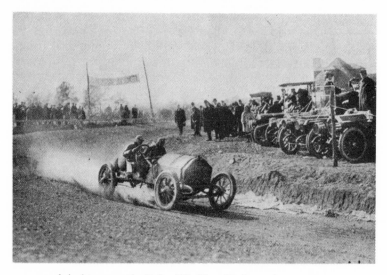

A bad turn on the Briarcliff, New York, road race course.

of which he offered to the navy. A commentator in *The Technical World Magazine*, more confident than the public who, in the main, regarded Wheaton's idea as chimerical, said that "the invention, if kept a close secret, would render the United States invincible." * * * *November* 1. "A great newspaper no longer needs a clown," asserted, confidently, the Boston *Herald*, in announcing its dropping of comic supplements from Sunday editions. *The Herald* felt that not only had public taste in Boston risen above the level of comic supplements, but that these "have ceased to be comic; they have become as vulgar in design as they are tawdry in color; there is no longer any semblance of art in them, and if there are any ideas they are low and descending lower." * * * *November* 4. President Eliot of Harvard University resigned, after a service of thirty-nine years. * * * *December*. In this month, for the first time, the Red Cross sold Christmas seals to raise funds for a campaign against tuberculosis. Receipts were $135,000. * * * *December* 26. At Sydney, Australia, a negro stevedore from Galveston, Texas, "Jack" Johnson, won the world's heavyweight championship from "Tommy" Burns, Canadian. Immediately James J. Jeffries, former world champion, living in retirement on a farm in California, was besieged with suggestions that he re-enter the ring to bring back the heavyweight title to the white race. Jeffries replied that he had made an irrevocable decision never to fight again. Two years

President Roosevelt and Governors of States making inspection tour of Mississippi River, 1908.

later, however, on July 4, 1910, he fought Johnson and was defeated. * * * *December 27. *Sunday*. At Nyack, N. Y., followers of Prophet Lee J. Spangler arose early for what they expected would be their last day on earth. In white dresses "specially made for the occasion" they assembled and journeyed to South Mountain to await, in a snow-covered graveyard, Gabriel and the trumpet-call. The day drawing to a close, and nothing having happened, the crowd dispersed and returned to their homes. Prophet Spangler departed without farewells.

The Books of 1908

Books popular during 1908 included: "The Trail of the Lonesome Pine," by John Fox, Jr. . . . "The Circular Staircase," by Mary Roberts Rinehart. . . . "The Firing Line," by Robert W. Chambers. . . . "Mr. Crewe's Career," by Winston Churchill. . . . "Old

Wives for New," by David Graham Phillips. . . . "The Barrier," by Rex Beach. . . . "The Ancient Law," by Ellen Glasgow. . . . "The Fruit of the Tree," by Edith Wharton. . . . "Together," a novel of many mismatings, by Robert Herrick. . . . "The Shuttle," a story of an international marriage, by Frances Hodgson Burnett.

Photograph by Pach Bros.
From the Albert Davis Collection.
George Arliss.

In 1908, on January 25, the death of "Ouida" (Louise de la Ramée) recalled to many Americans a novel about the French Foreign Legion, "Under Two Flags." On July 3, Joel Chandler Harris, one of the very few American authors of an indisputable classic, "Uncle Remus," died at his home in Atlanta, Ga. Among his best-known books were "Told by Uncle Remus," "Uncle Remus and His Friends," "Uncle Remus and Br'er Rabbit."

The Theatre in 1908

"The Melting Pot," by an English author, Israel Zangwill, produced in America during October, pictured the complete absorption by America of Jewish immigrants, with the "utter obliteration of their race history, their religion, and those separate institutions which they have cherished for forty centuries." . . . In another English play, "The Servant in the House," by Charles Rann Kennedy, the spirit of Christ was personified, by no means irreverently, in an English butler.

. . . Mrs. Minnie Maddern Fiske played in "Salvation
Nell."[16] . . . Maude Adams in "The Jesters" and in a
repetition of Barrie's "Quality Street." . . . Ethel Bar-
rymore in "Her Sister" and "Lady Frederick." . . .
George Arliss in "The Devil." . . . Blanche Bates in
"The Fighting Hope." . . .
Thomas A. Wise and Doug-
las Fairbanks (in that order) in "A Gentleman from
Mississippi." . . . William
H. Crane in "Father and the
Boys," by George Ade. . . .
John Mason in "The Man
from Home." . . . Mabel
Taliaferro in "The World
and His Wife." . . . James
K. Hackett in "The Prisoner
of Zenda." . . . John Drew
in "Jack Straw." . . . Max-
ine Elliott in "Myself Bet-
tina." . . . Annie Russell in

From the Albert Davis Collection.
James K. Hackett.

"The Stronger Sex." . . . Robert Edeson in "The
Offenders." . . . William Hodge in "The Man from
Home." . . . Mabel Taliaferro in "Polly of the Cir-
cus." . . . DeWolf Hopper in "The Pied Piper."
. . . Marie Dressler in "The Boy and the Girl." . . .
George M. Cohan in "The Yankee Prince." . . . Ed-
die Foy in "The Orchid." . . . Two colored comedians,
Williams and Walker, played in "Bandanna Land."
. . . Anna Held in "Miss Innocence."

In 1908, a group of talented Irish players, from the
Irish National Theatre Company in Dublin, produced
in New York and elsewhere in America, "The Rising of

---

[16] This was the first play to come on the stage as a direct result of college instruction in playwriting; it came from the course just started at Harvard by
Professor George P. Baker.

the Moon," "The Birthright," and other Irish plays.
. . . Madame Luisa Tetrazzini made her first appearance in America, at the Manhattan Opera House. . . .
Despite perennial deploring about neglect of the older
drama accompanied by meretriciousness in the new, Robert Mantell played Shake-
spearean rôles in New York
for three months. . . . In
1908, in October, at Car-
negie Hall, New York, a
young violinist named Mischa
Elman played for the first
time in America.

Isadora Duncan, in a short,
loosely hung Grecian dress,
with bare feet and arms,
danced a series of Greek
dances from Gluck's "Iphi-
genie en Aulide," reproduc-
ing the postures of Greek
dancers as portrayed on ancient vases. A New York poet,
who at the time was very young, Charles Hanson Towne,
wrote:[17]

From the Albert Davis Collection.
William Hodge.

> I thought her a wonderful April morning,
> A blossom of loveliness white from the earth,
> As, whirling and twirling, our cruder speech scorning,
> She danced to our hearts like the spirit of Mirth.

Pessimism said that "the ingenue will soon become
extinct as the buffalo; our girls burst from childhood
into womanhood; there is no intermediate period of girl-
hood." Since the stage holds the mirror up to life there
was in the current drama a tendency which Elizabeth
Marbury, entrepreneur between playwrights and produc-

[17] *Theatre Magazine,* October, 1908.

ers, epitomized: "The drama of the sweet young girl who is separated from her lover by the machinations of a wicked villain has gone out of date with crinolines and slavery and other monuments of foolishness." With whatever relevancy, Miss Marbury added: "The big drama is being born. That is the writing on the theatrical wall."

Meantime, in spite of prophecies of changing taste, Denman Thompson played — again — "Josh Whitcomb" in "The Old Homestead"; it was still "one of the most valuable pieces of theatrical property in existence." The 1908 production was comparatively brief, for Denman Thompson was now an old man, seventy-five. As a young actor in the 1850's he had played "Uncle Tom" in "Uncle Tom's Cabin"; his impersonation of "Uncle Joshua (pronounced Joshuay) Whitcomb" dated from the 1880's. The newspaper announcements

From the Albert Davis Collection.
Eddie Foy, in "The Orchid."

of the 1908 performances promised that "not a thing in the play has been changed or brought up to date" — real hay, real oxen, the farmer's double quadrille; the singing of "All Bound Round with a Woollen String," accompanied with a quaint old solo dance, and "Denman Thompson will positively appear as 'Uncle Josh.'" "The Old Homestead," so Eugene Field had written years before, "can be enjoyed over and over again.

Amid all the changes and fluctuations to which our stage has been subjected there has obtained a strong demand for a purely American drama, a play which should truthfully illustrate a type of humanity. This demand is fully answered in 'The Old Homestead,' a production so complete in naturalness that it seems not a play but actual bits of Yankeedom and of Yankee flesh and blood plucked from the Down East and spread before us for our delectation and benefit. Denman Thompson does not act. He is."

From the Albert Davis Collection.
E. H. Sothern, as "Lord Dundreary."

Similarly, the America of 1908 still got pleasure from Edward H. Sothern's revival of the character "Lord Dundreary" in "Our American Cousin," which Sothern's father had made famous more than a generation before. "Our American Cousin," a farce about life in the British aristocracy, and about American ways as seen from that standpoint, had been first produced on October 18, 1858, at Laura Keene's Theatre, New York City. A minor part, "Lord Dundreary," having only 47 lines to speak, had been given to Edward A. Sothern, then young, but destined to be known (after his son Edward H. became famous) as "the elder Sothern." Sothern, Sr., during his early strolling days had happened to know, among the British officers at the garrison at

Halifax, Nova Scotia, a young titled Englishman whose mannerisms were those of the conventional "English fop." Him Sothern, Sr., had copied, expanded and embellished with fantastic exaggerations, until "Lord Dundreary" became, during the 1860's and 1870's, one of the half-dozen most familiar characters on the American stage. His flowing whiskers set a vogue that the post-Civil-War generation of young American males imitated; his "ulster" made that garment a style; his hesitating speech, his lisp, his twisted proverbs, his half-earnest, half-foolish, wholly amusing figure provided laughter to America from 1858 until the elder Sothern's death in 1881. The younger Sothern's revival of the character in 1908 gave delight to a new generation — and more to aging folks who remembered it as part of the glamour of their youth.

At Ford's Opera House, Baltimore, on May 16, 1908, Kellar, a magician, completed forty years on the stage. . . . In 1908, on August 26, died Antonio ("Tony") Pastor; about the same time passed his name from the sign of the theatre in the lineal predecessor of which he had, in 1865, created the first American "music hall." . . . In 1908, on August 4, Bronson Howard died. The best known of his plays was "Shenandoah." Bronson Howard could fairly be described as the first American dramatist, in the sense of the first American who made his living wholly out of writing plays. In that uniqueness Howard continued until the early 1890's; by the time of his death American playwrights were numbered by scores.

INDEX

INDEX